Apocalyptic
Marvell

Apocalyptic Marvell

The Second Coming in Seventeenth Century Poetry

Margarita Stocker

Research Fellow in English,
University of Liverpool

OHIO UNIVERSITY PRESS
Athens, Ohio

First published in the United States of America in 1986 by
OHIO, UNIVERSITY PRESS
Athens, Ohio 45701

Library of Congress Cataloging-in-Publication Data

Stocker, Margarita
  Apocalyptic Marvell.

1. Marvell, Andrew, 1621–1678—Religion and ethics.
2. Apocalyptic literature—History and criticism.
3. Revelation in literature. I. Title. II. Title:
Second Coming in seventeeth-century poetry.
PR3546.S76 1986   821'.4   85–15429
ISBN 0–8214–0830–5

Printed in Great Britain

For David

'And the angel said unto me, Why didst thou marvel?'
(Revelation 17:7)

Contents

List of Abbreviations

Andrew Marvell, *The Rehearsal Transpros'd* . . .	RT
An Account of the Growth of Popery . . .	GP
John Milton, *Paradise Lost*	PL
Paradise Regained	PR
Edmund Spenser, *The Faerie Queene*	FQ
Bucknell Review	BuR
College English Association Critic	CEA Critic
Critical Quarterly	CQ
Durham University Journal	DUJ
Etudes Anglaises	EA
Essays in Criticism	EIC
A Journal of English Literary History	ELH
English Language Notes	ELN
English Literary Renaissance	ELR
English Studies	ES
Huntington Library Quarterly	HLQ
Journal of English & Germanic Philology	JEGP
Journal of the History of Ideas	JHI
Journal of the Warburg & Courtauld Institutes	JWCI
Modern Language Notes	MLN
Modern Language Quarterly	MLQ
Modern Language Review	MLR
Modern Philology	MP
Notes & Queries	N&Q
Publications of the Modern Language Association	PMLA
Philological Quarterly	PQ
Review of English Studies	RES
Renaissance News	RN
Renaissance Quarterly	RQ
Studies in English Literature	SEL

Studies in Philology	*SP*
Shakespeare Quarterly	*SQ*
Times Literary Supplement	*TLS*
University of Toronto Quarterly	*UTQ*
The Yearbook of English Studies	*YES*

Note on References

I am grateful to Oxford University Press for permission to quote from *The Poems and Letters of Andrew Marvell*, 2 vols., ed. H. M. Margoliouth, Pierre Legouis, and E. E. Duncan-Jones (3rd edn, Oxford, 1971). Reference is made also to *The Rehearsal Transpros'd and . . . The Second Part*, ed. D. I. B. Smith (Oxford, 1971); for the other prose works reference is to Vol. IV of *The Complete Works of Andrew Marvell*, ed. A. B. Grosart (Fuller Worthies Library, London 1872–5). For Milton's poems reference is to *Poetical Works*, ed. Douglas Bush (London, 1970).

Note on Terminology

In the effort to analyze the apocalyptic tradition, certain terms will occur with some frequency. In my discussion of eschatological ideas, I shall be referring to the features of mainstream eschatological belief (whereas in the minutiae of eschatological speculation there was a considerable degree of sectarian variation, and such variations will be discussed where relevant). The term "eschatology" itself implies this restriction to the mainstream. "Millenarianism" refers to a belief in the thousand-year-old rule of the Church on earth before the Last Judgment. "Apocalyptic" refers to the mode of writing proper to the biblical Book of Revelation, and of texts which aspire to revelational characteristics. "Chiliasm" refers to belief in an approaching millennium, usually with a connotation of expectation and hope. Eschatology comprises the doctrine of the universal last things—the end of the world, the Second Coming of Christ, the resurrection of the dead and the Last Judgment.[1] Since this book is concerned mainly with Protestant eschatological belief between 1600 and 1680, my use of the term "eschatology" can be understood usually to imply also that Protestant version of history which was associated with eschatological beliefs during this period in England. The nature of this historical ideology is discussed below.

Two matters of attitude also bear mention here. We should recognize that in this period, chiliasm was not limited to extremist groups or radical sects, and that such belief was not considered unusual (as it might be in the twentieth century). Equally, we must grasp an attitude of mind which—in distinction from our own age, with its apprehensions of nuclear holocaust—regarded the end of the world with hope and enthusiasm, as the triumph of God's saints and of His Justice, and as the prelude to bliss. To this degree seventeenth-century eschatology was optimistic.

Introduction

The essential purpose of this book is to alter radically the received image of Andrew Marvell. Two things are wrong with this image. First, he has been seen as a difficult, elusive, elegant, poised—one might say even etiolated—poet, celebrating Nature and withdrawal from the world: too poised to be committed, his every statement undermined by unresolved ironies which render the location of "meaning" impossible. So admired has been this enigmatic effect that it has become the central cliché of Marvell studies, an expression of Marvell's "exquisite impartiality" or his inability to take sides.[1]

Second, his works are considered in discrete groups—the Cavalier or courtly poems, the political poems, the pastoral poems, the "degenerate" satires and inaccessible prose works. His Latin poems are largely ignored, as if irrelevant to the oeuvre. Hence the overall effect is as if there were several Marvells, the last disastrously opinionated in contrast to the Marvell of the great early lyrics.

These supposed categories, and the hospitably empty vessel of his "inconclusiveness", have allowed critics of Marvell to foist upon the lyrics a wide variety of speculative and mutually exclusive readings, ranging from Platonist and Buddhist to resolutely impressionistic.[2] Emptied of individuality, Marvell has become fair game for all comers.

This book hopes to show that the traditional view of Marvell is mistaken, both in premise and in interpretations. Its salient features—the dissolving Marvell and the fragmented canon of his works—disappear when we recognize that he is committed to a distinctly larger ideology than has been considered hitherto: that of apocalyptic belief. In the light of this ideology we will find that he is a trenchant and contentious poet, committed to his convictions. Because of that commitment the whole range of his works should be seen

xiii

as a coherent and integrated expression of his apocalyptic preoccupations, encompassing his attitudes, his life, and his writings.

The shape of the book is designed to manifest this integration. The first chapter is concerned to show that Marvell's thought is determined by an apocalyptic system, evincing its effect upon his career and his controversial prose works; in this context his poem *The First Anniversary*—in some respects the simplest case—becomes intelligible, and indeed this poem becomes the focus for his poetry as a whole. The second chapter will suggest the apocalyptic origins of Marvell's poetic structures, reinterpreting *A Dialogue Between the Soul and Body* and *Upon Appleton House*. The third chapter will show that *An Horatian Ode* and *Tom May's Death* are examples of Marvell's fusion of classical sources with apocalyptic topics, while the fourth chapter demonstrates his revision of the classical Golden Age in terms of the Second Coming, showing how this innovation affects equally poems of public address, personal lyrics like *The Coronet* and *The Picture of Little T. C.*, and the extended narrative of *Upon Appleton House*. The fifth chapter discusses the relationship between 'New World' mythology and apocalyptic ideas, and shows how they affect *The Last Instructions to a Painter*, *Upon the Victory Obtained by Blake* and *Bermudas*. The sixth chapter then demonstrates how such national myths are transformed into private myths in *To His Coy Mistress* and other love lyrics, the *Mower* poems, and *The Garden*. The final chapter demonstrates that both national and private elements of apocalyptic are vital to an understanding of *The Unfortunate Lover*.

Because of this reinterpretation, involving the complex ramifications of an apocalyptic vision, persistent questions raised by Marvell criticism are answered. The unity of *Upon Appleton House*, long sought for in vain;[3] the rational structure of *The Garden*, especially the elusive meaning of the central stanzas;[4] the oddities of *To His Coy Mistress*, and especially the baffling images of its last paragraph;[5] whether *Bermudas* is simple or ironic or otherwise complex; whether *Blake* is an odd diversion from Marvell's characteristic voice; the poet's political stance and his tone in *An Horatian Ode*;

the puzzle of what *The Unfortunate Lover* "means";[6] the relation of the Latin poems to the English, of the satires to the lyrics; the sources of Marvell's peculiar tone; all these questions are resolved, and his poems seen in their truly witty light, only once we recognize Marvell as the great lyric exponent of apocalyptic.

This is a version of a doctoral thesis submitted to the University of York in 1981. I would like to express my thanks to Dr Graham Parry, of the University of York, for his unfailing encouragement, advice, criticism, and patience while I was engaged on this work. I am so grateful to Dr Peter Thomas of University College, Cardiff, for both the kindness and the rigour of his comments; and Professor Kelsey Thornton, of the University of Newcastle, for his reading of and comments upon some chapters. Last but not least, I thank my husband, whose patience and help have been inexhaustible and invaluable.

A Revelation for the Times: The Context of Marvell's Poetry

Andrew Marvell is a poet in constant engagement with his own time, whose poetry largely arises out of, and presupposes knowledge of, its historical context. Interpreted without pertinent reference to that context, it remains as obscure and as elusive of tone as the canon of Marvell criticism would tend to suggest. The historical and historico-theological studies of recent years have indicated that the mid seventeenth century—the period in which his poetry was written—was marked by an upsurge of chiliasm, especially of the millenarian variety, and that this chiliastic tendency exerted a major influence upon the religious and political thought of the time.[1] Particulary in the crisis of Civil War, the doctrines and the historical methodology of current eschato-logical belief helped to determine men's analyses of the conflict, providing them with an explanation of the causation and events of that war.

For, since the reign of Elizabeth, eschatology had harnessed to itself a peculiarly Protestant version of history, in which England was regarded as the Elect Nation of God. The English Reformation had extirpated Antichrist, the "popish" church, and had reinstituted the 'true religion', of which the Roman Catholic Church was merely an impostor. It was, so the thought ran, a false image of Christianity, a superstition distinguished by idolatry, hypocrisy, and clerics who were 'wolves in sheep's clothing', betraying the faithful to the maw of the Beast. Thus the English Reformation was understood as a victory in the age-long war between Christ and Antichrist, and England was to be in the forefront of the Christian effort to prepare the world for the Second Coming, which would vanquish Antichrist and inaugurate the Millennium.

Promulgated expecially by the works of the Protestant martyrologist John Foxe, this version of history was the inheritance of the seventeenth century. By the 1640s, the decade of Civil War, the majority of Englishmen might be described as chiliasts. Revelation, the biblical book of the war against Antichrist, was regarded as a textbook for contemporary events and politics; the current age was believed to correspond to the Latter Days; wars—and the Civil War in particular—were 'Signs of the End', which was fast approaching.

On the royalist side, Charles' cause was underpinned by *Dei Gratia* doctrines implying the messianic resonances of kingship, doctrines which harnessed the mythologies of the Millennium and the Second Coming. On the parliamentarian side, the Civil War represented a holy crusade, the 'reformation of the nation' by the eradication of the "popish" king, ministers, and prelates. The anticlericalism which, since the days of the Lollards, had been a salient factor in resistance to the Catholic Church had retained its force in the virulent anticatholicism of the decades to 1640; but, equally, it had fomented anticlerical resistance to the Laudian dispensation and its Arminian 'heresy' and characterized Laudian high Anglicanism as a form of 'popery' perpetrated by the episcopal agents of Antichrist. It was considered that episcopacy had reverted to its true nature, as manifested by its Roman Catholic predecessors. The climactic issue of this attitude, which was the impulsion behind the parliamentarian abolition of episcopacy, was the widely held view in the 1640s that the bishops had vitiated the pure religion of the Elect Nation by the antichristian error and thereby damaged its spiritual integrity; they represented a 'national sin' that had visited England with God's retribution. The Civil War was, then, the visitation and the purgation of this national sin.

[The] Popishnesse of the English Clergye [is such that] . . . there is no way to vindicate the Honour of our *Nation, Ministry, parliaments, Soveraigne, Religion, God*; but by causing the punishment [to be effected] . . . that our [Antichristian] adversaries that have triumphed in their sinne, may be confounded at their punishments . . . the personall acts of these *sonnes of Beliall* [are] . . . become Nationall sinnes.[2]

Such a national sin of 'Popishnesse' evoked the wrath of God upon a nation;[3] by purging England of her antichristian episcopacy,[4] Parliament enacted, they thought, the judgment of God, and to this degree the Civil War was regarded as purgative.[5] The consequent restoration of England's godliness would reactivate her reforming role in the world and thus hasten the Second Coming.

Such was the nature of contemporary attitudes to history when the crisis of Civil War occurred. The Puritan Marvell himself contributed to the polemical eschatological literature which bulks so large in the publications of this century, when he appended to one of his later tracts *An Essay Concerning General Councils* (1677).[6] His examination there of the early history of doctrinal elaboration in the Christian Church was an eschatological exercise, intended to demonstrate the antichristian infiltration of the true religion and to supply an historical model for current episcopal heresies.[7] Such heuristically historical, chiliastic tracts were a consistent feature of reformist anti-episcopal literature, and the *Essay* exemplifies Marvell's participation in this stream of thought.

Recent studies have emphasized that Marvell's friend and fellow poet, John Milton, was a Puritan reformer and chiliast,[8] but Marvell has always been considered a character of more delicate constitution, unlikely to espouse extravagant causes and indeed chary of all ideological commitments. However, eschatological belief was widespread amongst all classes and tempers of men,[9] and Marvell's prose tracts manifest both his eschatological assumptions and his trenchant religio-political commitment.[10]

In Marvell's career as a Puritan reformer his background was, no doubt, formative: his father's lectureship at Holy Trinity Church, Hull, was a civic preaching office, independent of the church, of the type which in towns of an advanced Protestant character—like Hull—were established precisely to evade episcopal pressures for conformity.[11] Marvell senior himself penned a commentary upon that salient chiliastic text, II Peter.[12] While his home and his education must have reflected this progressive cast upon the state religion, Marvell's matriculation at Cambridge coincided with that university's strengthening reputation on the European scene for chiliastic and millenarian scholarship[13] (theology was still the major subject of study, of course).[14] Like Hull, Cambridge had been in the vanguard of the Tudor movement for Reformation,[15] and since the late sixteenth century its members had produced expositions of Revelation along lines which complemented the decisive influence of John Foxe upon English chiliasm.[16] (Quite orthodoxly, Marvell recommended Foxe's *Book of Martyrs* as a gloss upon the Last Day.)[17] One of the seminal exegetes of Revelation, Joseph Mede, had taught at Cambridge, where Milton was one of his pupils.[18] In what may be seen as an understandable moment of juvenile rebellion against the pressures of such a background, Marvell seems at this time to have undergone a brief conversion to Roman Catholicism at the hands of Jesuit agents.[19] Certainly, this experience must have exacerbated that vehement opposition to popery which is evinced in his tracts, confirming, as it did, contemporary fears of a Jesuit fifth column at work in England.[20] The poetic vituperation of his early antipapist satire, *Fleckno, an English Priest at Rome* (1646), is matched by the forceful rhetoric of his prose tract *An Account of the Growth of Popery and Arbitrary Government* (1677):

> That Popery is such a thing that cannot, but for want of a word to express it, be called a Religion: nor is it to be mentioned with that civility which is otherwise decent to be used, in speaking of the differences of humane opinion about Divine matters. Were it either Judaism, or plain Turkery, or honest paganism, there is yet a certain *bona fides* in the most extravagant belief . . . but this is compound of all the three, an extract of whatsoever is most ridiculous and impious in them, incorporated with more peculiar absurdities of its own . . . and all this deliberately contrived, knowingly carried on, by the bold imposture of priests under the name of Christianity.
>
> (*GP*, 250–1)

This identification of popery as the false image of Christianity is the essence of its antichristianism, and here, as in all his tracts, Marvell manifests that combination of anticatholicism and anticlericalism which is characteristic of reformist chiliasm. In respect the essential similarity between *GP* and

Fleckno is instructive since they are symptomatic of a consistency in Marvell's views from the mid-century crisis to the very different circumstances prevailing after the Restoration.

Similarly, just as Protestant reforming opinion had always identified 'true religion' with 'godly government',[21] so Marvell is committed to the integrity of 'True Worship and True Government' (*GP*, 289), which distinguishes England as the chosen nation:

> as we are thus happy in the constitution of our State, so we are yet more blessed in that of our Church; being free from that Romish yoak, which so great a part of Christendom do yet draw and labour under.
>
> (*GP*, 250)

For him popery and absolutism have a symbiotic relationship (reflected in the title of the tract): Antichrist conspires 'to subvert the government and religions, to kill the body and damn the soul of our nation' (*GP*, 261).

Marvell's analysis of the contemporary popish threat is closely comparable to that of Milton, four years earlier, in *Of True Religion . . . and what best means may be used Against the Growth of Popery*. Milton contends, for instance, that 'Popery is a double thing to deal with, and claims a twofold power, ecclesiastical and political, both usurped, and the one supporting the other'.[22] For him the Pope's is a 'Babylonish yoke',[23] while for Marvell it is a 'Romish yoak'; both represent the reformist view that Antichrist imposes a spiritual and political tyranny. That 'bondage' is the aim of the prelates (*General Councils*, 81), a sentiment in which Marvell echoes Milton's *Eikonoklastes* of 1649.[24] Two decades after the headiest days of chiliasm, Marvell reveals himself to be as consistent as his friend in his tenacious reformism. In the 1670s he points to the bishops as *agents provocateurs* of civil war and catalysts of national sin, whose aim is:

> to make the good people of England walk in peril of their souls, to multiply sin and abomination thorow the Land, and by ingaging men's minds under spiritual bondage, to lead them canonically into temporal slavery.
>
> (*General Councils*, 21)

This could well have been written in the 1640s, and it is a symptom of the way in which Marvell's views had been indelibly stamped by the reforming chiliasm of that period.

With Marvell's entry into public life as an MP, after the Restoration, he achieved recognition as 'a shrewd man against Popery',[25] reflecting therein popular opinion, which retained its mid-century antipathy to the 'Scarlet Whore of Rome'.[26] After the Great Fire of London, for which rumour blamed papist incendiaries,[27] Marvell was one of the MPs appointed to investigate its cause,[28] and in 1675 he was created a commissioner for recusancy in his home county of Yorkshire.[29] In view of this distinguished career as a champion of the 'true religion' it is not surprising that at his death it was opined that he had been poisoned by Jesuits;[30] nor that his posthumously published *Growth of Popery* contributed to the national hysteria over the Popish Plot of 1678.[31] The fact that his was not an isolated voice on this occasion should remind us that his resistance to the Restoration establishment should not be interpreted as radical or extremist. The consistently eschatological origins of his tracts chimed with popular feeling precisely because, even after 1660, the mainstream of eschatological belief retained a vestigial power against the new forces of suppression marshalled against it by the religio-political establishment; in the 1640s eschatology had ultimately proved to be a subversive force, and the post-Restoration period saw a backlash against it.[22] To that degree Marvell was a representative of the mainstream, which the new masters of the nation sought to redirect.

The exact nature of Marvell's political allegiance, before the Restoration, has been a subject of considerable uncertainty. The Civil War is first explicitly mentioned in his poetry in 1648; it is thought probable that by 1648 or 1649 Marvell was moving in London literary circles that would have been largely royalist in sympathy. *To His Noble Friend Mr Richard Lovelace* (1648) seems to express a royalist viewpoint, and *An Elegy upon the Death of My Lord Francis Villiers* (1648) is explicit in its royalist sympathies.[33] Similarly, in 1650 Marvell attacked the parliamentarian laureate in *Tom May's Death*. This pattern of royalist loyalties appears to be interrupted by a poem written slightly earlier in 1650, *An Horatian Ode upon Cromwell's Return from Ireland*, the political sympathies of which are still a subject of dispute (for that reason it shall be left aside just for the moment). From late 1650 or early 1651 until some date in 1652, Marvell was tutor to the daughter of Lord Fairfax, former commander of the parliamentarian forces. This so-called parliamentarian phase in Marvell's life continues with his appointment as tutor to Cromwell's ward, William Dutton, in 1653, and further in 1654 with his poem *The First Anniversary of the Government under his Highness the Lord Protector*. Other poems written in support of Cromwell followed, and in 1657 he was appointed Latin Secretary to the Council of State, under Milton. Yet after the Restoration in 1660 he escaped odium, retained a seat as MP for Hull and travelled on at least one diplomatic mission, to northern Europe.

Much has been made of this apparent alteration in Marvell's allegiance, from "royalist" to "parliamentarian".[34] In some cases commentators have gone so far as to suggest that he was never a royalist; or, accepting a royalist phase, that his enthusiasm for Cromwell was limited by vestiges of royalism; or that his attitude to Cromwell was ironic to the last. These are strongly defined, one might say even simplistic, attitudes to Marvell's allegiance. The main issue of recent historical studies of this period has been to warn us against speaking too glibly of Puritans, parliamentarians and royalists, as if they were strongly defined groups with immutable characteristics. Many of the original parliamentarian generals and spokesmen were conservative in outlook, regarding themselves as defenders of the "Elizabethan" status quo; they came from the solid ranks of the gentry and in many cases are best described as constitutional monarchists. Respect for Charles' office was such that, when the king was condemned, it was a difficult task to find the required number of signatories for the death-warrant. Cromwell himself, who by 1649 was convinced of the necessity for regicide, had done his utmost to treat with the king while the latter was in the custody of the Army.[35] At the outset of the war hardly anyone could have imagined that events would precipitate a course as drastic as regicide. Indeed, 'Puritans were as devoted to monarchy as their Anglican opponents were', despite propaganda to the contrary effect; for the majority of parliamentarians regicide was a matter for acquiescence rather than enthusiasm.[36] Difficulties of loyalty afflicted the royalist camp also, for although they adhered to the king, some were not unsympathetic to Parliament's complaints.[37]

In political aims, divisions on the parliamentarian side surfaced most obviously after the first Civil War, when common antipathy to the bishops had been largely satisfied.[38] Most of the political events occuring during and after the Civil War arose out of circumstance rather than calculation. Hardly anyone had a cut-and-dried view of the issues involved, or indeed of the great men on either side. Response to Cromwell in particular was ambivalent on both sides—a fact which should not be obscured by party propaganda.[39] Neither is it surprising that the question of Marvell's loyalties is a vexed one. It should be remembered that many other poets altered their allegiance, some more than once—Dryden, Waller, and Tom May amongst them. It is difficult to say whether conviction or mere policy provided the dominant motivation for such shifts, but one can say, with certainty, that those who lived through the Civil War were themselves confused by events.

Marvell's political views are illuminated especially by *The First Anniversary* and *The Rehearsal Transpros'd (RT)*: dating respectively from the Interregnum (1654) and the Restoration (1672-3) periods, they reveal the consistency of Marvell's principles across the boundaries of political change, principles consequent upon a belief in providential history. In *RT* Marvell gives his analysis of the true cases of the Civil War, that Charles I—'the best Prince that ever wielded the English Scepter'—was ruined by self-seeking churchmen:

> For his late Majesty being a Prince truly Pious and Religious, was thereby the more inclined to esteem and favour the clergy. And thence, though himself of a most exquisite understanding, yet thought he could not trust it better than in their keeping . . . But he that will do the Clergyes drudgery, must look for his reward in another World. For they having gained this Ascendent upon him, resolv'd whatever became on't to make their best of

him; and having made the whole business of State their Arminian
jangles . . . did for recompence assign him that imaginary
absolute Government, upon which Rock we all ruined.

(*RT*, 134)

Marvell's praise of Charles I in this passage may be partly
motivated by prudence. On the other hand, even during the
1640s few had disputed that Charles I was 'Religious';
simply, some thought him pious in the wrong—Popish—
manner. The irony of 'he that will do the Clergyes drudgery,
must look for his reward in another World' is incisive
enough—it does not spare Charles I, and it challenges Charles
II to avoid a repetition of his father's disastrous mistake.
Similarly, even in the 1640s, on both sides it had been
common to attribute the king's fall to the episcopal influence
upon him.[40] Because of their papist tendencies and their
urging of absolutism in the monarch, the Civil War had
ravaged the nation: the 'Good Old Cause' had some reason in
it, because of their activities, but it need never have occurred
had the bishops restrained themselves (*RT*, 242). By recalling
the corruptions of the English Church at the hands of the
clergy—ever since the Reformation itself—Marvell places the
Civil War in the perspective of eschatology (130–4, 240),
asserting that only true and continuous 'reformation' averts
such national tumults. 'For all Governments and Societies of
Men, and so the Ecclesiastical, do in process of long time
gather an irregularity, and wear away much of their primitive
institution', requiring a constant review of 'those errours . . .
that have insensibly crept on' (239). This principle of constant
reformation is evidently derived from eschatology, which
described history as a process in which the corruptions of
Antichrist had vitiated the 'primitive religion' and 'crept on'
in the institutions of the world. The proper vigilants of
reformation are the government and the Church (239); for
Marvell the active intervention of the people in resistance or
revolution is a last resort (240), and this principle distinguishes him as a reformer rather than a revolutionary.

This attitude had an international as well as a national
context. Mainstream chiliasm had proposed that zeal should
comprehend the worldwide struggle against Antichrist.[41]

During the Interregnum Cromwell's attempts to implement a European "Protestant Alliance" had included overtures to Sweden; Marvell supported these attempts in the form of three poems presented to Queen Christina during the period of negotiations.[42] This diplomatic offensive was symptomatic of the 'last ditch' militancy of Protestant feeling in England,[43] which Marvell shared in his poem *A Letter to Dr Ingelo*. For him as for other chiliasts, zeal motivates an army crusading for the purposes of providence, which is the arbiter of history, driving it to its fulfilment in the *eschaton*.

On the international as well as the national scene, that Fifth Kingdom is an antirevolutionary concept: 'although Christ did not assume an earthly and visible Kingdome, yet . . . he knew very well that without dethroning the Princes of the World at present . . . opposition would be worn out, and all Princes should make place for a Christian Empire' (236)— that which, for Foxe, was prefigured by the Protestant Christian Emperor on earth. His antagonists, the 'Princes of the World', are in fact the 'kings of the earth' which Revelation had said would ally with the Whore until the Last Day (17:2f.). The radicals—Fifth Monarchists and their ilk—thought to attain the Fifth Kingdom by 'dethroning' such monarchs, but against their view, and equally against that of his high Anglican opponent, Marvell expresses the belief of moderate chiliasm that Christ wears out 'all opposition', without the assistance of either camp. The 'wearing out' of the kings of the earth finds an analogue in the words of a chiliastic divine, that the Coming would occur when 'he [Christ] hath worn them [kings] all out'.[44] For mainstream eschatology emphasized those biblical texts which stated that the time of the Coming was not 'revealed' to men,[45] deriving the moral that men must be 'patient' for Christ's Coming, remaining 'vigilant' in the meanwhile.[46] Any attempt to precipitate that Coming was presumptuous, for the 'timing' was in God's hands. Marvell's version of the inexorable *eschaton*, independent of human effort, allies him with moderate chiliasts, and is the source of his antagonism towards those sectarians who would seek to anticipate that process. 'God only in his own time, and by the inscrutable methods of his Providence is able to effect' the extirpation of popery (15): the limits of revelation proscribe human activism in the cause of the *eschaton*.[47]

This theme of confident 'patience' is the salient feature of his remarks on the Civil War in *RT*:

> the War broke out, and then to be sure Hell's broke loose. Whether it were a War of Religion, or of Liberty, is not worth the labour to enquire . . . I think the Cause was too good to have been fought for. *Men ought to have trusted God*; they ought and might have trusted the King with that whole matter. 'The Arms of the Church are Prayers and Tears', the arms of the Subjects are *Patience* and Petitions . . . *For men may spare their pains where Nature is at work, and the world will not go the faster for our driving.* Even as his present Majesties happy Restauration did it self, so *all things else happen in their best and proper time, without any need of our officiousness.*
>
> (135; my italics)

If we disregard the flourishes deferring to Charles II, the main thought emphasized here is that history is not of human making. God knows what He is doing, and drastic activism of the kind that characterized politics before the Restoration is futile interference. It follows that, despite the revolutionary interlude of the Interregnum, history recovered its course and the Restoration was effected by the 'Providence of God' (43). Of necessity, Marvell's statements here justify both the king and the 'Good Old Cause' of Parliament, which had responded to an obvious need for reformation in the absence of monarchical reforms. Equally, however, 'Men . . . might have trusted the King', for if history is providentially directed, Charles was willy-nilly God's agent: the godly cause was 'too good to have been fought for' because one way or another God's plan would achieve its destined objectives. The ruler's authority is God-given (232–3), and revolution is outside the sanctions given by Christ the Fifth King:[48] a view which, confirming the distinction between Christ's and earthly kingdoms, is characteristic of mainstream eschatology and was ratified even by conservative parliamentarians of the Civil War period.[49] 'Subjects are bound both as Men and as Christians to obey the [ruler] actively in all things where their duty to God intercedes not' (232–3). The question was, where did the boundary lie between the subject's duty and the believer's? In locating that boundary the subject had to be sensitive to the fact that obedience was demanded for kings precisely on the basis of obedience to God, and that rebellion could merely recapitulate 'Man's first disobedience': 'Tis Pride that makes a Rebel. And nothing but the over-weening of our selves . . . that raises us against divine Providence'.[50] It might well be that the potential revolutionary mistook God's complicated scheme, in which even tyrannous monarchs might play their part, and substituted his own personal programme under the colour of godliness.

We are unaccustomed to a philosophy in which religion and politics are so thoroughly fused, and at first sight the political concomitants of Marvell's views may seem fatalistic. Belief in providential history might seem to warrant any government, simply on the basis that its existence is *de facto* proof of its favour in the eyes of God. However, what is in question here is the individual's ability to comprehend God's purposes in history, which is hardly an easy task. Aware that he might have misread God's intentions, he had to ensure a certain circumspection in his political actons;[51] but, equally, the Puritan chiliast was enjoined to be active in the furtherance of God's purposes. These conflicting considerations of activism and quiescence placed the individual in a dilemma. Just how active for God's purposes, and how passive to His hand in history, could one be? Could one be both? Such questions vexed the parliamentarians during the Civil War,[52] and (as we shall see) they bedevil Marvell's poems too.

In *RT* Marvell suggests that 'the Arms of the Subjects are Patience and Petitions', a submission to the given order which is equally a legal enterprise to change it. This gradualist political philosophy, amalgamating passivity and activism, allows a shifting emphasis to each in response to the necessities of the time. Such an emphasis, for instance, separates the writing of *RT* (which at least seemed—for its own reasons—favourable to Charles II's latest controversial action) and *The Growth of Popery*, which was evidently subversive of the government, although careful to avoid explicit treason against the king. Despite the moderation of Marvell's activist stance, the vigour of his convictions is never more evident than in the fact that at times he endangered both his small income[53] and his freedom to promulgate them, a commitment which is equally decisive in his poems.

An explicit example of such commitment is his *The First Anniversary of the Government under his Highness the Lord Protector* (1655), in which the younger Marvell had celebrated the apparently effective agency of Cromwell. Between this poem and the *RT* of two decades later there is a gulf, not of commitment to eschatological politics but of disillusionment with the conscious assistance of men in the divine plan. The Puritan William Prynne, surveying the waste and futility of the mid-century and the self-interest that had vitiated even 'godly' projects, expressed his disgust with 'mutabilities and perfidiousness in men of all' parties and concluded that 'I dare trust none. . .but God alone'.[54] For similar reasons Marvell came to rest in the thought that 'Men ought to have trusted God'. We may imagine, then, how he looked back upon his panegyric of Cromwell as God's agent, as a proof that he had himself mistook the course of providence in the 1650s.

The poem was issued under government sponsorship[55] presumably because, answering the radical sects, it verified the godliness (and therefore, necessarily, the legitimacy) of the Protectorate. In this poem mainstream chiliasm answers its revolutionary critics: since Marvell is as chiliastic as his opponents, he is able to hoist them by their own petard. It has been generally recognized that one section of the poem (100–40) is explicitly millenarian, but this is usually treated as a digression and its so-called 'millenarianism' as something of an aberration.[56] The poem has never been understood in its basic premise, its context, and (as will become evident) its centrality to Marvell's poetry as a whole.

While it has been noted that time and its various aspects are ubiquitous in the poem,[57] this motif is, in fact, a context for Marvell's polemical proposition that Cromwell is the chosen 'Captain' of God in the Latter Days, who reforms and reconstructs the state at home and prosecutes the struggle against Antichrist abroad. This is the justification of Cromwell's regime.

Now that peace has been restored, reformation and reconstruction involve the composition of national factions. Since peace is 'a harmony and an agreement of different things',[58] that is precisely the manner in which Marvell describes Cromwell's activity as 'Architect' of a new state:

> The crossest Spirits here do take their part,
> Fast'ning the Contignation which they thwart;
> And they, whose Nature leads them to divide,
> Uphold, this one, and that the other Side;
> . . .
> While the resistance of opposed Minds,
> The Fabrick as with Arches stronger binds
> *(The First Anniversary*, 89–96)

The pacifying 'harmony' is compared to Amphion's similarly architectonic music (73). This vision of the reformed state's architecture has its source in Milton's description of the reformed Church (they are, of course, symbiotic institutions in Puritan reformist thought). In *Areopagitica* (1644) Milton is arguing for religious toleration—as Marvell would, too, thirty years later—in a Church which could encompass minor sectarian differences:

> there must be many schisms and many dissections made in the quarry and in the timber ere the house of God can be built. And when every stone is laid artfully together. . .it can but be contiguous in this world. . .the perfection consists in. . .that out of many moderate varieties and brotherly dissimilitudes that are not vastly disproportional, arises the goodly and the graceful symmetry that commends the whole pile and structure. Let us therefore be. . .more wise in spiritual architecture, when great reformation is expected.[59]

Milton and Marvell share the vision of a spiritual architecture which builds a harmony out of tension, recognizing that 'Contignation' rather than uniformity is all that can be expected in this world and all that God requires. The tensions which provoked war are portrayed as a providential advantage to the strength of godly institutions. This is 'The Commonwealth[s]. . .willing Frame', because true reformation evokes the will of men themselves; just as Milton called for reconciliation rather than 'the forced and outward union of cold. . .and inwardly divided minds',[60] so Marvell affirmed that 'Reformation is most easily and with least disturbance to be effected' by individuals (*RT*, 239). Here, however, when men are embittered by civil war, reformation must fall to the ruler, who may compel 'The crossest Spirits'. Hidden in these lines is a careful *legerdemain* implying that most are submissive to Cromwell's statesmanship, but even the intractable are subsumed. Cromwell's power, metaphorical-ized as the divine magic of music, metamorphoses into architectural art and finally figures a supernatural power to reconcile 'the Minds of stubborn Men', out of whom no-one else 'can build'. By such means the extended metaphor "proves" Marvell's contention that 'Such was that wondrous Order and Consent,/When *Cromwell* tun'd the ruling Instrument' (*The First Anniversary*, 67–8)—compounding the Instrument of Government (issued in December 1653) and the divine harmony which, like David, Cromwell receives as God's appointed. Such ratification is necessary because he is not God's anointed.

Since ratification must be eschatological, too, Cromwell is portrayed as a statesman 'in tune' with the urgent tempo of the Latter Days, contrasted to the dilatory ineffectiveness of 'tedious Statesmen' (69). These—the previous Caroline regime, in effect—are, like the monarchs of Europe, recur-rently contrasted to Cromwell's celerity by images of stagnancy, paralysis and retardation. Marvell insists upon the contrast because, in the light of the imminent End, time itself is at a premium. 'Cromwell* alone with greater Vigour runs,/(Sun-like) the Stages of succeeding Suns' (7–8), thereby echoing the haste with which Christ the sun of righteousness (Malachi 4:2) hastes to His Second Coming. Cromwell's celerity, 'contracting' time, is that activism or zeal proper to the Latter Days, in which the saints must be constantly 'Looking for and hasting unto the coming of the day of God', the Last Day (II Peter 3:12).[61]

> 'Tis he the force of scatter'd Time contracts,
> And in one Year the work of Ages acts:

> While heavy Monarchs make a wide Return,
>
> . . .
>
> And though they all *Platonique* years should raign,
> In the same Posture would be found again.   (13–18)

Like the pre-Cromwellian regime, which 'many years did hack,/Framing a Liberty that still went back' (69–70), the remaining kings of Europe are frozen in ungodly inactivity: '(Image-like) an useless time they tell' (41), like a stopped clock. The motive for this inactivity is self-interest, since at the end of time 'the kings of the earth' are destroyed (Revelation, 18:9); by delaying the retributive justice of God, they preserve 'From the deserved Fate their guilty lives' (40). Similarly, the notion of a 'Liberty' which constantly reverts to tyranny is an obverse image of ongoing reformation. In contrast to antichristian reversion ('When the Wheel of Empire, whirleth back': *Tom May's Death*, 67), the reformer must 'brush the dust off the *Wheels*, and oyl them again, or if it be found advisable. . .chuse a set of new ones' (*RT*, 239). As such, a reformer put it, 'a worke done in season. . .is a worke upon its wheels. . .that goes on to purpose'.[62] Time itself is a 'Wheel' (*Hastings*, 12) that reformation must drive on towards the day when the perfect Kingdom will come. Cromwell's haste is thus macrocosmic and apocalyptic in its implications.

Thus his political actions are described in terms of a control exercised over time, in step with God's will. Having 'tune[d] this lower to that higher Sphere' (48), Cromwell has brought human time into pace with heaven's. 'One day is with the Lord as a thousand years, and a thousand years as one day' (II Peter 3:8); Cromwell 'in one Year the work of Ages acts'—and 'All the Year was Cromwell's day', as Marvell states in another poem,[63] making a conceit out of the fact that the divine time made a 'day' in Revelation an elastic temporal unit.[64] Building the Protectorate is an exercise in this divine control, that 'still new Stopps to various Time apply'd' (66).

But this control and speed are not personal. Cromwell is impelled by the irresistible forward movement of providence, as an instrument:

an higher Force him push'd
Still from behind, and it before him rush'd,
Though undiscern'd among the tumult blind,
Who think those high Decrees by Man design'd.
(239–42)

In emphasizing Cromwell's god-given rights as agent, Marvell is also implementing the poet's own spiritual necessity, which is the 'worthy speculation of the great order. . .of God's wise providence, through the whole contexture of these exterior, seeming accidents' (*General Councils*, 139); obeying the imperative of the chiliast to look beyond events,[65] even as he responds to the political moment in an activist proponence of Cromwell. In the light of this diagnosis the fall of the monarchy and the institution of the Protectorate— 'Here pulling down, and there erecting New', as Marvell carefully expresses it, just for the Miltonic 'Proportions' of the thing (247–8)[66]—are to be regarded as providential: ' 'Twas Heaven would not that his Pow'r should cease' (243).

If Cromwell is God's 'Captain' in the Latter Days (321), his reform of the state must be seconded by that of the Church, in contrast (again) to those antichristian rulers who 'neither build the Temple in their dayes. . .Nor sacred Prophecies consult within,/Much less themselves to perfect them begin' (33–6); that is (expressing Cromwell's virtues negatively for variety's sake), Cromwell does implement the saint's duty by consulting God's 'inner promptings' in his soul as well as the sacred prophecies of the Bible.[67] Thereby he is enabled to 'build the Temple' in England, the church which is an antitype to Solomon's in Jerusalem—the church-in-glory of the New Jerusalem. This project affirms Cromwell's godliness, and provides a basis for Marvell to extend Cromwell's reforming role to the international arena where chiliasm must find effect.

At once a portent and an agent of the divine will in history, Cromwell 'like a Star,/Here shines in Peace, and thither shoots a War' (101–2). Rather than fear him, other princes should be apprehensive of what he represents, and convert themselves into Puritan saints:

> O would they rather by his Pattern won
> Kiss the approaching, nor yet angry Son;
> And in their numbred Footsteps humbly tread
> The path where holy Oracles do lead;
> How might they under such a Captain raise
> The great Designes kept for the latter Dayes!
> (105–10)

Marvell's advice to the unregenerate kings of the earth is drawn from Psalm 2:2-12—though they have 'set themselves. . .against the Lord. . .Be wise. . .O ye kings. . .Kiss the Son, lest he be angry, and ye perish from the way, when his wrath is kindled'. The Son of God is 'nor yet angry' because He is yet to come in His role as the Judge of men, but that event is imminent,[68] and a wiser self-interest on the part of such kings would dictate that they save themselves and the world together rather than turn from the true way. As yet, however, they serve the antichristian powers who obstruct the Coming, for 'still they sing Hosanna to the Whore,/And her whom they should Massacre adore' (113–4). As read in England at this time, 'the kings of the earth' in league with the 'Scarlet Whore of Popery' against the godly (Psalm 2, Isaiah, Revelation 17:2) are the Catholic powers of Europe.[69] While they adore her, time remains arrested at the point ('still') where, as prophesied by Revelation 17, they 'fornicate' with her spiritual idolatry, disregarding that 'sacred Oracle' (17:16) which prophesied that they would turn upon the Whore as the Last Day approached. Similarly, ignoring the Pauline prophecy of the conversion of the Jews and heathens, which would signal the ingathering of the nations to Christ's Kingdom (Romans 11), such princes 'Indians whom they should convert, subdue;/ Nor teach, but traffique with, or burn the Jew' (115-6). Some readers might mistake for modern anti-imperialist liberalism—one suspects that they often do—what is, in fact, eschatological dogma. Marvell is completing the contrast between God's antagonists and Cromwell, who not only executes the 'great Work' (56) of England's reformation but, as 'Captain' in the Holy War, may accomplish the 'great Designes' of history in Europe (110).

The warning to Europe is given a personal signature:

> Unhappy Princes, ignorantly bred,
> By Malice some, by Errour more misled;
> If gracious Heaven to my Life give length,
> Leisure to Time, and to my Weakness Strength,
> Then shall I once with graver Accents shake
> Your Regal sloth, and your long Slumbers wake;
> Like the shrill Huntsman that prevents the East,
> Winding his Horn to Kings that chase the Beast.
>
> (117–24)

To prosecute the godly cause in poetry as Cromwell does in war is the properly activist role for the poet-saint. These are the finest lines in the poem, resonant with Miltonic fervour. Indeed, the prophecy of Marvell's 'graver Accents' echoes Milton's own early statement of his epic ambitions, that 'I had rather, if I were to choose,/Thy service in some graver subject use'.[70] In these lines we must recognize that for Marvell, no less than for Milton in his determination upon the chiliastic *Paradise Lost*, epic was the logical poetic consequence of the saint's duty. Although Marvell's talents seem essentially lyrical in scope, he might not yet have discovered that, and eschatological commitment pointed to the great historic poem. Amongst other things, Marvell requires for epic 'Leisure to Time', and that might well be lacking if the End comes as soon as he hopes. In epic voice the poet's 'Horn' is his equivalent to Cromwell's similarly musical and reforming 'Instrument'. (Since this puns on the 'horns' of the Beast, which were understood as the kings who served Antichrist, the poet's weapon matches his opponents.) Both prince and poet are implicated in the *eschaton*, pursuing their preferred modes of activism—not least in writing this poem.

Having stated his own sanction as the poet who celebrates God's agent, Marvell uses this to elevate Cromwell further:

> Till then my Muse shall hollow far behind
> Angelique *Cromwell* who outwings the wind:
> And in dark Nights, and in cold Dayes alone
> Pursues the Monster thorough every Throne:
> Which shrinking to her *Roman* Den impure,
> Gnashes her Goary teeth.
>
> (125–30)

The Antichristian powers are (as often) compounded in the image of the Beast who is also the Whore, and such powers were always characterized as devourers ('Goary teeth')[71] of the faithful. If the Whore is forced to retreat from temporal power back to Rome, the heart of impiety in this world, the Latter Day battle would be all but won: Cromwell would be the forerunner of Christ Himself, for the extirpation of Antichrist is the prerequisite of the Coming.

This is the climax of Marvell's claims for the Prince of the Elect Nation, sealing his legitimacy. There is an implicit contrast with the pre-Cromwellian regime, when English statesmen had proved to be instruments of the Whore, 'Whose num'rous Gorge could swallow in an hour/That Island, which the Sea cannot devour' (71–2). Thus Cromwell's ability to gag the Whore in Europe is read back into his reformation of England, justifying the destruction of the English monarchy (although not, be it noted, regicide). Now Marvell may indulge his own vision of the future:

> Hence oft I think, if in some happy Hour
> High Grace should meet in one with highest Pow'r,
> And then a seasonable People still
> Should bend to his, as he to Heaven's will,
> What we might hope, what wonderful Effect
> From such a wish'd Conjuncture might reflect.
> Sure, the mysterious Work, where none withstand,
> Would forthwith finish under such a Hand:
> Fore-shortned Time its useless Course would stay,
> And soon precipitate the latest Day.
> But a thick Cloud about that Morning lyes,
> And intercepts the Beams of Mortal eyes,
> That 'tis the most which we determine can,
> If these the Times, then this must be the Man.
> (131–44)

While Marvell must complete his vision of Cromwell as God's captain, his expressed horror of presumption in such matters must moderate the terms in which he locates Cromwell's coincidence with prophecy.[72] His portrayal of the warrior saint—the *Resolved Soul*—had commended 'a Soul that knows not to presume', rejecting the proffered temptation that he could 'know each hidden Cause;/And see the future Time' (*Resolved Soul*, 69–70); so, here, the 'ifs' and 'wishes' formalize the wistfulness of a vision which may not, after all, be fulfilled by Cromwell, though fulfilled it must be. Uncertainty does not enfeeble eschatological hope, though human frailty may postpone the consummation. Here Marvell is deferent to God's 'mysterious Work', in the same fashion for which he would later praise Milton's *Paradise Lost*.[73] The question is one of timing, since activism must achieve coincidence with the timing decreed by God Himself:[74] 'All things happen in their best and proper time'. If the 'Man' and the 'Times' must be in conjunction, so the 'seasonable People' is a timely nation, in tune with the urgency of the Latter Day crisis. Once such a 'Conjuncture' does occur, time will cease altogether—the climax of the poem's theme of temporal adjustment. Paradoxically, the total cessation of time is the desirable effect of speeding it up. But this would demand the fulfilment of the ambiguity in 'seasonable', that the English nation be not merely temporally responsive but true to its Chosen character.

This political warning, that it may be the nation that fails Cromwell and God, not vice versa, is the topical diagnosis of an uncertainty about 'the Times' which must anyway be present in Marvell's poem. He is capitalizing on his reverent discretion in political terms, quite rightly, since the political polemic of the poem is itself eschatology in action.

The "cloudy" terms in which Marvell envisages the End provide a conceit which turns an eschatological commonplace into an expression of his discretion. At the Second Coming 'they shall see the Son of Man coming in the clouds of heaven with power and great glory' (Matthew 24:30),[75] 'clouds' which became a byword in contemporary descriptions of that Coming.[76] Marvell's 'thick Cloud [that] about that Morning lyes,/And intercepts the Beams of Mortal eyes' makes of the signal of Second Coming the source also of its mystery for those who would locate it in time. This necessary secrecy, even for the chiliast sensitised to God's historical signals, recalls the metaphor in which Marvell described the majority of men as impercipient of the providence behind Cromwell's rise. The difficulty of achieving the *eschaton* is that the elect activist is hampered not only by its necessary mystery but also by those who are not even conscious of that mystery. By the optical motif, Marvell recalls that at the Coming 'every eye shall *see* him' (Revelation 1:7; my italics), a metaphor for the full revelation which will be manifested at the End.[77] The political point, re-animating the doctrinal one, is that by then it will be too late for some—those enemies of Cromwell who are also God's enemies, whose sins even of omission will reap a dreadful reward on that day.

The strategy whereby Marvell turns the reverence of his expression of the chiliastic vision to political capital, is also applied to the characterization of Cromwell here. When the poet discreetly averred that 'If these the Times, then this must be the Man', he was addressing an audience which largely believed these to be the Latter Days, and who should take the point that this man was indeed the instrument of God. If Cromwell has been "timely", it must be the 'People' who need, like the kings of the earth, to imitate his 'pattern' without demur:

> And well he therefore does, and well has guest,
> Who in his Age has always forward prest:
> And knowing not where Heavens choice may light,
> Girds yet his Sword, and ready stands to fight;
> But Men alas, as if they nothing car'd,
> Look on, all unconcern'd, or unprepar'd;
> And Stars still fall, and still the Dragons Tail
> Swinges the Volumes of its horrid Flail.
> For the great Justice that did first suspend
> The World by Sin, does by the same extend.
> Hence that blest Day still counterpoysed wastes,
> The Ill delaying, what th'Elected hastes;
> (*The First Anniversary*, 144–56)

The greatest obstacle to Cromwell and the *eschaton*—by now almost synonymous quantities in the poem—is the unregenerate torpidity of those who 'Look on' rather than 'see': since the meaning in events escapes them, time is extended during a tug-of-war in which their sluggishness counterweights the galvanizing forward movement of elect saints like Cromwell. The moral for the nation is the constant readiness and responsiveness to God which scripture enjoined upon the activist.[78] The alternative is the continuance of Antichrist's persecution of the faithful in the Latter Days under the power of his Red Dragon, whose 'tail drew the third part of the stars of heaven and did cast them to the earth' (Revelation, 12:3–4). The pun on 'still'—arrested time and constant imperfection—voices the poet's frustration as the preceding vision of *eschaton* recedes before human negligence.

If these are the supine enemies of God's great design, equally malignant are those whose activism is misdirected, like the Fifth Monarchists who 'the Scriptures. . .deface' by their belief that the Kingdom will be established by violence. 'Whose frantique Army should they want for Men/Might muster Heresies, so one were ten' (299–300), a Hydra-headed army which is recognisably an antichristian Beast. Such sects, opposing the Protector, provide the dangers signified by portents of disaster which had appeared when Cromwell suffered a near-fatal accident (175–214). 'The Shame and Plague both of the Land and Age' (294), they represent the new, postwar national sin. Cromwell 'Our Sins endanger, and shall one day kill' (174), a martyr to that domestic national enemy in which Antichrist is disguised as the most fervent of saints—a particularly virulent form of the normal antichristian mode of impersonation, and therefore more dangerous than the avowedly popish enemies derided earlier in the poem. By paronomasia Marvell includes in condemnation the Quakers and Ranters (298, 307), and the major charge is that these are of 'Mahomet's' kind (303f.), identifying them with antichristianism in its Muslim aspect. The evil spirits of antichristianism are implied in the reference to Mohammed's 'Falling-sickness', which puns on sin, physical fits, possession by demons,[79] and fits of heresy. The same epileptic image is used by Marvell in later years to deride the heresies of a high Church opponent as popish (*Mr Smirke*, 32). Specifically their tribulation of the nation is identified as that of the Locusts from the Bottomless Pit (Revelation 9:2–3,11):

> Accursed Locusts, whom your King does spit
> Out of the Center of th'unbottom'd Pit;

> Wand'rers, Adult'rers, Lyers, *Munser's* rest,
> Sorcerers, Atheists, Jesuites, Possest;
> You who the Scriptures and the Laws deface
> With the same liberty as Points and Lace;
>   (311–16)

The liberties which they take with scripture reveal them as the agents of Antichrist, corrupting the Word; they may claim to serve Christ the Fifth King (296) but in truth they serve Satan, who inhabits the Pit. Inverting their Monarchy, Marvell similarly inverts the significance of the 'Fifth': the Locusts of the Pit are agents not of the Fifth Kingdom, but of the Fifth Trumpet of Wrath (Revelation 9:1–3, 11)—not saviours, but destroyers. Joseph Mede had glossed the Fifth Trumpet's 'smoke' as Mahommedanism, obscuring the true Christian doctrine.[80] Like the Fifth Monarchists here, the Locusts were traditionally interpreted as heretics who oppressed God's people in the Latter Days, 'Bent to reduce us' (318) like Satan's original temptation and its deadly effect on man (319–20).

The catalogue of abuse which introduces this condemnation echoes the invective of II Timothy 3:2–5, which describes the sins which ravage the Latter Days: 'men shall be lovers of their own selves. . .proud, blasphemers, disobedient. . .unthankful, unholy. . .false accusers, incontinent. . .Traitors. . .Having a form of godliness, but denying the power of it'. Marvell's lines similarly subsume the pride, heresy, political and spiritual disobedience, ingratitude to Cromwell, malignancy, slanders, adultery, treason, and hypocrisy of the Fifth Monarchists. The comparison to the extremists of Munster and their characterization as witches, Jesuits, atheists and madmen encompasses the wide range of antichristianism and would have been understood by a contemporary audience in that sense. This invective has a topical political resonance, since in 1654 (the year of this poem's composition) the government suspected that the major radical groups might combine with royalists in subversion.[81] The poem implies that such a combination would empower Antichrist in England. The tight logical structure of this passage has both imagistic and polemical logic, impeccably based (as Fifth Monarchist ideas are not, in this account) upon scriptural reference. Misinterpretation of scripture is what impels such revolutionaries and makes them both heretics and traitors 'who the Scriptures and the Laws deface'. At once spiritual and political, this offence provides Marvell with a periphrastic assertion of the legitimacy of Cromwell's government, which must consist in its godliness.

The First Anniversary articulates the chiliast's perennial effort to discover in current events that providence which is generally 'undiscern'd by the tumult blind,/Who think those high Decrees by Man design'd' (241–2), and to commit himself—in virulent polemic if need be—to the political consequences of that diagnosis. When this eschatological principle is recognized as the basis of Marvell's political views, the question of how his political allegiances developed is clarified. Despite periodic critical assertions that Marvell was a republican, the first thing to recognize is that he was a constitutional monarchist, a 'Parliament's man' in the traditional sense. Never in any of his works does Marvell express a republican idea, as one critic has correctly noted.[82] In effect, Marvell's problem was to experience the reigns of two kings who were less than sensitive to constitutional restraints, and to see in Cromwell a statesman who, while lacking dynastic right, seemed fitted for the English form of government. In *The Growth of Popery* Marvell describes the English constitutional form at some length, in contradistinction to the tyranny of such European absolutists as Louis XIV (248–9). The contrast is also religious, since the English are Elect in the nature of both Church and state (250), combining a 'Providential Constitution' (*RT*, 250) with freedom from antichristian religion. This symbiotic relationship provided for Englishmen like Marvell problems of allegiance, especially during the Civil War. As the poems on *Lovelace, Villers, Hastings*, and *May* indicate, Marvell was a royalist at least between 1648 and 1650. In *Hastings* he reviles the 'Democratick Stars' (25); in *May* he derogates the republican image of the parliamentarians and reverses the usual description of royalists as 'Malignants' by re-applying the epithet to the parliamentarian laureate. Since most early parliamentarian leaders equally respected the king's as a sacred authority, and (at first anyway) regarded Charles I as misled, Marvell in the

1640s was a royalist in a manner only finely distinguished from orthodox parliamentarian principles which emphasized the combination of constitutional government with true religion. However, as a Puritan chiliast hostile to Laudian episcopacy—with which Charles' cause was inextricably involved—Marvell shared the dilemma of a number of royalists who were required to make a crucial choice between loyalty to the king and opposition to the episcopal influence over him. While in *Tom May's Death*, Marvell asserted the 'ancient Rights' of monarchy (69), the division between civil and spiritual 'right' in his mind seems to be recalled in William Fairfax's similar difficulty:

> What should he do? He would respect
> Religion, but not Right neglect:
> For first Religion taught him Right,
> And dazled not but clear'd his sight.
>   (*Upon Appleton House*, XXIX)

William can resolve his problem because he opposes the false image of that religion. While Marvell's choice was apparently more difficult, it is evident from his royalist poems that he finally chose to support the civil right. In the case of Thomas Fairfax, Marvell's employer in the early 1650s, a similar dilemma issued in allegiance to Parliament; by then, however, he had resigned his position, and his attitude to the regicide had confirmed that—like several other parliamentarian leaders—he was a constitutional monarchist horrified by the execution of an anointed king.[83] But personal contact with Fairfax would have mitigated Marvell's view of the original objectives of the parliamentarians, an alteration signified by the difference between his youthful vision of 'how slow Death farre from the sight of day/The long-deceived Fairfax bore away'[84]—a bitter partisan wish-fulfilment—and the paean to Fairfax's moderation in *Upon Appleton House*. Equally, more immediate acquaintance with Cromwell and Milton's commitment to the Cromwellian regime accounts for the distance between Marvell's early dream of how 'heavy Cromwell gnasht the earth and fell'[85] and his eloquence as unofficial laureate in *The First Anniversary*. By 1657 Marvell's Latin Secretaryship formalized his commitment to Cromwell.

That the basis of Marvell's allegiance had not altered is evident from his description of the Protectorate as precisely that combination of liberty and restraint which he defined as proper to English constitutionalism in *Growth of Popery*:

> 'Tis not a Freedome, that where all command;
> Nor Tyranny, where One does them withstand:
> But who of both the Bounders knows to lay
> Him as their Father must the State obey.
>
> (*First Anniversary*, 279–82)

Many contemporaries recognized in this Father-Protector a king under another name, and some decried his ambition in ousting a king merely to usurp his place.[86] When offered the crown he refused it, probably to obviate such calumnies.[87] But for Marvell in 1654 monarchy was precisely the form which he approved for Cromwell, as his description of the Protectorate makes clear; and later, in *Upon the Victory Obtained by Blake* he averred that 'The best of Lands should have the best of Kings' (40).[88] If monarchy was proper to England, Cromwell was superbly qualified for kingship despite his lack of dynastic right. In Marvell's support for Richard Cromwell's succession to the Protectorate[89] it is evident that he was attempting to forward a dynastic pattern even for the new regime. Nor was he much to be distinguished from Cromwell himself in constitutional monarchism, since this was usually a feature of Independency, and if Cromwell was an Independent, the signs indicate that Marvell was also.[90]

After the Restoration his position required more "radical" proponence than it might have done under a less reactionary regime and a king less inclined to popery. Marvell's views were constant in the providential relationship of Church and state within the Elect Nation: it was governments which changed, swiftly and extremely, between 1640 and 1670. Marvell's political affiliations after 1660 reflect this pattern. The 'Country' opposition in the Commons with which he was associated—the constitutional and anti-French platforms of which were essentially his own as well[91]—were in many ways the heirs of the original parliamentarian position. The major figures in this group, Shaftesbury and Buckingham, were amongst the Four Lords whose commitment to the Tower on a constitutional quarrel was denounced by Marvell (*GP*, 321–2). A Presbyterian favouring toleration, Shaftesbury had liaised between his co-religionists and the established Church,[92] a conciliation which Marvell as an Independent would have approved; the terms in which he commends Shaftesbury are characteristic, that the latter may yet become 'a martyr for the English liberties and the Protestant religion' (409). With Buckingham, Marvell's connexions were closer, since the Duke had married Maria Fairfax, Marvell's former pupil; he is the champion of 'the due liberties of the English Nation' (299). In the 1640s and 50s Buckingham had been active for royalist interests both in the field and in post-war intrigues. While his father was the favourite of both James and Charles I, his brother Francis died in the royalist cause, an event commemorated in Marvell's eponymous elegy with appropriately royalist sentiments. While in 1671 Marvell was described by a government informer as an 'agent' of Buckingham, by 1674 he was probably also a spy and an agitator, since he had become involved in a fifth column established by William of Orange[93]. It is possible that Marvell's own pamphlets were financed and promoted by this organization, since its brief was to disseminate propaganda against the 'growth of popery' and the complicit 'French Interest'. In 1673 William's organizing agent, Peter du Moulin, himself published a pamphlet expounding the vital connexion between popish and French menaces, precisely Marvell's thesis in *Growth of Popery*. Such an analysis lies behind the possibility that Marvell aided the Dutch in the destruction of the Anglo-French alliance in 1673–4.[94] Marvell's motivation for espionage is readily comprehensible, given his fear of a Catholic succession by James and his community of Protestant interest with William. It would seem that the occasioning circumstance for *Growth of Popery* was the marriage of William to James' daughter Mary in November 1677;[95] Marvell makes veiled reference to the popish motives for the marriage, as fundamentally advantageous to the French.[96] Although the connexion has not been recognized, it is evident that this provocative event is linked to Marvell's pro-Dutch activities, and that his motive in the tract's diagnosis is largely anticatholic. Hitherto overlooked, Marvell's explicit reference to William is placed in the tract's closing pages for maximum effect upon the sympathetic contemporary reader. Marvell repines 'The abandoning [by Charles' regime of] his Majestie's own nephew for so many years, in compliance with his and our nation's enemies [the French]' (411), a reminder particularly telling since William was commonly regarded in England as a champion of Protestantism.[97]

Marvell's contacts with Holland were doubtless the basis of his entry into the Dutch organization,[98] connexions refreshed by a visit in 1662 the purposes of which remained mysterious but may have involved secret diplomatic aims.[99] His friend John Ayloffe was a member of the fifth column for similar reasons,[100] as (although a double agent) was Thomas Blood[101]—celebrated in Marvell's epigram *Bludius et Corona*, with an anticlericalist emphasis. Several prominent men felt happy to marshall foreign aid against domestic enemies, and while some were doubtless merely venal in intention, the salient motive for international loyalties in this period was militant Protestantism, retaining its chiliastic universalism.[102] In league with the Protestant champion of Europe against popery and absolutism, Marvell would have regarded his espionage as implementing the most fundamental loyalty of all. This involvement, like his controversial prose works, is his form of zeal; he was well aware that ends need means, for 'in this world a good Cause signifys little'—as little as the Good Old Cause had amounted to—'unless it be as well defended. A Man may starve at the Feast of Good Conscience' (*Letters*, 324). Reflecting an earlier disillusionment, he had opined that 'the antient Rights. . .do hold or break/As Men are strong or weak' (*Horatian Ode*), a fact which does not derogate such rights but is an inevitable function of the imperfection of men and 'this world'. Marvell's form of defence was obviously readjustable according to the political vicissitudes of the time, and we should not—as modern casts of thought tend to encourage us to—underestimate the way in which Puritan chiliasm could integrate pragmatism into idealism. Timeliness was a virtue not only sanctioned but demanded by chiliastic thought.

Marvell's political consistency resided in an ideology distinctly larger than partisanship, and that consistency is the source of his variations in allegiance. Perhaps the greatest value of a providential belief was that it could assimilate the enormous changes which England underwent in the seventeenth century. When in his poetry Marvell confronts historical change, his resource is always to deploy the complex strategies of chiliasm, most especially to define his own relationship to history in the making.

2

A Revelation for the Poet

Since the *eschaton*, and the religio-political ideas associated with it, dominated contemporary thought, it should be no surprise that the literature of the time reflects that preoccupation. Once that historical context is recognized, it can be seen that Marvell is the lyric poet of apocalypse—as Spenser and Milton are its exponents in epic. The influence of the Book of Revelation upon these two poets has been regarded as a significant factor in the *Faerie Queene* (*FQ*) and *Paradise Lost* (*PL*),[1] but the crucial nature of eschatology in Marvell's work has not been recognized. His case is a focus for the critical relationship between a poet and his own times, not only because that relationship has remained obscure but because, once understood, it is so illuminative for his poetry. His poems have long been characterized as "difficult", highly allusive, even cryptic.[2] In fact, it is precisely because of their close engagement with their own times that they are difficult of access now.

Even at their original publication this problem manifested itself. When the *Miscellaneous Poems* were posthumously published in 1681, the apogee of chiliasm had passed and its 'enthusiasm' was not merely unfashionable but actually repressed, so it is not surprising that their reception was unenthusiastic.[3] Marvell's proper audience was that of the 1640s and 50s, as the official endorsement of *First Anniversary*, one of the few poems published "in season", demonstrates. After the Restoration, only a few with similar views recognized in the published Marvell an apocalyptic—a prophetic—voice,[4] a voice which has not been heard for three hundred years. It is perhaps not inappropriate that the times should have been vital to the reception of a poet engaged with time in its dynamic aspect.

If we recognize that the implications of eschatological

31

belief were salient factors in the national life between 1600 and 1660, it is possible to see how profoundly they affected Marvell's overtly public writings. But we must also take account of the prevailing mood fostered by such beliefs. To an age still dominated in every aspect of life by its religious sense, the expectation that the new paradise was imminent generated great excitement.[5] Individual involvement was demanded by the need to observe the 'Signs of the End' and to act to accelerate the Coming,[6] and this 'integration of the individual in the historical process' was echoed within his own soul, the microcosmic battleground where the macrocosmic struggle between Christ and Antichrist found its echo.[7]. Antichrist and the Whore were at once historical and spiritual entities, involving at both levels the immediate experience of the believer. The emotional and intellectual repercussions of this attitude could animate any lyric form, whether public or personal in address, and provided structures and motifs of great literary power.

(i) THE POETICS OF HISTORY

The cryptic nature of Marvell's poetry is due to a range of factors, all of which spring from his relationship to his own times and the formulation of a poetics that may engage with history in its eschatological process. In order to understand his poems we must analyse the sources and the peculiarity of his poetic tone and structures.

The major issue of Marvell studies has been the problem of how to evaluate Marvell's poetic statements: he is a highly ambiguous poet, and frequently considered to have undermined the seriousness of his poems by a proliferation of irony and ambiguity.[8] In fact, ambiguity in Marvell is a constructive force, carefully manipulated precisely in order to create "meaning": he utilises ambiguity in order to make statements, not to evade them. Ironies and ambiguities are constituents of his characteristic procedure, which I shall term the "problematic". Before outlining that procedure, it is necessary to highlight another component, the "Final Image". This is, in general, the last few lines of a Marvellian poem (where it is not punctuated by stanzas), or its last stanza: it usually consists of a pithy couplet or a distinctively self-enclosed image, often of a descriptive or iconographical kind. Two such examples are the last stanza of *Upon Appleton House* or the final couplet of *The Unfortunate Lover*. More descriptive than enlightening, they have provided great difficulties for critics, none of whom has given a satisfactory account of (for instance) how the last stanza relates to—let alone finalises— the concerns of *Appleton House*. Highly resistant to explication, because not overtly conclusory, Marvell's Final Images are nevertheless summations of the poems' arguments; each providing a unit of meaning within his procedure, the problematic.

The problematic involves the use of *two* continuous arguments or narratives within a single poem; sometimes they run parallel, each reinforcing the meaning of the other. On other occasions they appear to contradict one another (rather like the thesis and antithesis of dialectic). This "double" narrative is achieved by the almost constant use of ambiguity, a form of language which may even allow two contradictory meanings to coexist within one statement. Thus the bifurcation of meaning that constitutes ambiguity also creates, in the aggregate, a bifurcation of the narrative of the whole poem. At the conclusion of the poem, these two narratives synthesize—are resolved—within the Final Image; in cases where the two narratives of the poem appear irreconcilable, the Final Image reconciles them. In this manner a conclusory force is achieved.

This procedure can be demonstrated only in the course of analysing a whole poem (as we shall see), precisely because the problematic builds ambiguities into a complex structure. In some cases a component ambiguity may imply more than two levels of meaning, but each meaning is subordinate to one of the poem's two narratives. (This is a system of meanings, not a proliferation of possibilities such as Empson might suggest.) As long as this procedure remains unrecognized, Marvell's poems look 'out of joint' (as indeed they have for many readers) because elements of the poem are omitted or misplaced in the experience of reading and explication. Once the problematic is recognized, it is possible to reveal the status and function of a statement in a Marvellian poem, which otherwise might appear confusing in its implications.

(In this relation it is not insignificant that Marvell also wrote a deal of satiric poetry, in which the double level of statement is a simple and traditional method.) By means of the problematic, ambiguity and irony become contributory factors in a highly organized poetic structure, and this intellectual procedure is the manner in which Marvell's 'wit' functions— structurally.

Ambiguity is poetic because subtle, harnessing the energies of language precisely as one expects that poetry should. That subtlety is underwritten by the covert nature of the problematic itself. That term I have redefined: in one school of criticism the term denotes in part a system of relationships within a literary work which is not recognisable by the author. That proposition I have turned on its head because Marvell's case requires it to denote a system of meaning not explicit within his work, and unnoticed by most readers, but of which he himself is conscious. Capable of variations from poem to poem, the problematic is in effect a means of codifying Marvell's poetics for the purposes of analysis.

Marvell's motivation for such a covert procedure comprises several factors, the first of which is his obsession with self-protection; for there are traces both in his life and his works of a deliberate self-effacement. When John Aubrey wrote his tantalisingly 'Brief Life' of Marvell, he characterized the poet as one who bordered on the anti-social. Mentioning a few of Marvell's close friends, he nevertheless observes that 'He had not a generall acquaintance'. His Marvell is a cautious man who, in hard-drinking times, 'was wont to say that he would not drinke high or freely with any man with whom he would not intrust his life'.[9]

This pronounced element of caution is nowhere more evident than in Marvell's letters, in which he rarely expresses overt opinions on political or other sensitive issues—even when writing a private epistle to his nephew. When he does express an opinion, it is usually in an ambiguous or even enigmatic fashion: a peculiarly apt example is 'they that discourse the lest and thinke the best of it will be the wisest men', commenting on Charles II's attitude to the Commons (*Letters*, 234). One suspects, indeed, that the habit of ambiguity became ingrained with him and may eventually have been an almost unconscious reflex.

He did, however, have reason for caution. In letters dating from the Restoration period his reticence may partly be attributed to an awareness that his mail might be intercepted by government agents.[10] A typical example of this motive is a letter to his nephew in which, referring to one 'Andrew Marvell' (who, it seems, is not numbered among the writer's 'generall acquaintance'), he continues:

> There came out, about Christmass last, here a large Book concerning *the Growth of Popery and Arbitrary Government*. There have been great Rewards offered in private, and considerable in the Gazette, to any who could inform of the Author or Printer, but not yet discovered. Three or four printed Books since have described, as near as it was proper to go, the Man being a Member of Parliament, Mr. *Marvell* to have been the Author; but if he had, surely he should not have escaped being questioned in Parliament, or some other Place. (357)

Here caution and humour are mingled in his indication to his nephew of the commotion caused by his latest tract. At one point, however, his anxiety for concealment becomes explicit, in the cause of concealment itself, of course. He rebukes his constituents for divulging to a stranger the contents of a previous letter:

> seeing it is possible that in writing to assured friends a man may giue his pen some liberty and the times are something criticall beside that I am naturally and now more by my Age inclined to keep my thoughts private, I desire that what I write down to you may not easily or unnecessarily returne to a third hand. (166)

Here Marvell admits to a congenital desire 'to keep my thoughts private', supplementing his assertion of the political wisdom of secrecy, that 'the times are something criticall'. Moreover, his asseveration that 'neither do I write deliberately any thing which I feare to haue divulged', while seeming to confirm his ingenuousness, actually indicates that he takes pains to couch his statements cautiously.

Doubtless his circumspect choice of drinking companions was due to a sense that in his cups he might let loose a dangerous word. And in general, according to Aubrey, 'He was in his conversation very modest, and of very few words'.[11] All of these observations sort well with Marvell's involvement with espionage, which one may see as both a cause and a symptom of his cautious *modus vivendi*. Possibly Marvell himself is responsible for the paucity of materials available to his biographers.

This reticence, the fostering of enigmas, is no less marked in his poetry, as many readers have testified. There is a tendency to assume that the allegedly unresolved or ambivalent stances of his poems reflect his own lack, or repudiation, of commitment to specific views.[12] On the contrary, it was because of his tendentious writings of the Restoration period that Marvell adopted politic language in his letters; his advertisement in those tracts of his committed views justified a caution in his personal life. In his poetry as in his letters his statements are habitually circumspect expressions of his views; that is, his self-protectiveness affects mainly the manner in which he chooses to express himself.

It is hardly surprising, then, that Marvell should have adopted the arcane procedure of the problematic, nor that this procedure should depend upon ambiguity. Since verbal ambiguity is by nature indirect and 'non-committal', it produces statements which appear to contain their own qualification. At a basic level, ambiguity provides a smokescreen for the poet. On the other hand, Marvell made of it a tool which, by its very indirections, might express his views in a covert manner: ambiguity is a 'two-handed engine', at once protecting and expressing his meaning. (And, since a conclusion is the ultimate commitment, it is notable that his Final Images are self-enclosed and resistant to such a degree.)

By these means his poetry imitates its creator, since it does not court a 'generall acquaintance'. While his manuscripts may have circulated privately,[13] his lack of interest in publication reflects this fact (also, possibly, that belief in an imminent *eschaton* belied the concept of posterity). The majority of the lyrics unpublished in his lifetime manifest what is essentially a self-reflexive verse, intended for an audience of one. If the problematic is a supremely difficult procedure for the reader to comprehend, that is because

Marvell was usually writing for himself—a privacy that perhaps even a coterie might not be allowed to penetrate fully.

If Marvell's temperament, interacting with the 'criticall' nature of the times, affected the language of his poetry, it must be said that the times were such as to affect men deeply.[14] Both civil war and regicide evoked a variety of strong reactions in men of all political colours, and the ensuing Protectorate revised many aspects of the national life. There were conflicts of loyalties at all levels of human relationship. The Civil War presented to Englishmen of the time a puzzling and disturbing picture, and the propaganda of both sides should not obscure the fact that psychological repercussions were inevitable when one nation split into two. In Marvell's works this national fissure provoked images of division at various levels, and decisively affected his choice of a poetic procedure.

One of those who meditated upon the unfortunate consequences of the times was the royalist poet Abraham Cowley, who mourned the loss of 'Reason'—and, with it, of the 'Thracian lyre'—in the Civil War: 'In sensless Clamours, and confused Noise,/We lost that rare, and yet unconquer'd Voice'.[15] Similarly, in his poem *To His Noble Friend Mr Richard Lovelace, upon his Poems* (1649), Marvell expatiated upon his fellow poet's "victimization" at the hands of Parliament, averring that 'th'infection of our times' had drastically affected the nature of poetry:

> Our times are much degenerate from those
> Which your sweet Muse with your fair Fortune chose,[16]
> And as complexions alter with the Climes,
> Our wits have drawne th'infection of our times.
> That candid Age no other way could tell
> To be ingenious, but by speaking well.
> . . .
> These vertues now are banisht out of Towne,
> Our Civill Wars have lost the Civicke crowne.
>
> (1–12)

Here, the 'Civicke crowne', which is implicitly compared with the crown of 'Bayes' (8) proper to the poet, represents the virtues of civic life, since it was the reward for virtuous action in that sphere. Thus Marvell draws a parallel between the breakage of social virtues in civil war and the destruction of true poetic values. Because of this vital connection between the social and literary orders, Marvell asserts that in time of civil war it is not possible to write good poetry: 'Our *wits* have drawne th'infection of our times'. Such is the poetic effect of the "national sin".

With this recognition of the effects of division on poetry, we can connect Marvell's frequent use of images of division or "doubleness". It would appear that a divided nation provoked a keen sense of internal division within men themselves. Thus one contemporary divine chose to stress anew that:

> there is since the fall, a separation betweene God and man, betweene Angels and man, betweene man and the creatures, *betweene man and himselfe.*[17] (my italics)

Similarly, noting this inner division, Marvell remarks the 'double Heart' of man, and his 'double. . .Mind' (*A Dialogue Between the Soul and Body*, 10; *The Mower Against Gardens*, 9). Such a sensitised attention to man's doubleness is equally apparent in the writings of Thomas Browne at this period of civil strife, when he notes that each man is a 'world of contraries'[18] imitating the antagonisms of civil war within his own psyche.

Marvell's fullest statement of this internal civil war is his *Dialogue Between the Soul and Body*. Here Soul and Body clash in a traditional Christian *agon*, each reproaching the other for its persecutions. However, Marvell has departed from tradition by allowing equal weight and space of argument to both interlocutors; normally the Soul overwhelmed the Body in this argument.[19] In this manner Marvell maintains an equipoise of argument, so that man's internal division between flesh and spirit is seen to be at once absolute and equal in its elements. The *moralitas* of the poem is a covert one, that the internal civil war is unwinnable in these terms. Equally tortured by one another, Soul and Body reveal the futility of their antagonism:

Soul. O who shall, from this Dungeon, raise
    A Soul inslav'd so many wayes?

. . .

Body. O who shall me deliver whole,
    From bonds of this Tyrannic Soul?

(1–2, 11–12)

Here Soul and Body make an identical complaint each against
the other (pointed up by the symmetry in line-numbers)—the
grievance of 'enslavement'. This internal echoing marks the
whole poem, showing the essential identity of Soul and Body
even in their quarrel; an identity which is at once the source
of that quarrel, since they each chafe against it, and the
obstacle to a resolution until death itself breaks their bond.

And there is a political lesson here. In essence, the lesson,
for those who prosecuted civil strife at this time, was that
division was both innate and intractable; but that also this
division merely expressed and confirmed the problems of
what must be, willy-nilly, a single entity. In other words, like
the Soul and Body, the two warring parties within this one
nation must learn that such differences have to be lived with,
that they are intrinsic elements of the 'Body *politic*', which
could not be resolved by outright war.

At this covert level of its argument, the poem reflects
Marvell's characteristic analysis of the causes of the Civil
War—that the clerical establishment, itself draconian, had
misled Charles into absolutist postures. We recall that for
Marvell the recurrent problems of human polities reflected
the inroads of antichristian ambition, which drove clerics to
desire political power, too. The combination of clerical and
secular antichristianism had the result:

> that men, instead of *squaring* their governments by the rule of
> Christianity, have shaped Christianity by the measures of their
> government. . .and bungling divine and humane things together,
> have been always hacking and *hewing* one another, to frame an
> irregular figure of political congruity.
>
> (*GP*, 281; my italics)

The same metaphor of 'squaring' and 'hewing' closes this
poem:

> What but a Soul could have the wit
> To build me up for Sin so fit?
> So Architects do square and hew,
> Green Trees that in the Forest grew.
> (41–4)

While serving the ostensible level of the poem, the architectural metaphor here also comprehends that sense of "a political order" which it signifies in *The First Anniversary* and *An Horatian Ode Upon Cromwell's Return from Ireland*,[20] denoting, here as in *GP*, political error and confusion. The state (or Body politic) is 'buil[t] up for Sin so fit' by the Soul (or Church) because of clerical meddling; thus the English state is 'A Body that could never rest,/Since this *ill Spirit* it possest' (19—20; my italics). Here antichristian error renders the Anglican Church an 'ill Spirit' corrupting the national body, just as Marvell would later diagnose in *GP* a similar antichristian conspiracy 'to subvert the government and religion, to kill the *body* and damn the *soul* of our nation.' (*GP*, 261; my italics). This is the inescapable obverse of the Elect Nation's character, which is properly an integral combination of 'True Worship and True Government'. That integral reciprocity is the motive for the Body's equality of role in this poem.

Thus the *Dialogue* points a moral for the nation by analogy with its traditional counterpart, man himself. Civil strife is figured by the conflict between flesh and spirit; in both cases, identity, whether national or personal, involves integrity too, and both forms of strife occasion damage to that integrity. Marvell makes that relationship between selfhood and nationhood explicit in the political metaphor of 'Tyranny' (12), the crime of which Charles I was accused at this time. The metaphor highlights the fact that the body of man had long been a simile for the political order. Thus, in a time of schism, the same metaphor relates the riven body politic to the divided self.[21]

Another Marvellian image of the divided or double man is the 'Amphibium': literally a creature able to live either in water or on land, it becomes in Marvell's poetry a symbol of human and national doubleness. Thus, in the last stanza of

Upon Appleton House, some fishermen are described as 'rational *Amphibii*' (XCVII), representing at once the divided nature of man, the 'rational' creature, and the more acute 'doubleness' of men who inhabit a nation split in two. (The line has another meaning, relevant to these concerns, which shall be discussed in context.) Similarly, in *The Unfortunate Lover* the eponymous hero is described as 'Th' *Amphibium* of Life and Death' (v). He is—as Christian man is said to be—a double creature, with a vital soul and a mortal body. Moreover, as we shall see, he is more acutely "double" because he experiences the divisions of the English Civil War. In all these cases, the traditional Christian image of man is given a contemporary force by public events; tradition and contemporaneity reinforce each other, as past and present collude in the making of history.

These images of doubleness are important in Marvell's case because they reflect his problems as a poet in 'th'infected' atmosphere of civil war. To realize the spiritualized force of his characterization of it thus in *Lovelace,* it is sufficient to notice there that Marvell is making a play on Sidney's famous description of the results of the Fall, that men have now both an 'erected wit' and an 'infected will'. Thus the enormity of this poem's situation, where 'wit', too, has 'drawne th'*infection*'. This view of the War as a sort of 'Fall', which recurs in other poems,[22] here dramatizes the poet's problems in the face of the catastrophe. In order to approach these problems, it is useful to observe that Thomas Browne also chose to describe man as an 'Amphibium':

> thus is man that great and true *Amphibium,* whose nature is disposed to live not onely like other creatures in divers elements, but in divided and distinguished worlds.[23]

This remark is interesting for the present purpose, because—having here remarked the 'divided' nature of man—Browne later reuses the amphibious metaphor to convey a similar quality in language, his term 'amphibology' denoting a statement with two opposite meanings.[24] The relationship between these terms in Browne's conception points to an analogy between the double man (amphibium) and the ambiguous or double statement (amphibology); it could be said that the double man was the incarnation of ambiguity, and ambiguity the semantic sign of the 'double Mind' of man. These analogous quantities, the divided man, the divided statement, and the divided nation, provided the poetic structure which Marvell chose for his writings in time of civil war. In this manner the bias of his times inspired the problematic of his poetry.

In particular, the *manner* in which the problematic made use of ambiguity—the double statement—meant that Marvell could not only reflect the doubleness of things, but could also redress it. The reflection of doubleness is, of course, achieved by the use of a double narrative based upon a series of ambiguities. In turn, the resolution of doubleness—the reattainment of singleness and certainty—is achieved by the synthesis of these two narratives in the Final Image. In this manner Marvell can simultaneously reflect the state of man and the nation in his times, and stand off from that division, recreating in poetry the unity that his times have lost. The problematic acknowledges and expresses doubleness in the times, but it also attempts a rehabilitation.

As a chiliast Marvell was indeed required to engage with the nature of his own times, and that engagement is achieved in his poetic structure also. The rehabilitation of the times is, however, a matter of recognizing the providential pattern concealed by events. If the problematic reflects and redresses the times, it must also reflect providence in the process of redeeming the course of history. The providential concept and the problematic's "dialectic" are analogous.

Dialectic involves the argument of two contrary elements which are eventually brought together in synthesis. The same procedure characterizes the providential directive in history, which is the argument of good with evil in the world, resulting in a synthetic product which is God's design. The resulting principle, that evil is necessary to the purposes of God, was emphasized by Marvell when he stated that God has:

> distinguished the government of the World by the intermitting seasons of Discord, War, and publick Disturbance. Neither has

he so ordered it only (as men endeavour to express it) by meer permission, but sometimes out of Complacency.

(RT, 231–2)

Accordingly, the idea of a providential directive at work in history is based upon the notion that evil is redeemed by its participation in God's design. Augustine had compared this providential dialectic to the creative ability of the poet:

> For God would never have created a man, let alone an angel [Lucifer], in the foreknowledge of his future evil estate, if he had not known at the same time how he would put such creatures to good use, and *thus enrich the course of the world* [sic] *history by the kind of antithesis which gives beauty to a poem*. . .a kind of eloquence in events, instead of in words.[25] [my italics]

The point of Augustine's comparison of providential history to a poem is that both are founded upon antithesis. And dialectic, the poetry of God in history, is also the problematic of Marvell's poetry. In this sense, it is capable of acting as a poetic equivalent of Marvell's view of history.

One other feature of Marvell's technique requires elucidation before we can go further: that stylistic peculiarity of Marvell which has been described, since the very inception of Marvell criticism, as his combination of 'levity and seriousness'.[26] The sources of that peculiar tone have remained obscure. Essentially, Marvell is accustomed to treat a serious theme of which he is convinced and to which he attaches the highest importance. However, his mode of expression for this theme exploits both wit and comedy, even at times to the verge of irreverence. Such use of comedy and wit is not only true to Marvell's temperament, but also fully sanctioned by Christian tradition and the devotional attitudes of his time.

Noting Marvell's predilection for self-protection, it should be recognized that the most effective form of defence for a writer tender of his own convictions is wit, a protective and even tolerant wit. Marvell proved his sensitivity to this fact in his controversial prose works, where wit and comedy are at once defensive and a sharp weapon of attack against his opponents. To present one's beliefs in comic form—or rather, in a manner acknowledging comedy—allows their affirmation while anticipating any assault upon them; paradoxically, to treat such beliefs without pomp is to make their contradiction appear a great deal too serious for its own good. Equally, wit can lend a cutting edge to one's own convictions. Thus, describing his method in *RT*, Marvell asserted that:

> That which is solid and sharp, being imp'd by something more light and airy, may carry further and pierce deeper, and therefore I shall look to it as well as I can, that mine Arrows be well pointed.   (187)

Wit and comedy are instruments of conviction, sharpening the impact of statement. He further described this style as 'betwixt Jest and Earnest' (187; echoing Bacon), an admixture that, as it has been rightly observed, distinguishes his poetic style as well.[27] When he said that it was possible to be at once 'merry and angry' in a serious religious debate (145), Marvell was confirming both the seriousness of his convictions and the witty efficacy of the mode he had chosen for their expression.

The best test of that mixed style, 'betwixt Jest and Earnest', is that it succeeded admirably in its aim of impressing Marvell's points, for his tract was judged to have worsted his opponent 'in the severest but pleasantest manner possible.[28] Part of this success is due to another effective quality of a mixed style, that an injection of comedy into a crucial argument guarantees the "good sense" of the writer; that, despite the strength of his convictions, he has enough sane detachment to treat them in this joco-serious manner.

That impression of "sanity" given by comedy was already well understood within the Christian tradition and supplemented by Renaissance ideas. It had already been recognized in the Middle Ages that such wit and comedy could both impress Christian ideas and create an atmosphere of "saneness" about them. Even "vulgar" laughter—at, for instance, a shrewish wife in a Miracle play—was valued 'as an indication of sanity, indeed almost of holiness'.[29] In extreme cases, even blasphemous wit has a niche in the Christian tradition, for as T. S. Eliot observed, 'It is only the irreligious who are shocked by blasphemy. Blasphemy is a sign of Faith'.[30]

Renaissance tradition confirmed the joco-serious mode of religious expression, in the form especially of *serio ludere*. This form of expression involved a sort of inverse decorum which acknowledged the distance between divine and human levels by wrapping the divine in the insulation of comedy. In a way, beliefs were too serious to treat seriously without still falling short of them, so one chose to fall deliberately short of them. A similar rationale—which, in essence, avows humility before sacred things—could motivate a Calvinist like Marvell. For Calvinism stressed the irretrievable corruption of man and nature, and the consequent imperfection of all things—a doctrine memorably expressed by Marvell himself.[31] To understand how this doctrine of imperfection could underwrite the joco-serious treatment of Christian beliefs, one has only to recall Eliot's further observation that the irreverence of the believer 'retains its respect for the divine by showing the failure of the human'.[32] This timeless form of Christian affirmation was seconded by 'the spirit of sacred *drôlerie*' in the Renaissance.[33] In the seventeenth century the joco-serious treatment of strong beliefs is apparent not only in the poetry of the period (Donne's *To His Mistris Going to Bed* is a good example), but also in its general writings. Religious devotion was, of course, strong in this period; the obverse side of this devotional coin, its "sane" and inevitable concomitant, was the obsessive treatment of religion in jokes. Thus one recent study remarks on not only the 'sheer obsessiveness' of religious topics but also that one of its effects was that 'Coarse ballads, innumerable mock-litanies, even the chapbooks of jokes of the period, all focus on religion'.[34] This was the reflex not of disrespect but of familiarity and conviction.

As such, it is apparent not only in Marvell but also in the clergyman, Marvell Senior: it was noted by a contemporary that the latter was 'Facetious and yet Calvinistic',[35] a mixture comprehensible in terms of the joco-serious tradition. Similarly, Marvell himself was observed to be at once a caricatured Puritan and a coffee-house wit,[36] and an encomiast of the time, lauding his "prophetic" matter, equally approved him as 'Mirrour of Mirth, and Prodigie of Witt'.[37] In his adoption of a mixed style for his sublime theme Marvell was, as in everything else, a man of his time.

(ii) APOCALYPSE AND *UPON APPLETON HOUSE*

The literary response to the times as 'the Latter Days' is most fully comprehended if we recognize that Marvell is an heir of Spenser and a companion of Milton. These poets represent the enterprise to construct an apocalyptic literature adequate to such an historical crisis. For both Spenser and Milton epic was to prove the vehicle best fitted for this enterprise, although it affects their shorter productions also. In Marvell's case the enterprise remained essentially lyrical; to that degree it is both less evident (epic is more readily seen as "historical" in its pretensions) and perhaps more subtly difficult. Indeed, in this respect the sophistication of his problematic is a response to such difficulty.

The most extended of his lyric poems is *Upon Appleton House*, which is best seen as an epic in miniature. In its reflection of the Civil War, encompassed by means of the owner Fairfax's role in hostilities, the poem attends particularly to the war's significance as a Latter Day phenomenon: 'ye shall hear of wars and rumours of wars. . .for all these things must come to pass, but the end is not yet. For nation shall rise against nation, and kingdom against kingdom' (Matthew 14:6–7). In joco-serious mode the poem imports this resonance into its record of the common view that the Civil War was a visitation upon the national sin.

> Oh Thou, that dear and happy Isle
> The Garden of the World ere while,
> Thou *Paradise* of four Seas,
> Which *Heaven* planted us to please,
> But, to exclude the World, did guard
> With watry if not flaming Sword;
> What luckless Apple did we tast,
> To make us Mortal, and The Wast?
> 　　　　　　　　　　　　(XLI)

Guarded by its island fastness as Eden had been by 'flaming Sword', pre-war England was a treasury of reformed religion protected from the antichristian sin that predominated elsewhere. As Marvell stated in *Mr Smirke*, 'we in England. . .are another world. . .are under an imperial crown [the Christian Empire]. . .are "none of them" [Papists and Lutherans]. . .but have a distinct Catholick faith within "our four seas'.[38] That Elect Nationhood is what England seems to have lost here, a characterization of a "post-lapsarian" England that comes to a climax in the penultimate stanza:

> 'Tis not, what once it was, the *World*:
> But a rude heap together hurl'd;
> All negligently overthrown,
> Gulfes, Deserts, Precipices, Stone.

There is no greenery left in the national 'Garden', for the conditions of life have been radically altered by Civil War—the metaphor of devastated landscape signifying that a national integrity has been lost. England, too, now partakes of the antichristian ruin which dominates the Latter Days as the world degenerates towards its End. Neither is 'what once it was'. The transformation of England from 'Garden' to 'Desert' indicates the alteration in the national environment, the overthrow of all that is familiar and the resultant chaos of the 'rude heap'. In the breakdown of order 'Chance' and force rule: when the Mowers of Death 'massacre the grass along' they inadvertently kill its inoffensive inhabitants:

> Unhappy Birds! what does it boot
> To build below the Grasses Root;
> When Lowness is unsafe as Hight,
> And Chance o'retakes what scapeth spight?
>   (LII)

Even the humble and the civilian are at risk in such a conflict, the universality of the Mowers' death-bringing function being figured in the 'Grass' which is the biblical symbol of Mankind: 'all flesh is grass' (Isaiah 40:6). (Indeed, several critics have understood the Mower section as a full-scale imitation of the civil war.)[39]

Reacting to this insecurity, Marvell takes refuge in the woods:

> How safe, methinks, and strong, behind
> These Trees have I incamp'd my Mind;
> Where Beauty, aiming at the Heart,
> Bends in some Tree its useless Dart;
> And where the World no certain Shot
> Can make, or me it toucheth not.
> But I on it securely play,
> And gaul its Horsemen all the Day.
>
> (LXXVI)

'Safety', the overriding consideration here, is at once a caution in one's personal life—Marvell's death as a bachelor proves him indeed resistant to female 'Beauty'[40]—and a security from public events with their unpredictable consequences. This twofold security gives Marvell an opportunity for playfulness, on the subject of playfulness itself: 'I on [the World] securely play,/And gaul its Horsemen all the Day'. Like a guerrilla Gaul eluding Roman cavalry, his playing 'galls' them: having encamped himself behind the carapace of his poetry, Marvell can tease 'the World'. His playfulness is, as it were, made possible by his caution.

If the persona of Marvell within the poem represents the personal effects of civil war—fear of disorder, insecurity, and caution—the national characterization as the New Israel is also wittily drawn:

> The tawny Mowers enter next;
> Who seem like *Israalites* to be,
> Walking on foot through a green Sea.
> To them the Grassy Deeps divide,
> And crowd a Lane to either Side.
>
> (XLIX)

The Mowers' progress through the parting grasses is a 'green Sea' counterpart to the Red Sea crossing by the original Chosen People, the Israelites.[41] Characteristically, Marvell conveys the typology of Old Israel to New with a delicate humour which nevertheless points to the destiny of the English.

Such national motifs are properly present in a poem which, through General Fairfax, can intimate in the 'lesser World'

(XCVI) of his estates the greater world of national events:[42] 'Things greater are in less contain'd' (44). Of England the chiliast and reformer Samuel Hartlib remarked that 'these 3. *Corn*, *Cattel*, and *Wood*, are the very *strength* and *sinews* of this Land'.[43] By the same token, the action of the poem's central portion includes a harvest of corn (XL–LV), a herd of cattle (LVII–IX), and a wood (LXI–LXXVIII), providing a truly representative microcosm of England's topography.

Upon Appleton House describes a train of events which not only imitates the national circumstances but also rehearses the eschatological destiny of the Elect Nation. Its eschatological theme first comes to the fore when Marvell meditates upon the history (suitably enough) of Nunappleton's own parochial Reformation, the transformation of a popish nunnery into a Puritan house:

> We opportunly may relate
> The Progress of this Houses Fate.
> A *Nunnery* first gave it birth.
> For *Virgin Buildings* oft brought forth.
> And all that Neighbour-Ruine shows
> The Quarries whence this dwelling rose.
>
> (XI)

'The Progress of this Houses Fate' imitates that of England: popery in ruins, Reformation represented by the reconstruction of a building. The Tudor Reformation of England is implicitly compared to the immaculate conception of Christ, at once elevating Protestantism and, by a salacious joke about the morals of Roman Catholic nuns, derogating that religion as the spiritual fornication denounced in Revelation. The nunnery's dedication to the Virgin thus wittily subserves Marvell's conclusion that Appleton House was 'no *Religious House* till now' (XXXV),[44] when it is inhabited by Puritan saints. While it was the residence of 'Suttle Nunns' (XII)—deceptive and inveigling as all antichristianism is, seducing Isabel Thwaites from her true destiny—it was a place of popish idolatry. Stanzas XII to XXXIV are an ironic evocation of the wrong kind of religious observance—ritualism, materialism, and hypocrisy, which a reforming

Fairfax extirpates. Marvell celebrates the demise of a superstitious religion in the Henrician Dissolution of religious houses:

> Thenceforth (as when th'Inchantment ends
> The Castle vanishes or rends)
> The wasting Cloister with the rest
> Was in one instant dispossest.
>
> (XXXIV)

The portrait of popery as 'Inchantment' alludes to the idea that the antichristian church was an illusion, a matter of 'lying wonders';[45] just as the nuns as 'Witches' (XXVI) recall that witchcraft was regarded as an aspect of Antichrist.[46]

The national event of the Henrician Reformation is reflected in the poem by means of Fairfacian family history, an incident in which William Fairfax rescued his betrothed from the cloister. This event has itself a reforming resonance, since the true Church was seen as the 'Bride' of Christ, requiring rescue from antichristian captivity.[47] To this imagistic end Marvell has already evoked 'the great Bridegroom' Christ, of whom the nuns claim to be 'Each one a spouse' (XIV, XV), in the usual antichristian mode of impersonation. As a parochial incident which may personalize the national experience, this occurrence is suitable to a poem of microcosmic significance for the national life.

Apart from the little Reformation and the harvesting Mowers, Marvell makes extensive use of comedy as a miniaturizing device. Thus when the nuns are alerted to William's assault upon their convent:

> Some to the Breach against their Foes
> Their *Wooden Saints* in vain oppose.
> Another bolder stands at push
> With their old *Holy-Water Brush.*
> While the disjointed *Abbess* threads
> The gingling Chain-Shot of her *Beads.*
> But their lowd'st Cannot were their Lungs;
> And sharpest Weapons were their Tongues.
>
> (XXXII)

The farce in this stanza has a religious point, directed against the idolatry of wooden saints and the formalism of holy water and rosary, which is embodied in the puppet-like 'disjointed' abbess. Such things 'in vain oppose' the militancy of a Puritan saint. At every point in the poem's *historia paula* this controlling comedy mediates between the greater world and this country estate, simultaneously highlighting, as here, the reformist message.

In keeping with this scale, William Fairfax's experience personalises the Puritan attitude to Catholicism. When he fears for his beloved—'Though guiltless lest thou perish there' (XXVIII)—he is referring to the spiritual death entailed by popery, and is moved to a prophecy (fulfilled by Marvell's time) that 'sure those buildings last not long,/Founded by folly, kept by wrong.' (XXVIII). To such a popish building Appleton House stands in contrast, in its humility (VI) contrasting antichristian pride and symbolizing the reforming spirit. This symbolic use of houses recurs at a later stage of the poem, when Appleton House bears antipathy towards Cawood Castle, a representative of episcopacy: 'As if it quarrell'd in the Seat/Th'Ambition of its *Prelate* great' (XLVI), John Williams, Archbishop of York.[48] At the "contemporary" stage of the poem's chronicle, Appleton House's opponent is not the ruined nunnery of the past but the episcopal threat of the present. Such an animus in the poem would have been congenial to Fairfax himself, who was as virulently anticatholic as any of his contemporaries.[49] To reflect the proper nature of the Elect Nation the poem recalls not only the break with Rome but the popish Arminianism of Thomas's day.

Involved with reformation by the nunnery episode, the family history is also brought into connection with the history of 'all the *Universe*' (XXXI), the eschatological process of which reformation is part. William Fairfax's reforming power is devolved upon Thomas:

> Is not this he whose Offspring fierce
> Shall fight through all the *Universe*:
> And with successive Valour try
> *France*, *Poland*, either *Germany*;

Till one, as long since prophecy'd,
His Horse through conquer'd *Britain* ride?
Yet, against *Fate*, his Spouse they kept;
And the great Race would intercept.
(XXXI)

In time the 'great Race' of Fairfaxes expands its activist
mission throughout Europe, a destiny cumulative ('Till one'),
so that Thomas is seen as the prophetic *telos* of the race, its
destination in time. The teleological pattern which he
represents within familial history is analogous to the eschatological tendency of time itself, thus welding together the
parochial and universal dimensions of the poem. When the
nuns attempted to 'intercept' this pattern, they withstood not
only the family destiny but the universal 'Fate' in which the
Fairfaxes participate. The malign attempt of the nuns to
frustrate destiny contrasts with the Fairfaxes' elect activism to
forward it, by which they 'make their Destiny their Choice'
(XCIII).

This accord with history is also incumbent upon the nation
as a whole. When the New Israelites/Mowers cross their sea
they enact the antitype of the Jews' exodus to the Promised
Land. I say its antitype—the passage is normally understood
by reference to the type alone[50]—because the Promised Land
of the *New* Israel is the New Jerusalem. In this fulfilment of
the type the Red Sea, figure of baptism,[51] alludes to the
baptism of fire at the Last Day, 'when that world and this and
all that shall be all born hereafter, shall passe through the
same Red Sea, and be all baptized with the same fire'.[52] This
eschatological typology represents the journey towards the
national goal, the 'Rule of the Saints' in the millennial
Kingdom—national counterpart to the teleology of Fairfax's
race. Numerically speaking, this stanza (XLIX) is the central
stanza of the poem, a place signifying its thematic importance
in characterization of the Elect Nation, its figural identification of their destination, and its inauguration of the "Civil
War" in the poem.

The episode in which the harvest becomes a bucolic
metaphor for war (L–LIII) provides that sort of amalgam of
levity and seriousness common in Marvell:

> The Mower now commands the Field;
> In whose new Traverse seemeth wrought
> A Camp of Battail newly fought:
> Where, as the Meads with Hay, the Plain
> Lyes quilted ore with Bodies slain:
> The Women that with forks it fling,
> Do represent the Pillaging.
>
> (LIII)

No seventeenth-century reader, recalling the Civil War, would have found such stanzas completely comic, unless perhaps in the grim mode of black comedy. The communal phenomenon of harvest is a microcosm of the countrywide war, its humour reflecting the distance between bucolic triviality and the momentous events of civil conflict. Only in this way can it successfully provide an intimate reflection of public cataclysm.

It is natural that the military metaphors earlier employed to describe Fairfax's garden should re-emerge in the description of the war in which his military talents had been recently displayed. The harvesting of men-as-grass places the war in its eschatological context, where the last Mower, Christ, will harvest mankind in the universal death: 'the Son of Man, having. . .in his hand a sharp sickle. . .Thrust in thy sickle, and reap. . .for the harvest of the earth is ripe. And he. . .thrust in his sickle on the earth, and the earth was reaped' (Revelation 14:14–16). This consummating devastation is mimicked by the Mowers as if in rehearsal of the real event, and the Civil War is located as one of the Latter Day wars which contribute to the last harvest. As usual, then, the national reference of the passage is extended to the universal.

One of the stages of Latter Day destruction, the plague of Locusts of the Apocalypse, appears in stanza XLVII as the 'Grashoppers' (identified with locusts in this period)[53] which preside over the Mowers' 'Massacre':

> And now to the Abbyss I pass
> Of that unfathomable Grass,
> Where Men like Grashoppers appear,
> But Grashoppers are Gyants there:
> They, in there squeking Laugh, contemn

> Us as we walk more low then them:
> And, from the Precipices tall
> Of the green spir's, to us do call.

Not only do these creatures introduce the harvesting of flesh in the poem, but they are associated with 'Precipices', a feature of the wasted world in stanza XCVI, and hence with the motif of devastation. In fanciful form they recall their apocalyptic counterparts:

> And there came out of the smoke [of the pit] locusts upon the earth, and unto them was given power. . .that they should not hurt the grass of the earth, neither any green thing. . .but only those men [who are not of the Chosen]. . .they should be tormented. . .And the shapes of the locusts were like horses prepared unto battle. . .and their faces were like the faces of men.   (Revelation 9:3–7)

From these cryptic images Marvell builds his fantastic conceit. The locusts orignate in the 'pit', while their playful equivalents inhabit the 'Abbyss'; 'Men like Grashoppers appear', whereas the locusts have 'faces. . .like the faces of men'. The grasshoppers are 'Gyants', the locusts the size of horses; the grasshoppers 'contemn' men, while the locusts 'torment' them; the latter have power over men, while the grasshoppers overtop the men who are 'more low'. The sinister nature of the Locusts of the Apocalypse is carefully miniaturized into the uneasy 'squeking Laugh' of their counterparts. According to the Geneva Bible, 'Locustes are false teachers, heretikes, and worldlie suttil Prelates. . .which forsake Christ to mainteine false doctrine', with power over those who are susceptible to error. They are the bishops, who 'affected pre-eminence . . . Lording it over Gods inheritance' (*RT*, 238), like the 'Prelate great' of Cawood, their overweening nature represented here by their disproportionate size. From their church-'spir's they condemn men to spiritual degradation, hence exacerbating the distance between their worldly eminence and the status of the men in their ironic care. As presiders over the war-harvest, they are placed in their true light as provocateurs—a contemporary, Protestant form of the menace represented by 'Suttle Nuns'.

Such resonances are controlled by the diminution of the poem, especially by the device here of a theatrical perspective. Recurrent reference to dramatic devices transforms such events as the harvest into the scenes of a play or masque:[54]

> No Scene that turns with Engines strange
> Does oftner than these Meadows change.
> . . .
> This *Scene* again withdrawing brings
> A new and empty Face of things.
> . . .
> And see how Chance's better Wit
> Could with a Mask my studies hit!
>
> (XLIX, LVI, LXXIV)

By means of these linking passages the poem proceeds like a theatrical spectacle: like actors, 'The. . .Mowers enter next'. In formal terms, the world of Nunappleton is seen as a theatrical mime of the greater world, preserving the decorum of the microcosm. Just as the comic devices in the poem had both miniaturizing and thematic functions, so this theatrical metaphor has eschatological significance too. One of the persistently popular books of the century was Thomas Beard's *The Theatre of Gods Judgements* (1631), a survey of the retributive providences of God in human history, suitably relished: it implemented the notion that history was God's dramaturgy,[55] in which the Last Day 'shall include and comprehend all that went before it, wherein as in the last Scene, all the Actors must enter, to compleate and make up the Catastrophe of this great peece'.[56] The scenes of *Appleton House* record current historical events as acts in the eschatological drama, the theatrical metaphor uniting the theme and the frame of the poem.

In that drama the harvesting of the earth is part of the purgative desolation of the Latter Days, in which wars participate. So the poem's harvest is succeeded by an image of England cauterized: 'A levell'd space. . ./The World when first created sure/Was such a Table rase and pure.' (LVI). This *tabula rasa*, while chiming with the parliamentarian view of the war as purgative, bodes ill in its premonition of the Levellers who appear in the next stanza.[57] The topographical pun on this faction also implies the claims of the Diggers for common ownership of land,[58] wordplay which allows their incorporation into the metaphoric landscape. The Levellers' appearance signifies the rise of radical groups in the vacuum created by the breakdown of the established order:

> to this naked equal Flat,
> Which *Levellers* take pattern at,
> The Villagers in common chase
> Their Cattle, which it closer rase;
> And what below the Sith increast
> Is pincht yet nearer by the Beast.
> Such, in the painted World, appear'd
> *Davenant* with th' Universal Heard.
> (LVII)

By the cattle who crop the grass even closer we should understand that England suffers further depredation, by faction: 'Levellers' and 'in common' give overtones of the rabble to 'th' Universal Heard'[59] but maintain the tone of the poem by an arty and witty distance. This 'Beast' is not just a cow but *the* Beast, figuring antichristian dissension and devouring in domestic grazing.

In similarly play-ful form the subsequent stanzas portray the vulnerability of the nation, and the havoc wreaked by faction. The river and the land become confused, and the species are compounded; the cows become hallucinatory images (LIX, LX, LVIII). These effects of disjunction convey not only the disordered aftermath of war, but also the uncertain perception that such disorder may cause.[60] By flooding:

> The River in it self is drown'd,
> And Isl's th'astonisht Cattle round.
>
> Let others tell the *Paradox*,
> How Eels now bellow in the Ox;
> How Horses at their Tails do kick,
> Turn'd as they hang to Leeches quick;
> How Boats can over Bridges sail;
> And Fishes do the Stables scale.

How *Salmons* trespassing are found;
And Pikes are taken in the Pound.
(LIX, LX)

Here nature, too, like the nation, is out of joint, the elements
of earth and water become indistinct from one another, and
natural categories are confused; figuratively reflecting a war
which divides a nation against itself and throws men into
unfamiliar categories and relationships. Such disarray of
nature was characteristic of the Latter Days:

> The terrors of the Judgement shall be spoken aloud by the
> immediate forerunning accidents, which shall bee so great
> violences to the old constitutions of Nature, that it shall break
> her very bones, and disorder her till shee be destroyed. . .The
> sea. . .shall rise fifteen cubits above the highest mountaines, and
> thence descend. . .then all the beasts and creeping things, the
> monsters, and the usuall inhabitants of the sea shall be gathered
> together, and make fearfull noyses. . .the wild beasts shall leave
> their dens and come into the companies of men, so that you shall
> hardly tell how to call them, herds of Men or congregations of
> Beasts.[61]

The deluge, violence to nature, compounding of species, even
the noises (as of the 'Eels') are mimicked by the flooding
river, which is itself a Latter Day sign: 'The decay of the parts
argues the dotage of the Whole [world]. . .The sea now
rageth where the ground was dry: and fishes swimme, where
men walked';[62] 'Fishes do the Stables scale'. These are both
effects of war and Latter Day signs, just as the war itself was
such a sign.

The river concludes these playful rehearsals by flooding the
meadows,[63] for of the Last Age 'the end of it shall be with a
flood' (Daniel 9:26).

> Then, to conclude these pleasant Acts,
> *Denton* sets ope its *Cataracts*;
> And makes the Meadow truly be
> (What it but seem'd before) a Sea.
> For, jealous of its *Lords* long stay,
> It try's t'invite him thus away.
> (LIX)

The second couplet here intimates a typological fulfilment of the metaphor whereby, earlier, the meadows seemed a 'green Sea'. Now truly a sea because of their flooding, they figure the way in which time will fulfil the signs of the End rehearsed here. On another level, this indicates that the war which was a sign of the End has been succeeded by that End. Since the deluge is part of the final 'Act' of the historical drama, it is aptly described as concerned to 'conclude these. . .Acts'. In the third couplet, on the literal level, the 'Lord' is Fairfax, "invited away" by his Denton estate, which has caused the river joining the estates to flood, thus indicating its jealousy that he should prefer to stay at Nunappleton.[64] This familial meaning adumbrates the analogous national meaning of the lines: that Fairfax is "invited away" from his retirement by his standing (represented by Denton, the more splendid estate), and by the political turbulence of the times (the flood). In this muted manner Marvell expresses the thought that men like Fairfax are badly needed in public life, since he could have repaired the wasted landscape of England (XLIV). At the figurative level the couplet invokes another deliverer for England, the divine '*Lord*' Christ: the meadows (England) 'invite him thus away' from heaven, 'jealous of [his] long stay'; that is, his Coming is too tardy for the Elect Nation, and she brings upon herself a deluge (the war) in order to signify that His time is come. In so doing her haste invokes the biblical assurance that 'He will not tarry' but hurry to His Coming.[65] This playful statement of impatience for the Last Day wittily envisages the chaos of the war as in a sense a virtue, because it hastens the Latter Day devastation and thus accelerates the Coming. Poetically it imitates the biblical phrase which echoed through contemporary life: 'Come quickly, Lord'.[66]

At this point Marvell himself comes into the foreground.

> But I, retiring from the Flood,
> Take Sanctuary in the Wood;
> And, while it lasts, my self imbark
> In this yet green, yet growing Ark;
> Where the first Carpenter might best
> Fit Timber for his Keel have Prest.

> And where all Creatures might have shares,
> Although in Armies, not in Paires.
>
> (LXI)

Here eschatological resonance subsumes typologies. The first Ark and carpenter appeared at Noah's Flood, type of the final deluge:[67] that from which Marvell takes refuge in this rehearsal of the eschaton. As carpenter, Noah was a type of Christ, the Nazarene carpenter, whose Coming effects the *eschaton*. The Ark itself was traditionally a type of the Church Militant, of which Marvell as saint is a member, and she is the heroine of the eschatological drama.[68] Having thus implicated his personal stake in the *eschaton*, Marvell in the wood meditates upon the natural phenomena that surround him, until he can claim to interpret natural signs and prophesy:

> Out of these scatter'd *Sibyls* Leaves
> Strange *Prophecies* my Phancy weaves:
> And in one History consumes,
> Like *Mexique Paintings*, all the *Plumes*.
> What *Rome*, *Greece*, *Palestine*, ere said
> I in this light *Mosaick* read.
> Thrice happy he who, not mistook,
> Hath read in *Natures mystick Book*.
>
> (LXXIII)

The contents of the classical poets and the Old Testament (line 5) are relevant to the 'one History' of progressive revelation because of the Christianization of classical authors and the Old Testament's typological relationship to the New. In the 'light Mosaick' of the dappled wood-floor Marvell puns on the Mosaic Books of the Bible,[69] and on the 'leaves' or pages of books. To read in the 'book of Fate'[70] is the appropriate occupation of the elect, especially in a doubtful time of civil war, and their interpretative activity should be twofold: directed simultaneously at the sequence of historical events and the patterns or portents evident in Nature— 'speciall providence' and 'common providence'.[71] Attending, therefore, both to revelation and to 'Natures mystick Book', Marvell's interpretation of history relates especially to the events just witnessed in the meadows, which are themselves both natural and historical.

Returning from wood to meadows, from privacy back into history, Marvell finds that the war-harvest has passed and the flood has receded: so it was understood, that after the deluge 'The sea. . .shall. . .thence descend into hollownesse'.[72] The evening which begins to fall over the landscape (LXXXIII–IV) is in a metaphorical sense also the twilight of England and the world. Suitably, this sunset period is marked by a 'Coming'—not yet that of Christ, but the parochial Coming of Maria Fairfax:

> *Maria* such, and so doth hush
> The *World*, and through the *Ev'ning* rush.
> No new-born *Comet* such a Train
> Draws through the Skie, nor Star new-slain.
> For streight those giddy Rockets fail,
> Which from the putrid Earth exhale,
> But by her *Flames*, in *Heaven* try'd,
> *Nature* is wholly *vitrifi'd*.
>
> (LXXXVI)

Maria affects 'The World' and 'Nature' itself, is derived from Heaven, and likened to a portent. The stanza's expansive terms—at first a rather peculiar characterization of a little girl—overgo the genre of "the beloved in a landscape" in order to achieve an apocalyptic dimension. The 'putrid' earth is in its decay, which will be purged by Christ's Second Coming as 'a refiner's fire' (Malachi 3:2), and by the final conflagration it will be 'vitrifi'd' into the 'Sea of Glass' foretold by Revelation.[73] Similarly, Maria is compared to the halcyon, symbol of peace, recalling the character of Christ as the Prince of Peace even as she imitates His coming. The placing is appropriate not only because the war was a sign of the end but because Maria's appearance is as the war recedes, figuring the final peace that supervenes after the End. Maria's 'lesser World' (XCVI) is inspired to order itself by her presence, imitating the divine restoration of the ruined world at the End (XCIV). As 'Paradice's only Map' (XCVI)[74] her restoration of nature is a premonition of the last paradise, and her "Coming" is like a typological fulfilment of her father's character as Christ-like "Deliverer".

In the last stanza tortoise-like fishermen appear. The reference to the tortoise recapitulates an earlier reference where tortoises reflected the twofold nature of men, who carry souls within their bodies/shells.[75] Naturally this makes the fishermen 'Amphibii' too, mortal and vital; more especially so because they inhabit the time of Civil War doubleness, and of Latter Day confusion, when sea and land are compounded and men too must become 'Amphibii'. These resonances are, however, only the first answer to critics who have puzzled over and even derogated this stanza,[76] since the tortoise's implication of men's mortality provides an image of the *telos* which here participates, by reference to their amphibiousness, in a vision of the *eschaton*. The evening is, then, moving into darkness:

> But now the *Salmon-Fishers* moist
> Their *Leathern Boats* begin to hoist;
> And, like *Antipodes* in Shoes,
> Have shod their *Heads* in their *Canoos*.
> How *Tortoise like*, but not so slow,
> These rational *Amphibii* go?
> Let's in: for the dark *Hemisphere*
> Does now like one of them appear.
>
> (XCVII)

In the allusion to mortality and universal End this Final Image ends an eschatological poem with the only image that could properly do this—an image of the End itself. The initial image of *eschaton* is the oncoming of the night. Then the fishermen are upside down, as if their feet were in the air—Antipodeans in the wrong hemisphere. But, since the hemisphere is 'like. . .them', it, too, must be upside down, the right hemisphere upended upends them also. At the last Day, indeed, the world is turned upside down: 'the Lord maketh the earth empty, and maketh it waste, and turneth it upside down, and scattereth abroad the inhabitants' (Isaiah 24:1). We have already seen the earth made desert in the penultimate stanza, an emptiness foreshadowed in the *tabula rasa* of England, and its turning upside down is the final stage of the eschatological ruin. 'The land shall be utterly emptied, and utterly spoiled. . .the foundations of the earth do shake. The earth is utterly broken down' (Isaiah 24:3, 18–20):

> 'Tis not, what once it was, the *World*;
> But a rude heap together hurl'd;
> All negligently overthrown,
> Gulfes, Deserts, Precipices, Stone.
>
> (XCVI)

This 'overthrow[ing]' of nature at the End extends also to the human race, a fact with great political force in the period. To radical chiliasts like the Fifth Monarchists the overturning motif had a political moral implying the overthrow of traditional hierarchies.[77] For them the disruption of social and political orders was positively demanded by the Book of Ezekiel's advocacy of the destruction of the kings of the earth in the cause of Jesus the Fifth King:[78]

> profane wicked prince of Israel, whose day is come, when iniquity shall have an end, Thus saith the Lord God:. . .take off the crown. . .exalt him that is low, and abase him that is high. I will overturn, overturn, overturn it, and it shall be no more, until he comes whose right it is; and I will give it him.
>
> (Ezekiel 21:25–7)

This text was one of those adduced to justify the radical position both during and after the war against the king. It could be associated with such texts as Psalm 146:9 ('the way of the wicked he turneth upside down') and Isaiah 24:21 ('in that day. . .the Lord shall punish the host of the high ones. . .and the kings of the earth') in the service of revolution. By this means such factions could associate themselves with the first Christians—highly desirable when 'Primitive Religion' was the watchword—who had been described by their opponents as those who 'turned the world upside down' by their convictions.[79] This motif was frequently used to denote the activities of those groups who took it literally, such as the Levellers mentioned in the poem.[80] 'If we. . .consider the great revolution and turning of things upside down in these our days, certainly. . .the Lord hath prepared the instruments of death against Antichrist';[81] so the last stanza refers to such current political tumults as the final signs of the End.

The 'overturning' of the world was prefigured in the poem when the Locusts of the Apocalypse lorded it over men, who were appointed the lords of creation. The grasshoppers' eminence was associated with 'Precipices', a presage of those which figure in the overturned world of the penultimate stanza. The last stanzas thus "fulfil" this type in the poem in a biblically eschatological manner. That the final stanza represents not such a rehearsal but the End itself is indicated by the injunction of the last line, 'Let's in', which echoes Isaiah's advice to the elect of the Last Day. 'Come, my people, enter thou into thy chambers, and shut thy doors about thee; hide thyself. . .until the indignation is overpast' (26:19–20). As members of the elect, it is incumbent upon Marvell and Maria to obey this injunction. Here that directive to the faithful is personalized by Nunappleton's inhabitants, maintaining the microcosmic focus of the poem even at the End.

Appleton House is distinguished by this light touch throughout, and in explicating the poem one cannot help but do violence to this delicacy. The poem wears its eschatology lightly, although it is no less serious for that. The characteristically playful fishermen are, of course, very aptly amphibious by their calling, and this calling is also the basis of their integration in the motif of 'overturning'. As fishermen they recall the nature of the very first Christians, the 'fishers of men'. It was because 'The Apostles were so many fishermen' (*The Character of Holland*, 58)[82] and nothing more, in worldly terms, that Christ chose them. This Christian emphasis upon humility was embodied earlier in the poem by the tortoises to which the fishermen are compared, in contrast to antichristian pride. Christ Himself embodies the notion of spiritual exaltation in a humble station, for 'He who was "Lord of all". . .was nevertheless contented to come in the "form of a servant", and to let the emperours and princes of the world alone'.[83] This paradox of high spiritual destiny within humble social status underlies the fishermen's relationship to the motif of social inversion, since Marvell himself explicitly related the notion of the world turned upside down

to its source in the characterization of the first Christians, and
Christ Himself as one of those "inverters".[84] If the Marvellian
fishermen represent the capacity of the humble to be exalted,
Isaiah predicts that at the End 'it shall be, as with the people,
so with the priest; as with the servant, so with his
master. . .the Lord shall punish the host of the high ones that
are on high, and the kings of the earth' (24:2, 21). The Geneva
Bible, a great authority of the time, moralizes this: 'the
Prophet signifieth an horrible confusion, where there shalbe
nether religio(n), order nor policie. . .There is no power so
high or mightie, but God wil visite him wth his roddes.' The
priests in particular will get what is coming to them, and the
fishermen will end up on top in a fortunate inversion. Perhaps
this idea reflects Marvell's sense that the 'high ones' were at
fault in England, the Civil War the peculiar sin not only of
great prelates but of the politicos also, making 'Lowness
unsafe as Hight' for the humble mass of Englishmen. While
the apostolic resonances of the fishermen counterpoint
episcopacy, the same critical stance comprehends the current
powers of the nation, the military 'Grandees' of the early
1650s, when this poem was probably composed. Marvell's
characterization of Fairfax as unique amongst the 'high ones'
supports this interpretation, for he alone possesses the virtues
required of her leaders in England's parlous hour, and he has
retired from their ranks:

> And yet there walks one on the Sod
> Who, had it pleased him and *God*,
> Might once have made our Gardens spring
> Fresh as his own and flourishing.
>
> (XLIV)

But it did not please either Fairfax or God, the author of
destiny. This remark has often been misread, as if Fairfax
were at fault,[85] but in fact it was axiomatic that even when
men followed their own bent—as Fairfax did by retiring from
public life and compromise—they were obeying God's will in
His historical purposes.[86] It must follow, with personal pain
for Marvell, no doubt, that England's eschatological role
required otherwise than that England should have remained a

'Garden'. It is this thought that determines the 'one History' of the rest of the poem, the movement to 'the world turned upside down'.

In this stanza the relationship between the gardens of Appleton House and England's national Garden is explicit. Fairfax is a gardener in both literal and political senses:

> For he did, with his utmost Skill,
> *Ambition* weed, but *Conscience* till.
> *Conscience*, that Heaven-nursed Plant,
> Which most our Earthly Gardens want.
>
> (XLV)

Can it be that in his 'Conscience' Fairfax is unique especially amongst ambitious parliamentarians, who in their opponents' analysis sought only to advance themselves? At any rate, this relationship between England's destiny and Fairfax's is what binds together the poem's familial portrait and its vision of current national events.

Without comprehending the eschatological theme, we cannot fail to find much in the poem obscure, as the many and diverse critical accounts of the poem in recent years amply demonstrate. Indeed, more recent criticism has tended to attempt to justify this poem, which has so often been found wanting—not unified, or overlong, or even 'rambling'.[87] In fact, it is only by recognizing the eschatological theme and its witty variations that the poem *can* be seen in its unity. D.C. Allen recognized that the harvesting mowers had a connection with the Civil War; Maren-Sophie Røstvig suggested some typological motifs in the poem; and Joseph Summers saw 'some apocalyptic strain' (a vague one, admittedly) in Maria's arrival on the scene; while Leishman realized, in isolation from his overall reading of the poem, that her 'vitrifying' was in some way related to the vitrefaction of the earth.[88] None of these commentators has understood these motifs in the way that I have suggested they function, and they have failed to see the eschatological theme of the poem, its complex and ubiquitous effects, and its relationship to the comprehensive doctrines of the period. Their intimations may be seen as at once a lack of thematic recognition and as an indication that the true theme of the poem has forced, here and there, an opening within their respective accounts of the poem. Above all, the longstanding question of the poem's unity is answered by the comprehensive function of the eschatological vision in the poem. Far from prolix, *Appleton House* compresses an epic theme into miniature form.

While the function of this theme is at once universal and parochial, the personae of Marvell and the Fairfaxes in the poem give to the eschatological theme a personal dimension, expressing the intimacy of providential destiny to the life of the poet as well as the public face of the *eschaton*. It was innovatory to create a vision of universal events in what was, generically speaking, a "Country House" poem,[89] the mode of which was essentially parochial and intimate. (The true scale and nature of this innovation will be discussed later.) *Appleton House* comes to embrace its intimations of the national life within the great design: the Reformation, the destined race of Fairfaxes, the character of the Elect Nation, the Civil War, post-war tumults, the deluge, a Coming, the benighting of the world, and finally the world turned upside down. Of this national destiny the history of the Fairfaxes is a suitable microcosm: an earlier Fairfax strikes a blow against Antichrist and for spiritual freedom by rescuing his bride, while Thomas Fairfax could have been the deliverer not merely of a bride, but of England herself. His estates represent, through the theatrical metaphor, what England is now—a meadow reaped in blood and razed by faction. Equally, his gardens, in their careful order (XXXVI–XL), represent what England might have been; they are a diagram of what England has lost, but like the loss of the first 'Garden of the World', that dreadful alteration is subsumed by divine design. Fairfax is in retirement; England and the world are in eclipse.

3

The Revelation in Action:
The Poet and Contemporary History in
An Horatian Ode

Like *Appleton House, An Horatian Ode upon Cromwell's Return from Ireland* is concerned to place contemporary events within a chiliastic context. It exemplifies Marvell's use of the problematic as a poetic structure congruent with the processes of providential history.

From the sizeable corpus of critical comment on the *Ode* it transpires that the essential puzzle of the poem lies in its attitude to Cromwell:[1] very simply, is Cromwell here right, wrong, or 'impartially' viewed? The poem has proved remarkably ambiguous. One can say of pro-Cromwellian, anti-Cromwellian, and neutral readings of the *Ode* that they represent respectively an 'unequivocal' poem; an 'equivocal' poem which results in an unfavourable view of Cromwell; and an 'equivocal' poem which results in the purist's interpretation of 'equivocation', that the poem is 'impartial'. In fact, the *Ode* does not render up its meaning easily because it is an example of Marvell's consistent use of ambiguity, within the problematic. The portrayal of Cromwell here is a product of the dialectic of providential history within the poem, a dialectic imitated by its problematic.

When Marvell writes, ' 'Tis Madness to resist or blame/The force of angry Heavens flame', he is expressing the *moralitas* of providential history: that, whether one likes it or not, any historical event is willed by God and must be accepted as such. Perhaps the clearest statement of how one should respond to such events is made by Augustine:

> Divine providence. . .warns us not to indulge in silly complaints about the state of affairs, but to take pains to enquire what useful purposes are served by things.[2]

The same doctrine motivates Marvell's repudiation of the capacity to 'resist or blame' what heaven has decreed.[3] This thought is reiterated later in the poem when Marvell states that Charles 'call'd [not] the *Gods* with vulgar spight/To vindicate his helpless Right'; neither Marvell nor his king will 'indulge in silly complaints'. As the poet asserted in his *First Anniversary*, the correct response was—like Augustine—'to take pains to inquire what useful purposes are served by things', to diagnose the providential pattern behind events.[4]

At this time—1650—Marvell was still royalist in his political sympathies (his last royalist poem, *Tom May's Death*, was written after the *Ode*).[5] Since the nature of such allegiance was complex, it should not surprise us that the *Ode* is not a blood-and-thunder philippic against Cromwell, especially when we recall the general ambivalence of response to Cromwell at this time. Furthermore, the *Ode* was written after the execution of the king, in the consciousness of regicide and defeat. The point is not an emotional but a formal one, for Marvell chose to write his *Ode* in Horatian form. There is a distinct similarity between Horace's situation after the Roman Civil War and Marvell's after the English, for in both cases the poet's allegiance had lain with the losing side. The Horatian form of Marvell's *Ode* is an acknowledgement of the fact that Marvell's own cause had lost.

The emotional point is not that of defeat itself but rather of how Marvell was to respond to that defeat, for his beliefs demanded that he do his utmost to understand the divine purpose behind it. What some have called the 'impartial' tenor of the *Ode* is not a matter of Marvell's political 'neutrality'—he was not neutral. It is not truly impartiality either; it is in fact a matter of Marvell's personal reconcilement with the courses of providence, and in that sense the *Ode* is a very personal poem. At the same time it has an impersonal element, in the sense that it defers to the absolute nature of providence. The tension in this poem is that of a personal disappointment vying with faith.

While providential belief demanded of Marvell that he see Cromwell's rise as, *de facto*, sanctioned by God, it did not require that he view Cromwell himself as intrinsically good.[6] If he felt that Cromwell was an unrighteous rebel, he could allow himself to state this view, but at the same time he had to acknowledge that providence had decreed Cromwell's rise and the triumph of his cause. The dialectic set up by the royalist's view of Cromwell and the believer's view of history is the problematic of the *Ode*.

(i) THE ROMAN PARALLEL: *TOM MAY'S DEATH*

At this point it is necessary to explore what might be the advantages for Marvell's purpose of an Horatian form, and what effects he may have intended it to have. Of Horatian form the most obvious consequences are the Roman allusions and concepts that are sprinkled through the poem: 'Caesar's head' (23), the anecdote of the Capitol (68), 'Caesar' again (101), and 'Hannibal' (102).[7] If Marvell seems to be drawing some analogy between the Roman and the English states, then he himself provided its proper perspective; fashionable at the time, such analogies are the subject of a critique in his *Tom May's Death*[8], written so soon after the *Ode* itself.

May appears to have elected himself for Marvell's vilification on three counts; he was a poetaster, a parliamentarian propagandist, and a turncoat from the royalist cause. After his defection to Parliament he became in the 1640s its apologist. Such writings as his *History of the Parliament* prompt Marvell to decry him as 'Most servil' wit, and Mercenary Pen' (40). To Marvell, May's historical philosophy was as false as his poetry, comparable to the least reputable historians of the past: 'Polydore, Lucan, Allan, Vandale, Goth,/*Malignant Poet and Historian both*'.[9] May's version of history was repugnant to him since it involved, in part, a use of Roman analogies to justify the triumph of Parliament in the Civil War—as if England were another Rome.[10] That comparison Marvell reviles in a speech "delivered" by Ben Jonson, when the arbiter of poets evicts May from the poets' Elysium with these words:

> Go seek the novice Statesmen, and obtrude
> On them some *Romane cast Similitude*,
> Tell them of Liberty, the Stories fine,
> Until you all grow *Consuls* in your wine.
> Or thou *Dictator* of the glass bestow
> On him the *Cato*, this is the *Cicero*.

> *Transferring old Rome hither in your talk,*
> *As Bethlem's House did to Loretto walk.*
> Foul Architect that hadst not Eye to see
> *How ill the measures of these States agree.*
> And who by *Romes* example *England* lay,
> Those but to *Lucan* do continue *May.*
>
> (43–54; my italics)

For Marvell, England under Parliament and republican Rome are quite dissimilar; "historians" like May prove their speciousness when they 'by Romes example England lay', transferring to parliamentarian rule the famed honours of the Roman Republic.

Accordingly, Marvell takes his revenge upon this 'Romane cast Similitude' by turning it against the oligarchs of Parliament. He remarks that May has turned 'chronicler to *Spartacus*' (74), the rebel who led an army of slaves against Rome: the derogation in this remark consisting equally in Spartacus' rebellious character, and in the implication that the parliamentarians are "slaves" (like the 'servil' May). By this 'Spartacus' it has been suggested that Marvell referred to any one of several generals, but in view of Fairfax's eclipse and the ascendancy of Cromwell at this time, the latter would seem to be the more likely referent here, most especially in view of his lionization by May. Turning May's own Roman parallel against Cromwell is Marvell's congruous revenge: the parallel becomes a method of dispraising republicanism.

The same inverted use of the parallel occurs earlier in the poem. As May approaches, Jonson is reciting, 'Sounding of ancient Heroes, such as were/The Subjects Safety, and the Rebels Fear' (15–16). In ancient times, Marvell implies, heroes were servants of the ruler, protecting loyal 'Subjects' and terrorizing 'Rebels'. Equally, he indicates that May's ancient heroes are such rebels as Spartacus: his own are monarchists, May's are subversives.

May's sort of hero also figures in Jonson's speech, but as a 'Cheat': 'a double-headed Vulture Eats/Brutus and Cassius the Peoples cheats' (17–18). Here Marvell is alluding to the last canto of Dante's *Inferno*, where Satan is a 'monstrous bird' with three mouths, two of which are devoted to the mastication of Brutus and Cassius.[11] Marvell has reduced the

number of mouths, as if the monster were devoted solely to
the punishment of the Roman rebels (in Dante Satan
consumes Judas too). In Marvell's formulation their revolt
and assassination are qualifications for the ultimate torment
of hell, and evidently there is an implied comparison with
those who rebelled against and executed Charles.

Throughout *Tom May* Marvell's use of the Roman parallel
is contemptuous; republican Rome is not to his taste as a
model for England. Therefore we may conclude that the
presence of such a parallel in the *Ode* is not intended to
elevate the English republic. This interpretation is supported
by a particular analogue to the *Ode* in *Tom May*. Marvell
states the role of the true 'Poet and Historian' (*viz.*, himself)
in these degenerate times:

> When the Sword glitters ore the Judges head,
> And fear has Coward Churchmen silenced,
> Then is the Poets time, 'tis then he drawes,
> And single fights forsaken Vertues cause.
> He, when the Wheel of Empire, whirleth back,
> And though the World's disjointed Axel crack,
> *Sings still of ancient Rights and better Times,*
> Seeks wretched good, arraigns successful Crimes.
>   (63–70; my italics)

Marvell's vision of the current political scene is bleak: the
'successful Crimes' are those of the victorious rebels; the law
has been corrupted by intimidation, the 'Sword'; 'Churchmen', confirming Marvell's perennial view, prove unwilling
to resist the unrighteous regime. In the face of this general
submissiveness Marvell states his own militant mission, to
'single fight forsaken Vertues cause', an aim proper to poetry
since this 'is the Poets time'. This passionate statement of
opposition manifests Marvell's attitude to the English republic in 1650. It also clarifies a statement in the *Ode*, where he
states that Cromwell's success provokes 'Justice against Fate
[to] complain,/And plead the *antient Rights* in vain'. In *Tom
May* he professes his own devotion to those 'antient Rights',
as a poet who 'Sings still of ancient Rights and better Times'.
This is the monarchism that redirects the force of the Roman
parallel.

There are several reasons for Marvell's use of a Roman parallel and a Horatian form in the *Ode*. He shared Horace's situation of defeat; he could turn the Roman parallel to his own purpose; generically speaking, the Horatian Ode was a mode proper to his "occasional" purpose, which was to consider Cromwell as he appeared on his 'Return from Ireland'. It was a suitable genre for a private man whose subject was a public figure.[12] Thus the form possessed several recommendations for Marvell's purposes, apart from the fact that he was a classicist. Nor should we forget the utility of this form for a poet tender of his own freedom. The political climate of 1650 was such that, had Marvell's *Ode* fallen into the wrong hands,[13] it might have been interpreted as subversive. *Tom May* makes clear Marvell's low opinion of the judiciary at this time, which may have heightened his almost congenital feelings of insecurity. Against this possibility of reprisal, the form of the *Ode* was a useful safeguard; the Horatian form tended to be associated with praise of a public figure, and thus generically could assist Marvell in resisting any anti-government interpretation of the poem. Not that this generic factor prevented Marvell's criticism of the regime. An interesting comparison for this point is Alexander Pope, who chose an Horatian imitation to satirize his king; the mere appearance of praise was sufficient to secure Pope from litigation over the poem.[14] This protective quality of the Horatian form, its apparent positiveness, may well have appealed to Marvell in his own circumstances.

Nor did the Roman colour of Horatian language preclude Marvell's statement of Christian belief. On the contrary, poets of this period frequently used "pagan" or classical formulations for Christian ideas[15] (notions of "impropriety" in such matters become current only in eras when faith is on the defensive: they did not deter the generally devout seventeenth century). Simply, when in the *Ode* Marvell refers to 'the Gods' (61), he is using a classical formulation for God.[16]

The Roman parallel also provides a pertinent historical flavour for the *Ode*: a relationship between separate ages—that of the Roman Civil War and Augustan period as against the recent civil war in England. This relationship is not necessarily that of exact similarity, such as might endorse the new regime; rather, on a more general level, it places the English Civil War within the *process* of history, as part of a long series of events, which is the perspective of providential history.

Finally, and most important, the Augustan/Horatian period was of particular significance for chiliasts. It had long been an orthodox tenet that the reign of Augustus had established the conditions proper for Christ's First Advent, a world-empire and universal peace. To chiliasts this foreshadowed the nature of the Second Coming, which would follow the establishment of a Christian world-empire.[17] Marvell used this chiliastic Augustan motif on several occasions, as we shall see in later chapters. In the *Ode* the Augustan timing of Christ's First Advent becomes a suitable parallel for the current time, when His second advent was expected.

(ii) AMBIGUITY IN *AN HORATIAN ODE*

The ambiguities of the *Ode* focus upon Cromwell himself. The first approach to his portrayal is oblique: the poem opens not with Cromwell, but with a 'forward Youth':

> The forward Youth that would appear
> Must now forsake his *Muses* dear,
> Nor in the Shadows sing
> His Numbers languishing.
> 'Tis time to leave the Books in dust,
> And oyl th'unused Armours rust:
> Removing from the Wall
> The Corslet of the Hall.
>
> (1–8)

The forward youth must *now* appear because it is at this point in English history that the Civil War calls him to military action. These lines provide a valediction to the time when it was possible to attend to the cultural pursuits of 'Books' and the 'Muses'; in time of war different values obtain. In this manner the initial couplets provide an atmosphere for the rest of the poem, the atmosphere of war's ruder values:

So restless *Cromwell* could not cease
In the inglorious Arts of Peace,
But through adventrous War
Urged his active Star.

(9–12)

'So', "in just this fashion", Cromwell left the 'Arts of Peace' for the 'active' life. He, too, was 'forward', 'urg[ing]' his star of destiny voluntarily. The word 'So' compares Cromwell and the youth—they are not one and the same; that is, Cromwell is shown to be like other men faced with war, in so far as war demands of men that they turn to action. If we are to see any specific 'Youth' here it is, rather, one who has shared the impact of the war—Marvell himself, a poet who 'Must now forsake his *Muses* dear'. He can no longer be (as youthful poets tend to be) the amorous poet of 'dear' loves, 'languish[ing]' in adoration of the beloved.[18] His muses are 'dear' both because they are the ladies who inspire his poems and because poetry itself is 'dear' to him. This highly personal occupation with poetry and love puts Marvell in the 'Shadows' of life, these being one's existence as a private person. From these shadows war invites him to 'appear', to take part in the lighted arena of public events.

Yet his private existence is, precisely, 'dear'. His 'appearance' is a matter of leaving what he best likes, whereas Cromwell '*could not* cease/In the inglorious Arts of Peace'. War alone is 'glorious' in this particular sense; when Marvell describes the Arts of Peace as 'inglorious' he does not derogate them, for they have already been denoted 'dear'. Rather he is revealing that characteristic which made such Arts unacceptable to Cromwell, for he is a man of ambition, 'urg[ing]' his destiny, 'the Wars and Fortunes Son'. By that aptness for 'adventrous War' he is differentiated from the poet. This contrast returns in the finale of the poem, where Cromwell's have become the 'Arts' of power. One is a man whose artistry depends on peace, the other's depends on war; one is concerned with order ('Numbers'), the other with the vagaries of fortune ('adventrous'). The contrast turns on the similarity of their situations since both are 'called' by war; the difference is in their reaction and defines Marvell's stance vis à vis his subject, Cromwell. It is men like Cromwell who have compelled Marvell to abandon the muses of love for poetry of a more public nature. While Cromwell has entered public life as a general, the poet has entered it by turning to a public theme; the Horatian Ode as a form is the medium of such private excursions into the public realm. In a sense this exordium is Marvell's protest against writing this poem at all.

His attitude to Cromwell is that of a private citizen to a national figure, a reflective man to an active man. That contrast between the poet and his subject throws into relief Cromwell's 'active' nature, emphasizing his force, his 'fiery way', 'Courage high', and 'industrious Valour'. But this also detaches the poet from his subject—because he is not of Cromwell's kind, he can observe him from a distance. 'And, if we would speak true,/Much to the Man is due': the statement is equable and evaluative. That kind of evaluation is possible precisely because the poet has defined his own exclusion from Cromwell's values. This exclusion is not used as the springboard for an assault upon Cromwell; it shows the poet's bias but does not indulge it. The "objective" perspective defers to Marvell's belief that his personal feelings about Cromwell are not absolute, for they are not the arbiters of history.

Thus Marvell's initial statements about Cromwell manifest neither aversion nor approval, describing the latter in such a way that either is possible. They are ambiguous, both in kind and in intention. Cromwell is 'restless', ambitious; we are not given any guidance on whether this ambition is praiseworthy:

> So restless *Cromwell* could not cease
> . . .
> But through adventrous War
> Urged his active Star.
> And, like the three-fork'd Lightning, first
> Breaking the Clouds where it was nurst,
> Did thorough his own Side
> His fiery way divide.
>
> (9–16)

Cromwell is at once a portent and the occurrence portended (the simultaneity reinforces his "urgency"). He is portentous like the 'Lightning' and acts as the lightning, carving a 'fiery way', both presaging a cataclysmic event and effecting that event. But this fact simply implies that he is a force; at first sight that force is neutral, but in the last couplet it becomes ambiguous. 'His own Side' refers, in one sense, to Cromwell as a cloud 'nurs[ing]' lightning, which Cromwell as lightning then breaks 'thorough': he is at once that which is broken through and the force that breaks it. What does this mean? Does it imply that Cromwell's innate force, hidden so long in the 'Clouds' of obscurity, erupts into prominence with such violence that he himself is a victim of it? That he is not in control of his own force? The poetry here is neutral in feeling, so the statement remains ambiguous. How much control Cromwell exercises over his own force, and what sort of force it is, remains substantially in question. Cromwell:

> Did thorough his own Side
> His fiery way divide.
> For 'tis all one to Courage high
> The Emulous or Enemy;
> And with such to inclose
> Is more then to oppose.
>
> (15–20)

Here the second pair of couplets seems to say that a force like Cromwell takes little account of whether it meets friend or foe, 'Emulous or Enemy': *any* opposition will attract the enmity of 'Courage high'. Thus, when Cromwell breaks through his 'own Side' Marvell is referring, among other things, to his emergence from the ranks of his own party, to a place at its head. The implication may be (since 'Emulous and Enemy' are equally vulnerable to him) that he is prepared to 'divide' or break up his own party, an implication reinforced by the next couplet, where the poet remarks that 'with such to inclose/Is more then to oppose'. He may mean that it is more dangerous to join cause with such men than to oppose them.[19]

Yet, as a statement, the couplet is almost blatantly mysterious (if such a thing is possible). It could mean that it is 'more' to support than to oppose Cromwell, in the sense that it is "better". But even in this sense the statement's difficulty

multiplies, since one might ask, "better" in what way? 'More'
virtuous, or simply 'more' politic? What value is the poet
placing on the word 'more'?

In fact, the most that can be said of these concatenations of
ambiguity is that the passage is ambiguous. Cromwell may be
in some sense "genuine", an awesome man of destiny; or in
some sense malign, a terrible man of destiny. This consistent
use of ambiguity in the passage is a mode of presentation—
presenting Cromwell as himself ambiguous. Is he the force
straight from the heavens which men must not oppose
because his force is righteous; or is he an avatar of malignity
signified by the wracking of the heavens, whose power is
indiscriminate in its destruction? He is both. If one chooses
either possibility, and ignores the other, one is denying the
ambiguity of this passage, which is a function of the
problematic. The other ambiguities in the poem to this point
have a similar character of "doubleness": one meaning is
reconciled to Cromwell, the other critical of him, and thereby
two "narratives" are built up in the course of the poem. This
double narrative of the problematic reflects Marvell's attitude. Hostile to Cromwell's cause, Marvell expresses that
hostility in the "negative" narrative of the poem. On the
other hand, 'to resist or blame' the triumph of Cromwell and
his cause would be to criticize God Himself, who decreed it:
in some way Marvell must reconcile himself to that triumph.
That reconciling impulse motivates the "resigned" narrative
of the poem, that which consists of meanings not unfavourable to Cromwell.

This pattern of opposites provides the dialectical movement
of the poem, each ambiguity providing a simultaneous thesis
and antithesis. Therefore the poem's ambiguities tend to
focus upon the portrayal of Cromwell himself. From the
opening (1–20), Marvell moves to a chronicle of Cromwell's
activities (21–90):

> Then burning through the Air he went,
> And Pallaces and Temples rent:
> And *Caesars* head at last
> Did through his Laurels blast.
>
> (21–24)

Cromwell is 'burning' because Marvell is still describing his 'fiery way': he is, in fact, a destroyer, one who 'rents' and 'blasts', climbing 'To *ruine* the great Work of Time' (my italics). These feats develop his character as 'active', and prove his force. 'So much one Man can do,/That does both act and know' (75–6). His force characterizes the 'forced Pow'r' of the republic, which is based upon a martial victory. This typification of Cromwell as martial man, force, and destroyer, is seconded by a motif of Cromwell as hunter. 'The English Hunter' (110) terrorizes the Scots, and chases royal quarry:

> He wove a Net of such a scope,
> That *Charles* himself might chase
> To *Caresbrooks* narrow case.
> (50–52)

Marvell makes him Charles' executioner, too: 'That *thence* the Royal Actor born/The Tragick Scaffold might adorn' (my italics), 'thence' meaning, "as a result of Cromwell's stratagem"; he not only pursues his prey, but dispatches it also. This predatory quality in Cromwell moves Marvell to describe him as a falcon:

> So when the Falcon high
> Falls heavy from the Sky,
> She, having kill'd, no more does search
> (91–93)

Although the motifs of the hunter and the destroyer endow Cromwell with an almost superhuman efficiency, they do not make him an attractive figure.

In such passages feeling is remarkable by its absence, but the portrayal of Cromwell as hunter-destroyer—however neutral in feeling—is itself an adverse comment. Exactly the same motif appears with virulence in royalist propaganda. Two examples of such propaganda, in pictorial form, portray Cromwell accompanied by beasts emblematic of a rapacious nature.[20] One portrays him, ironically, as a preacher, with a wolf resting on his shoulder; the other portrays him as a

regicide, with an axe in one hand and a bleeding head in the
other, and a leopard behind him: both the leopard and the
wolf characterize Cromwell as a predator. Marvell's adoption
of this royalist imputation in the Ode reveals his hostile
attitude to his subject.

But he is careful to avoid any virulence of feeling in this
portrait, and his language appears descriptive rather than
didactic, a calm descriptiveness which perhaps convinces the
reader of Marvell's point about Cromwell rather better than
diatribe could. This restraint is intended to keep Cromwell's
rapacity in its place, in such a way as to allow a larger
perspective upon him. This abstraction of statement from
feeling recurs throughout the poem and is what has puzzled
readers most when they attempted to comprehend Marvell's
attitude to Cromwell; it is an effect of Marvell's double
perspective, which requires that he neither enthuse nor revile.

A comparison of the *Ode* with *First Anniversary*, written
after Marvell's change of heart towards Cromwell, is instructive in this matter of "feeling". An instance is that passage
where Marvell describes Cromwell's abandonment of a
secluded life on his estates for the burdens of power:

> For all delight of Life thou then didst lose,
> When to Command, thou didst thyself Depose;
> Resigning up thy Privacy so dear,
> To turn the headstrong Peoples Charioteer;
>
> (221–4)

Here Cromwell has come to share the values of the poet who
at the exordium of the Ode was called away from his 'Muses
dear'; in *First Anniversary* for Cromwell, too, 'Privacy' is
'*dear*'. This passage is encomium, more formal perhaps than
Marvell's enthusiasm for Fairfax in *Appleton House*, but still
very positive. One may contrast the same phase of Cromwell's life in the *Ode*:

> Much to the Man is due.
> Who, from his private Gardens, where
> He liv'd reserved and austere,
> As if his highest plot

To plant the Bergamot,
Could by industrious Valour climbe
To ruine the great Work of Time.
                                    (28–34)

The feeling of this passage is confined to surprise—that a
relatively obscure member of the gentry could rise to the
height of power: no other explicit feeling seems to animate it.
Reflected in these passages is the difference in Marvell's
attitude to Cromwell in 1650 and in 1654. The feeling of the
Ode is in appearance at least neutral, which is another way of
saying that it is ambiguous.

The ambiguous portrayal of Cromwell as hunter stretches
through his capacity as Parliament's hunter in Ireland, his
similarity to the 'Falcon', his potential martial conquests in
Europe, to his terrorizing the Scots. Throughout, Cromwell
is a man of the 'Sword' (116), 'the Wars and Fortunes Son'
(113). Is his force unselfish—applied in the interests of
England—or is he some ghastly machine? This "political"
ambiguity of the 'Hunter', the question of his motives and
purpose, provides local ambiguities throughout the poem.
Each of these tends to consist in a "statement of fact" about
Cromwell, or a comment on his rise, which also contains a
defamatory potential.

One of these was 'inclose. . .oppose', another his 'restless-
[ness]', both of which might imply his personal ambition in
an unattractive sense. In fact, both royalists and parliamentarians had doubts about how many of the parliamentarian
leaders were truly revisionist, and how many were simply
striving to advance themselves.[21] This doubt about Cromwell
appears again in other sections of the poem. In the couplet,
'And Caesars head at last/Did through his Laurels blast', the
Roman adornment for the *princeps*[22] is metonymic for
Charles' kingship. The couplet can be read either transitively
or intransitively: "Cromwell blasted Caesar's head through
the laurel crown", or, simply, "Caesar's head was blasted
through the crown". The ambiguity reflects two distinct
views of Cromwell's part in Charles' downfall, one level of
the ambiguity suggesting that it was the particular agency of
Cromwell which overthrew Charles. At this point in the

poem Marvell merely implies that perhaps Cromwell was the Prime Mover of the regicide. Possibly also the new "vacancy" of the laurel crown allows an inference that Cromwell wished to release the crown for himself.

The potential, of Cromwell's monarchical pretensions, is maintained in Marvell's description of Cromwell's life before he gained national prominence.

> As if his highest plot
> To plant the Bergamot,
> (31–2)

W. R. Orwen has described, in reference to these lines, the traditional association of the Bergamot pear with kingship.[23] Known as the 'pear of kings', it would have been recognized as such by a seventeenth-century reader. Marvell is joking here: he pretends to trivialize Cromwell's youthful occupations as harmless and unpolitical, his 'highest plot' being his garden plot; but the monarchical associations of these pears imply that perhaps even at that time Cromwell was 'plotting' for kingship.

A similar ambiguity characterizes a later quatrain:

> Nature that hateth emptiness,
> Allows of penetration less:
> And therefore must make room
> Where greater Spirits come.
> (41–4)

The 'greater Spirit' is Cromwell, who now occupies Charles' place or position—perhaps that "empty" laurel crown links with this subsequent image of political dominance: Charles had to be crowded out if Cromwell was to take his place, an idea which introduces the next passage, concerning Cromwell's pursuit and execution of the king. But in what sense is Cromwell a 'greater Spirit': is he "stronger", or simply more ambitious? This ambiguous line is succeeded by praise of Charles, who 'nothing common did or mean', implying the nobility of *his* spirit; consequently the 'greater Spirit' in Cromwell is even more difficult to locate precisely.

The emphasis of this continuous ambiguity, its leaning towards defamation, becomes more acute in the lines:

> And *Hampton* shows what part
> He had of wiser Art.
> Where, twining subtile fears with hope,
> He wove a Net of such a scope,
> That *Charles* himself might chase
> To *Caresbrooks* narrow case.
> That thence the *Royal Actor* born
> The *Tragick Scaffold* might adorn.
>
> (47–54)

Here Marvell suggests that Cromwell allowed Charles to escape to 'Caresbrook' in order that eventually Cromwell would be able to instigate his execution. The idea that Cromwell had connived at Charles' escape was a common slander against him, and much emphasized by royalist propaganda;[24] Marvell chooses to state this slander as fact, knowing that to do so constituted an explicit defamation of Cromwell. By his use of this imputation he makes of his attribution of 'wiser Art' to Cromwell a statement that Cromwell was underhand in his methods. Although his passage is the only *explicit* defamation of Cromwell in the poem, it contains no element of vituperative feeling; as usual it is presented as a statement of fact.

That restraint is again preserved in Marvell's description of Charles' execution. '*He* nothing common did or mean/Upon that memorable Scene'. This '*He*' is Charles, an impressive figure in Marvell's account; the italicization of the pronoun[25] seems to imply that, while Charles 'nothing common did or mean', someone else did; the ready identification of this personage with Cromwell is an invitation made by the line. That invitation, however, remains inexplicit.

Ambiguity returns in the description of Cromwell's relationship to Parliament. Marvell seems to portray him as the deferent servant of the republic:

> Nor yet grown stiffer with Command,
> But still in the *Republick's* hand:
> How fit he is to sway

> That can so well obey.
> He to the *Commons Feet* presents
> A *Kingdome*, for his first years rents:
> And, what he may, forbears
> His Fame to make it theirs:
> And has his Sword and Spoyls ungirt,
> To lay them at the *Publick's* skirt.
>
> (81–90)

The first line here says that Cromwell is 'Nor yet' overbearing, seeming to mean that "despite" his power he is not tyrannical to the state; but it could also mean that he is not overbearing *now*, although he might become so in the future.[26] A similar ambiguity features in the second line: 'But still' could imply that Cromwell is consistently deferent to the republic, or that he is as yet deferent; that he might cease to be. This passage is ambiguous also in historical terms. The realities of power in 1650 were quite otherwise than would appear from these lines: Cromwell was in control of the Army, and in the Army resided the effective power of Parliament. In other words, while the military Grandees agreed amongst themselves, Parliament's actions had to be sanctioned by them.[27] Marvell is misrepresenting the political situation, not because he is concerned to maintain the fiction of a republic in England but precisely to portray the relationship of Parliament to Cromwell ironically. As throughout the poem, Cromwell is portrayed ambiguously so that Marvell can imply his personal antipathy to Cromwell and his cause, without making this the absolute arbiter of the poem: ambiguity is a principle of Marvell's presentation of his subject.

(iii) CHILIASM AND CLASSICISM

The Horatian cast of the *Ode* provides a vehicle for Marvell's double perspective on Cromwell. While Horace wrote of Augustus Caesar, Marvell portrays an Augustan Cromwell—figure alike not only in that both were victors in a civil war but also in that Cromwell like Augustus is apprently 'in the Republick's hand' while in fact his personal power is beyond that appropriate in a republic. While Augustus was technically answerable to the Roman Senate, this was largely a fiction which Augustus himself was anxious to maintain because of vestigial Roman antimonarchism. The position of Cromwell in the English republic was increasingly similar to that of Augustus in the Roman, and the congruity provides Marvell with a Horatian form for his subject.

Thus Cromwell is portrayed as a new 'Caesar' (101), one who transforms the state from one kind of political entity into another (35–36). He 'casts the Kingdome old' into the 'Republick', whereas Augustus transformed the fictional republic of Julius into his own incipient empire. In fact, Caesar's title of *dictator* and Augustus' protean title *princeps* were different names for much the same degree of power; Augustus' "tranformation" of the Roman state was really a development of what it had been already—a proto-monarchical state.[28] The same development is implied by Marvell's ambiguous references to Cromwell's monarchical pretensions, and his ironic portrayal of Cromwell as servant of the republic could as well describe Augustus' position in the state. Another parallel is implied when Marvell envisages a "Roman" career of foreign conquest for Cromwell (97–104), since Augustus' foreign conquests were much vaunted, especially by Horace. Equally, just as in Marvell's portrait of Cromwell, Augustus had spent his youth in provincial obscurity and was notorious for being 'reserved and austere'.[29]

While Augustan-Horatian tropes have of course been discussed in relation to the *Ode*, they have not been understood in their true function, and the significant ones have not been recognized at all. Far from implying admiration for Cromwell, as some have suggested, such tropes are—as in *Tom May*—used for Marvell's dialectical purpose. The ironic function of the parallel is to maintain the *Ode's* implications of Cromwell's Monarchical ambitions; and to compare Cromwell's foreign activities to those of Caesar in Gaul gives them an imperialistic tinge.[30] An Augustan model was antipathetic to the parliamentarian "republican" public image, as their foremost propagandist Milton makes clear:

> Dio. . .tells us in. . .his History. . .that Octavius Caesar, partly by force, and partly by fraud, brought things to that pass, that

the emperors of Rome became no longer fettered by laws. For he, though he promised to the people in public that he would lay down the government, and obey the laws, and become subject to others; yet, under pretence of making war in several provinces of the empire, still retained the legions, and so by degrees invaded the government, which he pretended he would refuse. This was not regularly getting from under the law, but breaking forcibly through all laws, as Spartacus the gladiator might have done, and then assuming to himself the style of prince or emperor, as if God or the law of nature had put all men and all laws into subjection under him.[31]

Here Augustus is an archetype of the worst possible rule: autocracy. Thus for Marvell the Augustan format provides a critique of Cromwell's and the 'Republick's' public postures.

While, in this sense, the Augustan format subserves Marvell's personal view of Cromwell, it was also necessary that it should work in concert with his providential role in the poem: while damaging to him as a politician, this format can also comprehend a sense of his 'usefulness' in history. The providential focus of the poem begins in its very exordium, where Marvell characterizes the 'times'—of War and Fortune. But the very existence of the old 'Corslet' signifies previous wars and implies that this moment is a part of the *process* of history, thus providing the setting for the poem's historical and chiliastic view of its subject. The Civil War is a punishment for England's sin by heaven itself, 'the force of *angry* Heaven's flame'. The agent of this devastation is Cromwell the malign rebel, the 'flame' of heaven consisting in his 'Lightning':

> like the three-fork'd Lightning, first
> Breaking the Clouds where it was nurst
> . . .
> His *fiery* way
> . . .
> Then *burning* through the Air he went
> . . .
> The force of angry Heavens *flame*.
> [my italics]

Cromwell's fiery power is the agent of Heaven's punishment. As the 'Lightning' is both portent and agent of punishment, it is also both a portent of Cromwell's emergence and the emergence itself. Cromwell's destructive 'force' is ordained of heaven as the scourge of England,[32] and his personal control of his force is not apparent precisely because it is *heaven* which directs that force.

The 'three-forked Lightning' was that of the Roman supreme deity, Jove: a punitive instrument,[33] avenging the sins men committed against him. Thus this image provides a Roman symbol for God's punishment of England. And the punitive nature of the lightning provides a Roman analogue for the punitive aspect of Cromwell as the agent of *'angry Heaven'*. As a Roman parallel, this image is particularly appropriate to the "Augustan" presentation of Cromwell. Augustus was frequently connected with lightning and thunder by classical writers. Suetonius, for instance, describing a dream prophetic of Augustus' destiny, says that the future *princeps* appeared:

> mortali specie ampliorem, *cum fulmine et sceptro exuviisque Iovis Optimi Maximi* ac radiata corona.[34]
>
> [my italics]

Here Suetonius invests Augustus with the attributes of Jove himself, including his *fulmen* (thunderbolt). Marvell had certainly read this work,[35] but the association was a common one, intended to convey the notion that Augustus' power was divinely decreed. Similarly, Horace's *Ode* 1.12. is a statement of this divine authority of Augustus, describing him as 'right hand' and 'lieutenant' on earth of Jove the Thunderer. While that connection with Jupiter Tonans was echoed by others, Suetonius in his account says that lightning was a portent of Augustus' destiny.[37] The destiny of Divus Augustus is thus attached to Cromwell as agent of heaven, and Cromwell too is the lieutenant of God. The difference between classical laudatory portraits of Divus Augustus and Marvell's portrait of Cromwell lies in his treatment of the image of 'Lightning', which specifically conflates Cromwell with the *punitive* instrument of Jove. It is as a destroyer in God's hand that Cromwell's malignity is providential. In the dialectic of the poem, Cromwell as destroyer may be personally unattractive, but his efficiency as a predator suits the purposes of God.

Cromwell's punitive aspect is seen in action when 'burning through the Air he went,/And Pallaces and Temples rent' (21–2)—the palaces metonymic for the monarchy, and the temples for episcopal religious institution. Marvell's writing is, as always, much more specific than commentators have understood. The association of monarchy and episcopacy here reflects that interrelation of their interests which was the bugbear of Charles' cause. What Cromwell has done is to destroy the antichristian force in the Church, for Antichrist made his home in the very 'temple' of God (II Thessalonians 2:4) impersonating Christianity.[38] Therefore a preacher insisted that against the bishops Parliament must 'take *thunderbolts* out of the hand of God, and so save. . .the Nation.'[39] So here Cromwell as the 'Lightning' of God's wrath blasts the episcopal source of the national sin which has evoked heaven's anger. But to root out antichristianism Cromwell of necessity had to destroy its monarchical ally: his motives for this, and the actual destruction of the monarchy, are not favourably presented by Marvell because of his loyalty, but to the religious issue of Cromwell's action Marvell must assent, for in purging this element Cromwell helps to purify England for her role in the last act of the *eschaton*.

In destruction Cromwell is described as 'burning through the Air' because in the last tribulations of the world the final vial of wrath is the 'plagues of the air'. These cause an earthquake in which 'the cities of the nations' fall, just as Cromwell in implementing heaven's wrath 'rent' the palaces and temples of England. It is Cromwell's providential role that causes his element of destruction to be the 'Air',[40] and as an embodiment of the Seventh Vial of Wrath in his military destruction he here recalls that the Civil War itself was God's 'viall of his revenging justice'.[41] Equally, the Seventh Vial is accompanied by 'thunders, and lightnings' (Revelation 16:18), Cromwell's character here.

By this destiny Cromwell is called from his 'private Gardens' into the acts of history:

Much to the Man is due.
Who. . .

. . .

Could be industrious Valour climbe
To ruine the great Work of Time,
And cast the Kingdome old
Into another Mold.

(28–36)

He is an actor in history, affecting 'the great Work of Time';
functioning within God's plan, which was the 'great Work' of
creating England as Elect Nation. What Cromwell does is to
remold the 'Kingdome' of England into a republic. In the
eschatological view, history was a succession of kingdoms or
empires of which the fifth and final was God's Kingdom;[42]
hence Marvell's play on 'Kingdome', for by destroying a
kingdom in England Cromwell has accelerated the achievement of the last Kingdom in time. In that light Cromwell's
'ruine' of the monarchy is a contribution to the final ruin of
the world and time itself.

Marvell cannot let this providential thought pass without a
balancing statement of his personal chagrin:

Though Justice against Fate complain,
And plead the antient Rights in vain:
But those do hold or break
As Men are strong or weak.

(37–40)

Human values of 'Justice' complain against the providence of
'Fate'. In the course of providential history Marvell's own
cause has been defeated, and 'antient Rights' violated. This is
Marvell's statement of the personal cost of the divine plan; he
does not 'resist or blame' heaven (human 'Justice' does that),
but rather he expresses his sense of how strange heaven's
purposes are in human terms. Yet this distance between the
human perspective and providence is something to which
Marvell can reconcile himself. He notes that 'antient Rights'
'do hold or break/As Men are strong or weak': presaging his
later asseveration that 'A good Cause signifys little, unless it

be as well defended'. The onus is on 'Men' to be 'strong'; obviously Charles was not, and it is men, not providence, who are at fault.

As Charles was not strong enough to defend the old Kingdom, it was to redress this weakness in the Elect Nation that providence imported Cromwell:

> Nature that hateth emptiness,
> Allows of penetration less:
> And therefore must make room
> Where greater Spirits come.
>
> (41–44)

Cromwell is 'greater' than Charles in the sense especially that he is 'stronger'; he is, after all, a 'force'. If that strength has dubious motives—like ambition, 'greatness'—then that is a facet of his malignity. 'Nature' decrees his supremacy, and as in another statement of Marvell's, 'Nature' here means providence:[43] the image from physics in this passage demands the word, as the physical aspect of God's providential order in the world.[44] It is in terms of this order that Cromwell's strength replaces Charles' weakness.

Marvell's resignation to this fact is something that he attributes to Charles also:

> Nor call'd the *Gods* with vulgar spight
> To vindicate his helpless Right,
> But bow'd his comely Head,
> Down as upon a Bed.
>
> (61–64)

The salient feature of this quatrain is Charles' acceptance of the fact that 'the Gods' are willing to see his 'Right' violated, and himself dead. He 'bow'd his comely Head,/Down as upon a Bed'. The gesture of submission is not a *political* acquiescence[45] but rather, as Marvell states it, acquiescence to the divine edict that Charles must die.[46]

When he sets the scene for Charles' execution, Marvell describes it as a theatrical occasion, complete with audience and applause:

> That thence the *Royal Actor* born
> The *Tragick Scaffold* might adorn:
> While round the armed Bands
> Did clap their bloody hands.
>
> (53–56)

The scaffold becomes a stage ('Scene'), with Charles in the leading role of his own "tragedy". This theatrical image is not a derogation of the event:[47] Charles is portrayed with sympathy throughout the passage describing the execution. In fact, the theatrical motif is derived from the providential 'Theatre' of history, placing Charles' execution in that providential context. Thus Charles is described as 'the Royal Actor *born*'. As the future king, he had been 'born' to be an actor in history, his position demanding that role of him. This fact places him in contradistinction to Cromwell, who was not 'born' to act in history, but had to 'climbe' (33) to it. Providence has thus removed Charles from his 'antient Rights' of *Dei Gratia* kingship,[48] the right to be the lieutenant of God. Charles' virtue is to acquiesce in this overruling of legitimacy by the dictates of providence. This providential view of the regicide was common, in fact, both to the king and to his executioners: the latter truly believed that in executing him they were enacting the will of God,[49] and Charles himself, although conscious of injustice, described his imminent execution as a part of God's historical design.[50] It was understood that in the last phase of His design, horrors, destruction, and tribulation would disturb the nations. Marvell describes Charles' 'Tragick' end as a part of this human 'tragedy' of the Latter Days.[51]

> For now is the last Act begun of a most long and dolefull *tragedy*, which shall wholly overflow with scourges, slaughters, destructions.[52]
>
> [my italics]

Charles' tragedy on the scaffold is one of these,[53] and Cromwell is the instrument of this as of other divine 'destructions'.

The point of the Latter Day 'tragedies' was to purge the

earth for the establishment of the next Kingdom: their issue was ultimately fortunate.[54] Thus Charles' execution, however distasteful to Marvell, must be one of these preludes to bliss, a 'sign' of future good:

> This was that memorable Hour
> Which first assur'd the forced Pow'r.
> So when they did design
> The *Capitols* first Line,
> A bleeding Head where they begun,
> Did fright the Architects to run;
> And yet in that the *State*
> Foresaw it's happy Fate.
>
> (65–72)

Charles' 'bleeding Head' is a prophecy of England's 'happy Fate'. Intrinsically, the execution is a horrifying event (it 'Did fright the Architects') but in terms of what it prophesies—the approach of the Last Day—it is the forerunner of a 'happy' end. That peculiarly 'happy Fate' is England's favoured position in the *eschaton*. Thus, although the immediate horror of the regicide is not forgotten in this passage, it is placed in a chiliastic perspective. Marvell emphasizes that '*This* was that memorable Hour/Which first assur'd the forced Pow'r'. The new regime is based upon this act of force: it is illegitimate. The regicide in fact characterizes the new regime as a '*forced* Pow'r'.

For the prophetic sign represented by the execution, Marvell uses a Roman parallel, the discovery of a human head during excavations for the building of the Capitol at Rome.[55] An augur interpreted its appearance as a sign of Rome's future prosperity, and this fortunate nature of the Roman event is proper to Marvell's own prophetic purposes concerning England's destiny. This Roman parallel is especially apt because the excavations were for Jupiter's first temple, a monument to their supreme god: an analogy for the notion that God's 'temple', His new Kingdom, will be erected by the English, who are His chosen people. Thus the Roman event reflects Marvell's purpose, which is to show a providential aspect of the regicide.

When Marvell notes that the *Caput* 'Did fright the Architects to run', he is alluding especially to those parliamentarians who were outraged by the regicide.[56] Marvell notes that they 'ran' from the phenomenon of regicide, and yet were 'Architects' of that state which the regicide was intended to 'assure'. This incongruity between their belief in the sanctity of kingship and their allegiance to a non-monarchical state gives Marvell an opportunity for such ironic allusion; the Latter Day sign is too strong for *their* stomachs, even if the poet himself can be reconciled to that sign.

The 'happy Fate' of England depends upon her industrious pursuit of her mission, which is to promote the Kingdom of God by opposing popery in the nations. Therefore, having described the omen of this fortunate fate, Marvell proceeds to chronicle the way in which England pursues that mission under the new regime. The first instance is Ireland, the conquest of which is the occasion for the poem. As one Englishman stated the matter, 'arise oh Lord and scatter the Irish rebels! arise oh Lord and confound Antichrist!'[57] To the English, Ireland (or most of it) represented a running sore of antichristianism in the British Isles themselves.

Thus when Charles came to an agreement with the disaffected in Ireland, this concord aroused fears of the introduction of popery at home: fears that the king had allied himself with the Catholic cause, which greatly damaged Charles' reputation in England.[58] Later, indeed, Marvell recalled the damage inflicted upon Charles' cause by the Irish rebellion, and attributed the Irish troubles to a popish conspiracy intended to ruin that monarch:

> in the time of his late Majesty, King Charles the First, (besides what they contributed to the Civil War in England) the Rebellion and horrid Massacre in Ireland. . .the Pope's Nuncio [there] assuming. . .the temporal as well as spiritual power. . .[and] breaking the treaties of peace between the King, and, as they stiled themselves, the confederate Catholicks;. . .all which ended in the ruine of his Majestie's reputation, government, and person; which, but upon occasion of that [Irish] Rebellion, could never have happened.
>
> (*GP*, 259)

Here Marvell manifests that he shared the popular view that the Irish, tools of Antichrist, were part of the popish conspiracy to subvert the Elect Nation.[59] The topic was an emotive one, for the so-called "Irish massacre" of English Protestants in 1641 had alienated English feeling. When Cromwell was entrusted with the reconquest of Ireland in 1649, he defended his severity by claiming that his policy of severe reprisals was God's retribution for the massacre of 1641.[60] This notion that Irish *Catholicism* was the target of suppression was the salient feature of English thought on the matter. Thus, when Cromwell suppresses the Irish, he is God's instrument, promulgating the mission of the English:[61]

> And now the *Irish* are asham'd
> To see themselves in one Year tam'd:
> So much one Man can do,
> That does both act and know.

Marvell says 'and *now* the Irish are asham'd'; '*now*' that the sign of England's mission has defined her 'Fate', "purification" from her own antichristian elements has made her strong enough to quell antichristian Ireland. The source of this strength is Cromwell: 'So much *one Man* can do'. His fitness for the task is due to the fact that he both 'acts' and 'knows', a classical formulation in the *Ode* for the Puritan faculty of 'zeal'. Caesar, for instance, (to whom Cromwell is compared in 101) was a celebrated example of this classical combination of action with knowledge,[62] and that combination was in general a Roman ideal.[63] So, here, the Roman parallel provides this formulation for Puritan 'zeal', which denoted a similar combination[64] of an alertness to 'Truth' with the ability to enact God's purposes. In suppressing the Irish, Cromwell's zealotry manifests England's mission.

For this and other reasons, the Irish "encomium"[65] on Cromwell is ironic in intention.

> And now the *Irish* are asham'd
> To see themselves in one Year tam'd:
> . . .
> They can affirm his praises best,

> And have, though overcome, confest
> How good he is, how just,
> And fit for highest Trust:
> Nor yet grown stiffer with Command,
> But still in the *Republick's* hand:
> How fit he is to sway
> That can so well obey.
>
> (73–84)

We may note first that this—the only explicit "praise" of
Cromwell in the poem—is attributed to the Irish, not the
poet himself. 'They can affirm his praises best' is, with
reference to Cromwell's notoriously bloody suppression, a
caustic attribution; moreover, to the contemporary English
reader, steeped in anti-Irish propaganda, the reverse of
recommendation. As we have seen, the poet and the reader
accorded in this prejudice. These factors, counterbalancing
Marvell's endorsement of Cromwell's zeal, maintain the
poem's equilibrium between personal irony and the affirmation of England's mission.

In the transition to Cromwell's relations with Parliament,
one commentator has noticed a logical difficulty: that 'Trust'
in Ireland and 'Trust' in England are not equivalent, while the
passage appears to equate them.[66] In fact, as in the "Irish
encomium" itself, Marvell here deliberately affronts English
feeling, by seeming to equate the political needs of the
"primitive" Irish (as contemporaries saw them) with those of
England herself. The implication is that Cromwell's military
mission in Ireland is no basis for entrusting him with political
power in England. The difference between the two 'Trust[s]'
is that between Cromwell as providential instrument (the
Destroyer versus Antichrist) and as political tyrant at home
(the Destroyer loose in the Elect Nation). Overseas he is the
representative of England's mission: at home his malign
aspect is uppermost.

It is as providential instrument that Cromwell 'to the
Commons Feet presents/A *Kingdome*, for his first years
rents': the Catholic 'Age' or 'Kingdome' which he has
subdued in Ireland. For Ireland was a part of the so-called
antichristian empire of the Pope, which was the power of

popery in the world;[67] to the destruction of which nefarious Kingdom Cromwell has contributed by his exploits in Ireland.

The ambiguity of Cromwell at home consists, here, in his relationship to Parliament. Marvell portrays this relationship ironically, as if Parliament were in control of its War Machine, the control of a handler over his hawk: 'Where, when he first does lure,/The Falckner has her sure'. The irony is that the 'Falckner' truly in control of Cromwell is God: Cromwell is *His* tame "Destroyer",[68] and God can certainly 'ha[ve] him sure' when destruction is not His purpose. In his choice of a bird of prey to represent Cromwell as divine instrument, Marvell is using a Roman motif. The eagle was Jupiter's messenger; Horace calls this bird the 'servant of the lightning', agent of Jupiter's decrees.[69] Marvell describes Cromwell as the 'Lightning' of God, and to compare him to the 'servant of the lightning' is further to characterize him as the instrument of God. (In fact, the eagle was a common attribute of Jupiter.)[70] In this comparison Marvell is also maintaining the Augustan aspect of the Roman parallel; Horace describes Augustus in war as a hawk bearing down on his prey,[71] and Marvell uses the same image for Comwell in his Holy War.

This description of Cromwell as agent of God's judgments introduces a passage in which Marvell considers Cromwell's ability to enact them. Properly to do so he must perform England's mission by extending the struggle against popery into Europe:[72]

> What may not then our *Isle* presume
> While Victory his Crest does plume!
> What may not others fear
> If thus he crown each Year!
> A *Caesar* he ere long to *Gaul*,
> To *Italy* an *Hannibal*,
> And to all States not free
> Shall *Clymacterick* be.
>
> (97–104)

Cromwell has '*crown*[ed]' the year with the '*Kingdome*' in Ireland, for Ireland was one of the 'crowns' of the Beast (his horns were interpreted as kings in his power).[73] Marvell looks for such 'crowns' wrested from Antichrist elsewhere in the world,[74] and specifically to the conquest of 'Gaul' and 'Italy'. At this time France and Italy were the strongholds of Catholicism in Europe, France the foremost Catholic power and Italy the homeland of popery. By extirpating the two major antichristian powers, Cromwell would 'to all States not free/. . .Clymacterick be', emancipating them from the power of the Beast (the characteristic antichristian 'tyranny').

A 'Clymacterick' is a critical moment, marking the end of one epoch and the beginning of another.[75] Cromwell will provide this to 'all States' yet under the yoke of the Beast; thus he will be the 'Clymacterick' to the world-empire of Antichrist, marking the end of the antichristian era and the onset of the new Kingdom. As God's instrument against Antichrist, Cromwell is the 'Clymacterick' to the Antichristian Age, a purgative instrument not only in England but in Europe also. This moment is the climax of Cromwell's providential role in the *Ode*. It portrays him as an agent of God in *world* history, who thus "realizes" the peculiar mission of England.

This vision of Crowell's destiny is suitably contained in the Augustan format of the *Ode*. Augustus was considered the conqueror of the world; he too represented a 'Clymacterick' to classical authors. Horace, Virgil, and Ovid all saw him as an all-conquering ruler, and Virgil in particular portrayed him as a man of destiny who would inaugurate a new Golden Age—his equivalent of the seventeenth-century 'Kingdom'.[76] It is his similarity of vision, a Golden Age and a man of destiny, that makes Virgil's description of Augustus' fate a source for Marvell's description of Cromwell's. The relevant Virgilian passage is that at the end of the sixth book of the *Aeneid*, where the statement of Augustus' destiny is clearest.

> hic Caesar et omnis Iuli/progenies magnum caeli uentura sub axem./hic uir, hic est, tibi quem promitti saepius audis,/ Augustus Caesar, diui genus, aurea condet/saecula . . ./Cuius in aduentum iam nunc et Caspea regna/ responsis horrent diuum et Maeotia tellus. . ./et dubitamus adhuc uirtutem extendere factis. . . ?[77]

Here Virgil states that Augustus is the fulfilment of prophecy: 'hic uir, hic est'. In the same way Marvell envisages Cromwell as the man who can fulfil the prophesied defeat of Antichrist. Both are men of destiny with a divinely ordained purpose on earth. Virgil says that Augustus will bring a Golden Age for Rome, 'aurea condet/saecula', while Marvell states that Cromwell is harbinger of the Kingdom Age: both represent 'Clymactericks'. As his destiny, Augustus will extend the conquests of Rome; similarly, Cromwell's conquests will extend to 'all States not free'. Virgil's final thought is that with Augustus at their head, Romans cannot hesitate 'uirtutem extendere factis'. This thought appears also in Marvell's description of Cromwell's leadership in England's mission: '*What may not then our Isle presume*/While Victory his crest does plume?' Cromwell, like Augustus, inspires his country's militant spirit. Hence the Roman parallel of Augustus' inauguration of a Golden Age provides a format for Marvell's Cromwell as agent of the Kingdom.

From this climactic vision of Cromwell's destiny Marvell returns to the struggle at home. This matter, like the rest of the poem, is still a part of the historical process: the Irish problem belongs to the *past*, the vision of Cromwell in Europe belongs to the *future*, as a prophecy of his role. The *present* matter concerns what Cromwell will be doing in Scotland, which is his current 'Trust':

> The *Pict* no shelter now shall find
> Within his party-colour'd Mind;
> But from this Valour sad
> Shrink underneath the Plad:
> Happy if in the tufted brake
> The *English Hunter* him mistake:
> Nor lay his Hounds in near
> The *Caledonian* Deer.
>
> (105–112)

This is Cromwell as Hunter again. Marvell portrays the Scots as cowards cringing from Cromwell's might: 'Happy if. . . The English Hunter him mistake', the fearful Scot goes into hiding, timid as the notoriously nervous 'Deer' of his land.

The trouble with the Scots (as opposed to the Irish) was, in the immediate sense, their proclamation of Charles II—Parliament's current problem—and Cromwell was to be dispatched to rid them of it. If the Scots had declared for the new king, why should Marvell derogate them, both by imputations of cowardice and by describing them as 'party-coloured', deceitful? In order to gain Scottish aid for his cause Charles II had agreed perforce to a Presbyterian settlement in England, should he regain his throne.[78] This was an outrage to many in England: remember Milton's famous remark about the 'New Presbyter' being worse than the 'old Priest' of episcopacy?[79] The Independents in particular feared an established Presbyterian Church;[80] thus Marvell too was antagonistic towards the Presbyterians.[81] This religious question is the source of Marvell's antipathy to the Scots, not mitigated by the fact that the Scots seemed prepared to turn coats for anyone who would promise them an English Presbyterian settlement. If Cromwell quells the Scottish threat he is defending **the true character of English Protes**tantism. As in the case of Ireland, the Scots represented a religious as well as a political threat, exacerbated by outrage at the idea that the Scots could see fit to invade England.[82] In this passage the contemporary English prejudice against the Scots as a 'perfidious' nation[83] goes hand in hand with a religious issue.

With the prediction of Cromwell's success in Scotland Marvell closes the chronicle, turning to apostrophize Cromwell himself:

> But thou the Wars and Fortunes Son
> March indefatigably on;
> And for the last effect
> Still keep thy Sword erect:
> Besides the force it has to fright
> The Spirits of the shady Night,
> The same *Arts* that did *gain*
> A *Pow'r* must it *maintain*.
>
> (113–20)

This direct address to Cromwell inevitably involves a renascence of Marvell's personal feelings towards him. He has characterized Cromwell as the instrument of providence, 'Fortune';[84] but he has not forgotten that Cromwell is the '*Wars* . . . Son' also. Cromwell rose by. military means: his power is still an illegitimate power. The fact that he is providentially sanctioned but politically illegitimate, the collision of divine and human values, is reflected in the division of this line between Cromwell as Son of Fortune and Cromwell as Son of War. This line defers to providence even while it puts Cromwell in his place.

The illegitimacy of Cromwell's 'Pow'r' evokes a warning from Marvell that to maintain that power Cromwell must remain 'industrious' (33); force is the basis of 'the forced Pow'r', and to retain that power Cromwell must hold to force: 'And for the last effect/Still keep thy Sword erect'—in the sense that Cromwell's sword *is* his power, this sword represents government by force. In this way Cromwell the Destroyer becomes a Defender, but because of his nature— and the nature of his power—that defensiveness is as much a matter of force as his destructiveness. They are the same 'Arts'. This thought, originating in Sallust,[85] is a warning in classical form.

The efficacy of Cromwell's sword is that it 'has force to fright/The Spirits of the shady Night'. These are, on the political level, the dead, the Roman 'shades' or ghosts of men: those who, earlier in the poem, chose to 'oppose' Cromwell, and the 'bleeding Head' of Charles must be amongst them. Perhaps Marvell suggests that they come to haunt Cromwell; perhaps also, that their memory inspires his living enemies. This too would seem to be a warning, and the political level of this final passage is a sinister one. Marvell sees fit to warn Cromwell both of his political future and of the fact that he must remain eternally vigilant. 'March indefatigably on', Marvell advises, even if he does not sympathize with, Cromwell. And this personal element in the lines recalls the exordium of the *Ode*, where the 'Arts' of the poet and the 'Arts' of Cromwell were opposed: the poem's closure on the Arts of Power circles back upon that opening thought. Cromwell has committed himself to the 'adventrous' life, and the distance of the poet from that *modus vivendi* is here reasserted.

But this finale takes account also of Cromwell's 'usefulness', his providential aspect. As the Final Image, it synthesizes the dialectic of personal and providential perspectives in the poem. It does so, first, by re-emphasizing Cromwell's efficiency: he is 'indefatigable', a thought which recalls that he is the 'industrious' instrument of God. He must be so 'still' (116), because it is that quality which ensures him the favour of providence. He must maintain a vigilant sword 'for the *last effect*', which is the end of history itself, the Last Day. (It is worth recalling that in *The First Anniversary* Marvell describes the Last Day as the 'wonderful *Effect*' [135]). Reference to it completes the historical context of the poem. It was in the service of that day that Cromwell was called to power, and he must continue to serve it. His service is in the nature of the 'Sword', militant; to keep that 'Sword erect' is to remain in readiness for that service, and readiness was the Puritan ethic of chiliasm.

Cromwell is still an Actor in history, and his activity in this department is, like his political activity, a matter of force. He is at once 'the *force* of angry Heaven' and 'the *forced* Pow'r'; on both levels his sword 'has *force* to fright' (26, 66, 117). Both his illegitimate (political) aspect, and his providential (historical) aspect depend upon this faculty of force. In this way a synthesis is made.

Thus, in the providential sense, the enemies of Cromwell are not only his enemies amongst men but those "powers" which oppose his providential function. Like the ghosts of men the agents of Antichrist come from the underworld, the 'shady Night'. The Roman underworld was both the region of the dead and the infernal domain of Pluto, their Devil.[86] Hence Marvell's use of the Roman trope of 'the shades' can contain within it both the dead and the infernal enemies of Cromwell, for, as the agent of God against Antichrist, he must have both mortal and 'Spiritual' enemies. These are both, then, the 'Spirits' of the dead and 'Spirits' in the old sense of "demons".

Cromwell's function now, having quelled the antichristian element in the British Isles, is to maintain the struggle against the antichristian enemies of England: the force of his 'Sword' defends England against them, just as earlier Marvell saw his force as England's militancy towards them. The Holy War is fought on two fronts, aggressive and defensive. This is the providential aspect of Cromwell's defence, as opposed to the personal defence of his own power. It is a *spiritual* war, against 'Spirits':

> For we wrestle not against flesh and blood, but against principalities, against powers, against the rulers of the darkness of this world, against spiritual wickedness in high places.
>
> (Ephesians 6:12)

'The rulers of the darkness of this world' are the most powerful 'Spirits of the shady Night', the avatars of the Beast on earth,[87] and in England these Pauline terms were constantly reiterated during the struggles of the 1640s and 50s. Ephesians further advises:

> take unto you the whole armour of God, that ye may be able to withstand in the evil day. . .and take. . .the sword of the Spirit.
>
> (Ephesians 6:13–17)

This 'sword' and this vigilance are Cromwell's during the antichristian tribulations of the Latter Days (for so Paul's 'evil day' was understood)—that period of 'destructions' diagnosed earlier in the poem, which precedes the 'last effect' of the End.

Springing from the Pauline metaphor of the 'sword of the Spirit', Cromwell's sword carries specific iconographical meanings. In classical literature, and particularly in Virgil's *Aeneid* VI, it was believed that the spirits dwelling in the underworld feared the "cold metal" of the sword;[88] thus, in the Roman parallel, the sword of the Spirit frightens the dead mortals ('spirits') at least. However, this Final Image has also a chiliastic level of meaning, and as elsewhere in the poem this Roman parallel provides a format for a chiliastic view. Cromwell is a warrior in eschatological history, and in this Final Image he is the guardian of England against the forces of Antichrist. In this role the 'Sword', as an iconographical attribute, has a direct connexion with eschatology, for it is the attribute of Michael the Archangel who wars with the Dragon

in Revelation 12. Michael provided the type for Spenser's Red
Cross Knight in the latter's encounter with the Dragon: he
was the most significant of the angels in the fight against
Antichrist. In medieval legends he is represented as captain of
the host of heaven against Lucifer and his fallen angels, and as
such he appears in *Paradise Lost* VI.[89] For the parliamentarians, the Civil War itself had been a conflict between 'Saint
Michael and the *Serpent*'—between the Angel of the saints
and Antichrist.[90] Thus he was usually represented as a
warrior, with a sword as his special attribute.[91] The analogy
between Cromwell's function as warrior in the *eschaton* and
Michael's is very close. Cromwell and the Angel also have the
same guardian and Prince of Israel, and Cromwell in the *Ode*
is the guardian and Prince of the New Israel, England. Both
Michael's protective function and his militancy are present in
the Cromwell of the Final Image.

This characterization of Cromwell is not peculiar to
Marvell. An example of its applicability to Cromwell in terms
of the English eschatological preoccupation is William
Faithorne's emblematic portrayal of Cromwell: 'The
Embleme of England's Distractions' appeared in 1658[92] and
provides an instructive parallel to Marvell's Final Image.
Faithorne's engraving shows Cromwell as 'Pro De lege et
grege', the Lord Protector and therefore guardian of England;
he carries an erect sword, symbol not only of state but of his
strength and guardianship. That this might is holy is evident
from the iconography of the emblem. Cromwell is the
warrior-guardian with the sword, and crushed beneath his
feet are the Beast and the Whore of Babylon.[93] Thus
Cromwell in the emblem is Michael to the New Israel, the
three kingdoms guarded by his might. This is the figurative
level of the Final Image which as it were emblematizes
Cromwell's providential function. At this level it admonishes
Cromwell to remain the forceful instrument of God, while
the political level advises him to retain his own power by the
same force. The malign and the providential aspects of
Cromwell were thus incipiently reconcilable, for his force as
Destroyer *constituted* his suitability to the purposes of God.
Thus his 'sword' has at once tyrannous and fortunate aspects,
synthesizing Marvell's double attitude.

Although providential Cromwell is not legitimized, his 'Pow'r' still 'the forced Pow'r' (120, 66). This characterization of the Parliamentarian regime echoes that of the king, who when at his trial admonished to remember that he was before a court of justice, remarked, 'I find I am before a *power*'.[94] Marvell makes the same distinction between 'antient Rights' and mere 'Pow'r'—Cromwell's requires to be 'maintained' because it cannot rest on legitimacy.

For the synthesis in the Final Image between Cromwell as tyrant and Cromwell as guardian, the Roman parallel provides a format, as has the Augustan portrayal of Cromwell throughout the poem. And the Horatian equability of tone that stamps Horatian form[95] provides a vehicle for Marvell's balance of perspectives on Cromwell, reflecting his not neutral but neutralized feeling. Also, by placing Cromwell in an historical "typology" as analogue to Augustus, the *Ode* embodies its sense of history: just as Christ was born in Augustus' empire, so would He come again in this poem's own age. This is the major motive for Marvell's Roman parallel, for Cromwell is one of those who prepare the world for His Coming.

Marvell's complicated view of the Cromwellian phenomenon was far from unusual at this time. Thus a polemical pamphlet, *An Honest Discourse between Three Neighbours, Touching the present Government in these Three Nations* (1655) similarly evinces that an eschatological view of Cromwell could "overcome" the author's hostility to him. This Puritan opponent sets himself the problem of understanding the Protectorate in terms of the providential purposes of God and the imminent *eschaton*.[96] In his view there is no doubt of Cromwell's political malignity and selfish ambition:[97] 'The Cavaliers say now, Did we not prophesie true, These Reformers sought themselves?'[98] Nevertheless, like Marvell, the pamphleteer must acknowledge that Cromwell's authority is divinely sanctioned, since 'Gods wise providence doth nothing amiss, and suffers nothing but for good', and (as chiliasts were fond of citing) 'all worketh for good to them that are good'.[99] Cromwell's utility within God's plan is that, like Cyrus, he is the involuntary instrumental of providence: 'the counsel of God prospers in this Cyrus his hand, though he comprehend it not when he is thus girded' with the sword of the Spirit. His malignity, that 'obstructs good things', is proscribed by his providential character as he 'keepeth off evil also as an instrument'.[100] Marvell's poem issues from a similar process of dialectical control of feeling, for he has done what was required of him, 'to take pains to enquire' into the utilitarian and provocative direction of providence within current events. It is this quality of personal reconcilement to history that gives the *Ode* its peculiarity.

In this reconcilement the *Ode* reflects poetry as a formulation of reality. Bacon had distinguished between the 'feigned history' of the writer and the phenomenal event:

> The use of this *feigned history* hath been to give some shadow of satisfaction to the mind of man in those points wherein the nature of things doth deny it, the world being in proportion inferior to the soul; by reason whereof there is, agreeable to the spirit of man, a more ample greatness, a more exact goodness. . . than can be found in the nature of things. Therefore, because the acts or events of *true history* have not that magnitude which satisfieth the mind of man, *poesy* feigneth acts and events greater and more heroical: because *true history* propoundeth the successes and issues of actions not so agreeable to the merits of virtue and vice, therefore poesy feigns them more just in retribution, and more according to revealed providence:[101]

According to Bacon, the value of poetry is that it redresses the morally dissatisfactory nature of 'history', consoling 'the mind of man'. So does Marvell's poem, revealing providence; yet the stringency of Marvell's acknowledgement of harsh reality—not merely of event but also of the bleak providential directive too—strives for something more adequate to the peculiar crooked ways of God. God is an ironist; and the *Ode* can afford that irony too.

4

Revelation and Renovation: The Poetics of Prophecy

The Ode's chiliastic redeployment of a Roman parallel is an innovation within that English Renaissance tradition whereby classical and Christian *topoi* are fused. For Spenser and Milton, too, classical inclinations interacted with chiliastic convictions. From that interaction there evolved, in the works of these three poets, a genre which I shall call "revelatory eclogue", remodelling Virgil's Fourth Eclogue. Marvell's *Upon Appleton House* particularly provides a highly developed example of the genre, and shows that, just as Horace provided a classical framework for the *Ode*'s historical present, so Virgil's Fourth Eclogue became for Marvell a similarly potent historical formula for the understanding of his own times. The seventeenth-century recasting of Virgil's Eclogue is a further step in that progressive indentification of the poem with history which is the hallmark of the apocalyptic literary tradition.

(i) THE PROBLEMATIC AND THE PROCESS OF HISTORY
Recalling the Augustinian analogy between history and a poem, we may remember the way in which Marvell's problematic reflected the dialectic of history itself: how, in a sense, eschatology and his poetry have in common the features of the problematic. Now I want to develop this comparison of the problematic with the historical process and with the way in which that process was customarily interpreted by the individual saint.

Earlier I described that characteristic element of Marvell's poetry, the Final Image at the close of a Marvellian poem at which synthesis is achieved, completing the problematic. I also observed the way in which the problematic reflects that dialectic of history, whereby the eschatological design subsumes both evil and good to produce the final triumph of God. In this analogy, therefore, the end of the poem—the Final Image—corresponds to the end of history. Both evince a teleological movement: just as the problematic of the poem moves inevitably towards resolution in the Final Image, so history tends ineluctably towards the Last Day, which is the resolution of eschatology. In this manner Marvell's procedure imitates the 'great Design' which is his major theme.

This correspondence between the Final Image and the universal End is evident, on the thematic level, in *Appleton House*, where the conclusion of the poem is an image of the end of the world. Similarly, the Final Image of the *Horatian Ode* looks to 'the last effect' of history, urging Cromwell to imitate the poem by acting in cognisance of that 'last effect'. Moreover, there the Final Image performed that synthesis of the problematic, thereby exemplifying both its thematic and its structural significance. (In all poems there is, as one theorist has noted, a problem of closure, to achieve a sense of completed design.[1] But Marvell's poetry, concerned as it is with many aspects of 'ending', overcomes this problem almost as a matter of course.) As we shall see, there are many more examples of the correspondence of the two teleologies—historical and poetic—in the Final Images of Marvell's poems, whereby the poems themselves insist upon their reciprocal relationship with the nature of history.

In Marvell, this relationship was peculiarly essential; but to mimic the design of history in less thoroughgoing manner was not unusual in this period. One may compare Herbert, whose anthology *The Temple* completes *The Church* with a *L'Envoy* expressing his anticipation of the Second Coming; indeed, the last few poems here are all concerned with the Four Last Things. In this fashion the culmination of *The Church* reflects her imminent triumph at the Last Day, although at a relatively simple level. Vaughan's *L'Envoy*, at the close of *Silex Scintillans*, has a comparable function; and Spenser's epic terminates with his imprecation of that 'Sabaoths Day'.[2] Thus Marvell was not the only poet to acknowledge in his poetry the teleological impetus of his beliefs, although he implemented them to an unusual degree.

Similarly, although it may seem evident that all poetry

exists "in time"—the time required to peruse it—this fact attains rather more importance than usual in Marvell's case. If this reading-time is, in little, an experience of the movement of time towards its end, it may readily accrue other patterns proper to chiliasm.

In the description of these patterns, one may begin with Augustine's formulation of the relationship between the "time" of a poem and Christian time. The latter is 'linear' time; considering this fact (and man's apprehension of it), he expounded the comparison of a Psalm—or sacred poem—in the course of recital:

> I am about to repeat a Psalm that I know. Before I begin, my expectation is extended over the whole; but when I have begun, how much soever of it I shall separate off into the past, is extended along my memory; and thus the life of this action of mine is divided between my memory as to what I have repeated, and expectation as to what I am about to repeat; but "consideration" is present with me, that through it what was future, may be conveyed over, so as to become past. Which the more it is done again and again, so much more the expectation being shortened, is the memory enlarged; till the whole expectation be at length exhausted, when that whole action being ended, shall have passed into memory. And this which takes place in the whole Psalm, the same takes place in each several portion of it, and each several syllable; the same holds in that longer action, whereof this Psalm may be a part; the same holds in the whole life of man, whereof all the actions of man are parts; the same holds through the whole age of the sons of men, whereof all the lives of men are parts.[3]

Thus, according to Augustine, the time-process of a poem is common to both its parts and its whole; and the same time-process characterizes the lives of men and the ages of the world ('the whole age of the sons of men'); men live in 'expectation' on three levels, of the end of a poem, of their own lives, and of the "historical" future. Doctrinally, of course, Augustine is expounding the futurist emphasis of Christianity, which lives for what is not yet—the afterlife, the end of the world. Eschatology above all provides the 'expectation' of the Christian, and seventeenth-century preachers enjoined that all actions should tend towards the service of that End.⁴ The ending was, as it were, always present, and the present was always referred to the End. The difficulty of this position was not only the "interval" between the two (that which is between expectation and end), the features of which are unknown, but also the way in which the present and the End are related to one another in the overall design; that is, without first *knowing* the overall design, it is impossible to undersand that interval of (as Augustine puts it) 'consideration' between 'expectation' and 'memory'.

This was by no means an abstract problem for the chiliasts of the mid seventeenth century. For the moment it is sufficient to understand the problem in essence. Augustine provides a clue to it when he says that the temporal process of a poem involves, for our perceptions, the elements of 'expectation' and 'memory', which mutually readjust as time proceeds; what is no longer in process falls into memory, waht is yet to be exists in expectation, and what is present is at the point of moving from expectation into memory. The chiliast's apprehension of history followed exactly this pattern, but the pattern was not self-sufficient.

For to relate one's own consciousness of time to God's was to try to adjust one's own pattern to the great design of history. The historical design was an integrated entity, and like all such entities it subordinated the parts to the whole, to the point where the parts are not only under the control of the whole but unintelligible without it. From one's own little portion of time one had to perceive that whole; and then one needed not only to fit the part into the whole but also actively to shape that part in a manner required by the whole design—to fit the whole, as it were, into the part. The only way in which this project became feasible was if that which was unknown, the interval between expectation and memory, was revealed—if one foreknew, and if one knew also the whole design *as* a design in which past, present, and future cohered. This project was an unavoidable issue for the chiliast, and it was feasible because what he needed to know had been 'revealed' in the Book of Revelation.

As I have indicated, "interpretation" was the fundamental requirement of the chiliast; Revelation had displayed to him the whole course of history after Christ's advent, providing him with the whole design. He was supposed to take it for his guide, to identify the events to which its prophecies referred, and thus to "place" himself in history. He had to be apprised of that place, because he was enjoined to act in a manner which forwarded the fulfilment of those prophecies which were as yet unfulfilled.

The problem of the "interval", as I have called it, supervened because God rationed one's ability to understand His Revelation. By nature, apocalyptic is symbolic and secretive, and it is precisely for this reason that interpretation is so necessary. Thus, in the course of stating the imperative nature of interpretation, at least one seventeenth-century writer finds himself indicating its fundamental difficulty:

> *history of prophecy*, consisteth of two relatives, the prophecy, and the accomplishment; and therefore the nature of such a work ought to be, that every prophecy of the Scripture be sorted with the event fulfilling the same, throughout the ages of the world; both for the better confirmation of faith, and for the better illumination of the church touching those parts of prophecies which are yet unfulfilled: allowing nevertheless that latitude which is agreeable and familiar to divine prophecies; being of the nature of their Author [God], with whom a thousand years are but as one day; and therefore are not fulfilled punctually at once, but have springing and germinant accomplishment throughout many ages; though the height or fulness of them may refer to some one age.[5]

This is Bacon's manifesto for 'the history of prophecy'; that is, these prophecies must be understood, but it is difficult to judge the time of their 'accomplishment' because Revelation has a prophetic, not a human, sense of time. The fact that God does not distinguish between a 'day' and a 'thousand years' was taken from Scripture (II Peter 3:8).[6] If one did not know the time ('age') to which a prophecy referred, then it was difficult to understand anything at all: for one does not know which prophecies can be consigned to 'memory' and which to 'expectation'.

The potential solution to this impasse was God Himself, who intended that His Revelation should *become* revelatory by stages. At appropriate moments He would provide 'signs' to enlighten men, 'For such is the order of God's enlightening his Church, to dispense and deal out by degrees his beam, so as our earthly eyes may best sustain it'.[7] Thus it was understood that, as time ran down towards its end, so God's revelation of truth increased, until, at the Last Day, there would begin the time of perfect knowledge:

> Truth [revealed truth] indeed came once into the world with her divine master, and was a perfect shape most glorious to look on: but when he ascended, and his apostles after him were laid asleep, then [under the Roman Church] arose a wicked race of deceivers, who. . .took the virgin Truth, hewed her lovely form into a thousand pieces, and scattered them to the four winds. From that time ever since, the sad friends of Truth, such as durst appear . . . went up and down gathering up limb by limb still as they could find them. We have not yet found them all . . . nor ever shall do, till her Master's Second Coming; he shall bring together every joint and member.[8]

Asserting a common tenet which Marvell also held,[9] Milton is here expounding the doctrine of progressive revelation, the perfection of man's knowledge which will be attained at the End. Thus the process of time and history is itself a progression in revelation; and the continuous readjustment of 'memory' and 'expectation', known and unknown, means that every historical event adds to the sum of knowledge. For these reasons the End reveals all, and only then is the whole Design truly understood. (Then, in Augustine's wry observation, it will even be revealed why what was unrevealed was such, at any particular moment in history.)[10] As Daniel 12:9 stated, 'the words are closed up and sealed till the time of the end.'[11]

To see how this 'progressive revelation' and interpretation affects Marvell's poetry, it is necessary to go back to Augustine's comparison of time and the psalm. For him the familiar temporal sequence of a poem known by heart is a model of the omnipresent knowledge of God:

> Certainly, if there be a mind gifted with such knowledge and foreknowledge, as to know all things past and to come, as I know one well-known Psalm, truly that mind is passing

wonderful, and fearfully amazing; in that nothing past, nothing to come in after-ages, is any more hidden from him, than when I sung that Psalm, was hidden from me what, and how much of it has passed away from the beginning, what, and how much there remained unto the end.[12]

That is, perfection of knowledge is absolutely related to the perception of the whole design, whether it be of a poem or of history. As a divine expressed it in 1649, men did not understand the providence in current events because 'we cannot see the whole frame of things, how sundry particular events in a mutuall relation do concurre to make up the beautie of the whole'.[13] Only the End of history reveals the shape of history.

Similarly, on the analogy of the poem, the 'beauty of the whole' is not evident until the poem is known, has been read to its end; integrity of design is common to both poems and history, and in both cases the End is the moment when all is revealed. This correspondence between the two 'Designs' becomes important in Marvell's case, because of the correspondence in his poetry between the Final Image and the universal End. Until the moment of the Final Image the problematic remains unresolved, just as history remains unresolved until the End; this involves also the reflection that the ambiguities and tensions inherent in the problematic do not become 'beautiful'—understood and solved—until the Final Image has so resolved them. In fact, the Final Image is decisive in a Marvellian poem not only because it is resolving and conclusive but also because (like the universal End) it 'reveals' what has gone before.

At the end of any poem, it has been noted, 'we should be able to re-experience the entire work'.[14] In our experience of a Marvellian poem the process is more complicated. If one has apprehended the nature of the problematic, the first reading involves the understanding of ambiguities and antitheses. As one progresses through the poem one follows their mutual readjustments until, in the Final Image, the pattern is complete; that is, throughout one's reading one is constantly retaining and readjusting elements because the problematic demands it, just as, in the experience of history, 'interpretation' constantly retains and readjusts the relationship between prophecy and event. Similarly, if one is familiar with the problematic, one is aware that this process of interpretation will be resolved by the Final Image—that the progressive revelation of the *poem* will be perfected by its End. Equally, like the chiliast, one reads in expectation of that end, an expectation as sharp because as sure of resolution. The tension generated by the unresolved antitheses of the problematic, like the antitheses of history, is relieved only by the End.

Just as important, because antecedent to this process, is the assumption that it is participatory. Just as the chiliast is required to understand and explicate prophecy—prophecy is otherwise useless as guidance[15]—so the problematic requires of the reader a greater involvement in the "structuring" of a poem than is normal, for the problematic is, equally, useless as a key to the poem if the key is not utilized. Without it Marvell's poems display that mystery which has puzzled so many of their readers and produced such varied interpretations.

The problematic is particularly demanding of this "participation" because it is an arcane procedure. But once its pattern is apprehended, it operates as a key, and the poem is "revealed" so that 'nothing. . .is. . .hidden'. These features, of cryptogram and revelation, relate the problematic to prophecy on another level, for prophecy is a paradoxical quantity, at once secret and revelatory.[16] For the chiliast who was also a poet, the relationship between poetry and prophecy could be founded upon several traditional ideas about the function of a poet. Puritan poets assimilated the time-honoured idea that poetry was divinely inspired to the Calvinist notion of election by God, so that a poet might become the chosen voice of God's will in literary form.[17] Thus poetry of a prophetic type was itself a form of activism, directly related—as all such activism has to be—to the interpretation of God's revealed will. And a certain apocalyptic "secrecy" was proper to it, as an especial form of that religious decorum which Marvell celebrated in his poem *On Mr Milton's "Paradise Lost"*: 'things divine thou treat'st of in such state/As them preserves, and thee, inviolate' (33–4).

There also Marvell defended Milton's theological sanction for his "sacred" epic on the basis that Milton was truly a latter-day prophet (many doubted that there could be "modern" prophets), a vatic poet. Thereby Marvell dispels his own dramatized horror of antichristian presumption meddling with the divine mysteries of providential history,[18] absolving Milton's blindness of its potential analogy in Samson's "un-revealed" (i.e. Old Testament) nature as the blinded destroyer, and reinvesting it with comparison to the true prophecy of the blind Tiresias. As in *First Anniversary* it is all a matter of 'seeing'—and secret writing, like blind seeing, is a paradox enactive of prophecy. For Marvell divine sanction and his personal secretiveness are complementary.

Moreover, the Renaissance idea that the poet imitated God in so far as he was a "creator", to which Marvell refers in *On Mr Milton*,[19] had an especial emphasis for the chiliast, in that (as Bacon indicated above) God was the 'Author' of the Book of Revelation and thus the model for all prophetic poetry. In an age when so many—learned and otherwise—were attempting with urgency and enthusiasm to "reveal" the Revelation—under such titles as *Clavis Apocalyptica*, *The Key of the Revelation* and *A Revelation of the Revelation*—it is understandable that Marvell should have appropriated the design of history *in revelatio*. (For Augustine, we recall, history was itself God's poetry.) It has been noted that the appeal of the Hebraic view of history, upon which Protestant eschatology was based, was that it 'showed an all-absorbing interest in the significance and place of each event within great patterns.'[20] This eschatological procedure—to retain the sense of a real, individual event within a grand supertemporal scheme—is the basis of the formal relationship of the problematic to the historical process; just as 'expectation', the emotional relationship of men to the Last Day, has a counterpart in the poetic impetus towards the Final Image. The processes of revelation provide the prophetic structure of Marvell's poetry.

(ii) RENOVATION: *THE CORONET*

If the End was full revelation it was equally complete renovation. The Latter Days moved to the rhythm of patterns of 'desolation' and 'renovation', in which the dire destruction of the imperfections of this world was a necessary prelude to reconstructed perfection. Apocalyptic thought imitates and expresses this pattern, whether in the political arena or in the structures of Marvell's poems, which break down experience in order to achieve the Final Image and its redemptive power.

The phase of 'desolation' in history is itself realized in three stages. The first consists of the tribulations of the faithful by the Latter Day 'tragedies', 'the abomination of desolation' in which the world labours under antichristian domination: wars, plagues, earthquakes, the persecution of the faithful and their affliction, after which Christ will come (Matthew 24:3–14). In this period it is darkest before the dawn. The second stage of desolation involves the destruction of Antichrist and the Whore (Revelation 17f.); the third, the destruction of the earth when the world is turned upside down (Isaiah 24), and 'In the city is left desolation' (12).[21] Then is the renovation: 'a new heaven and new earth; for the first heaven and the first earth were passed away. And I. . . saw the holy city, New Jerusalem, coming down from God out of heaven. . .And he. . .said, Behold, I make all things new' (Revelation 21:1–5). To this end of newness the purgation by desolation contributes and makes of apocalyptic destruction a process like that of the Fortunate Fall itself. Like the world, the faithful are purged, for 'by trials and persecutions the chosen people undergoes purification'.[22] Men, like the world, decay in spirit and faith during this period, which was understood to be currently operative.[23]

Such distressing signs were, however, the index of hope, since they promised an imminent End and renovation. The political moral of this paradox was the call for reformation: for parliamentarians, that of Church and state by the desolations of civil war; for radicals in the Army, to 'desolate' Antichrist in the person of 'that Man of Blood' the king.[24] Hence the prominent parliamentarian divine, Stephen Marshall, would in his sermon *Reformation and Desolation* call for the purification of the Elect Nation in these terms.[25] Since the same principle applied to England's mission in the international sphere, John Owen called for the 'Shaking' or desolation of the nations in the cause of eschatological renovation.[26] As the implementation of purgation by civil war was inevitably painful, Marshall urges as consolation the fortunate issue of Latter Day wars as signs of the coming bliss:[27] thus the eschatological theme of *desolatio et renovatio* became a model for diagnoses of contemporary events.

We have already seen the diagnosis at work in Marvell's Cromwell poems. In the Ode, Cromwell purged the national sin, and his 'ruine' of the kingdom 'cast [it] Into another *Mold*'; similarly, a contemporary described the *desolatio* as acting 'to purge out the dross. . .and then cast the Mass again into a new and better Mould'.[28] The *caput* of Charles' execution, horrible in itself, effects a sort of national atonement which addresses the happy End. While Cromwell in the Ode was a desolator, in *First Anniversary* he encompasses the renovatory effect as well, in his 'pulling down, and. . .erecting New' (247): the English 'rase and rebuild their State' (352). The culmination of this idea appears in the Final Image, where Cromwell 'as the *Angel* of our Commonweal,/Troubling the Waters, yearly mak'st them Heal.' Having become for Marvell the providential agent who 'Does with himself all that is good revive' (321–4), Cromwell is the angel of renovation or 'healing' to the nation. Marvell's lines recall the biblical source once invoked by Cromwell himself:[29] 'For an angel went down at a certain season into the pool, and troubled the water; whosoever then first. . .stepped in was made whole of whatever disease he had.' (John 5:4). Similarly Cromwell's 'troubling' of the national waters by reformation would restore the corrupt body politic. Not only was it understood that 'God's people, as well as worldlings, have their time to fish in troubled waters',[30] to undergo purification by tribulation, but this was the destiny of the chosen nation also:

> The *Common wealth* doth by its losses grow;
> And, like its own Seas, only Ebbs to flow.
> Besides that very Agitation laves,
> And purges out the corruptible waves.
> (*The Character of Holland*, 131–4)

Here Marvell's analysis of the Commonwealth's setbacks in the war against Holland ascribes them to the desolation/

renovation pattern, by means of which he who laughs last laughs loudest—as England will. The metaphor of the nation's 'own Seas', like that of 'Waters', picks up Revelation' symbolism, in which 'the great whore. . .sitteth upon many waters', and 'The waters. . .are peoples, and multitudes, and nations' (17:1, 15). The inevitability of the tide reflects the inexorability of the Elect Nation's victory by means of her eschatological purity, equally as it implies "the turn of the tide" in this war.

The renovation of the nations and ultimately of the world was reflected by analogy in the physical and spiritual state of the individual. The universal resurrection of men effected at the End is part of an omnipotent 'day of restauration of all thi[n]gs. . .For all things shalbe purged from their corruption, and the faithful shall enter into heauen'.[31] All aspects of renovation could be anticipated by the saints before the Last Day, not only in political, religious, and scientific reconstructions[32] but in their own spiritual lives—where Christ and Antichrist warred as bitterly as in the outside world. Since both man and nature were left depraved by the Fall (*The Mower Against Gardens*, 1–2), in order to become a saint the individual was required to purge that depravity by the process of 'Conversion': which involved the "death" of the natural man and his rebirth as 'the new creature'.[33] He must come to abhor his own sin and to loathe his own unworthiness, to the point where his personality lies in ruins. Only then does God vouchsafe His grace, and 're-create' him.[34] The transformation of the natural man into the new man, by means of destruction and re-creation, is analogous to the transformation of the old earth into the new by *desolatio et renovatio*. It is, in Milton's phrase, a 'paradise within',[35] attained by the combination of 'Mortification, or purging out corruption; and Vivification',[36] and in this sense it also anticipated the resurrection of the End.

This ontological experience of the *desolatio et renovatio* pattern defines the experience of *The Coronet*, where Marvell imitates the process whereby the regenerated man constantly monitors his own spiritual condition,[37] guarding against the incursion of the 'natural man'. When Marvell the shepherd, or 'natural man', turns from profane to sacred poetry (from the natural to the spiritual), he attempts to recreate Christ's crown of thorns, to transform it into a chaplet of flowers by means of his poetry. Detecting in these flowers the natural man's desire for 'Fame and Interest', he proffers the corrupted garland to his saviour, suggesting that He might renovate the garland by removing its 'serpent', or, if that proves impossible (sin being so recalcitrant), He might desolate it instead:

> Or shatter too with him my curious frame:
> And let these wither, so that he may die,
> Though set with Skill and chosen out with Care.
> That they, while Thou on both their Spoils dost tread,
> May crown thy Feet, that could not crown thy Head.
>
> *(The Coronet,* 22—6)

Here Marvell's own "creation" (produced by 'Skill' and 'Care'), which was intended as regenerative (transforming the merely natural), is offered up for destruction instead; the transformation has taken place but in a manner directly opposed to that which the poet originally intended. Regeneration requires destruction, as *renovatio* requires *desolatio*, and the ironic inversion of the poet's plan itself indicates a radical revision of natural into spiritual. We may recall, here, Marvell's witty description of the poems of his carnal or natural phase: 'my fruits are only flow'rs' (6), a paradox which, at that stage of the poem, mimed the frustration of spiritual 'fruits' (generating and regenerative) in favour of more carnal elements. (Just as, in *On A Drop of Dew*, the soul's dewdrop recoils from the blossoms of the flesh.)[38] Here the flowers and fruits are those equally of himself and his poetry: as the shepherd/swain he produces the flowers of pastoral love-poetry, which he attempts to transfer to the devotional poem here projected. He must fail *because* his fruits are only flowers—'by their fruits ye shall know them', says Matthew 7:15–20, of 'false prophets'. For the true prophetic poetry the flowers of carnality must be destroyed, for they cannot be merely adapted. Accordingly, just as the poet's own natural being is echoed in the flowers of his tainted poetic garland, so in the Final Image he offers to destruction both the ingenious verse and his own 'curious frame'. The ambiguity of that phrase subsumes the identity of poet and poem in their corruption. Speaking of such identity between man and his spiritual fruits, Matthew continues: 'every good tree bringeth forth good fruit, but a corrupt tree bringeth forth evil fruit. . .Every tree that bringeth not forth good fruit is hewn down, and cast into the fire';[39] that is, the natural man will be given to the fire of destruction which rages at the Last Day, when he is judged. Thus Marvell's Final Image here is made eschatological: his self/poem offered to that Judgment and destruction so that, by *desolatio*, they might be regenerated or renovated. The Final Image is proleptic, evoking an anticipation of the Last Day in the present experience of the believer.

This effect, whereby once again Marvell fashions a correspondence between the end of the poem and the end of time, is emphasized on several levels, all of which relate the poet's experience here to the renovatory pattern. First, we must recognise that, just as the natural man-poet's original intention was to provide a poetic act of atonement which might complement Christ's redeeming Passion (1–4), so in the end the poet acknowledges that such atonement, while sacrificial like the *Passion*, involves a specific sacrifice of the poem in offering to Christ as *Judge* (in the Final Image). Poet and poem simultaneously submit to judgment their natural 'frame'. Just as the poetic activity is analogous to that of God as creator, so Christ is wittily figured as both Judge, at the End, of the Creation and judge of poetic creation. The poet himself, of course, is part of the general Creation, so he submits to Christ as both created and "creator", submitting to the ultimate arbiter. Equally, in its movement from evocation of the crucified Christ at its beginning to its invocation of Christ the Judge at its end, the poem imitates the movement of time to the *eschaton*.

The movement from the moment of redeeming Passion to that when redemption takes effect—the universal ressurrection at the *Second* Coming—is that from the poet's repentance ('long, too long' sinning [1]) and "recognition" of sin to his call for Christ's aid. The sins of 'Fame and Interest' make the poem itself an embodiment of sin in the "flowers" of carnality. The submission of both poet and poem to the process of judgment and resurrection, *desolatio* and *renovatio*, is the moment of Conversion—of transformation from natural to spiritual man. It recapitulates in the believer the passage of Christ through death to resurrection and anticipates the converted saint's resurrection at the Last Day. So, like the poem, it looks back to the Passion and forward to the *eschaton*. On both universal and individual planes, the renovatory process has Christ as arbiter.[40]

Thus the Final Image, where Christ 'dost tread' 'both' poem and serpent, alludes to Christ *in majestate*, treading upon the serpent-Dragon of Antichrist in His final triumph. (In the service of this allusion Marvell's serpent, with his 'speckled breast', recalls the 'speckled brest' of the antichristian Dragon in Spenser's *Faerie Queene* I. xi. 5.)[41] That iconography of Christ treading the Dragon fulfilled Genesis' prophecy that He would bruise the head of the serpent[42] and was a traditional image for centuries,[43] symbolizing His ultimate victory over the principle of evil. So, here, enacting the various levels of the *desolatio/renovatio* pattern, it refers to Christ's supremacy in the heart of the now-converted saint. The Last Day occurred here and now, in the heart of every believer;[44] the critical moment for the saint was that conversion which implemented the victory of Christ. Marvell asks here for that desolation of the Antichrist within himself and his poem, invoking the renovation consequent upon Christ's aid.

So the imagery of these last lines—aiming to 'crown thy Feet'—echoes the contemporary chorus, that 'Christ shall reign till he hath put all his enemies *under his feet*' (I Corinthians 15:25),[45] for the triumph of His Kingdom was that 'of *Crowning* him, of putting all things *under his feet*'.[46] The desolation of Antichrist—'treading' him—precedes the 'crowning' of the Kingdom; as the Geneva Bible stated, glossing that passage from Corinthians:

> he maketh two parts of this reigne and dominion of the Sonne. . .
> to wit, the ouercomming of his enemies (whereof some must be
> depriued of all power, as Satan and all the wicked, be they neuer
> so proud and mightie, and other must be vtterly abolished, as
> death). . .the godly. . .cleauing fast vnto their head Christ, his
> kingdome and glory, as a king in his subietcs. Moreover, he

pvtteth the first degree of this kingdome in the resurrection of his Sonne, who is the head: and the perfection, in the full coniunction of the members [the Saints] with the head, which shall be in the latter day.

In this account of Paul's teachings on resurrection, the Geneva Bible shows how I Corinthians 15 provides the doctrines adumbrated in *The Coronet*. For 'vnlesse the dead doe rise againe. . .neither Christ be Lord of all: for neither should the power of Satan and death be ouercome'.[47] Upon 'ouercomming' depends the Kingdom—vanquishing to rule; upon treading depends the crowning. So, here, Christ 'treads' on the 'Serpent' of Marvell's sin and his poem's corruption— they are 'put under his feet'. Equally, they 'crown' His feet. Hereby Marvell recalls the conquest of evil and the reign of good at the *eschaton*—that the processes of resurrection and renovation find their 'perfection. . .in the latter day'.

In the poem, 'Christ, his kingdome and glory'—what here is called 'Heaven's Diadem' (18)—is implicitly contrasted with the crown of laurel attained by the successful poet; 'mortal Glory', the chaplet of flowers, is really a monument to that poetic success which its motifs (his motives) of 'Fame and Interest' weave through it. At a simple level, those motives imply that Marvell's poetic devotion is really devoted to his own promotion as a poet rather than deferent to Christ's glory; he has fallen into that trap which—for Herbert also—was implicit in poetic piety. Thus the identification between poem and sin, poetry and the natural man, 'mortal Glory' and antichristian motives, is sealed. Therefore the desolation of evil at the *eschaton* is (in the Final Image) related to Christ's extirpation of the Serpent from another order of creation, the poem. In its constituent 'flowers' the poem was as carnal as the poet, so 'shatter too with him my curious frame' refers to the poet's person as instigator of the poetic frame; he, like his poem, requires the desolatory purgation, and as both are instinct with earth so—like the earth at the end—they will be purified only by destruction. Both submit to the Creator who is also a Destroyer, whose treading is equally a crowning; in that paradox the Final Image imitates that of *desolatio et renovatio*.

So Marvell rejects the earthly coronet of the poet for the

heavenly crown of the Kingdom and its saints. He abrogates the perpetuity of poetic 'Fame' for that of resurrection (the former a pagan or classical desideratum, the latter the Christian alternative). He rejects his 'Interest', the self-advertisement implicit in his 'curious' or ingenious poem, replacing the latter by the *traditional* religious icon of *Majestas* in his Final Image. This abrogation of the sin of pride in his individual achievement is an individual enactment of that universal submission to Christ which is effected at the End, 'that [we may]. . .lay down our reason, lay down our goods, lay down all we have *at the feet* of God'.[48] The poem's intention, to crown Christ, becomes the crisis of Conversion, whereby the chiliast will 'Crowne Christ in our owne hearts, to set up his Kingdome within our selves'.[49] That triumph of the internal *eschaton*, anticipating the universal transforma-tion, requires the recapitulation of the *desolatio-renovatio* pattern within Marvell the poet.

(iii) RENOVATION OF THE GOLDEN AGE

The most significant feature of the final renovation is its uniqueness: unlike the classical notion of the Golden Age, it is not a phenomenon recapitulated within a cyclical model of history. Christian history is linear, pointed to a triumphant end. Christ's Coming fulfils where His first advent merely promised: 'His kingdom of grace. . .began with his first advent. . .but his kingdom of glory will not commence till his second advent.'[50]—'the last and full performance shall be, when all things shall be new indeed', the triumph of the Church, when the saints shall inherit the earth.[51] Dissolving the distinctions of imperfection, 'Earth be chang'd to heav'n, and heav'n to earth,/One kingdom, joy and union without end' (*PL* VII. 161—2; Revelation 11:15). Far from a return to the Edenic state, the New Jerusalem Kingdom shall be 'far happier place/Than this of Eden, and far happier days' (*PL* XII 461f.). Such emphasis upon the completeness of renovation is the basis of Milton's connexion with the chiliastic attitude, and indeed the cornerstone of all Christian prophecy.[52]

It was not lost on chiliasts of this period that, in terms of the partial revelation dispensed to classical writers, the

Golden Age was analogous to the Kingdom. The divine Richard Sibbes called the renovation 'golden times',[53] and Milton envisaged the moment when 'The World shall burn, and from her ashes spring/New heav'n and earth. . .golden days' (*PL* III. 334f.), the 'age of gold' (*Nativity Ode*, 135). In an Iron Age of civil war, this modified concept of the Golden Age aptly expressed hope for the future. From the Middle Ages onwards, the most influential classical statement of the Golden Age had been Virgil's Fourth Eclogue. Celebrating the expected birth of a child to the consul Pollio, this poem takes the birth as a signal of the Golden Age's return, when Astraea, the goddess of justice, will come back from the heavens, invited by the new Augustan Age of Peace in the Roman Empire. The earth will be inspired to lavish her bounty upon mankind, nature will be transformed to paradisal effect, men will live in harmony and without the necessity for toil, and as the child grows to adulthood all sin will be gradually eradicated. The prophecy has its political level, in which the reign of Augustus restores to a Rome wracked by civil war the virtues of a Golden Age. As interpreted especially by Augustine, this Eclogue must prophesy—in imperfect pagan form—the advent of Christ the saviour;[55] as interpreted by Lactantius, who exerted a considerable influence upon sixteenth- and seventeenth-century thought, the eclogue referred to the last paradise which Christ's Second Coming would bring into being.[56] Another strong tradition affirmed that the Augustan *Pax* had created those conditions on earth proper to the coming of the 'Prince of Peace';[57] since Virgil's *Aeneid* was associated with this tradition,[58] Marvell's invoking of that epic and its historical framework in his *Ode* was especially apt to his eschatological theme. After the English Reformation the Golden Age motif could express the blossoming of reformed religion in England,[59] providing also a political mythology for the Tudor regime in which Elizabeth I was the new Astraea.[60] In this guise Elizabeth as Foxe's 'Christian Emperor'[61] appropriated classical as well as Christian prophecy.

At his Coming Christ was both Prince of Peace and Sun of Righteousness, and justice was God's gift to man at the Last Day,[61] redeeming the long history of earthly injustices. It was foretold that 'righteousness and peace have kissed each other' (Psalm 85: 10), a thought echoed by Marvell's 'Kiss the approaching. . .Son'; Peace and Justice distinguish the Kingdom of Christ (Isaiah 9: 6–7). Hence Astraea, the goddess of Justice whose return inaugurates the Age of Peace, could signify Christ's harbinger, as indeed she is in Milton's *Nativity Ode*.[63] There, in a poem addressed very much to its own time, when the Coming was imminent, Milton's vision stretches from Astraea's annunciation of the Incarnation to the promised Last Day, when Christ's saving power will be consummated.[64] Here Milton explicitly over-goes his Virgilian model by recasting it in "fully revealed" Christian form,[65] combining the moment of Incarnation with the prophecy of Second Coming. A staging-post on the way to this seventeenth-century Puritan recuperation of Virgil, whom they regarded as having received intimations of the Christian truth,[66] was the fourth eclogue in Spenser's *Shepheardes Calender*. Imitating Virgil's pastoral form, Spenser portrays Elizabeth as a shepherdess on the Astraean model. Since Astraea is associated with the perpetual Spring of the Golden Age,[67] and its natural fecundity, her eulogy is aptly placed in the month of 'April shoure', when Spring renews and refreshes the earth. While in exile from earth, Astraea was stellified as the constellation Virgo (*FQ* V. i. 11), the astrological virgin: thus the flowers of spring and the magical virtue of Astraea as a virgin—reminiscent of the Virgin Mary's agency as Christ-bringer—are compounded in a compliment to the Virgin Queen, 'that blessed wight:/The flowre of Virgins. . .In princely plight.' Like Astraea, Elysa is a 'goddesse' (97), 'of heavenly race' (53); her deification is placed at the seventh line of the seventh stanza, because the sacred number seven could signify her immaculate and virginal qualities.[68] Since by Justice peace is established, Elysa's righteousness merits the gift of the irenic olive branch (123–6). Just as Virgil's Astraea caused peace to supervene upon the Roman Civil War, so Elizabeth—as the daughter of both Yorkist and Lancastrian houses—in herself embodies the resolution of the Wars of the Roses in England, an Astraean 'flowre' of national regeneration (68). In *FQ* Astraea as the handmaiden of God's justice is an *exemplum* for the princes who are His lieutenants on earth (V Proem 10–11). As Virgo, she is 'the righteous Virgin' led by the month of August (VII. vii. 37) and bearing the corn symbolic of harvest and Golden Age plenty; in September, the month in which Virgo hands over to Libra, the (now thematized) scales of Justice hold sway (38). Symbolically, the first Virgoan month brings peace, and the second effects the Coming of Justice; August and September figure the Autumn of the world itself.

This symbolic pattern whereby months represent the great 'year' of the world's duration is implicit in *First Anniversary*, where both Cromwell and Marvell were huntsmen chasing the Beast: Autumn, after harvest, is the hunting season. Elsewhere in Marvell the whole system whereby Virgil's Eclogue is recast into revelatory eclogue—the prophecy of Second Coming—is brought to its generic perfection. As I have shown elsewhere, his Latin poem *A Letter to Dr Ingelo* portrays the Protestant Queen Christina of Sweden as Astraea in the Latter Days.[69] Unlike Milton, Marvell by this contemporary identification of Astraea can preserve the integrity of the Virgilian model, since here Astraea is harbinger not of the first but of the Second Coming.

(iv) ACTIVISM AND ASTRAEA

Like Milton, Marvell located in Virgil the classical vatic poet whom he was determined to imitate, recuperate, and surpass as a Latter Day poet. He withheld from himself the prophetic sanction which he vouchsafed to Milton, but in his expression of epic ambitions there is a Virgilian strain:

> If gracious Heaven to my Life give length,
> Leisure to Time, and to my Weakness Strength,
> Than shall I once with graver Accents shake
> Your Regal sloth. . .
> (*The First Anniversary*, 119–22)

This vision of a poetic activism subsumes its echo of Milton's epic promise in an echo of Virgil's:

> o mihi tum longae maneat pars ultima vitae,
> spiritus et, quantum sat erit tua dicere facta:

non me carminibus vincat. . .Thracius Orpheus.
(Eclogue IV, 53–5)

While *Ingelo* imitates Eclogue IV, the lines from *First Anniversary* almost directly translate Virgil's statement of epic ambition there. Just as Virgil desires a longer life with 'spiritus', so Marvell needs longevity and 'Strength': even the rhythms echo, from 'spiritus et' into 'Leisure to Time'. While Virgil waits upon the deeds of Pollio's golden child, Marvell waits upon those of 'Angelique' Cromwell—'Till then my Muse shall hollow far behind' him. As Virgil invokes the mythic poet Orpheus, Marvell invokes Virgil in his vision of a Cromwelliad that might recast the *Aeneid*. Since, unlike Virgil, he was not fated to see his hopes realized—either in longevity or in Cromwell—it is not surprising that the Marvellian epic remained a dream.

Yet, if *Appleton House* is epic in miniature, it achieves that feat by enlisting Virgil and the revelatory eclogue derived from him. Both in *First Anniverary* and in *Ingelo*, Marvell associates the Virgilian model with activism, whether public or poetic in form. It is the problems of activism that *Appleton House* addresses through revelatory eclogue. Before we can see how it does so, however, it is necessary to attend a little more closely to the poetic effects of eschatological activist pressures.

If eschatology required of the individual that he act to promote God's will in history, the timeliness, appropriateness, and aims of activism could only be ascertained by a threefold effort of interpretation: of prophecy, of God's promptings within the self, and of historical events.[70] At any point this interpretative process might go awry. Similarly, man's life must become a divinely ordained process in which activism (responding to God's call) alternated with quietism (when action would be inappropriate to His purposes). Puritans were conditioned to regard the external battle against Antichrist as the counterpart of their internal struggle with the promptings of the serpent, so that at both levels 'permanent warfare was the central myth' of Puritanism.[71] Thus Marvell's *Resolved Soul*, in combat with *Created Pleasure*, is the armoured Puritan warrior; Oliver Cromwell,

Puritan warrior without peer, 'first put Armes into *Religions* hand . . . The Souldier taught that inward Mail to wear,/And *fearing God* how they should *nothing fear.*' (*Upon the Death of O.C.*, 179-84). Because the Civil War was a spiritual war against Satan himself, when the Army came to debate its policy in the Putney Debates of 1647, the problems of activism bedevilled discussion.[72] It is possible to outrun God's will, and act precipitately; equally, it is fatally easy to ignore His call, mistaking negligence for quietism. In either case 'carnal imagination, and carnal reasonings', tools of Antichrist, may lead to the wrong choice.[73] The fault of precipitate action may compound that of negligence: 'If we have lost the opportunity of appearing against God's enemies, let us take heed, when we be sensible of God's displeasure, that we do not run before he bids us go a second time.'[74] In such statements spiritual language and political reasoning go hand in hand, linking self-interest to antichristian error and assimilating eschatological anxieties into political manoeuvres. Not that their sincerity, on the whole, is questionable; pragmatism and idealism are compounded in the acknowledgement that activism requires no less than the willed surrender of self-determination to God's direction.[75] The possibility of misinterpretation or of mistaken forms of activism is both a political and spiritual problem for chiliasts. The Putney Debates record the public face of that problem addressed in Marvell's *Coronet*, where the carnal reasonings of 'Fame and Interest' vitiated the new creature's attempt at a poetic *renovatio*. Spiritual alertness such as that enjoined in *First Anniversary* sought to obey the injunction to be 'ready... for in such an hour as ye think not the Son of Man cometh' in history or into the heart (Matthew 24:44).[76]

That crucial linkage of activism to the seasons of action involves the problems of the "interval", of placing oneself within the great design, when the reference-points in that design are known only to God. The basic difficulty may be compared to an individual's ignorance of the time of his own death, which renders him unable to anticipate its contingencies. This problem of the interval is present also in the activism/quietism complex: between the moments when activism is appropriate there fall intervals of quietism which "wait upon" such moments. Because the boundaries of these intervals are not known, it is possible for quietism to impinge upon the times of activism, becoming negligence; or for activism to invade the interval proper to quietism.

In *First Anniversary* Cromwell brings divine and human times into tune, collapsing the intervals so that 'scatter'd Time contracts'. The music of divine time in that poem— assimilating the traditional notion of the 'music of the spheres'—is reflected in *Musicks Empire*, where Marvell portrays world history in terms of musical development. The 'Organs City' (8) represents civilization in a manner which links it to the harmony of the higher region, like Cromwell's musically constructed state in the renovation described by *First Anniversary*. So it is when time is correctly apprehended.

The problems of assessing the gulf between divine and human times are rendered personal in Marvell's elegy *Upon the Death of Lord Hastings* (1649). Amongst other poets, Marvell was contributing to a memorial volume a conventional lament,[77] but he individuates it as a vehicle for his own preoccupations. Hastings' untimely death, in his youth and before his marriage, is one of those 'observable passages'[78] which require the chiliast to investigate their significance; it provokes in Marvell a meditation upon the relationship between the timing of an individual's death and the divine apprehension of time.

> Alas, his *Vertues* did his *Death* presage:
> Needs must he die, that doth out-run his *Age*.
> The Phlegmatick and Slowe prolongs his day,
> And on Times Wheel sticks like a *Remora*.
> What man is he, that hath not *Heaven* beguil'd,
> And is not thence mistaken for a *Childe*?
> While those of growth more sudden, and more bold,
> Are hurried hence, as if already old.
> For, there above, they number not as here,
> But weigh to Man the *Geometrick* yeer.
>
> (9–18)

Heaven's year is not man's. 'They number not as here': the geometric year—for which one scholar has supplied an extensive background[79]—has in fact the essential explanation that it is universal time, the 'All-circling point. All centring sphere./The world's one, round, Aeternal year.'[80] The difference between this "circular" year (which is like the eternity in circling of the spheres) and human time is rendered initially by the fact that human life must have its stop. And human life in divine computation can look like a mere 'yeer', just as 'All the Year was *Cromwell's* day' because he had achieved the divine timing of Revelation (*Death of O.C.*, 142). Here divine and human times look out of joint because Hastings was 'hurried hence, as if already old'. Yet in heavenly computation Hastings did look old because of his activist haste: 'more sudden, and more bold'. True maturity is spiritual, the process of full Conversion; each man has his peculiar tempo for 'growth' (15): 'there may be great difference thereof in several men. . .every man hath a measure appointed to which he must grow; but men are brought to this fulness several ways. . .Some die sooner, and therefore God fits them for heaven sooner. . .often they that live shortest grow fastest'.[81] This was Hastings' case, in which 'growth [was] more sudden', and also 'more bold' because of his activist cast. 'Needs must he die, that doth out-run his *Age*.' As elsewhere in Marvell, the current age is portrayed as culpably negligent, replete with men 'Phlegmatick and Slowe' whose laxity delays the course of time: 'vivit at in praesens maxima pars hominum' (*Illustrissimo Viro*, 36). They drag on 'Times Wheel', thus prolonging their lives (or 'day') by appearing spiritually and actively immature. Like Cromwell, 'who in his Age has always forward prest' (*First Anniversary*, 146), Hastings 'doth out-run his Age'. But the age cannot be outrun if God's purposes are to achieve timely fulfilment, so Hastings has used up his ration of activism and time. Because the age is dominated by the unregenerate, delaying time, Hastings is sacrificed to the negligence of others; worse, he is sacrificed in fact to the national sin, since in the Civil War 'the *Democratick* Stars did rise,/And all that worth from hence did *Ostracize*' (25–6). While the parliamentarians are in the ascendent, Hastings' 'Vertues did his *Death* presage' because the times themselves are tainted.[82] Unregenerate action and unregenerate inaction combine in malignity to God's elect.

While this is an expansive compliment to pay a youth who, although of impeccably royalist family, was not killed in the War, it presses Marvell's own concerns rather than those of Hastings' parents. But in his own terms the compliment is capable of infinite extension, since heaven does not represent the terminus of Hastings' activism. 'So he, not banisht hence'—the parliamentarians do not possess such power— 'but there confin'd/There better recreates his active Minde' (31–2). In heaven there is another mode of eschatological activity, to experience and participate in re-creative *renovatio*: just as there is a heavenly form of time, so there is a heavenly mode of activism. It was understood from Revelation 5:10 that the saints in heaven 'expect' the Last Day's renovation no less anxiously than their earthly counterparts, for the Kingdom 'on earth to come is a far more glorious condition for the saints than what their souls have now in heaven. . .their thoughts fly to comfort themselves with this, "we shall reign on earth" '.[83] The 'new song' which the saints sing before God's throne (Revelation 5:9) refers to the newness of *renovatio*: the pastime or recreation of song is also the renovation therein, and to this combination Marvell's pun on 'recreate' refers. Hastings' participation in the heavenly choir is allowed because he was unmarried, and the 'new song' in Revelation is sung by those who have no carnal knowledge of women (14:4). The recreating activism of heaven is as militant as the saints' on earth, for there 'The armed *Angels* hold their *Carouzels*' (34).

In this manner Hasting's death and ascension are portrayed as a divine counterpart to the quietist intervals that punctuate earthly activism, a more ingenious form of consolation to the bereaved than most poetic elegies achieve. The individual's internal form of renovation was Conversion, by which alone he could become an activist saint; therefore any preparation for activism was a little *renovatio*. Preparing for the next summons, a quietist interval was a 'recreation' in both senses of the word, a spiritual refreshment. To the individual personalities of men, God adjusts His demands; not only not imposing 'upon them what they could not be patient of, but [prompting] so as that their powers and faculties might be put upon the exercises whereof they were capable. . .that neither their passive capacity should be overcharged, nor their active be unemployed' (Marvell quoting Howe, *Defence of John Howe*, 185–6). Having fitted them for their particular roles, God influences them to act at the appropriate moments: 'faculties may be sometimes unapt for action. . .if every moment when they act they be not rendered apt by a superadded influence, which may habilitate them for action' (*Howe*, 187). Addressed against a determinist view of predestination by God, this argument asserts rather His 'spiritual promptings', which encourage the saint to join cause with destiny in a free choice; such as that made by the Fairfaxes when they 'make their *Destiny* their *Choice*' (*Appleton House*, XCIII), in what has been rightly called the 'Puritan integration of freedom and necessity'.[84]

In this poem Hastings' nature is seen as 'apt for action', and since it did not require recreative intervals on earth, he receives his proper interval in heaven. An ingenious element in Marvell's eulogy, this implies that Hastings was so replete with the 'Vertues' of activism—punning on *virtus* or martial courage—that in order to persuade him into a quietist interval heaven has to kill him off. Just as his life was crammed with activism, so his quietist interval is remarkably extended in the afterlife. As the dead saints wait upon the End in heaven, theirs is the equivalent in divine time of earthly intervals which wait upon God's punctuation of the temporal design. Like an individual experiencing an earthly interval, Hastings is not permanently 'banisht' but may return, at the End— another ingenious twist on consolatory conventions of elegy. In heaven Hastings' long renovatory interval expects that moment when he will taste of the 'Tree of Life' (20–4) which stands in the 'new heavens and new earth' and is thus symbolic of the final *renovatio*. It, too, recreates, since it is 'for the healing of the nations' (Revelation 22:2): it will provide remedy not only for the saints after the End but also for the long period of tribulation in which war has wracked the nations. The Civil War's sins and activism are equally recalled when from heaven Hastings 'views the *Turnaments*/ Of all these Sublunary *Elements*' (35–6). Such earthly contests will establish the renovation which Hastings anticipates when he 'His Thought with richest Triumphs entertains' (29), a line with intimations also of the militant activism necessary to this establishment, since Roman 'Truimphs' were victory celebrations. While Hastings' heavenly interval is thus properly sensitive to activist imperatives, it is also of course restorative, 'And in the choicest Pleasures charms his Pains' (30). The conventional consolation whereby the bereaved family of saints (37f.) is reminded of the dead man's 'better' state in heaven is extended into an assurance that Hastings will return to earth with the other dead saints at the End; that he will be even more spectacularly activist than before ('there better recreates his active Minde'), and that the healing of his "wounds" in heaven's quietist interval foreshadows that of the family and the nation too. His death is symbolic not only of national sin but of national regeneration also.

The last extravagant touch to this portrait of time-consuming activity is Marvell's echo of the classical tag that '*Art* indeed is Long, but *Life* is Short'. This, the sixtieth line of the poem, signifies thereby the normal life-span:[85] the art of the poem has achieved that longevity, which is self-mockingly measured by Hastings' short but active life. Equally, however, if Marvell's poem is wittily envisaged as longer than the life it celebrates, this makes a compliment to Hastings by aligning the poem with those 'Slowe' lives to which his was contrasted. The final bow to Hastings' meta-activism and meta-quietism must be the poet's own playful humiliation before them. At the same time, the inordinate length of the poem in comparison to Hastings' brevity does imitate the *spiritual* amplitude of his life. Since Hastings died at the age of nineteen, it was in the nineteenth line that Marvell observed the tempo of his life: 'Had he but at this Measure still increast'. The whole structure of Marvell's ingeniously fanciful memorial can be traced back to the simple and traditional thought that the good die young (1), which is fleshed out in remarkably timely fashion by Marvell's play on the gulf between divine and human times.

The topics of the activism/quietism alternation and of the interval have their own peculiar language. Many years after *Hastings*, Marvell in his *Last Instructions to a Painter* muses that '*Rubens*, with affairs of State,/His lab'ring Pencil oft would recreate' (119–20). In this case there is no religious burden intended, but the recreating is again a matter of interposing intervals of recovery within Rubens' pursuit of his true vocation—a joke, of course, since politics are here seen as more important than art and Rubens as an example of political irresponsibility. But the 'recreate' is still characteristic of interval language. Milton's sonnet *To Lawrence* states in relatively simple terms the problems and the spatial conception of the interval. There he celebrated the restorative pastimes of withdrawal, whereby 'time will run/On smoother' (5–6), a thought reiterated in the sonnet *To Cyriack*, where the 'measure' of time is the basis of action:

> To measure life, learn thou betimes, and know
> Toward solid good what leads the nearest way;
> For other things mild heaven a time ordains,
> And disapproves that care, though wise in show,
> That with superfluous burden loads the day,
> And when God sends a cheerful hour, refrains.
>
> (9–14)

Milton recalls two versions of the same parable, which indicate that 'sufficient unto the day is its evil'. God does not require the saint to burden himself with care as if thereby only he will satisfy Him. For those who truly serve the Kingdom all needs and joys will be supplied as a matter of course, without diurnal anxiety (Matthew 6:34, 33). The moral—learning to punctuate activist imperatives with quietist refreshment—is eschatological, for Luke concludes this parable with the warning that timeliness acknowledges the fact that, although the time of the Coming is not known, men must be alert for that moment (12:35–40). At all times men's responses must be suitable to His purposes, and sometimes those are merely 'cheerful': in other words, failing to recognize which stance is appropriate at any given moment, and anxious to obey the activist imperative, Cyriack has been overdoing things. A variation on this intimate address to the activism/quietism problem ends *To Lawrence*: 'He who of those delights can judge, and spare/To interpose them oft, is not unwise.' The word 'spare' is ambiguous, leading critics to disagree about the point of Milton's sonnet.[86] He may mean that one should refrain from such pastimes (in which case, what of the foregoing lines in the sonnet?), or that one should "spare time for" these delights. However, correctly interpreted, the ambiguity is intentional: on some occasions quietist withdrawal is appropriate, on others it is not. Milton's ambiguity imitates the ambiguities of time and the saint's interpretation of it, the difficulty of judging the legitimacy of a quietist interval. The final line is cautionary, reminding the reader that even godly 'delights' must be regarded as 'interpos[itions]' in the alert and activist *modus vivendi*. As such they are valuable, but their status requires 'judge[ment]'. The fact that the quietist interval must acknowledge its activist teleology is signified in Marvell's ubiquitous usage of the phrases 'Mean while' and 'in the meane time'. Recurring frequently in the prose works, and especially in *Growth of Popery*,[87] they occur at significant points in the poems too. His fondness for these phrases is owing to their denotation of an interval, especially of the eschatological interval that remains before the fulfilment of a prophetic event. In *RT* Marvell rebukes his opponent's attitude to the Nonconformist heirs of Puritanism by remarking that only Christ may be their judge: 'In the mean time, 'tis not for you to be both the *Enemy* and their *Judg*' (89)—the phrase denoting that interval of time yet to elapse before 'that supreme Judge and Judicature' appear at the End (89). Such use of the phrase to signify the interval between the present and the Last Day was not uncommon. Richard Sibbes, remarking the saints' anticipation of their final glory, enjoins 'patience' 'In the meane time',[88] a moral similarly emphasized by Marvell in *RT*, where precipitate activists are informed that patience is necesary 'In the meantime' before the Last Day (15). 'Patience' was the appropriate attitude as one 'waited upon' moments of activism and fulfilment,[89] and such patient intervals are spaces or lacunae in time to which the phrase 'in the meantime' is appropriate. It denotes the expectation of an event, a terminal point for the current phase, the 'meane time' being that yet to elapse before the terminus is reached; hence its appropriateness to Latter Day expectation. Thus Milton, looking to the full revelation of the

End, argues that 'In the meanwhile' men must be free to investigate unrevealed truth;[90] in the Putney Debates the Army is told that in expectation of the *renovatio* they must be vigilant against its enemies 'In the meantime'.[91]

By analogy such phrases denote also spiritual intervals for persons and nations. In *Appleton House*, while the Fairfaxes wait upon the destiny of Maria in marriage, the landscape too must imitate Maria's virtues 'Mean time'; both nature and the Fairfaxes attend upon the End, occupying themselves appropriately in the interval before it. In *The Picture of Little T.C. in a Prospect of Flowers* the 'prospect' is also future time, in which the flowers of the flesh have both their life and their necessary mortality. Envisaging the little girl grown up into an adult beauty—the tyrannous beauty of women which he fears in *Appleton House* also—Marvell wishes that he might 'in time compound' with her prepubescence. '*Mean time*, whilst every verdant thing/It self does at thy Beauty charm,/Reform the errours of the Spring.' (25–7 [my italics]). Here the phrase denotes the period before the death of innocence, stressing its impermanence: it demarcates the interval wherein the Spring itself may be 'reformed' by T.C. Her little reformation, like the interval of childhood, is a *renovatio*, 'her golden daies'; in the same way as adult quietist intervals anticipate the last *renovatio*. Of course, the interval of growth has its destined teleology, as yet unrevealed: 'Who can foretel for what high cause/This Darling of the Gods was born!' (9–10). But yet the poet may be mistaken, and the child betrayed by an error of untimeliness: he begs the 'young Beauty of the Woods' (pastoral locale of quietist withdrawal):

> Gather the Flow'rs, but spare the Buds;
> Lest *Flora* angry at thy crime,
> To kill her Infants in their prime,
> Do quickly make th'Example Yours;
>   And, ere we see,
> Nip in the blossome all our hopes and Thee.
>   (V)

The continuous indentification of T.C. with the plants is underlain by the spiritual metaphor of growth: her spirit may fail to fulfil the promise seen by the poet. Equally, the rate of infant mortality being what it is, T.C. may not grow in the literal sense either. She is an individuated instance of the 'hopes' of *renovatio*, signified by the *tabula rasa* of a child's personality. Like that of England, the 'Table rase' may prove hospitable to renovation and a bright future, but equally it may fall into the state of further desolation by sin. In one of Edward Fairfax's surviving eclogues, preserved in Thomas Fairfax's manuscript book[92] (and therefore possibly available to Marvell), Flora is a pastoral embodiment of the Scarlet Whore and her flowers of carnality: a resonance which informs Marvell's fear that T.C. may fall into error and her life be forfeit therefor. Similarly, the antichristian carnality of Flora in this aspect reflects also his fears of T.C.'s sexual maturity. In reforming the Spring, T.C. must not merely 'Roses of their thorns disarm' (30) but disarm the rose that is herself. Turning on the notion of childhood as a renovatory interval before the time of love and action, Marvell's poem touchingly if playfully encapsulates the vulnerability and mystery of a child's development. The fear of a premature *telos*[93] is adumbrated by the Final Image, synthesizing mortal and antichristian menaces.

Marvell's own experience of the activism/quietism complex is demonstrable in the prophetic urge of *First Anniversary*, and his description of God's prompting (as he hopes) him to write *RT*, that 'I am (if I may say it with reverence) drawn in, I hope by a good Providence, to intermeddle in a noble and high argument'.[94] *RT*'s 'patience' is itself quietism in the service of political activism. But he himself stated that one had to 'guess' and 'prepare', not simple matters. In this respect his personal weakness, the obsession with self-protection, might collude with apocalyptic cryptology, but it also complicated his responsiveness as an active saint. 'I am naturally. . .inclined to keep my thoughts private',[95] and this militated against even his writing, for 'not to Write at all is much the safer course of life'.[96] In his poetic activity this privacy is not the stuff of which bold epic statement is made, and the private problematic in particular distanced Marvell from the 'vast Design' which he admired in *On Mr Milton's "Paradise Lost"*. In general, Marvell's 'natural' inclination to

quietism was of a kind which could interpose between him
and the correct interpretation of God's will, militating against
directives to activism. His own articulation of this problem
we shall look at presently.

For the moment we must recall something simpler,
manifest in Marvellian criticism as Marvell's liking for
"withdrawal" or "retreat", usually linked with the notion that
he retreated from commitments too. The obvious example of
withdrawal is *The Garden*, but the notion is best instanced, I
would suggest, by Marvell's classicist use of the word 'Shade'.
In the *Horatian Ode* he opposes his 'shadowy' poetic abode
to the public life of Cromwell; in *The Garden* he prefers to
society the 'narrow verged Shade' of his leafy retreat; in *Little
T.C.* he desires to 'be laid,/Where I may see thy Glories from
some Shade' (24). As *umbra*, shade is the classical image for
the *vita otiosa*, the abode of poets who write rather than act.[97]
For most critics, what they regard as Marvell's desire for
withdrawal tends to represent some variation on the argument between "action and contemplation", whether in
secular or Neoplatonic terms.[98] On the contrary, the tension
in Marvell's poetry between action and retreat reflects his
consciousness of the demands of an eschatological commitment, and is in fact a personal engagement with the problems
of the activism/quietism complex as I have described them.

Marvell's articulation of the pressures of activism usually
takes a classicist form, as in his echo of Virgil's epic project in
First Anniversary, his portrayal of Christina-Astraea as
eschatological activist in the revelatory eclogue of *Ingelo*, and
his echo of Virgil's *Aeneid* in the invocation to national
militancy in the *Ode*. As a model for the prophetic zeal of
poetry, Virgil also provides the models for expressions of the
activist imperative generally. Therefore, celebrating the
heroic Douglas, who in the brief interval of dying yet
'entertains, *the while*, his time too short/With birding at the'
enemy (*Last Instructions*, 665–6), Marvell pays tribute to an
enforced quietism which yet remembers activist responsibilities: the 'recreation' whereby Douglas 'entertains' the interval
is as hostile to the spiritual enemy as his fighting had been.
Marvell's tribute imitates *Aeneid* ix. 446–7,[99] but in its
promise to confer immortal fame on Douglas Marvell's

reminiscence is especially poignant because eschatological; the closing line here numerologically signifies 666 as the Number of the Beast, which chiliasts used to compute the date of the End.[100] Covertly, Marvell implies by the line-number of Douglas' demise that "after Douglas, the Deluge", England's state is so parlous now. Hence these are thematically, as well as polemically, the '*Last* Instructions'. The Virgilian echo signals poetic activism subserving public militancy, for it is the poet's job to 'fight forsaken Vertues cause' (*May*, 66); such moments of crisis are 'the Poets time', the timeliness of his work as he attempts to turn the wheel of time forward (65–70).

To imitate the prophetic role of Virgil in eschatological terms is the function of the revelatory eclogue in *Appleton House*, which provides a framework for Marvell's microcosmic epic. Maria Fairfax is not only like Christ in her Coming: specifically, she is a Reformation Astraea who harbinges the Coming. If Queen Christina is like Elizabeth-Astraea, Maria's portrait is closer to the Virgilian original in her conflation of Astraea and the golden child. By making that child female, Marvell comprehends the conflation with ease. On the other hand, Maria is a parochial figure upon whom the Astraean figure can be superimposed as an effect of Marvell's microcosm; his later application of the figure to Christina was, because of her station, more suitable to its directly political and serious import. In *Appleton House*, as in Virgil's eclogue, things lesser figure things greater (VI); in both poems the pastoral mode expands to national reference, 'Si canimus silvas, silvae sint consule dignae' (3). If the consul Pollio is for Virgil the *eminence grise* of the national regeneration, so Marvell's Fairfax is the potential deliverer of the nation, and as Fairfax is to Pollio, so is Maria to the golden child. The national timing is also appropriate, marking the end of a civil war: 'sacred Peace shall lovingly perswade/ The warlike minds. . .civile Armes to exercise no more;/Then shall a *royal virgin* raine' (FQ III. iii, 49); Spenser's Virgin Astraea is by Marvell more closely related to her origins in consular rank.

His first reference to Maria describes her as 'the *Virgin Nymph*' (XXXVIII). Positively rather than merely naturally virginal, she resists the wiles of Venus: 'Blest Nymph! that couldst so soon prevent/Those Trains by Youth against thee meant' (XC), recalling also Astraea's divinity in 'Blest'. Her heavenly provenance is further emphasized by the observation that she is 'in *Heaven* try'd' (LXXXVI). In XC her militant virginity is linked to Astraean piety,[101] whereby from the temptations of earthly love—easily associated with antichristian spiritual fornication—'She scap'd the safe, but roughest Way'. This is, of course, the narrow way of salvation (Matthew 7:13–14).

The details of Maria's portrayal all reflect her Astraean character, especially the major attribute of Justice. She has 'judicious Eyes' (LXXXII) and 'Supplies beyond her *Sex* the *Line*' (XCIII); as the goddess law-giver, Maria is 'the *Law*/Of of her *Sex*, her *Ages Awe*' (LXXXII). Also like the Reformation Astraea, she bestows order upon her environment: herself 'Pure, Sweet, *Streight*, and Fair', '*She* streightness on the Woods bestows' (LXXXVII). Images of straightness or rectitude, order and line and strictness, define the Astraean attributes: 'all *Virgins* She preceds' (XCIV), reflecting Astraean power and its association with the foremost Christian Virgin, the Mary whose name is recalled in Maria's own. If her ancestor was like an Eve tempted by antichristian nuns, Maria's rectitude counterpoints their hypocrisy and also stands as a typological fulfilment in the poem, the new Eve/Mary who truly was the Bride of Christ that they claim to be. It is in terms of this miniature eschatological pattern that Maria can be the little world's Astraea, described in terms that would otherwise be remarkably exaggerated.

So Maria evinces the Astraean association with Spring (*renovatio*) and flowers: 'the *Virgin Nymph*. . ./Seems with the Flowr's a Flow'r to be' (XXXVIII). She has the Astraean inspiritive effect, for ''Tis *She* that to these Gardens gave/That wondrous Beauty which they have' (LXXXVII). The Astraean implementation of *renovatio* is related to her holy wisdom, signified in her Virgoan form;[102] the golden child, too, was not only innately wise but acquired greater wisdom in time (Eclogue IV, 26–7). So Marvell, emphasizing Maria's wisdom and precocity, associates with them her piety: making of her reputed plainness the compliment that her beauty is spiritual:

> She counts her Beauty to converse
> In all the Languages as *hers*;
> Nor yet in those *her self* imployes
> But for the *Wisdome*, not the *Noyse*;
> Nor yet that *Wisdome* would affect,
> But as 'tis *Heavens Dialect*.'
>   (LXXXIX)

When he praises Maria's facility for languages, Marvell's role as her tutor personalizes the Astraean motif, for Virgo was considered skilled in all aspects of speech.[103] The resonance of 'Heaven's Dialect' is that the Reformation Astraea, who signals renovation to all peoples, can 'speak in tongues' of the revelation (Acts 2:4). Controlling such universal implications, the recollection of the pupil–teacher relationship is one of those intimacies that maintain the decorum of the poem; as in the Virgilian model, where while compliment expands to prophecy, it also recollects itself in such notes as the child's relationship with his mother (60).

Like that child and Elizabeth and Christina, Maria must issue from a distinguished line. Marvell gives her parents' status a mysical value:

>   the after Age
> Shall hither come in *Pilgrimage*,
> These sacred Places to adore,
> By *Vere* and *Fairfax* trod before
>   (V)

While themselves 'sacred' to later times, Maria's parents are of course also heirs to the 'great Race' of activist Fairfaxes. Marvell recalls especially 'The blooming Virgin *Thwaites*,/ Fair beyond Measure' (XII), whose blossoming (spring-like) virginity finds its true 'Measure' in the straightness and renovation of her descendant Maria; and William Fairfax, 'First from a Judge, then Souldier bred' (XXIX), from whom Thomas' military role and Maria's Justice are derived. Like Pollio's child, she has benefited by her parents' example:

> Thus 'tis to have been from the first
> In a *Domestick Heaven* nurst,
> Under the *Discipline* severe

> Of *Fairfax*, and the starry *Vere*;
> Where not one object can come nigh
> But pure, and spotless as the Eye;
> And *Goodness* doth itself intail
> On *Females*. . .
>
> (XCI)

Signifying the inherited virtues and the nurture of the golden
child, this is the terrestrial counterpart of Maria–Astraea's
divine provenance. The reference to her mother as 'starry
Vere' may allude to the Vere coat of arms,[105] although this is
merely the literal level of the image. Until her return to earth
Astraea was stellified as Virgo, and her 'starry' mother here
reflects that heavenly provenance at the astrological level. The
Maria in whom she has returned inhabits the abode of
'Discipline severe', domestic counterpart of Justice. The
Astraean figure is contained by this conflation of the homely
and heavenly. Hence the miniaturizing joke in which,
referring to Maria's status as heiress of Fairfax, Marvell
implies also the immaculate conception whereby Goodness
entailed itself on the Virgin Mary. Similarly, the Latinist pun
on 'Vere'—as the spring from which Astraea springs—evokes
the Latinist potential in 'Fairfax': his motto, 'Fare Fac', being
an eponymous pun ("do the will of God"). By such means
Maria's lineage is made emphatically Astraean.

Naturally this account of her provenance climaxes in the
prophecy of the 'universal good' which Astraea-Maria
signifies:

> Hence *She* with Graces more divine
> Supplies beyond her *Sex* the *Line*;
> And, like a *sprig* of *Mistleto*,
> On the *Fairfacian Oak* does grow;
> Whence, for some universal good,
> The *Priest* shall cut the sacred Bud;
> While her *glad Parents* most rejoice,
> And make their *Destiny* their *Choice*.
>
> (XCIII)

Here the prophecy of Maria's marriage, her social integration, symbolizes her analogous universal significance as the
bringer of Astraean harmony. This is directly related to her

parents' saintly posture, as those who submit in free will to the universal destiny; the 'Fairfacian Oak', assimilating the usual pun on godly action, implies their public service in the metonymous 'Oak' (the reward of civic virtue). This arboreal metaphor for the national significance of the Fairfaxes runs into that of mistletoe—recalling the magical rites of druids— to sanctify the marriage rite as significant of universal good. This characteristic combination in the poem of universal and national resonances echoes, in a chaster Christian form, Virgil's remark that the golden child may expect a goddess as his consort (63). That Maria's good is eschatological in kind is evident from its linkage to her parents' activist posture. From that she derives her power as harbinger and renovator.

Implementing renovation, then, she brings 'descent Order tame' to the landscape—imitating that which, because of the golden child, restores peace to a landscape in which the lion may lie down with the lamb (Eclogue IV, 18–25):

> Employ the means you have by Her,
> And in your kind your selves preferr;
> That, as all *Virgins* She preceds,
> So you all *Woods, Streams, Gardens, Meads.*
>
> (XCV)

Because of her renovation, the pastoral landscape can imitate the paradise of Eden, 'preceding' all other landscapes just as she 'precedes' all other virgins—the temporal pun on 'precede' seconding its notion of pre-eminence. Maria's renovation of the landscape is founded upon her Astraean 'Peace', supervening—as it had in Virgil— upon the desolation of war. So she comes after the harvest of the Civil War has reduced the landscape by purgation:

> For now the Waves are fal'n and dry'd,
> And now the Meadows fresher dy'd,
> Whose Grass, with moister colour dasht,
> Seems as green Silks but newly washt.
> No *Serpent* new nor *Crocodile*
> Remains behind our little *Nile,*
> Unless it self you will mistake,
> Among these Meads the only Snake.
>
> (LXXIX)

The landscape is washed, baptized, just as Milton had spoken of 'Man's Renovation' in terms of the 'washing of regeneration'.[106] Renovation founds itself upon such purgation by desolation. The 'No Serpent new' provides an implicit contrast with the 'old Serpent' or devil[107]—anticipating, in fact, the greater *renovatio* when he shall be destroyed forever, an event rehearsed in this expulsion of the national sin. In anticipation this looks to that moment when the deluge—like the flood here—recedes, and 'The sea. . .shall. . .thence descend into hollownesse':[108] 'the Waves are fal'n and dried'. Later ensues 'a prodigious drought'[109] which, as the devastation of 'Deserts', will inaugurate the end of the earth in the penultimate stanza of the poem. Coming to the purged national landscape, Maria's renovation takes effect in the September of the world, a Virgoan moment succeeding the world-harvest in its August. In her moment the serpent has been quelled, just as in Virgil's Eclogue 'occidet et serpens' (24). Plants (the human 'Grass' fallen and sinful in war) are themselves purified of their poison or malignity ('fallax herba veneni/occidet' [24–5]): 'Grass. . .newly washed'.

In the characterization of Maria's Astraean peace, Marvell found his source in Milton's equivalent, the 'Peace' who is Christ's harbinger in the *Nativity Ode,* a poem certainly known by Marvell.[110] Recalling Virgil's goddess:

> She. . .came softly sliding
> Down through the turning sphere,
> His ready harbinger,
> With turtle wing the amorous clouds dividing. . .
> She strikes a universal peace through sea and land.
>   (*The Hymn*, III)

Here Peace enacts the Astraean descent in her guise as Augustan *Pax*. Similarly, Maria's arrival is likened to the halcyon, emblem of peace in the sky:

> So when. . .
> The modest *Halcyon* comes in sight,
> Flying betwixt the Day and Night;
> And such a horror calm and dumb,

Admiring Nature does benum.
. . .
Maria such, and so doth hush
The *World*, and through the *Ev'ning* rush.
(LXXXIV–VI)

It is no accident that this passage, pivoting on the eighty-fifth
stanza, recalls not only Milton but the Christian Astraean
source in Psalm 85. Milton's 'turtle wing' is picked up by the
halcyon of Maria, and both transfix the world in peace:

The winds with wonder whist
Smoothly the waters kissed,
Whispering new joys to the mild ocean,
Who now hath quite forgot to rave,
While birds of calm sit brooding on the charmed wave.

The stars with deep amaze
Stood fixed in steadfast gaze
(*The Hymn*, V–VI)

In Milton's poem the halcyons appear finally in the 'birds of
calm'. The image of the world's transfixion is more emphatically developed in Maria's effect:

The gellying Stream compacts below,
If it might fix her shadow so;
The stupid Fishes hang, as plain
As *Flies* in *Chrystal* overt'ane;
And Men the silent Scene assist,
Charm'd with the *Saphir-winged Mist*.
(LXXXV)

This is the arresting of time as Astraea's arrival announces the
final Coming. The 'wonder' of it charms Milton's 'winds' and
'Charm'd' Marvell's men, the stillness of enchantment
locking men and nature both, as the Astraean effect should. If
Milton's 'charmed wave' is echoed by Marvell's 'gellying
Stream', this diminishes the effect to Nunappleton's scale,
the river supplying Milton's 'ocean', and the humorous
diminuendo of 'the stupid Fishes' is further refined to 'Flies in

Chrystal'. Such delicate adjustments of scale place Marvell's poem closer to the pastoral spirit of the Virgilian model. The charming enchantment, however, is the same in both of the revelatory eclogues, from Milton's 'whist/kissed' rhyme to Marvell's 'assist/Mist'. In Marvell's poem this renovatory effect implicitly contrasts with the sensuous delights (XXII–VI) extolled by the antichristian abbess, and her damning 'Inchantment' (XXXIV) or illusion. Maria's is the true wonder.

The image of time's transfixion can be compared to that in Edward Fairfax's eschatological *Egloge* (preserved in Thomas's manuscript book), where the poet imagines the Coming from the banks of the Isis:

> The heifer lett the hearbs untouched spring
> Forgott to feed, the stags amazed stood
> The siluer riuer staid her speedie flood
> Charmed was the Adder deafe, tamde was the Lion
> So trees hard Orpheus, Dolphins hard Arion.[112]

Recalling the Virgilian snake and lion, the *Egloge* may have suggested to Marvell his own location on the river bank at the Coming of Maria, merging with the suggestions from Milton's poem. Fairfax's *Egloge* similarly uses the Bridegroom motif for Christ, and a mower who provides a contextual figure of Death ('The sweatie sith-man wth his razor keene/Shore the perfumed beard from meadowes greene').[113] Assimilating such eschatological punctuation for the Virgilian model, Marvell's poem is distinguished from Milton's Incarnational placing of the Astraean Coming: thus further eschatological pointing is achieved by the word 'Scene', locating the Astraean moment in the eschatological drama as the pacificatory 'Act'—the 'silent Scene'. The next stanza defines Maria as a portent of the End: 'No new-born *Comet* such a Train/Draws through the Skie, nor Star new-slain.' (LXXXVI). The comparison implicitly recalls the Virgoan star which disappears when Astraea returns to earth—an appropriate thought at the moment when Maria–Astraea actually comes. From this point the Astraean figure is fully developed: her divine provenance (LXXXVI), her renovation of the landscape (LXXXVII), her wisdom (LXXXIX), her trenchant chastity (CX), her distinguished lineage (XCI), her 'knowledge' and 'Virtue' (XCII), her 'universal' destiny (XCIII), her gift of Justice and inspiration (XCIV), her 'decent Order' (XCVI). Such fluency ensues upon Marvell's preservation of the integrity of the Virgilian model: unlike Milton, who celebrates an Incarnational Astraea but must look forward to a Golden Age after the End, Marvell can celebrate the narrative of Astraea as harbinger of Second Coming. Most important, the portrait of Maria–Astraea's transfixion of her little world can anticipate the arrest of time and the peace of *renovatio* which must supervene upon it, providing a foretaste of the consequences of the End which occurs in the last stanza of the poem.

Her renovation imitates that effected by the golden child Christ in Milton's ode, where 'Nature in awe of him/Hath doffed her gaudy trim' (1), simpler and chaster because of His presence, and conscious of the fallen Creation. So Maria 'streightens' the landscape:

> See how loose Nature, in respect
> To her, it self doth recollect;
> And everything so whisht and fine,
> Starts forth with to its *Bonne Mine*.
> (LXXXIII)

In describing the renovated landscape Marvell echoes Milton's 'whisht' (V), punning to imply that this is the much desired 'restauration of all things'. The Astraean inspiritive effect is of natural beauty and bounty, imitating those in Virgil's Eclogue:

> 'Tis *She* that to these Gardens gave
> That wondrous Beauty which they have;
> *She* streightness on the Woods bestows;
> To *Her* the Meadow sweetness owes;
> Nothing could make the River be
> So Chrystal-pure but only *She*;
> *She* yet more Pure, Sweet, Streight, and Fair,
> Then Gardens, Woods, Meads, Rivers are.
> (LXXXVII)

Renovation purifies while it beautifies. Here as throughout this section of the poem all sentences are formulated so as to derive the renovatory effects from Maria alone—'only *She*'. In the Virgilian model the golden child's inspiration evokes the earth's desire to make returns by its tribute to him (18ff.):

> Therefore what first *She* on them spent,
> They gratefully again present.
> The Meadow Carpets where to tread;
> The Garden Flow'rs to Crown *Her* Head;
> And for a Glass the limpid Brook,
> Where *She* may all *her* Beautyes look;
> But, since *She* would not have them seen,
> The Wood about *her* draws a Skreen.
>   (LXXXVIII)

(It is as well to note that I am not supplying any of the italics in these quotations, pertinent as they appear to be.) The recollection of Astraean virginal modesty underwrites the idea that renovatory beauty is pure and sinless, whether in human beings or in nature. Since this renovation is a foretaste of that after the Second Coming, Maria's 'Crown[ing]' here properly recalls not only the royal virginity of the Astraean figure, but also the Kingdom itself. As in Virgil 'At tibi prima, puer, nullo munuscula cultu/errantes hederas passim cum baccare tellus. . .' (18–19), so here 'Admiring Nature' (LXXXIV) performs the same tribute to Maria. Even in the skies:

> The *Sun* himself, of *Her* aware,
> Seems to descend with greater Care;
> And lest *She* see him go to Bed;
> In blushing Clouds conceales his Head.
>   (LXXXIII)

Maria's ability to abash even the cosmic light by her purity recalls Milton's sun reacting to his golden child: 'The sun himself withheld his wonted speed,/And hid his head for shame' (VII). Maria has appeared at the sun's 'descent' into the night of the world, the appropriate time for her announcement of the Coming: when 'The moon shall be confounded, and the sun ashamed' (Isaiah 24:23). Marvell's several allusions to Isaiah in this poem are themselves relevant to his Virgilian model, since Christian exegetes had traditionally compared Eclogue IV to the prophecies of Isaiah in particular: and this was the Old Testament book of prophecies of desolation and renovation—Iron Age and Golden Age—to Israel. Thus Maria's eschatological coming, resonant of Isaiahan images, is crystallized in her specifically Christological 'vitrifying', recalling not only that He 'is like a refiner's fire' but also that 'he shall sit like a refiner and purifier' (Malachi 3:2–3). Since her renovation merely foretells His, Marvell is careful to emphasize that it affects only her 'lesser *World*' (XCVI), a 'Map' of the new earth to come. The picture of Maria as Reformation Astraea imports into the poem the promise of future renovation, balancing the desolation, confusion, and distress of the war. She mediates between war's Iron Age and final Golden Age, a twilight figure 'Flying betwixt the Day and Night', the day and night of the world, but also, in succession, the great and everlasting 'Day' of the Kingdom.

For this effect Marvell signalled his use of the Virgilian model when, in the wood, 'Out of these scatter'd *Sibyls* Leaves/Strange *Prophecies* my Phancy weaves'. To the Sibyl, Virgil had attributed his own prophecy in Eclogue IV. 4, and in similar fashion Marvell announces his prophetic vision of a new Astraea, speaking like Virgil himself from the 'Wood' or 'silvas' of pastoral. Like this exordium, Marvell's exit equally imitates Virgil's, where the classical poet also diagnoses the age that is to come from a great alteration in the world's normal appearance:

> aspice convexo nutantem pondere mundum
> . . .caelumque profundum;
> aspice venturo laetantur ut omnia saeclo!
>
> (50–2)

Marvell's use of the 'dark Hemisphere' directly recalls Virgil's 'convexo. . .pondere mundum', and in both poems the world itself signals its imminent transformation. The onset of (eschatological) night in Marvell's poem makes thematic use of the convention in pastoral whereby the poem follows the course of a single day—a recurrent feature of Virgil's Eclogues, several of which end with a description of the coming of evening.[114] Marvell refines the convention by bringing it into correspondence with his eschatological theme. And this thematic usage illuminates something that has puzzled several critics: *Appleton House* appears to record the action of a single day, but it also contains intimations of several different seasons of the year. In fact, a day at Nunappleton is a microcosm of the year, just as the place itself is a microcosm of the world. This simultaneous day/year is of course prophetic time, like that of Revelation itself. This prophetic sense of time is signified numerological-ly as the End approaches, and 'the Shadows. . ./From underneath these Banks do creep', announcing the night: the line's number is 666, the number of the Beast (Revelation 13:17–18). His number has come up, as it were. As his reign ends, Astraea-Maria 'The modest *Halcyon* comes in sight' (669), announcing the new and final Kingdom.

This Virgilian format for Maria founds itself upon the poem's insistence on the iron-golden contrast, which is the pivot of Eclogue IV. In its opening stanza *Appleton House* recalls the Golden Age of man's innocence and the current decay of the Latter Days. Contemporary architecture reflects man's growing presumption:

> Why should of all things Man unrul'd
> Such unproportion'd dwellings build?
> . . .
> What need of all this Marble Crust
> T'impark the wanton Mote of Dust,
> That thinks by Breadth the World t'unite
> Though the first Builders fail'd in Height?
> (I–III)

Marvell's characterization of the spirit of pride and presump-tion recalls the Tower of Babel (identified with Babylon and hence with antichristianism),[115] and looks forward to the proud prelates castigated later in the poem, especially for piles like Cawood Castle. Hence the joke, that sees Latter Day antichristian pride as to 'Breadth' what Babel was to 'Height', reflects also the wrong way 'the World t'unite'—by antichristian tyranny, predominant in this age, rather than by Christ's universal empire. Hence the eschatological as well as spiritual propriety of the house at Appleton, reflecting the 'sober' (I) spirit of Puritanism. Built upon the principles of 'holy Mathematicks' (VI), it recalls the holy 'arithmetic' which was recommended by Milton in the building of the reformed Church, evoking the Golden Section and true proportion, such as that of the 'proportion'd' Appleton House.[116] It is in this spiritual sense that the house is a recrudescence of past Golden Age, a throwback to the 'Primitive Religion' which Protestantism claimed to revive:

> In which we the Dimensions find
> Of that more sober Age and Mind,
> When larger sized Men did stoop
> To enter at a narrow loop;
> As practising, in doors so strait,
> To strain themselves through *Heavens Gate*.
>
> (IV)

In its compactness the house itself signifies the true religion, the strictness of which is the 'narrow way' to heaven's 'strait gate'. Such too is Maria's 'streightness', at once Astraean and Puritan—actively reformist. Here the lost Golden Age is recaptured in the golden proportion of the house, and with Maria–Astraea that Golden Age returns to earth.

That return is enacted by the distance between stanza XLII and Maria's entrance:

> Unhappy! shall we never more
> That sweet *Militia* restore,
> When Gardens only had their Towrs,
> And all the Garrisons were Flowrs,
> When Roses only Arms might bear,
> And Men did rosie Garlands wear?

This explicit elegy for the Golden Age implicitly counter-points to it the Iron Age of civil war, with its more sinister

'Militia'. Its 'restore'-ation is later effected by Maria, of course, when the 'Garlands' of the happy state are presented in tribute to her: 'The Garden [gives] Flow'rs to Crown *Her* Head' (LXXXVIII). Thus the poem enacts the Golden Age's return.

Similarly Virgil had mourned the Roman sin or 'scelus' of civil war,[117] which is dispelled by the golden child. If, in the garden, 'War all this doth overgrow:/We Ord'nance Plant and Powder sow' (XLIII), Maria–Astraea purifies its sin and reinspires nature. The garden's subjection to the 'Souldier' instead of the original innocent 'Gardiner', Adam, is of course amplified later by the Mowers' desolating activism, which Astraea's reforming activism will counterpoint:

> With whistling Sithe, and Elbow strong,
> These Massacre the Grass along:
> While one, unknowing, carves the *Rail*,
> Whose yet unfeather'd Quils her fail.
> The Edge all bloody from its Breast
> He draws, and does his stroke detest;
> Fearing the Flesh untimely mow'd
> To him a Fate as black forebode.
>
> (L)

Several attempts have been made to account for this incident in the poem, the most popular of which is singularly unconvincing.[118] The rail is the sort of victim that one would expect in the course of harvesting, and is not itself symbolic; the true significance of this event is explicitly indicated, that this was an 'untimely' death, caused 'unknowing' by the Mower, an involuntary murder in contrast to the 'Massacre', which is ordained and intended. The point of the Mower's distress is that such murderous activism as his requires to be both 'known' (understood by zeal) and 'timely' (in step with time). The ominous nature of this accident reflects—in diminished fashion—the individual's problems with the activism complex, and this allusion is aptly underpinned by the resonances of 'Fate' and portent in the last couplet. The key word in the stanza, 'untimely', is reiterated when the rail undergoes its 'untimely Funeral' (LII), and here Marvell repines the purely contingent effects of destruction as 'Chance'; the purpose of this incident is to embody chance and its offence against the principle of timeliness.

When in the subsequent stanza Marvell introduces 'bloody *Thestylis*' (a name suggested by Virgil's *Eclogues*),[119] her voracious character personifies an unregenerate action, destructiveness rather than activism. Her intention to cook and consume the rail, and trapping another, associate her bloodiness with the devouring aspect of antichristianism. She is heard to object to Marvell's characterization of the Mowers as the New Israel ('he call'd us *Israelites*'): failing to recognize the fundamental point of activism, that these are the militants of Protestantism and thus the New Israel. She and the murderous Mower are exemplars of mistaken and antichristian actions, characterizing the Civil War as a confusion in which militancy, unregenerate and malign action are compounded without distinction. This Iron Age of war, recalling Virgil, is summed up as '*Roman Camps*' (LV), and reflects in Roman form the desolating phase.

There is similar resonance in Marvell's retreat to *umbra* and the *vita otiosa* in the wood. This is the natural response to public events which are 'driving [the People] into Woods, and running them upon Precipices' like those of the penultimate stanza (*RT*, 234). But, while enacting Marvell's usual penchant for self-protection, his retreat into the wood ends even his passive role as *spectator* of history in the meadows. At first sight one might diagnose a fit of quietism here, a 'timely' withdrawal from action. But the 'Ark' in which Marvell finds refuge is the Church Militant, innately activist and even pressingly so when the time, as here, is one of war and desolation. By his recollection of the image of militancy Marvell provides an ironic comment upon his own retreat, as eschatological negligence: in this Ark the pairs of Noah become 'Armies', and Marvell should be part of the holy army. Just as Thestylis and the Mower represented wrong activism, so Marvell's persona in the poem embodies mistaken quietism. The wood section of the poem is its most extended joke, against Marvell himself (or "Marvell", as we should distinguish the poet's role from that of the poet himself, who reflects upon his past ironically).

From the very first the persona's voice has been that of dramatic monologue, conducting the reader/spectator from house through garden to meadows. Until the wood section the personal pronoun appears only once. Till now a companionable 'we' has comprehended both "Marvell" and the reader (e.g. XI), formalizing the properly participatory function of an alert reader in Marvellian poetics. In the house and garden episodes it seems that the Fairfaxes might be companions in the 'we', as the flowers' 'Vollyes' salute them in passing (XXXVIII). The group breaks up, and the persona's 'I' makes its first appearance in the poem, as "Marvell" leaves the garden: 'And now to the Abbyss I pass' of the meadows (XLVII.1). His identifying isolation is only momentary, since there he is swiftly included in the meadows' theatrical cast of mankind as 'Men', 'us', and 'we' (XLVII. 3, 6). But the moment of "Marvell's" individuation is significant, for at this point a crucial contrast is established between the two modes of eschatological struggle, activist militancy and antichristian intimidation. At the end of the garden episode Fairfax's militaristic garden provokes a juxtaposition, of his preference for industrious *'Conscience'* over self-serving *'Ambition'* (XLV), with 'Th'Ambition' of the prelatical Cawood (XLVI). This clerical hubris is then embodied in the 'Grashoppers' who, in the next stanza, preside over the war. In the face of their 'pre-eminence' "Marvell's" identity recedes, and he plunges into that mass of Englishmen who are subject both to the indiscriminate chances of war, and the great antichristian threat to the spiritual identity of the nation. As each saint's election—that which identifies him as God's—is in question at this moment of crisis, which way will "Marvell" go? Will he fall into the 'Abbyss'? At the flooding he retreats—'Let others tell' the rest (LX): 'But I, retiring from the Flood,/Take Sanctuary in the Wood' (LXI). In the wood episode, before he re-encounters Maria in her Astraean return to the 'lesser World', the first person pronoun recurs frequently because this is a private retreat. That retreat begins with an individuating 'But I,' which emphasizes at once his personal choice and his going against the grain of events. Fairfacian militancy is rejected for 'ease':

> I, *easie Philosopher*,
> Among the *Birds* and *Trees* confer:
> And little now to make me, wants
> Or of the *Fowles*, or of the *Plants*.
> (LXXI)

The individuality of Marvell has been introduced only to be absorbed into a sort of general species. This "natural" Marvell has receded from the human sphere of action into other orders of the creation, and his naturalness itself reflects the unregenerateness of 'the natural man' as against the 'new creature' or saint. The word 'easie' contrasts with the militancy and 'very hard duty' of the Puritan saint (*RT*, 246). Thus the double retreat into wood (LXI) and natural state (LXXI) take the same syntactical form ('But I. . .Thus I'), emphasizing in their precedent position in these stanzas the individual identity of "Marvell" at moments when he is making a crucial choice of role.

That he imagines that he is adopting the legitimate stance of quietism, rather than 'easie' negligence, is indicated as usual by the phrase 'while it lasts', characterizing his sylvan retreat from the war. Later in the poem this is contrasted by the Fairfaxes' activist 'Destiny their Choice', a readiness enjoined even upon the landscape:

> Mean time ye Fields . . .
> Where yet She leads her studious Hours,
> (Till Fate her worthily translates,
> And find a *Fairfax* for our *Thwaites*)
> Employ the means you have by Her,
> (XCIV)

In stanzas XCIII–IV Fairfacian activism is embodied in Maria, and Fate's expected 'translation' of her is a playful allusion to Marvell's translation of the Latin Astraea into the English Maria, foretelling indeed the eschatological destiny of her 'Fate'. The whiles and meantimes of these stanzas thus imply a familial interval in which readiness expects their activist roles. Here quietism and Fairfacian retirement are legitimated, while "Marvell's" in the wood was undermined by irony.

Instead of activism, "Marvell" in the wood takes to acting. Throughout the poem the forms of masque are evoked, and the dual role of spectator and actor proper to masques[120] is also that appropriate in the historical drama wherein the chiliast was supposed to be at once investigative of history and active in it. The dual role is evoked by "Marvell" as self-presented in the wood:

> And see how Chance's better Wit
> Could with a Mask my studies hit!
> The Oak-Leaves me embroyder all
> . . .
> Under this *antick Cope* I move
> Like some great *Prelate of the Grove.*
> (LXXIV)

Marvell has indeed assumed a role, but only in play; the accidental or contingent 'Mask' given by 'Chance' is in contrast to the carefully designed masque of history. Recalling the Mower's unlucky 'Chance', we may measure "Marvell's" delusion that chance has better wit than fate; patient of contingency, his attitude compares unfavourably with the destined 'Choice' of the Fairfaxes. Similarly, then, the 'Oak-Leaves' which are properly the reward of civic action and thereby granted to Fairfax in the poem are here ironic badges of negligence, emphasizing the continuous contrast between "Marvell" and his employers. Worse still, "Marvell's" role is as a 'great Prelate', hardly a legitimate disguise for the Puritan chiliast. The ecclesiastical 'antick Cope' (now 'antick' implies "demonic" as well as "frivolous") is derived from Milton's attack upon Arminian ritual[121] as 'an antick Coape upon the Stage of the High Altar',[122] already echoed in Marvell's *Fleckno*, where the hypocrisy of the papist priest is signified by his 'antick Cloak' (75).[123] The prelates as actors are:

> Companyes the worst that ever playd
> And their Religion all but Masquerade.
> The Conscious Prelate therefore did not Err,
> When for a Church hee built a Theatre.
> (*The Loyall Scot*, 166–9)

Such hypocrisy is "Marvell's" when he deludes himself that his retreat is legitimate, indulging his personal proclivity for privacy. The poet passes judgment upon his own lack of involvement in the eschatological war which ravages England.

In general, the wood section of the poem has been regarded by critics with much gravity, as some "mystic" vision of nature, with Marvell as an hermetic "priest" of the natural world, spiritually elevated.[124] This view, so contrary to the true significance of the stanza, is by them "read back" into Marvell's essentially frivolous meditations upon the phenomena of the wood, the tone of which is in fact an index of their parodic nature. The recollections here of the works of Saint-Amant and other French "libertin" poets[125] are in fact (as Annabel Patterson alone seems to have recognised)[126] a parody of libertine poses. More significantly, their supine, apathetic nature is Marvell's target, and we should relate this parody to the attitudes of those contemporary poets who retreated into hermeticism from the Civil War. When Marvell notes that:

> The *Nightingale* does here make choice
> To sing the Tryals of her Voice.
> Low Shrubs she sits in, and adorns
> With Musick high the squatted Thorns.
>   (LXV)

he is of course characterising pastoral poems, such as this, as the traditional apprenticeship of the poet destined for greater things, like Virgil in his Eclogue; this poem, like that, has its high theme in low pastoral. But when Marvell proceeds to specify the 'Sadder' poetry of the wood (LXVI), it is that of 'Stock-doves', of love. Self-love, indeed, since he has no other object here, and it is that 'carnal reasoning' that has misled him into this anticlimactic theme—anticlimactic because the higher theme should be activist and eschatological, not self-serving negligence.

Thus when Marvell speculates upon 'prophecies' (LXXIII), their context in the wood indicates that he is indeed 'mistook' in his reading of scripture and events. The activity of interpretation is proper enough, but "Marvell's" posture has made the 'light Mosaick' of the prophetic books not enlightening—revelatory—but frivolous in levity. The ambiguity in 'light' sums up both the difficulty of chiliastic interpretation and "Marvell's" 'mistaking'.[127] It is in the subsequent stanza that his prelatical disguise personifies this eschatological error. The *otium* of the wood emphasises negligence by exaggeration:

> Then, languishing with ease, I toss
> On Pallets swoln of Velvet Moss;
> While the Wind . . .
> Flatters with Air my panting Brows.
> (LXXV)

Ironically Marvell portrays his relaxation as effort ('toss' and 'panting'), a perverse recollection of the Mowers' sweatiness in action. Theirs was a 'wholesome Heat' (LIV), while "Marvell's" 'flatters' to deceive. Such ironic undercutting is continued when "Marvell" 'incamp[s]' defensively against the world and its Roman cavalry (LXXVI), describing retreat in the terms of military action and the 'Roman Camps' of the meadows. Such irony recalls again the Virgilian association with activism, but it is also eschatologically emphasized here, for the Roman 'Horsemen', pursuing "Marvell's" 'gaul', are also the Horsemen of the Apocalypse. They should harry "Marvell" into chiliastic activity, but he is yet content to 'play' for the duration of the eschatological 'Day' (LXXVI).

It seems that they prompt him only into paralysis, a comic fear of action and emergence:

> Bind me ye *Woodbines* in your 'twines,
> Curle me about ye gadding *Vines*,
> And Oh so close your Circles lace,
> That I may never leave this Place:
> But, lest your Fetters prove too weak,
> Ere I your Silken Bondage break,
> Do you, O *Brambles*, chain me too,
> And courteous *Briars* nail me through.
> (LXXVII)

Here self-criticism and self-mockery measure his self-protective neurosis. Not only will he languish, but he desires to become the passive victim of his own retreat. His request that the landscape assume his volition inverts the situation in the meadows, where the activist Mowers dictate the transformation of the landscape. The chiliast's 'Choice' is reduced to the choice of involution. Some time ago it was suggested that this stanza carries a reminiscence of the Crucifixion,[128] heretofore taken very seriously as an element in the wood's "mysticism". However, this muted reminiscence is—like the generally outrageous tone of the stanza—ironic. The triumphant victim of the Passion is equated with "Marvell's" similarly voluntary passivity and victimization here, and the extravagance of this equation measures "Marvell's" error. This is a frivolous and 'Silken Bondage', rather echoing the characteristic antichristian 'bondage' of men than the Passion which enfranchises them. The crucial historical climacteric of the Passion is therefore placed in its eschatological context here:

> Here in the Morning tye my Chain
> . . .
> But, where the Floods did lately drown,
> There at the Ev'ning stake me down.
> (LXXVIII)

In the prophetic time-scale of the poem, the Passion of the previous stanza signifies the dawn of the Church Age (or 'better world', as it is called in *Ingelo*)[129] and so must "Marvell's" Passion take place in the morning. The 'Ev'ning' of that age is the Last Day, approaching here: if then he wishes to be staked down in the meadows rather than the wood, this transference signifies that he will export his negligence from the wood (abode of quietism) into the meadows of history itself. And indeed so he does, compounding his error:

> Oh what a Pleasure 'tis to hedge
> My Temples here with heavy sedge;
> Abandoning my lazy Side,
> Stretcht as a Bank unto the Tide;
> Or to suspend my sliding Foot
> On the Osiers undermined Root,
> And in its Branches tough to hang,
> While at my Lines the Fishes twang!
> (LXXXI)

While "Marvell" clings to the 'Root' and 'Branches' he holds to his quasi-prelatical mistake; that which the Root and Branch Petition of 1640 had protested against on the national level. [130] That root is 'undermined' because the destruction of episcopacy is effected by the war and its destruction required by these Latter Days of the poem. All the ironies of "Marvell's" 'laz[iness]' here mean that he no longer looks like one of the elect. His forehead is disguised 'with heavy sedge' not only because this is detritus (like the inactive saint) but also because the elect are distinguished by God's sign in their foreheads (Revelation 7:3), and the badge of his negligence effectively cancels his sainthood. (This joke is seconded by a pun on 'Temples' as both forehead and the 'temple made without hands' which is God's elect saint.)[131] "Marvell's" 'sliding Foot' puts the seal on this portrait of his wandering from the true way. The wandering is spiritual rather than active in kind, 'a Bank unto the Tide' of history: likening "Marvell" to those 'Ill [men] delaying' the *eschaton* in *First Anniversary*. Even the poetry which he was seen to compose ('Sing') in the wood is tainted in the same way: the fish here make music with his Lines', [132] taking from his poetic voice just as the landscape was instructed to remove his volition. He is at once negligent chiliast and *poet manqúe*, for poetry too should be active for the *eschaton*.

Upon "Marvell" must come a nemesis of judgment, of course:

> But now away my Hooks, my Quills,
> And Angles, idle Utensils.
> The *young Maria* walks to night:
> Hide trifling Youth thy Pleasures slight.
> 'Twere shame that such judicious Eyes
> Should with such Toyes a Man surprize;
> *She* that already is the *Law*
> Of all her *Sex*, her *Ages Aw*.
>   (LXXXII)

Astraean activism and justice rebuke the poet's 'idle[ness]', as the roles of pupil and tutor are comically reversed. [133] Maria not only 'walks' in the night, contrasting his couch, but 'walks' *to* the night, moving towards the *eschaton* in the activist manner whereby the elect 'haste' to meet it. The pun records the injunction to zeal and causes "Marvell" to come to his senses, just as in her presence Nature 'it self doth recollect'. Her coming is elevated by contrast to the poet's supinity—the climax of Marvell's joke against himself. Whereas "Marvell" had implored the landscape to act upon him, Maria transforms it; the 'Fishes' who appropriate his muse are transfixed by her (LXXXV); while "Marvell" hides from 'Beauty' (LXXVI), Maria foils the wiles of *Amour*. To her fulfilment of the Sybilline prophecy of Astraea "Marvell's" placid interpretation of the Sybil in the wood is a counterpoint, subserving their representative characterization of negligence and zeal.

Maria–Astraea becomes a Virgilian fulfilment of the Fairfacian destiny, recalled in the wood to undermine "Marvell's" interpretation of fate:

> The double Wood of ancient Stocks
> Link'd in so thick, an Union locks,
> It like two *Pedigrees* appears,
> On one hand *Fairfax*, th'other *Veres*:
> Of whom though many fell in War,
> Yet more to Heaven shooting are:
> And, as they Natures Cradle deckt,
> Will in green Age her Hearse expect.
>   (LXII)

An extended play upon trees as a metaphor for genealogy[134] also utilises the biblical image of the righteous man as a tree productive of spiritual fruit.[135] Trees represent the Fairfacian dynasty, and just as trees provide timber for shipbuilding in wartime, so the Fairfaxes and Veres have provided numerous warriors: theirs is a holy warfare, 'shooting' upwards and imitating their elect translation into 'Heaven'. This swift and accurate vertical trajectory of their activism implies that zeal is indeed the true way of salvation.[136] Such vertical heaven-wards attitudes are those which distinguish the 'streightness' which Maria imposes upon the woods, and both she and her father are shooting upwards by means of zeal. The last couplet recalls Saint-Amant's 'la nativitie du temps',[137] and indicates thereby that 'Natures Cradle' refers to the beginning of the world. Thus the 'Hearse' is the End, concluding the stanza of course, and in this expectation the Fairfaxes act; 'green Age' implies not only the evergreen trees but the spring green of *renovatio*, which will make the Fairfaxes young again in their own resurrecton. The paradox of 'green Age' therefore characterizes the current 'Age', when the world is old and must die, and the 'green' renovation to which it will come by that means. At the familial level, the Fairfaxes retain youthful vigour because they are activists, and this notion sanctifies the 'sacred Bud' which is Maria on her wedding day. The implication, that regeneration of the family tree by successive generations produces a pattern similar to *desolatio et renovatio*, suitably locates Maria-Astraea as the *telos* of the 'great Race' and renovator of her world. The terminal position of 'Hearse expect' reflects the End here envisaged, and gives 'expect' a formally expectant quality, since it waits upon the continuation of the poem by the next stanza. This poetic enaction of the Fairfacian quietist interval rebukes "Marvell's" supposed quietism in the wood.

If the activism of the Fairfaxes legitimates their quietism, this paradox of Puritan readiness imitates that of *desolatio et renovatio* and 'green Age'. Fairfax's retirement contrasts with that of the nuns, whose locked and fortified nunnery is an antichristian prison, and with "Marvell's" 'Silken Bondage' of sloth, which is equally sensuous. Fairfax's militaristic garden signifies that militant virtues remain to him even in retirement, and are embodied in Maria as the figure of Virgilian activism.

By this problematic of revelatory eclogue with miniature epic, *Appleton House* not only reflects the national and universal destinies but memorably conveys the problems and responsibilities of the chiliast in response to destiny. Most specifically, it records Marvell's own sense of engagement with the activism complex during the Civil War period, and formalizes that engagement in a manner which may at once compliment his employers and overgo his Virgilian model. Here in the 1650s, as in *Ingelo* (1653) and *Illustrissimo Viro* (two decades later), the revelatory eclogue is a formulation of renovatory hope: *mutatis mutandis* Marvell holds to this consolation in the vicissitudes of the time, not forgetting to measure himself too.

The generic code of the traditional Country House poem involves the celebration of property and virtue, a fundamentally conservative pastoral code into which praise of the Fairfaxes is readily assimilated. The episodic construction of *Appleton House* imitates the generic model, Ben Jonson's *To Penshurst*, from the initial celebration of the primitivist ethic embodied in the house, through topography and familial history, to the political order and the moral education of the estate's heirs. At first Marvell's poem also appears to have a circular structure like *Penshurst's*, returning to the initial ethical proposition of the 'tortoise' emblem. But two significant differences should alert us to a deeper distinction between the poems. In effect Marvell's poem is End-dominated, committed to narrative and the linear course of history. It is also over seven times longer than *Penshurst*, for Marvell's macrocosmic theme demands such amplification. Equally, Marvell's version of the primitivist ethic is rather a commitment to the radicalized nostalgia of 'primitive religion'. In this symbolic opposition to the nunnery, Cawood, and the hubristic trajectory of clerical 'spir's' of 'Precipices' (places from which to Fall), the neat proportions of Appleton House (IV) paradoxically reflect the militant reforming spirit. In the context of the contemporary struggle the house implies a militancy equal to that of the conflict from which critics have thought its estate to be a retreat—so that the militaristic garden and the warlike meadows *enact* the militant significance of the house. Since in spiritual terms the estate is not properly a retreat, by subverting the recessive and reversionary implications of a conservative generic code, the poem makes of pastoral and war a continuum which is polemical.

This generic revolution is implemented also by the poem's joco-serious voice. Often critics regard the poem's 'comedy' as subverting whatever seriousness it may seem to claim for itself. Indeed, the apocalyptic theme that I indicate may appear to render more acute this apparent disparity between discourse and theme, since zealous Puritanism is not supposed to be elegant, witty and amusing. However, the poem's comedy has not only structural and satiric purposes (as I have suggested) but also an esthetic objective which is established at the very beginning of the poem. There the house's *'Humility'* (VI) sets the perspective on hubristic antichristian structures, typicalized by the reference to the Tower of Babel (III.24), and out of all proportion to the needs and dignity of man, 'the wanton Mote of Dust'. That incongruity, similarly evoked by Milton's Babel, promoted in heaven the response of 'great laughter' and 'thus was the building left Ridiculous' (*PL.* XII. 59, 62). A similarly evaluative ridicule mocks 'unproportion'd effects of 'unrul'd' mankind here (II). In stanza VII, where the house sweats and strains to contain Fairfax, the comically extravagant conceit signifies that the house does not recognize that its inhability to contain his greatness comfortably is precisely its spiritual proportion to him: 'too officiously it slights/That in it self which him delights'. In witty terms the house's humility is reintensified by its self-deprecating attitude. This attitude is glossed by the next stanza:

> So Honour better Lowness bears,
> Then that unwonted Greatness wears.
> Height with a certain Grace does bend,
> But low Things clownishly ascend.

This appears to refer to Fairfax's condescension towards his house, contrasted with the magniloquent piles in which meaner spirits seek to aggrandize themselves. However, at another level in this spiritual meditation his 'Grace' is implicitly compared to that vouchsafed by the greater 'Lord' God to mankind's essential 'Lowness', upon which the poem has already insisted. The poem itself is like the house, both in its embodiment of the militant spirit and in the relation of its 'low' generic kind of sylvan pastoral to the greatness of the addressee, Fairfax.

> *Humility* alone designs
> Those short but admirable Lines,
> By which. . .
> Things greater are in less contain'd.
>   (VI)

Just as the last line here characterizes the poem's procedure, so the poem like the house aims for proportioned 'Lines' of verse. Therefore its discourse must be, like the house, in some sense 'clownish'. Indeed, 'some will smile at this' humble house and poem (V). That reaction is proper to the spiritual ideal of humility, and crucially different in symbolic terms from the effect of antichristian modes which 'arch the Brows' of the spectator (V, I). Such pomp is abjured by the poem because deference to Fairfax and God is its mode. If in a religious discourse wit and comedy achieve reverence 'by showing the failure of the human', then the paradoxes of Fairfacian amplitude within pastoral containment and of apocalyptic theme within pastoral microcosm demand a style which can 'clownishly ascend'. For this reason the poem like the house opens with a paradoxical 'Stately *Frontispiece of Poor*' (IX), and ends with clownish—that is, rustic and humble—fishermen; at once embodiments of a low pastoral and, in their canoe-shoes, as radically unproportioned as the house is to Fairfax; yet equally significant of the hidden spiritual proportion which radically readjusts the status quo. Just as Marvell's comic/sinister Mower heals himself with 'Clowns-all-heal' (*Damon the Mower*, XI), so the poet who treats God's 'great Design' requires not a stately mode—that is the antichristian way (I)—but a mode which comically encodes his own limitations. The reformist combination of humility with militancy requires a similarly tense combination of joco-seriousness, in which jocosity guarantees the spiritual status of his expression of a high theme. In merging militancy with humility Marvell's joco-serious mode is, like his wittily 'unproportion'd' images, a way of turning the world upside down. Such a mode articulates apocalyptic.

Most important, both for the apocalyptic tradition and for literary history, is the way in which Marvell's development of revelatory eclogue effects a radical transformation of the genre of Pastoral.[138] Traditionally, Pastoral refers to myths of primitivism and Arcadianism, to a lost paradise (in the Christian tradition, Eden); in this evocation nostalgia is the dominant mood, reflecting man's loss of an original innocence and harmony.[139] However, as Milton develops and Marvell perfects revelatory eclogue, the Pastoral framework comes to include the 'new heavens and new earth' of the *last* paradise. This radically alters the orientation of Pastoral, from past to future, giving this normally backward-looking genre a dynamic forward thrust. The consequent injection of "expectation" into the Pastoral ethos, with its freight of apocalyptic destruction, gives new and unexpected twists to the genre. It is fitting that the revolution in thought which was effected by the Reformation in England should effect also a revolution in the ancient literary traditions of Pastoral. Since Pastoral is a mode reflecting crucial elements in Western consciousness, the implications of this revolution should significantly alter our view not only of this literary genre but of the history of ideas in general.

5

A Revelation for the Revolution: Maritime Images of the *Eschaton*

(i) SAILING TO THE NEW JERUSALEM

Marvell's increasing involvement with public events in the 1650s, implementing the activist role pressed by *Upon Appleton House*, is reflected in a group of poems which elaborate upon Revolution's image of the national 'waters'. These poems attempt to understand, come to terms with, and speak to contemporary events by means of the maritime images of the *eschaton*.

The maritime images of politics in the *eschaton* are intimately linked with the contemporary myths and motifs attached to England's character as a sea-borne power and hence to her imperialism. During Cromwell's Protectorate, England was the greatest sea-power in the world.[1] It was recognized that her trade and her influence both depended upon her maritime power and that, therefore, the navy was vital to her interests. That England was an island was a fact of great importance, since it was at once the source of her special character and of her impregnability—as *Appleton House* had emphasized. Because of the navy, 'The Ocean is the Fountain of Command' (*First Anniversary*, 369); by the same token, as the title of his friend, James Harrington's *Oceana* suggests, the sea was a metaphor for power.[2] While it was the instrument of her ambitions overseas, equally England's navy was the factor upon which her survival depended: 'our safety, our trade, our being, and our well-being, depend upon our forces at sea' (Marvell quoting Bridgman, *GP*, 268). In *GP*, therefore, the navy's strength is a major issue, crystallizing Marvell's argument about England's struggle to preserve herself as the Elect Nation (364, 383).

His appeal for the refitting and restoration of the navy in *GP* is anticipated, in his *Last Instructions* (1667), by a bitter diatribe against current politicking at the expense of the fleet, and by a lament of the Chatham naval disaster, at which British vessels were destroyed on inland waters (311-28, 397-410, 522f.):

> There our sick Ships unrigg'd in Summer lay,
> Like molting Fowl, a weak and easie Prey.
> For whose strong bulk Earth scarce could Timber find,
> The Ocean Water, or the Heavens Wind.
> Those Oaken Gyants of the ancient Race,
> That rul'd all Seas, and did our Channel grace.
> The conscious Stag so, once the Forests dread,
> Flies to the Wood, and hides his harmless Head.
>
> (573–80)

The fate of this once great and powerful navy is an image of England's degeneration, as Marvell views it; the reaction of Monk to this disaster is representative, in this poem, of all who treasure England's true role. Her power, reflected in this navy, once 'rul'd all Seas' but it is now reduced to 'a weak and easie Prey'. In this fall of the mighty England's naval power is compared to the stag, 'Once the Forests dread', but now 'harmless': an image which recalls the equally timid 'Caledonian *Deer*', which was used to denote Scots "cowardice" in the *Horatian Ode*. In both poems a fundamental political weakness is implied by the image. In contrast, Marvell's formulation of England's former glory—'Those Oaken Gyants of the ancient Race'—recalls his characterization of England's heroes, the Fairfaxes, as the 'great Race', whom in *Appleton House* he compared to the trees that provided the 'Keels' of England's navy. There, as here, England's greatness—and great Englishmen—are involved in that symbol and instrument of her power, the navy.

Related to England's sea-power was her characterization as a special kind of island. Traditionally, Britain was regarded as a manifestation of the mythical 'Fortunate Isles'.[4] The *locus classicus* for the motif of the Fortunate Isles was Pliny's *Naturalis Historia*, as islands of the Gods or Isles of Bliss.[5] Often identified with the Canary Islands,[6] these were a typically pliable conception, since they provided an image of a terrestrial paradise, 'Fortunate' in every respect, which could be, and was, frequently compounded with such other paradises as the Isles of the Blest, the Hesperidean Gardens and the Elysian Fields:[7]

> Or other Worlds they seem'd, or happy Isles,
> Like those Hesperian Gardens fam'd of old,
> Fortunate Fields, and Groves and flow'ry Vales,
> Thrice happy Isles.
>
> (*PL*. III. 567–70)[8]

These Christiano-classical conflations of the Fortunate Isles with other terrestrial paradises could also extend to the 'floating islands' of Pliny[9] and the 'flying island' of Macaria, satirized by Swift's 'Laputa' in *Gulliver's Travels*.[11] Deriving from the Renaissance mythographer, Comes,[12] such syntheses allowed much exotic reference, overlaying the usual paradisal qualities of pleasant aspects, effortless plenitude and 'eternal Spring': most specifically, the Fortunate Isles emphasize happiness,[13] always located in the West as islands off the Atlantic Ocean.[14] The significance of a "Western happiness" is eschatological, since there the sun declines to its End. Such significance came about because of a Renaissance tradition which identified the classically 'remote islands' of Britain, in the West and off the Atlantic, with the Fortunate Isles,[15] and which lies behind Shakespeare's eulogy of England as 'This other Eden' in *Richard II*—recalling, as usual in such instances, England's temperate climate and fertility.[16] For Elizabethan historians England as Fortunate Isle naturally came to reflect her especial fortune as the Elect Nation:[17] her "remoteness" took on the character of an isolation from the sins of a world dominated by Antichrist. In that character England provided a foretaste of the ultimate renovation or new world. While for Milton the Fortunate Isles were 'other Worlds', so for Marvell England's island was 'another world' because of her 'distinct . . . faith'.

The image of England as Fortunate Isle/Elect Nation was used by poets in conjunction with her peculiar naval character, symbolized by her archaic name 'Albion', Albion being the son of Neptune, god of the sea.[18] Exemplifying this idea in his description of the marriage of rivers Thames and

Medway, Spenser portrays England as Albion, her 'warlike people' heirs to Neptune's—naval—power (*FQ* IV. xi. 15). This stanza is the known source of a passage in Marvell's *Last Instructions*,[19]—heretofore not well understood—where the same rivers lament the fate of the navy at Chatham:

> When aged *Thames* was bound with Fetters base,
> And *Medway* chast ravish'd before his Face,
> And their dear Off-spring murder'd in their sight;
>
> . . .
>
> Sad change, since first that happy pair was wed,
> When all the Rivers grac'd their Nuptial Bed;
> And Father *Neptune* promis'd to resign
> His Empire old, to their immortal Line!
>
> . . .
>
> But most they for their Darling *Charles* complain:
> And were it burnt, yet less would be their pain.
> To see that fatal Pledge of Sea-Command,
> Now in the Ravisher *De-Ruyter*'s hand
>
> (743–58)

Here Marvell recalls that 'Father Neptune promis'd to resign/His Empire old' to England, as represented by the 'Line' of Thames and Medway. That power is proper to England's especial character,[20] and both that character and that power are represented by Marvell in this poem as lost due to a popish regime, and the debility of the navy. The loss of the *Royal Charles* has a symbolic import: just as, earlier in the poem, it represented for Monk England's 'sacred' power (611ff.), so here it is 'that fatal Pledge of Sea-Command'. Lost to the Dutch, it symbolizes the loss of England's naval supremacy. As a concomitant, it represents also a degeneration of England's 'Elect' *imperium*, a special implication of the ship's name as used by Marvell here; for 'Darling Charles', the heir to Neptune's 'immortal Line', is at once the ship and its eponymous owner Charles II. The king's power is precisely this 'fatal Pledge of Sea-Command'; the descendant of Albion and heir to his 'Empire' has lost that power. Marvell implies that Charles II has allowed the Elect Nation to lose her proper nature and with it her power.

Hence the thematic significance of Marvell's Spenserian reminiscence, since *FQ* celebrated the Protestant Empire of England under Elizabeth. This and 'Neptune[s] . . . Empire' are one and the same, for as *Smirke* stated, England is a Fortunate Isle because 'under an imperial crown'. Therefore in this poem England is a Fortunate Island 'ravished' by the Dutch admiral, De Ruyter:

> *Ruyter* the while, that had our Ocean curb'd,
> Sail'd now among our Rivers undisturb'd:
> Survey'd their Crystal Streams, and Banks so green,
> And Beauties e're this never naked seen.
> Through the vain sedge the bashful *Nymphs* he ey'd;
> Bosomes, and all which from themselves they hide.
> (523–8)

Here England is a virgin—undefiled by antichristian incursion, chaste in her uncorrupted religion, like Spenser's Una—whose 'Beauties e're this [were] never naked seen', exposed to the salacious gaze of the invader. These amorous metaphors for the invasion, like the sexual threat to Una, imply the antichristian mode of 'fornication', just as the invader's prurient enjoyment is metonymic for the antichristian idolatry that 'fornication' symbolizes. Thus the rape by De Ruyter the 'Ravisher' (758) is contrasted to the lawful 'Nuptial Bed' of Thames and Medway, the generation of England's power. In the subsequent lines, as the invader presses inland, England's religio-political virginity is linked to her 'Beauties' as the Fortunate Isle:

> The Sun much brighter, and the Skies more clear,
> He finds the *Air*, and all things, sweeter here.
> The sudden change, and such a tempting sight,
> Swells his old Veins with fresh Blood, fresh Delight.
> Like am'rous Victors he begins to shave,
> And his new Face looks in the *English* Wave.
> His sporting Navy all about him swim,
> And witness their complaisence in their trim.
> Their streaming Silks play through the weather fair,
> And with inveigling Colours Court the Air.
> While the red Flags breath on their Top-masts high
> Terrour and War, but want an Enemy.
> Among the Shrowds the Seamen sit and sing,
> And wanton Boys on every Rope do cling.

> Old *Neptune* springs the Tydes, and Water lent:
> (The Gods themselves do help the provident.)
> And, where the deep Keel on the shallow cleaves,
> With *Trident*'s Leaver, and great Shoulder heaves.
> *Aeolus* their Sails inspires with *Eastern* Wind,
> Puffs them along, and breathes upon them kind.
> With Pearly Shell the *Tritons* all the while
> Sound the Sea-march, and guide to *Sheppy Isle*.
>
> (529–50)

Here the Dutch invasion becomes a pleasure-cruise, because they 'want an Enemy'. England's navy is unprepared because of her government's folly—an improvidence at which Marvell's sarcasm is aimed, when he notes that 'The Gods themselves do help the provident'; in this case, England's enemy, since England and Providence are no longer at one, and thus Neptune, too, has defected to the Dutch (cf.749). England's degeneration from her Elect Nationhood and her loss of maritime hegemony are two faces of the same coin. Similarly, as her integrity was once *virgo intacta*, rape must be the antichristian form of her lost identity.

Certainly England displays here the 'Crystal Streams', the verdancy ('Banks so green'), the 'brighter' sun, and 'clear' air, and kind winds (547) which are characteristic of this terrestrial paradise: 'all things [are] sweeter here' in the Fortunate Isle. However, this beauty serves merely to delight the invader, to emparadise his fleet, and to forward their aims. Aeolus 'breathes upon them kind', speeding them to their work of destruction, while 'the Tritons' guide them to Chatham. What Marvell has done here is to represent a breakage of that vital connection, of England's 'Fortunate' character and her protective navy. Of this breakage Neptune's defection is an enaction. The Fortunate Isle gives 'complaisence' only to the conqueror, and thereby becomes unfortunate:

> So have I seen in *April*'s bud, arise
> A Fleet of Clouds, sailing along the Skies:
> The liquid Region with their Squadrons fill'd,
> The airy Sterns the Sun behind does guild:
> And gentle Gales them steer, and Heaven drives,

When, all on sudden, their calm bosome rives
With Thunder and Lightning from each armed Cloud;
Shepherds themselves in vain in bushes shrowd.
Such up the stream the *Belgick* Navy glides,
And at *Sheerness* unloads its stormy sides.

(551–560)

This "apotheosis" of the Dutch fleet is an ironic comment upon England's lost status: 'Heaven' is with the Dutch. They have assumed not only her erstwhile arbiter, Neptune, but also her fortunate character: the passage opened with England's 'Beauties'; in lines 530–550 they were enjoyed by the Dutch; and in these lines those beauties are actually assimilated to the Dutch themselves. By means of this carefully modulated description, England's 'fortunate' aspect passes over to the Dutch fleet: their "invasion" is an absorption of her character. By means of this character-transference Marvell conveys the Dutch usurpation of England's role as the foremost naval power.

To critics, the fleet's transformation into a 'fortunate' image may have looked curious at first sight,[21] but once Marvell's logic is understood the apotheosis of De Ruyter's navy can be seen to participate in his thematic pattern here. Moreover, the vital connection between this 'fortunate' character and maritime power is immediately enforced by the swift transition from apotheosis to destruction: 'all on sudden, their calm bosome rives/With Thunder and Lightning from each armed Cloud'. To assume the 'Fortunate' character is also to become militarily powerful, and this traditional linkage is enacted by the aggression of the 'Fortunate' vessels.

Reflected in the image of rape, that aggression is the antichristian mode of invasion, usurpation, and fornication, seconded by the image of devouring. The Chatham disaster is a 'Black Day! . . ./Thee, the Year's monster, let thy Dam devour' (737–40). The source of the disaster is, of course, Charles II, whom the poem has already characterized as "lost" to antichristianism in the form of his eponymous vessel. This covert attack upon the monarch is continued equally subtly (necessarily so, of course) in the poem's exit, where the king's notorious lechery is implicitly related to antichristian ravishment of England:

> Raise up a sudden Shape with Virgins Face,
> . . .
> Naked as born. . .
> . . .
> And silent tears her secret anguish speak. . .
> The Object strange in him no Terrour mov'd:
> . . .
> And with kind hand does the coy Vision press,
> Whose Beauty greater seem'd by her distress;
> . . .
> And he Divin'd twas *England* or the *Peace.*
>
> (891–906)

Here England the Virgin/Elect Nation reproaches Charles with the 'anguish' to which his policies have condemned her, her bound arms (893) symbolizing the 'French thraldome' which (as *GP* complained) had driven England into her impious war with the Dutch. Subsequently, the French 'Lewis' is seen to call the tune (914). Thus Charles' sexual designs upon the virgin intimate that vitiation from within that has exposed England to her vitiation from without. Similarly, as 'England or the Peace', this virgin is at once Una-like true religion and government, and Astraean power devolved upon England by Una's original, Elizabeth. That image recollects that England, not Holland, is the true imperial power on the Augustan model: Astraea and the Fortunate Isles are images linked by holy imperialism.

That linkage is at the heart of *Britannia and Rawleigh* (c. 1675), a satire once attributed to Marvell and generally assumed to be written by a colleague of similar views.[22] Here Charles' antichristian government, symbolized by 'Leviathans and absolute commands' (32), is opposed to Spenser's vision of his Virgin Queen's as the 'Golden dayes' (45) when England's naval might suppressed the antichristian Spanish armada (44). Elizabeth as 'Gloriana' is the Astraean Virgo recalling the star of Augustan imperial destiny (50–8),[23] counterpointed by a Duessan figure of antichristian pride and warmongering (59–70) who figures forth the French domination of Charles' regime. It is she who engineers the rape of Britain's virginal three kingdoms (99–101) by their own king. At the end of the poem England's resurrection is envisaged, as her activism throws off Antichrist and 'Freed by thy labours, Fortunate blest Isle,/The Earth shall rest' in the final Sabbath Day (191–2). Here the regaining of her chosen status makes of England's 'Fortunate Isle' an image of her reformation or renovation. That image implies at once England's proper nature at all times, and her final glory in the new world of *renovatio* after the End.

It is equally important to note that, in Jacobean and Caroline propaganda, the Fortunate motif was buckled to the sacred sanctions of monarchy. In Ben Jonson's masque *The Fortunate Isles, and their Union* (1626), King James is identified with Neptune, his son Charles with Albion, both personifying sea-power.[24] By naval means Britain achieves renovatory and messianic apotheosis, by the Coming of the Fortunate Isles to Britannia,[25] in the form of the floating island of Macaria.[26] As Macaria lands upon England, the country achieves her true identity as 'That where the Happy Spirits live', inspired by James as Macar, the happy or blessed one.[27] The paradisal features of Macaria[28] are thus politicized as emanations of divine monarchy, implemented as sea-power.[29] In *Neptune's Triumph*, the unperformed masque from which this was adapted,[30] Macarian England and her sea-power were characterized as Elect by the symbols in Inigo Jones' design, and by the typing of Prince Charles as the Prince of Peace Himself;[31] the prince's return from Spain hence signifying that Coming which brings renovation and Macaria.[32] Similarly, in *The Fortunate Isles* James as Macar recalls Christ the King,[33] appropriating the biblical portrayal of Christ as the King of the Isles (Psalm 97:1), an aspect of His final Kingdom.[34]

In this nexus of images, then, England as Macaria, Fortunate Isle, sea-power and Astraean *imperator* is envisioned in her religio-political propriety and in her future renovation within the final Kingdom of Christ. In the 1640s and 50s this admixture was capable of combination with other maritime symbols—like the Ark of the Church and the Ship of State—which carried equally significant political freight. In this context, traditional symbols achieved a new pointedness. The ancient notion of life as a 'voyage'[35] saw heaven as its destination, and the Soul is 'ready oft the Port to gain' of heaven (*Dialogue Between the Soul and Body*, 29). Works like Anthony Nixon's *The Christian Navy* (1602) described the Ship of the Soul negotiating the 'Tempests' of life and the 'rockes' of temptation as it sails to heaven through the 'sea' of the World.[36] While in Thomas Adams' *The Spiritual Navigator Bound for the Holy Land* (1615), heaven was also the destination; by the 1640s this trope had become specifically eschatological: to haste unto the Coming was to desire the port of the New Jerusalem, like a sailor longing for shore-leave.[37] Similarly, the classical image of the Ship of State[38] became, in the controversy leading up to the Civil War, a metaphor in the armoury of parliamentarians, which argued that if the mariners of a ship could oust an incompetent captain, a people could depose a king.[39] That justification for revolution was recalled in *First Anniversary*, where the 'lusty Mate' Cromwell rescues the storm-tossed Ship of State.[40] (However, against those who see this as a republican moment in the poem, it should be stressed that Marvell undermines the revolutionary idea by resubmitting the 'Passengers' to another individual authority, mate in place of captain: Cromwell is, as usual, the king who is not a king.) The goal of the state was the establishment of the New Jerusalem in England, the Millennium in which the saints rule on earth (Revelation 5:10; 20:4).[41] Towards the same goal sailed the Ark of the Church Militant. Herbert's eponymous poem envisages that Ark pressing its way ever westward— the locale of sunset and thus of the Last Day—pursued by tribulation and persecution which enforce that westward movement.[42] So would Marvell, describing the same Latter Day tribulation, recall 'when *Religion* did it self imbark,/And from the *East* would *Westward* steer its Ark' (*The Character of Holland*, 67–8). In Puritan thought the Church and the state were on the same journey, identifying the Ship of State and the Ark in the voyage of reformation.[43] The journey westward to renovation was the New Israel's antitype of the crossing of the Red Sea, Antichrist chasing after.[44] Since their destination is eschatological, the sea they navigate is at once the world—spatial—and the world's duration, in time. The image of the waters as Time complements the notion of life's voyage:

> Like the vain Curlings of the Watry maze,
> Which in smooth streams a sinking Weight does raise;
> So Man, declining alwayes, disappears
> In the weak Circles of increasing Years;
> And his short Tumults of themselves Compose,
> While flowing Time above his Head does close.
>
> (*First Anniversary*, 1–6)

The waters of Time are the location of the Ship of Church-State. Since only Cromwell's mastery of time can affect this 'flowing Time' under which other men 'sink', at the end of the poem the watery metaphor returns to show how Cromwell alone can make the waters 'Heal'. Since, in Revelation's image, the waters are nations, the image becomes self-reflexive: the Ship of State sails upon the waters of the-State-in-Time. The journey through political, temporal, and worldly waters is simultaneous.

The eschatological goal was not conceived in merely metaphorical terms: there was a sustained attempt to implement practical projects which imitated scriptural description of the final paradise. The New Jerusalem was to be a place where man controlled his environment,[45] and to this end Puritanism fuelled the scientific revolution in this century. If the New Jerusalem was to be built by the saints,[46] this practical effort was encouraged by the issue of manifestoes of reform at all levels, especially by the heirs of Bacon, who in the 1650s had a major impact upon Puritan thought.[47] His utopian *New Atlantis* (1626)[48] envisioned the reformed scientific paradise on a secret island in the West. Its scientific academy, 'Salomon's House', recalls the Temple's builder, who is the model for all modern builders of the new Temple; the paradise of 'Bensalem' is so called because Christ is 'King of Salem, King of Peace'[49] in the last Kingdom. This vision was imitated especially by Samuel Hartlib's *A Description of the famous Kingdome of Macaria . . .* (1641), where Macaria provided for the vision of England's parliamentarian renovation 'a Fiction, as a more mannerly way'.[50] The Macarian image apotheosizes plain religion, prosperity, fecundity, defensible security and might:[51] 'how the Kingdome of England may be happy'.[52] Macaria and the Fortunate Isles are visions of England's ideal renovated state, 'Oute from the worlde yet on the grounde, euen in a place of blisse', 'a new world beyond the ocean'.[53] England as Macaria is poised between present world and future world, in time and beyond it.

(ii) NEW WORLDS WON AT SEA: *BLAKE*

It was understood that the discovery of the New World was itself a sign of the Latter Days, the improved art of navigation that facilitated discovery being part of the Last Age's fuller revelation of knowledge.[54] The discovery of America, seemingly unknown for so many centuries, was a sign of the special revelation,[55] and divinely dispensed for acquisition by the Protestant *imperium* which was to arise in the Latter Days. God had reserved this revelation until the moment was ripe for the establishment of that *imperium*, and therefore the moment of empire was come.[56] The Astraean *imperator* hence symbolized the domination of the New World by means of her mystic sea-power,[57] and here England fought the same Holy War as in the Old World of Europe,[58] for Spanish power in the western lands was an extension of the Antichristian Empire.[59] Indeed, the Spanish threat came from within as well as without, fomenting domestic subversion even as two imperialist efforts clashed in the new territories. Pressed especially by clerical propaganda, pro-colonial and anti-Spanish aims were focused on the policy that England—always most fortunate at sea—must best Antichrist in naval warfare.[60]

Propagandists of godly colonization stressed that God had reserved the Americas for 'his Englishmen', and the settlement of Virginia, Bermuda, and Guiana would fulfil His will.[61] The notoriety of the Bermudas was God's fiction, preserving it from others until His English should acquire it.[62] The Americas were thus to be components of godly England, 'Daughters of England' and members of 'this English body'.[63] As another England yet the same, they provided the western destination for the renovated England,[64] divinely ordained Promised Land as Canaan had been for the Old Israel[65]—at once a present terrestrial paradise and the figura of the New Jerusalem.[66] As 'Englands out of England', 'New Britaines in another World',[67] the Americas could provide a transferred image of England in *renovatio*, a geographical destination which was also a terminus in time. Equally, if the Fortunate Isles which mythologized that image were also transferred to the 'Western Canaan',[68] they would by moving further westward regain their character as geographically remote, and the New World aptly embodied the New Earth. More specifically, the pleasant Bermudas could provide a real counterpart of the blissful Isles.

In Marvell's *Upon the Victory Obtained by Blake* the poetic process of transferal is under way, based upon the *desolatio/renovatio* motif as effected by the navy in *The Character of Holland*. In the latter the Dutch are vanquished by God's providential dispensation to the English navy:

> While the Sea laught it self into a foam,
> 'Tis true since that (as fortune kindly sports,)
> A wholesome Danger drove us to our Ports.
> While half their banish'd keels the Tempest tost,
> Half bound at home in Prison to the frost:
> That ours mean time at leizure might careen,
> In a calm Winter, under Skies Serene.
> As the obsequious Air and Waters rest,
> Till the dear *Halcyon* hatch out all its nest.
> The *Common wealth* doth by its losses grow;
> And, like its own Seas, only Ebbs to flow.
> Besides that very Agitation laves,
> And purges out the corruptible waves.
> . . .
> Their Navy all our Conquest or our Wreck.
> (122–40)

Here England's navy is repaired, and subsequently victorious, because of providential care. As for the individual saint, this is the godly navy's quietist interval, encapsulated by the words 'mean time' (127) and 'Now. . .now' (135, 137). Restorative like all such intervals, it is a fortunate *desolatio* or 'wholesome Danger' which 'purges' (134). Similarly, in *First Anniversary* the kings of the earth recognize England's navy as their scourge and the agent of Protestant *imperium*:

> Theirs are not Ships, but rather Arks of War.
>
> . . .
>
> Of floting Islands a new Hatched Nest;
> A Fleet of Worlds, of other Worlds in quest;
>
> . . .
>
> [Which] sink the Earth that does at Anchor ride.
>
> (357–64)

The navy that is the embodiment of apocalypse is the power that brings all nations into the one last Kingdom: 'those that have the Waters for their share,/Can quickly leave us neither Earth nor Air.' (371–2). English expansion *is* the Kingdom. Ultimately her navy is England, in quest of her apotheosized self—'A Fleet of Worlds, of other Worlds in quest'—and the timbers of her ships are herself in her 'Oaken Forrests' (353). When these 'floting Islands' land, so does Macaria on earth. This sanctification of Cromwellian England's imperial ambitions makes Cromwell the 'Monarch' of the seas, on the Messianic model (*Death of O.C.*, 167ff.). These images coalesce in *Upon the Victory Obtained by Blake over the Spaniards, in the Island of Teneriffe, 1657*. This poem has long lain under a critical cloud,[69] partly because of a distaste for its manner, but it is central to Marvell's vision of England in the 1650s, and its manner is condign to his theme. The poem is not merely politically partisan but an expression of the vital importance of Protestant *imperium*—that which, for Marvell, is in question when Blake attacks the Spanish.

In the current political analysis, it was believed that the harrying and capture of Spanish shipments of plate from the New World was the readiest means of weakening her antichristian empire.[70] Blake's success also proved the point that the true *imperium*'s best agent was her navy, here recapitulating the victory over the Spanish in 1588. The treasure-fleet itself represents Spain's tyrannous imperial ambitions and guilty dominion in the New World:

> Now does *Spains* Fleet her spatious wings unfold,
> Leaves the new World and hastens for the old:
> But though the wind was fair, they slowly swoome
> Frayted with acted Guilt, and Guilt to come:
> For this rich load, of which so proud they are,
> Was rais'd by Tyranny, and rais'd for War;
> Every capatious Gallions womb was fill'd,
> With what the Womb of wealthy Kingdomes yield,
> The new Worlds wounded Intrails they had tore,
> For wealth wherewith to wound the old once more.
>
> (1–10)

Here Marvell recalls the object of English policy, Spain's maintenance of her armies by means of the New World's riches: the fleet's is a 'rich load. . .rais'd for War', 'new Worlds. . .wealth wherewith to wound the old [World] once more.' This rape of the New World's 'Womb' is characteristically antichristian. Their voyage is furtive because knowingly guilty, fearing 'the Sun's light,/With *English* Streamers' (19–20); that is, the 'light' of revelation given by Christ the Sun to His chosen nation. The sea itself is 'that boundless Empire, where [Cromwell gives] the Law' (14), and on it they trespass like the antichristian usurpers they are, pretending to their false *imperium*. Such is the English monopoly on God's favour that 'To fight against such Foes' is useless, since the ocean that destroys others is where the English 'triumphantly do live' (85–8). By such means the Spanish themselves are brought to articulate England's true hegemony.

The Spaniards' invasion of the true empire's sea repeats their depredation of the New World: by their avarice (6–11) desolation plunders the New World, importing into it the sins of the Old. Their carriage of the New treasures to the Old World geographically enacts antichristian reversion to corruption, reversing the eschatological drive to turn old into new.

This inversion of renovation into desolation is developed into the variations upon the theme of *desolatio/renovatio* which form the body of the poem. As instigator of war (45–50), Spain is the agent of desolation; but because of the English right, Spain becomes her own victim in the act of provoking war: 'Peace, against you, was the sole strength of

Spain' (50). Thus Cromwell's 'Conquering Sword' (44) is the active instrument of renovation—a just war—while Spain's 'broken. . .Swords' (46) are symbols of a necessarily self-reflexive desolation. England's right is to defend the Canary Islands—traditionally the Fortunate—from antichristian invasion and desolation, such as Spain had imported into the renovation of the Americas, too:

> they behold the sweet Canary Isles;
> One of which doubtless is by Nature blest
> Above both Worlds, since 'tis above the rest.
> . . .
> And these want nothing Heaven can afford,
> Unless it be, the having you their Lord;
> (24–42)

Emphasizing that they are 'fertile', temperate, peaceful, and inhabited by a 'happy People', this passage has long been recognized as portraying the Fortunate Islands,[71] although its specific relation to England's character as Elect Nation has not been recognized. Teneriffe is specifically Macaria, 'above the rest' both in blessings and in its floating locale. Signifying a geographically distant *renovatio*, the island is caused to reflect back on England by its evocation as Cromwell's inheritance: 'Your worth to all these Isles, a just right brings,/The best of Lands should have the best of Kings' (39–40), in which the best land is England as Macaria, in renovation. Here Marvell hints that Cromwell should accept the crown, which was proffered to him at this time.[72] Since the Macarian England has not yet been realized, there is a short time lapse before Cromwell's activism gains it: 'this great want, will not a long one prove,/Your Conquering Sword will soon that want remove' (43–4). To acquire these islands is to implement the Protestant *imperium* which, simultaneously, involves the realization of a Macarian England: national and international renovation are identical goals. Contrasting with Spain's antichristian importation of Old into New, the English right brings New to match New World. England's is a just war because 'War will make [the islands] yours' and God's (52), an Ending war; that is,

English arms are renovators while Spain's are desolators. In this light it can be seen that the poem is not 'literal', as some have suggested, distinguishing it from Marvell's usual mode.[73] The problematic of *Blake* fuses a propagandist chronicle of the event with that event's peculiarly apposite signification of renovation. This problematic answers yet another critical cavil, that 'this naval victory has to be made into some sort of fairy tale before Marvell could be at home with it', because of course Marvell is much too fastidious to be at home with propaganda, and the fantastic mode of the poem is an index of his discomfort.[74] Marvell is far from fastidious where apocalyptic commitments are concerned, and the 'fairy tale' terms in which he portrays the engagement are an experiment in creating the otherworldly and mythic atmosphere proper to renovatory visions. The engagement is a parable of the world's fate as decided in the war of true and false *imperia*.

England's fleet is seen to preserve the ideal renovated place from antichristian despoliation:

> There the indulgent Soil that rich Grape breeds,
> Which of the Gods the fancied drink exceeds;
> They still do yield, such is their pretious mould,
> All that is good, and are not curst with Gold.
>
> (53–6)

The Canaries are a Golden Age, New Jerusalem place; traditionally, the presence of material gold corrupted the Golden Age,[75] and this is the threat represented by the advent of the Spanish plate fleet. The new earth, already figured as the Fortunate Isles here, is further specified by the 'rich Grape' or wine of Christ's redeeming blood, rich to purchase salvation in contrast to antichristian gold and worldliness. This is the New Jerusalem, indulgent to man in all things, as Milton had said it would be (*De Doctrina*, 493). In a Miltonic method, indeed, Marvell portrays this paradise as outdoing its classical counterparts, like the pagan 'fancy' of ambrosia as the immortal food. The Spaniards' 'fatal Gold' (57–64) is explicitly seen as having corrupted the Americas and threatening to corrupt *this* New World, too.

Because of the godly function of the English as warriors for renovation, the Spanish provocation of war and desolation is seen to rebound upon itself, imprisoning the Spanish in paradoxes which imply the great fortunate paradox of *desolatio et renovatio.*

> Peace, against you, was the sole strength of *Spain.*
> . . .
> For *Santacruze* the glad Fleet takes her way,
> And safely there casts Anchor in the Bay.
> Never so many with one joyful cry,
> That place saluted, where they all must dye.
> Deluded men! Fate with you did but sport,
> You scap't the Sea, to perish in your Port.
>   (52, 67–72)

Spain destroys herself by provoking war; in seeking refuge from Blake in the port, the fleet falls captive to him. For theirs is the false destination and haven, the true counterpart being the port of the New Jerusalem—this port, indeed, but it belongs to the English by renovating right. The paradoxes, semantic and conceptual, in which Marvell enmeshes Spain recall that the antichristian power is allowed by God in the cause of ultimate Christian victory at the End. Therefore the Spaniard's delusion of security here recalls that 'when they shall say, Peace and safety, then sudden destruction cometh upon them. . .and they shall not escape' the wrath of God at the End (I Thessalonians 5:3). The Spaniards' fate at Santacruze is a foretaste of the ending of all antichristian power. This is the antichristian confidence and hubris: 'So proud and confident of their made strength' (96). Their pride is countered by a fortunate paradox, that it is assimilated to England's glory: ' 'Twas more for *Englands* fame you should dye there,/Where you had most of strength' (73–4).

It is antichristian pride that causes wars, here disrupting the Macarian peace (at first there 'the jarring Elements no discord know' and 'coolness. . .with heat doth never fight' (35f.), recalling *Hastings'* image of war as 'turnaments of these sublunary Elements'). This desolating of the peace is enacted by a Babel-like pride in fortifications: the Spanish are 'Fond. . .restless. . .proud and confident. . .boasting', with a 'vast. . .pride' (92–102). Blake's breaching of their proud defences is thus further to the glory of the English in their successful assault upon so daunting a fortress. This antichristian presumption, assimilated into English glory, is associated with the image of *imperium*: 'Seas as vast as is the *Spaniards* pride' (102). In reasserting English right to the sea-*imperium*, Blake's 'renown' is effectively Cromwell's, since the latter is the Protestant Emperor (101). The antichristian Babel becomes his monument: 'They only Labour to exalt your praise' (94). This cumulative process of redeeming desolation into renovation is summed up when 'this [Spanish] Fleets design'd by fate' for the good of England (117).

Because this naval engagement anticipates the last apocalyptic battle, it is rendered in apocalyptic terms: 'enflam'd', 'War turn'd the temperate, to the Torrid Zone' (122–4), transforming the renovated place into a desolation. 'Fate these two Fleets, between both Worlds had brought./Who fight, as if for both those Worlds they fought' (125–6). Decreed by providence, this encounter brings English *imperium* into confrontation with its antichristian counterpart. Geographically, they meet 'between both Worlds', the Old of Europe and the New Americas; figuratively, this is the temporal moment of transformation which makes over old world into new earth. This encounter, representing the period of Last Day war and desolation before the renovation, decides the contest between Christian and antichristian empires that leads to the Kingdom: hence they 'fight, as if for both those Worlds they fought'. If the encounter is representative, so is the English victory, indicating and prophesying the inevitable triumph of Protestantism in the world. The inevitability of that outcome has been foreshadowed throughout the poem by the fortunate paradoxes which contain the Spaniards' activities. Marvell has already said to Cromwell that 'I draw that Scene, where you ere long,/Shall conquests act' (65–6); Macaria is a future 'Scene' in the historical drama, a visionary place. By such means Marvell achieves transition to the representative moment of battle itself—'Whilst I draw that Scene. . .your present [conquests] are unsung'—stipulating, in effect, that the Macarian image applies to the future time of which present conquest is just a foretaste. It is the so-called fantastic mode of the poem that allows such temporal and visionary shifts of perspective.

The prophetic context is made explicit in the description of an apocalyptic combat:

> Thousands of wayes, Thousands of men there dye,
> . . .
>   Urg'd by the active fire.
> Which by quick powders force, so high was sent,
> That it return'd to its own Element.
> Torn Limbs some leagues into the Island fly,
> Whilst others lower, in the Sea do lye.
> Scarce souls from bodies sever'd are so far,
> By death, as bodies there were by the War.
> Th' all-seeing Sun, neer gaz'd on such a sight,
> Two dreadful Navies there at Anchor Fight.
> . . .
> There one must Conquer, or there both must dye.
>
>   (127–40)

The images of conflagration, echoing that of the previous paragraph, imitate such features of the End as the 'lake of fire' of Revelation (19–20). Similarly, the apparently extravagant image of flying limbs combines eschatological with Fortunate Isles lore. Pliny had said that the Isles were vexed by the whale-carcasses washed up on their shores,[76] transformed here into human carcasses whose "invasion" of the island represents the incursion of desolation and death into the land of *renovatio*. The distribution of human remains imitates that of Revelation, where men can be judged only when 'the sea gave up the dead that were in it, and death and hell delivered up the dead that were in them' (20:13). This imitation of features of the universal cataclysm is supported by the next couplet's reminder of the *telos*, where the severance of soul and body in death is pertinent to the foregoing reminiscence of Revelation's resurrection of the dead, in which soul and body rejoin. Without such End-dominated connotations, the image would be gratuitous indeed. These recollections of Revelation 20 type this moment as envisaging the last desolation, upon which in Revelation 21 the 'new heavens and new earth' supervene; this combat is desolation subserving renovation, because of the English victory.

The context is established at the beginning and at the end of the passage. 'Thousands of wayes, Thousands of men' is an English equivalent of the '*Mille* modis monstrat *mille* per indicia' ('in a thousand ways and by a thousand signs') by which Marvell's *Illustrissimo Viro* introduces its Signs of the End,[77] looking forward to the Millennium. This numerological signal of the End is succeeded at the close of the passage by the signal of Coming: 'Th'all-seeing Sun' is especially the Sun of Righteousness, deciding the engagement as the omniscient Judge of the End.

The climactic and decisive nature of the engagement is stressed, that 'One must Conquer, or. . .both must dye' only 'There. . .there', in that representative location where the fate of the whole world comes to crisis. Their motives are crucially different: 'Necessity did them, but Choice did us' impel (142). Like the free choice of the Fairfaxes to go with destiny, the English 'Choice' to hazard themselves in war is a commitment to providence: 'A choice which did the highest worth express,/And was attended by as high success' (143–4). In other words, the English are guilty of neither piracy nor greed (as their enemies might contend) but look rather to the godly and inevitable spoils of providence's way.

The power of victory emanates from Cromwell, because he is the Protestant Emperor. Hence Marvell's attribution of Blake's victory to Cromwell is not just an awkward necessity of panegyric but an enactment of the imperial idea; as, in *First Anniversary*, Cromwell was the 'Star' of divine influence, so here he is like 'prosperous Stars' (147) whose influence decides the engagement at Santacruze by channelling the power of godliness through his agents. The issue is another fortunate paradox, 'Laurels reapt ev'n on the Mayn' (146), where no laurels grow.

Because their treasure is sunk, Spanish gold is prevented from vitiating the renovatory place (151–2), and this is symbolic of the permanent state of preservation and peace that is final renovation:

> Ages to come, your conquering Arms will bless,
> There they destroy, what had destroy'd their Peace.

And in one War the present age may boast,
The certain seeds of many Wars are lost.

(157–60)

When England makes war it is really making peace. This may
seem an awkwardly rhetorical justification of war, but in
terms of the poem's eschatological logic Marvell's point is
valid. The Spaniards provoke war, and because they are
antichristian a retaliatory warfare is not a desolation similar to
theirs but rather the force of renovation—destroying desolation itself forever. The paradox of the second line here means
precisely that, for 'Peace' is renovation. Sea-power is the
instrument of the new earth's creation: 'the Land owe[s] her
peace unto the Sea' (156). Thus it follows that 'fame. . .tells
the World, how much to you it owes' (167–8), a Final Image
which expresses the universal significance of Cromwell's navy,
which rescues the world itself.

(iii) A REVELATION FOR THE REVOLUTION:
BERMUDAS

Marvell's finest celebration of the New World is *Bermudas*,
dated by general supposition at 1653, when Marvell was
lodging with John Oxenbridge, a divine who had visited the
Bermudas and from whom Marvell may have received the
stimulus and some of the information for the poem.[78] The
date is condign to the poem's concerns first, because Marvell
was by 1653 tutor to Cromwell's ward and, second, because
it is in the early 1650s that the policies of Cromwellian
Protestant *imperium* gave a renewed stimulus to interest in
the New World. Related in its concerns to Marvell's other
poems of the 1650s, *Bermudas* is an *exemplum* and a vision
for Cromwell's revolution and its new era.

Critical comment upon the poem has been somewhat
confused, more especially since certain points have been
accepted as unquestionable without sufficient understanding
of their significance. The poem has been read in two ways:
first, as a celebration of extremist Puritan settlement and/or
an allegory of Eden or various other terrestrial paradises.[79] In
such accounts of the poem the several kinds of paradise are
confused, passing reference nearly always made to the

Fortunate Islands, and gestures at "millenarianism" in relative degrees of vagueness. The relationships between such elements in the poem are little recognized. Second, the poem is sometimes interpreted—presumably in despair at its apparent "simplicity", and a need to disagree with general critical opinion—as ironically iconoclastic towards its 'Puritan' sailors.[80]

In fact, the poem is built upon a prophetic problematic, providing a conjunction of reality and history with vision and exemplum. *Bermudas* is a vision, for Cromwell's England, of its arrival at a New Jerusalem character; an exemplum which recognizes the "interval" that yet interposes between England's current condition and the New Jerusalem to which she aspires.

The sailors of the poem have generally been identified as one or another set of those Puritan "extremists" who had been driven from England by Laudianism. In fact, by the 1650s Puritan voyages of this kind were no longer undertaken for such necessities. The topicality addressed by the poem is that Marvell's sailors are representatives of their England, and their boat—'the *English* boat'—is the contemporary Ship of State and Church, on its westward journey to the New Jerusalem. The islands of the poem are the real Bermudas, recalling the lore of those islands, and thus far the descriptions of Puritan voyage-literature are relevant to the poem.[81] But they are not, as some commentators would have them, paramount—and neither is it relevant to the poem that the Bermudas were subject to dissension and religious squabbles.[82] That Marvell's poem does not refer to the latter has been adduced by some, in a manner which patronizes his Puritanism, as a function of purblind partisanship. But the real Bermudas simply provide an effective historical scenario for an eschatological vision—a counterpart for the New-Jerusalem England, the identification of the two facilitated by the characterization of Bermudas as the Fortunate Isles.

Like the Mowers of *Appleton House*, *Bermudas*' voyagers are engaged in a crossing which is the Latter Day counterpart of the Old Israel's traverse of the Red Sea to their Promised Land. They sail through the Sea of the World, in the Ship of State and Church, to England's apotheosis. Bermuda is at once a material paradise of the New World, and the 'world to come': 'the glorious estate of the Church of God, even in this world; yet so, as it shall end and be consummate in future glory, in the world to come', as in Revelation's own twofold vision.[83] For the New Jerusalem itself was duplicate, earth and heaven joined at last, of this world and of God.[84]. Therefore the voyage to Bermudas enacts Jeremy Taylor's advice that 'we must look some where else for an abiding city, a place in *another countrey*'.[85]

The vision of Bermudas as New Jerusalem/Fortunate Isle is framed by an introduction and a peroration, each of four lines. By this means the vision is circumscribed, as a 'Song' sung by the sailors, and because a prophetic song it is suitably framed and separated from that description of situation which is provided by exordium and peroration. The time of the framing passages is current time, that of the song is visionary, referring to future time. This fact answers a perennial critical problem with this poem; for some critics complain that the sailors do not appear to have arrived at the island yet, but they describe it in their song as if they have already seen it.[86] All prophecy on the model of Revelation describes what is to be as if it had already happened, as St John did, and the features of their island New Jerusalem are known to the sailors because they have been "revealed" in prophecy—they are certain quantities. That description of the island is a vision, the "framing" quatrains are the present from which the vision is 'sung', the present in which they sail towards that destination adumbrated by the vision.

The first quatrain delicately, even mysteriously—as is proper to prophecy—establishes the nature of the poem:

> Where the remote *Bermudas* ride
> In th'Oceans bosome unespy'd,
> From a small Boat, that row'd along,
> The listning Winds receiv'd this Song.
> (1–4)

The islands are located in a fashion suitable to their significance, as "distanced" in time and space: they are 'remote' and 'unespy'd'—the latter word intimating their mysterious quality, as the New Jerusalem not yet "seen" in time. Later we are told that Bermuda was 'an Isle so long unknown' (7), recalling that its "revelation" was reserved for the Latter Days. Here the isles are "hidden" in a manner which intimates that deliberate concealment on God's part, till the English should possess it. Similarly, the location of the islands and of the boat is made self-reflexive: 'Where the remote Bermudas ride. . .a small Boat' locates the boat in an area of imprecise size ('Where. . .'), where the Bermudas also are—a geographic indication, but the 'Where' is vague enough to make us wonder how close the isles and the boat are to one another. They are at least in the same area; the implication of some imminent coincidence of boat and island figures the imminence of England's arrival at her destination, but its imprecise timing intimates also that the interval before that End is necessarily of unknown proportions. The distance ('remote') and mystery ('unespy'd') of this exordium imply the vague time and space of prophetic literature. Of this deliberate mystery the adverb 'along' is an element, since it disguises the direction of movement of the boat and we cannot know whether this movement is backwards or forwards. This may indicate that it is far from certain that England's Ship is progressing, since only the End itself can confirm that; equally, the 'small[ness]' of the boat as contrasted with the 'Ocean' conveys its fragility. These uncertainties are functions of the "interval" before prophecy attains fulfilment: the English boat in the present is interval-bound, the destination 'known' but as yet 'unespy'd'—for, as we recall, only the End makes all manifest and 'seen'.

The 'Bermudas ride/On th'Oceans bosome'; the islands are as it were unrooted, but riding at anchor.[87] This description is at once pertinent to the real islands and also indicative of their eschatological significance. Because very flat,[88] the islands could appear to be afloat on the sea; like the floating Fortunate Isle of Macaria, which in Jonson's masque "landed" on England, bringing her New Jerusalem. The "landing" is particularly appropriate since the New Jerusalem itself was understood to descend onto earth from heaven (Revelation 21:2).[89] So here the similarly floating Bermudas have come to rest as if at anchor; the 'Ocean' is once again the setting for a vision of England's destiny.

The mysterious ambience of this frame is further enhanced by the similarly unlocated 'Song'. The singers are neither present in the language, nor identified; a fact which supports the universalizing, prophetic mode of the poem. Similarly, the 'Song' does not seem to have a specific direction, since only 'the listning Winds receiv'd' it. Certainly the 'Winds' seem to carry a traditional spiritual connotation, which is here substituted for human auditors. The whole atmosphere is thus created for a mysterious and generalized effect proper to the prophetic mode.

The deliberately uninformative exordium is followed by the visionary 'Song', which alone must inform us *because* it is visionary. From the frame we move into the centre, the substance: the vision alone is precise, because it is a destination, whereas the frame was merely a "featureless" interval. It is prophetic and providential:

> What should we do but sing his Praise
> That led us through the watry Maze,
> Unto an Isle so long unknown,
> And yet far kinder than our own?
> Where he the huge Sea-Monsters wracks,
> That lift the Deep upon their Backs.
> He lands us on a grassy Stage;
> Safe from the Storms, and Prelat's rage.
> He gave us this eternal Spring,
> Which here enamells every thing;
> And sends the Fowl's to us in care,
> On daily Visits through the Air.
> He hangs in shades the Orange bright,
> Like golden Lamps in a green Night.
> And does in the Pomgranates close,
> Jewels more rich than *Ormus* show's.
> He makes the Figs our mouths to meet;
> And throws the Melons at our feet.
> But Apples plants of such a price,
> No Tree could ever bear them twice.
> With Cedars, chosen by his hand,
> From *Lebanon*, he stores the Land.
> And makes the hollow Seas, that roar,
> Proclaime the Ambergris on shoar.

He cast (of which we rather boast)
The Gospels Pearl upon our Coast.
And in these Rocks for us did frame
A Temple, where to sound his Name.

(5–32)

The 'Song' is a paean to God's care for His Chosen People; He guides, cherishes, and bestows. It is now evident why Marvell suppressed the singers' agency in the 'Song'—there are no agents in the poem who can match God's omnipresent agency. Apart from their praise of Him, they have no agency: 'What should we do but sing his Praise?'.Providence is the source of everything, the sailors its patients. He 'led', 'he. . .wracks', 'He lands', 'He gave', He 'sends', 'He hangs', He 'does close', 'He makes', 'And throws' and 'plants', 'he stores' 'And makes', 'He cast' 'And. . .did frame'; almost all the verbs belong to God, and the rest are products of or reactions to His agency. God is, as He must be, the arbiter of their destiny and the bestower of the New Jerusalem. And, as it should, the New Jerusalem serves every delight of man; if God is sole source of these gifts, so His elect are sole recipients: 'gave us', 'to us in care', 'our mouths', 'our feet', 'for us'.

These lines describe not only the New Jerusalem/Bermudas, but also the manner of the journey thither, through 'the watry Maze' (6). As in *First Anniversary*'s 'Watry maze' (1–4), these are the waters of the Sea of the World and Time. It is in the nature of the World-Sea that the Ship of the Church/State is driven westward by persecution, here represented by the 'Prelat's rage', which creates 'Storms' of desolation in the World-Sea, especially in these, the Latter Days when God's people suffer tribulation from the ungodly. That desolating prelude to the renovated destination is figured also by the 'Sea-Monsters', the 'hidious monsters' of antichristianism that infest the World-Sea towards the End.[90] Both leviathans and 'Prelat' are aspects of the antichristian persecution, the second specifying English antichristianism and former the antichristian power more generally, as 'Leviathan Hells proud beast',[91] equivalent to the Beast which rises from the Sea in Revelation 13:1. In the Last Day God 'shall slay the dragon that is in the sea' (Isaiah 27:1), a destruction effected here when He 'wracks' the whale-leviathans. For the persecutions of Antichrist must be withstood, and the Beast destroyed, before the godly can gain the port of the New Jerusalem.[92]

Adams had specified Leviathan as the enemy of the Soul/Church's Ship in the World-Sea, citing Psalm 104, which has often been linked to this poem in an unspecific manner:[93] Adams explicitly links it with the entity of Antichrist in Revelation, with his 'blustring tempest' of evil, rendered in Marvell's 'Storms'. (Bermudan lore backs up this motif of bad weather.)[94] Against this menace, God's providential care 'led us through the watry Maze', steering the godly Ship just as he steered 'the sterne of the world' itself.[95] 'His way is in the Sea. . .and his footsteps are not known' (Psalm 77:19); so is the 'watry Maze' the unknown path of God, that mystery of providence[96] which pervades the poem. Because He alone understands it, He is guide and agent throughout.

This eschatological narrative is fused by the problematic with a narrative of Bermudan and Macarian lore. The whales that figure Leviathan are such as those described by Pliny, spouting enough water to sink a ship:[97] 'That lift the Deep upon their Backs'. Equally, the 'watry Maze' recalls that the Hesperides (traditionally identified with the Fortunate Isles)[98] were protected by a winding inlet from the sea;[99] this maze similarly protects God's hidden paradise. It is also apt to the Bermudan narrative since the islands' navigational problems —'with such curious and narrow comming in'—contribute to their particularly defensible nature.[100] The islands' defensibility was seen by godly propagandists as at once providential and strategic;[101] a note sounded again when they described the rocky coastline, and which is in turn echoed in Marvell's 'Rocks' (31), conveying a providential protection of the island: 'the Rockes every way have so fortified the situation, that she would laugh at an Armada' like that of the Spanish in *Blake*—therefore 'she can know no other love or Lord but English'.[102] Destined to be and to remain English, the Bermudas' providential strength makes the sailors 'Safe' also because this is the New Jerusalem, which was itself 'walled for security'[103]—spiritually redeemed also, and therefore permanently 'Safe' in God.

So England's Ship moves to her transformed image as the New Jerusalem England. The sailors' landing, envisaged in the Song, confirms that the World-Sea is a mere interval, and 'onely is for waftage':[104] thus in the poem the voyage's *desolatio* is portrayed merely as a prelude to the *renovatio* of the destination. The 'Isle [is] far kinder than our own' because it is England's perfected self. The 'grassy Stage' upon which God lands them is a transformation of the real Bermudan landscape, which was in fact rocky and arid.[105] Its characterization as 'grassy' is the poem's introduction of the ideal renovated landscape and its fertility. The 'stage' is at once dry land and an equilibrium, a restful level which contrasts with the antichristian rising 'Deep' of the foregoing line, and hence indicates the 'Safe[ty]', peace and rest of the New Jerusalem. A similar contrast informs the 'hollow Seas, that roar' (27), since in the desolation of the World-Sea it was understood that there would be 'distress. . .the sea and the waves roaring' in the wracking of nations.[106] Here the English nation is envisioned as reaching that 'Stage' on which the drama of history comes to rest.

The passage through the World-Sea imitates Isaiah's description of the movement to the Elect Nation's renovation: God has 'wounded the dragon. . .made the depths of the sea a way for the ransomed to pass over. . .the redeemed of the Lord shall. . .come with singing unto Zion' (51:9–11). Recalling these prerequisites, Marvell's description, in the roaring seas, remembers also Isaiah's 'sea, whose waves roared' (51:15). Marvell's sailors also greet the New Zion with singing, not only in the form of the visionary Song but also within it: 'Oh let our Voice his Praise exalt' (33) For, according to Adams, when the saints have survived the perils of the World-Sea, 'setting their triumphant feete on the shores of happinesse; they sing a victorious song. . .Praising God' for bringing them safely to their renovation.[107]

This eschatological motif is seconded by the Bermudan narrative, since the pattern of guidance, landing, and grateful prayer marks the account of Bermuda's first colony as printed in Purchas' travelogue.[108] When Marvell's sailors begin their

Song by asking 'What *should* we do but sing his Praise', they are acknowledging that the proper activity of the saints in the New Jerusalem *is* to sing His praise.[109] The renovatory motif is supported by Fortunate Isles lore, which included the 'wonderful songs' both of human beings and of birds;[110] so, in this poem, the human 'Song' is also combined with reference to 'Fowl's', the only other creatures specified in the vision. The passage from sea to land effected in the Song is a literal enactment of the transformation effected at the *renovatio*: 'I saw a new heaven and a new earth. . .and there was no more sea' (Revelation 21:1), for the sea belongs to the old order, the world and its worldliness and desolation. This "landing" at *renovatio* is reflected also in *Bermudas*' near contemporary, *First Anniversary*, where, because of the malignity that slows time, 'landing Nature to new Seas is tost' (157). Nature—the Creation—is sea-borne in Time, aiming to 'land' and become new, a landing effected in *Bermudas*' vision.

Marvell's portrayal of the Bermudan New Jerusalem maintains the poem's double narrative. The islands manifest verdancy, fertility, 'care' for man: all features both of the New Jerusalem and the Fortunate Isles. Their 'eternal Spring' (13) intimates perpetual regeneration or constant newness, reflecting *renovatio*: the New Jerusalem was 'Euer grene and florishing'.[111] In contrast, in history:

> God has hitherto, instead of an *Eternal Spring*,
> a standing serenity, and perpetual Sun-shine,
> subjected Mankind to. . .Tempests. . .and . . .to
> the raging of the Seas.
>
> (*RT*, 231)

Such is God's will (231–2), which decrees that His chosen be purified by desolation—as are the sailors here—before the 'Eternal Spring' can be realized. Its visionary character is indicated by the fact that the Spring 'enamells every thing'; the landscape is enamelled as in a picture, visionary and exemplary. The word's connotation of deep and various colours[112] recalls the multicoloured New Jerusalem, flashing with gems (Revelation 21:11–21); a connotation picked up in the following lines, where:

> He hangs in shades the Orange bright,
> Like golden Lamps in a green Night.
> And does in the Pomgranates close,
> Jewels more rich than *Ormus* show's.

Here the jewels of the New Jerusalem appear, figured by the seeds of pomegranates, themselves a symbol of the Church[113] of which the New Jerusalem was the 'consummation' or glory. The Ship of the Church has undergone transformation into its renovatory fulfilment; thus the 'Jewels' are especially 'rich' because of their salvatory significance. The 'golden Lamps' recall the special 'lights' of the New Jerusalem, provided indeed by her jewels but also symbolic: she had no need of sun or moon 'for the glory of God did lighten it. . .And there shall be no night there. . .for the Lord God giveth them light' (Revelation 21:23; 22:5). In the same fashion God 'hangs. . .Lamps' for His saints in this poem. The only night manifested in Bermuda is the artificial 'green Night' of the forest, a common poetic motif[114] which is here rendered eschatological, because here even darkness is verdant and renovatory, illuminated by God's enlightenment in 'Lamps'. For prophecy itself is 'a light that shineth in a dark place' (II Peter 1:19): the enlightening effect here is that promised for the End.

It has long been recognized that the oranges here recall the golden apples of the Hesperides, although no one has explained why Marvell has converted the fruit. In fact, he is recalling Bacon's New Jerusalem in *New Atlantis*, in which the healing power of the place is represented by ubiquitous oranges, 'an assured remedy for sickness taken at sea'.[115] For, like Marvell's mariners, Bacon's have passed over the World-Sea and through tempest to their New Jerusalem,[116] and the oranges heal the sins and wounds inflicted on the desolatory voyage. They are Bacon's version of the New Jerusalem's 'tree of life, which bore twelve kinds of fruits. . .and the leaves of the tree were for the healing of the nations' (Revelation 22:2). Thus the poem's oranges are 'for. . .healing', agents of renovation, and the plenitude of fruits on the Tree of Life is imitated in this New Jerusalem, where there are 'Pomgranates', 'Figs', 'Melons' and 'Apples'.

These are given to, not gathered by, the saints because the New Jerusalem/Fortunate Isles are distinguished by an effortless plenitude: 'He makes the Figs our mouths to meet;/And throws the Melons at our feet.'

God's character as planter—in the actual colonies, of course, that is what the sailors would be—recalls the traditional notion that He is the 'Gardener', Creator and Renovator, of the first and final paradises. He 'Apples plants of such a price,/No Tree could ever bear them twice' (23–4). Controversy has raged over these 'Apples', some critics contending that they are pineapples, others that they recollect the Fall.[116] While they are indeed pineapples for the purposes of the Bermudan narrative, on the eschatological level they recall the Tree of Knowledge that at the *eschaton* is replaced by the Tree of Life, its renovated anti-type, which has already been introduced into the poem. Both Trees were identified with the Tree of the Cross, which redeemed the first and promised the latter: and in this tradition the apples of the first Tree become symbols of Christological salvation.[117] Since the apples of both trees are not merely the same but symbols of the "once and for all" salvatory Passion, it follows that 'No Tree could ever bear them twice'. Their 'price' is at once the mortality brought by the Fall and the ransoming of man's immortality by Christ; they are 'of price' because, like the pomegranates, 'rich' in salvation. By means of this imagistic process, Marvell's poem can encompass the redemptive pattern in history of which the New Jerusalem is the consummation.

Throughout these lines the eschatological narrative remains in touch with the Bermudan narrative, the closest analogue being More's travelogue in *Purchas*:[118] 'the Fowl's [sent] to us in care' recall that the islands contained similarly indulgent birds offering themselves for the eating—indeed, some of the islands were therefore called 'Bird Ilands'.[119] Marvell's pomegranates may have been suggested by the presence of 'Peares which have in them a red liquor, as the Pomgranat hath',[120] and the 'Melons' (22) had been planted by settlers.[121] Marvell's modifications of Bermudan lore into the portrait of the Western New Jerusalem are equally marked in the following lines, where 'Cedars. . .[of] Lebanon', 'Ambergris' and 'Pearl' represent renovatory transformations of real Bermudan features. The cedars on the island were of another type,[122] transformed by Marvell because it was with those of Lebanon that Solomon built the Temple.[123] In the New Jerusalem is its antitype, the new Temple: in *Bermudas* God 'in these Rocks for us did frame/A Temple, where to sound his Name' (31–2). The rocks at once imply a secure haven for the saints and recall the 'Rock' of the Church, which finds its—their—haven here (Matthew 16:18). The fact that this Temple is 'frame[d]' by God Himself reflects the belief that the temple of the new covenant was to be built without hands,[124] an immaterial internal temple which made of the saints themselves 'God's building' (I Corinthians 3:9). In the New Jerusalem comprised of the saints in glory, the 'walls and foundation is God.'[125] So the Bermudan Temple is made by and contains God, in the form of His 'Name'.

A similar renovatory transformation informs the 'Ambergris' here, the presence of which had been recorded by More.[126] Recalling this, Marvell fuses Bermudan lore with Pliny's description of the whales whose carcasses infest the shores of the Fortunate Isles;[127] in *Blake* their equivalents were the human bodies polluting the renovated isle. There a desolating allusion, here the stranded whales become a renovatory ornament: the 'Seas. . .Proclaime the Ambergris on shoar', this metonymy evoking only their useful and valuable product. Similarly, in this context the seas, too, are redeemed from their desolating function—they are 'hollow' (27) because at the Resurrection 'the sea gave up the dead that were in it' (Revelation 20:13); that is, not merely whales but the dead men whom *renovatio* revives, their delivery echoed in the sea's casting up of carcasses here. Another renovatory gift is cast upon the shore by God Himself—'cast. . .The Gospels Pearl upon our Coast'—in a transformation of those pearls which settlers claimed to have discovered on the island.[128] The gospels' pearls are the sacred truths (Matthew 7:6), made manifest to man by God at the End, and the 'pearl of great price' was the gospels' revelation of Christ as Redeemer (Matthew 13:46); already recollected in the poem, but here indicating the fulfilment of scriptural promise. That fulfilment is found particularly in the New Jerusalem's gates, each of which was 'one pearl' of unimaginable size (Revelation 21:21). In Marvell's lines the Bermudan 'Coast' where the Pearl lies is the equivalent of the gate of the New Jerusalem, and the new 'Temple' of the succeeding couplet is that described in the next verse of Revelation (21:22). Since the New Jerusalem is a spiritual paradise above all, the mariners 'rather boast' of this Pearl and Temple than of all the physical pleasures of their island. (Some commentators have wilfully misunderstood this line, as if the mariners were "rather boastful" types, in a distinctly modern usage which is not to be found here; there is nothing more orthodoxly godly than this moment in the poem.)

The subsequent couplets have given commentators some trouble to explain the 'rebounding' of praise: does it mean, some ask, that heaven will reject them for the "nasty Puritans" they are? It does not.

> Oh, let our Voice his Praise exalt,
> Till it arrives at Heavens Vault:
> Which thence (perhaps) rebounding, may
> Eccho beyond the *Mexique Bay.*
>
> (33–6)

The parenthetical 'perhaps' is yet another bait to those determined to see the poem, and these lines in particular, as iconoclastic. But the meaning of these lines, although it has eluded them,[129] is a secret not dreadful but renovatory. The first line enacts the purposes of the Temple, which is for the sailors 'to sound his Name' in the New Jerusalem. The 'rebounding' of that praise involves three complementary levels of meaning. First, the New Jerusalem is on earth (as it should be), and therefore the 'Praise' that reaches heaven quite properly 'rebounds' also upon the heaven-on-earth of the Bermudan New Jerusalem. Second, the harmony of heaven and earth at the *renovatio* is here intimated by the 'Eccho', an image of assent. That harmonious echo is exegized by a Puritan divine's remark that 'When we seale to the Truth of God, and cry *Amen*, it is a word that fills Heaven and Earth. . .When God says *Amen* in Heaven, if we presently can say *Amen* to his Truth upon the Earth, he will say *Amen* to our Salvation.'[130] This system of echoes represents an accord between heaven and earth, the New Jerusalem union echoes in the sense that it 'fills Heaven and Earth'. The image of New Jerusalem accord and salvation is wittily enfolded in a specific reference to the New Jerusalem especially as Kingdom of Christ: 'The Lord reigneth; *let the earth rejoice*; let *the multitude of isles be glad thereof*' (Psalm 97:1). This allusion recalls that in the renovation Christ is King of the Isles, here the Bermudan isles but also the British Isles to which this Christological aspect was attached by contemporary preachers.[131]

These images of the last renovation and apotheosis of England link with the reference to 'the Mexique Bay'. It has long been recognized that this is a reference to Spanish dominions in the New World,[132] although the implications of the reference have remained inchoate. The idea that the saints' 'Praise' may rebound with redoubled force to cover the antichristian areas of the New World is an image of godly activism made potent by renovation: it foresees the Latter Day Protestant *imperium*, which will ingather all nations into Christ's Kingdom. From small beginnings the Kingdom will 'fill the whole earth, notwithstanding all oppositions'.[133] Here the way in which the isles and waters of the 'Bay', and beyond, echo God's will is an image of desire for that moment of Christ's victory, when 'I heard, as it were, the voice of a great multitude, and *like the voice of many waters*. . .saying, Allelujah!' to Him (Revelation 19:6). As usual in the prophetic language, the 'waters' of Revelation and the poem are the nations, here united in the Kingdom vision. This holy expansionism informs the image of dilating and aspiring praise in Marvell's lines: they form an *exemplum*, indicating the course to be pursued by the saints of England at the current time, and supported by a vision of their destination in the New Jerusalem.

Similarly, the reference here to the enemy—the Spanish Antichristian Empire—is the imperial counterpart of Marvell's reference earlier in the poem to the domestic antichristian threat of the 'Prelats'; indeed, it was believed that Spain had a role in conspiring to subvert the English Church by means of the episcopal heresy of Arminianism.[134] The poem emphasizes that the eschatological struggle of England is at once internal and external, just as the Bermudas are at once England as New Jerusalem and the English presence in the New World.

Thus the qualification 'perhaps' of the 'rebounding' expansion is not ironic but an indication that this 'Song' is a *vision* of England's destiny and her destination, as yet unfulfilled but which will 'perhaps' be fulfilled quite soon. The word at once defers to the mystery of God's purposes and emphasizes that the vision is an *exemplum* requiring enactment. The distance between vision and fulfilment is that between Bermudas and the 'English boat', the parameters of which are unknown.

As the Song ends, the Final Image appears in the last four lines: we are back in the boat, in the frame containing this vision:

> Thus sung they, in the *English* boat,
> An holy and a chearful Note,
> And all the way, to guide their Chime,
> With falling Oars they kept the time.
> (37–40)

The ending of the poem at line 40 has a numerological significance, since the passage to the New Jerusalem was an anti-type of the Old Israel's journey to the Promised Land, before which renovation they underwent forty years wandering in the desert (or desolation). Such is the period of *desolatio* through which the English Chosen must pass in the Latter Days, keeping 'the time' of expectation. This numerological allusion warns of that purification that must be endured before the Song's vision can come into being. The *moralitas* is further enforced by the 'Note'—the Song itself, in fact—and here it has the force of *Nota Bene*: note well and note the good news, the Song is to be observed as an exemplary vision of 'chearful' import. By this means Marvell introduces the instruction: how that vision is to be attained, and the English Ship of Church and State to reach its destination. 'All the way, to guide their Chime,/With falling Oars they kept the time.' As more than one critic has puzzled, 'They might be expected [rather] to sing in order to keep their stroke in rowing'.[135] In fact, the Song is timed by the oars because the vision is brought into time by regulated action or activism. To row the English Ship towards its goal must be a communal effort: 'nothing more hinders the advancement of Christs *Kingdome*. . .then divisions among his people'.[136] So when here the English mariners row in concert to bring the Ship of State to its destination, it is an image of the unity necessary to the renovating effort. By this means they 'kept the time', according to the timeliness of activism.

That moral was reiterated frequently by Marvell, repining that men have failed to reap the advantages of 'that most perfect and practical model of humane society', the Christian religion, being left therefore with merely 'the speculation of a better way to future happiness' which is granted to them by revelation but which they are unable to enact because of schism, for on that 'way' 'the very guides disagree' (*GP*, 281). Thus, in *Bermudas*, only a communal and harmonious society of Englishmen can sail to the New Jerusalem, under the guidance of the only certain arbiter, God Himself, 'that led us through the watry Maze' of time.

Thus, fundamentally the message of *Bermudas* is that of its contemporary *The Character of Holland*: vigilant action by the new Commonwealth.

> For now of nothing may our *State* despair,
> Darling of Heaven, and of Men the Care;
> Provided that they be what they have been,
> Watchful abroad, and honest still within.
>
> (145–8)

The difference is that in *Bermudas* the prize—the New Jerusalem—is envisioned, and eschatological desire is captured in the fragile image of the beauty as well as the price of apocalypse.

6

Revelations of Love:
Amorous Images of the *Eschaton*

As the eschatological drama occurred both without and
within, in the soul and in the world, so even the most
personal lyric modes were susceptible of its influence—
rendering apocalypse in individual terms. It is the chiliast's
preoccupations that stamp Marvell's personal lyrics with their
peculiar tone and provide the explanation of their cryptic
images, and their dense arguments. In this light some of his
most puzzling as well as most attractive lyrics will be treated
in this chapter: *To His Coy Mistress*, *The Garden*, and *The
Mowers Song* (the concerns of which extend to the other
Mower poems, too). The latter poems fall into Marvell's
favoured Pastoral mode, melding it with apocalyptic signs; all
three poems are derived from classical genres, which were
so congenial to Marvell as he remodelled them for the times.
The Garden invokes the *Beatus Ille* tradition of *hortus
conclusus* poems,[1] *The Mowers Song* is a lover's complaint
such as those in Virgil's Eclogues, and *Coy Mistress* is on the
carpe diem model ultimately derived from Catullus. This
poem differs from other Latinist poems of Marvell in
exploiting not the vatic potential of Roman models, but their
significance as the pagan predecessors of Roman Catholic
antichristianism—for imperial Rome and the Roman Church
were contiguous from a certain chiliastic point of view. It is
such curious chiliastic transformation of genre that gives
Marvell's personal lyrics their famous if (hitherto) uncompre-
hended frisson: in this lies their wit.

(i) THE REVELATION OF HIS MISTRESS: *TO HIS COY
MISTRESS*

Although Marvell's most famous poem, *To His Coy Mistress*
has always seemed odd in its 'wittily lugubrious

grotesqueries';[2] and a massive critical effort has yet to explain them. Surveying *Coy Mistress* criticism, Fogle sums up three basic lines of approach underneath the various contexts suggested for the poem: 'it *is* a true *carpe diem* poem but spiced by typical Marvellian irony and wit; it is only *apparently* a *carpe diem* poem as a disguise for deep philosophical statement; it is not a *carpe diem* poem at all, but a sarcastic parody of the theme'.[3] In fact, the peculiar tone and dark humour of the poem are reflexes of Marvell's problematic, in which the classical *carpe diem* or persuasion-to-love poem is fused with an eschatological vision of love-as-activism. In a sense, then, the poem is ironic about the pagan mode of epicurean love-lyric, but only in the service of an eschatological transformation that is deeply felt: sexual energy and chiliastic fervour are identified.

In the conventional *carpe diem* poem the poet/lover tries to seduce his mistress from her virginal resistance to him, largely by means of stressing the brevity of life and hence the wisdom of enjoying sexual pleasures while time allows them. Essentially, sex and death are opposed so that the poet may press his suit. The *memento mori* is usually brief, since the prevailing seductive mode of the poem might be disturbed by too emphatic a stress on the morbid;[4] in the Catullan original the motif of 'Impossibles'—extravagant desire for impossible pleasures like countless kisses—balanced this emphasis. However, in *Coy Mistress* the evocation of death to frighten the mistress into submission is unusually intense and unpleasant, so much so that Stanley Stewart thinks the poem heavily indebted to the *ars moriendi* tradition.[5] However, the *memento mori* of the second paragraph is merely part of a sustained and detailed *chiliastic* narrative, in which this vision of the *telos* is subsumed. An eschatological narrative merges with the narrative of seduction so that the *carpe diem* notion—"seize the day"—is rendered as the eschatological instruction to be timely, to "grasp the time" of activism.

This transformation is predicated upon the conventional *carpe diem* addressee—a virgin reluctant to assent to the poet/lover's advances. Christ's parable of the Wise and Foolish Virgins (Matthew 25:1–13) portrays two distinct species of 'virgins' or souls, the first truly prepared by activist readiness for the Coming of Her Bridegroom, the second unprepared and negligent: the converted and the unconverted. The parable thus treats conversion of the saint and the activism in which conversion must express and ratify itself.[6] Since the time of the Coming is unknown and unnervingly sudden, only 'they that were ready went in with [Christ] to the marriage' of the End (10), for salvation is spiritual marriage to Christ the Bridegroom in the New Jerusalem (Revelation 21:9ff). Thus in Marvell's poem "seize the day" signifies, at this level, the love-as-activism of the elect, and the 'Coy' virgin is seduced to an eschatological purpose. This poem is a persuasion to elect love in which the aim is to 'convert' the mistress to (as it were) the 'true religion' of love, of which the speaker-lover is already an adherent—and best viewed as a persona rather than Marvell himself.

Marvell's chiliasm can easily assimilate the erotica of the *carpe diem* tradition. It is one of the more common misconceptions about Puritanism that it was hostile to sexuality: 'Far from suppressing the sensual and sentimental elements in sexual relationships. . .Puritanism exposed it to the full force of its habit of scrupulous analysis',[7] and herein lies the stringency of Marvell's love lyric. In this poem the sexual relationship is anatomized by means of eschatological modes of phenomenal diagnosis, and their psychological reference as personalized in the pattern of individual conversion. The imagery which enables Marvell's amatory-revelatory problematic is partly drawn from the Song of Solomon, an erotic biblical book which was explicated in eschatological terms as an allegorical history of Christ's Bride, the soul and the Church.[8] Merged with the Pauline doctrines of the soul's resurrection, this was influential upon Puritan attitudes to godly marriage. The latter was a saint's duty,[9] for such a union imitated Christ's Last Marriage to the soul and provided a foretaste of that renovation for which the saint longed: thus union was itself a renovation. St Paul's comparison of the Last Resurrection to a marriage is the basis of Marvell's apocalyptic version of the seduction poem. We do not need to see this poem as suggesting marriage (rather unlikely, in fact), in order to recognize Marvell's witty play upon the convention whereby amatory poems had traditionally pressed religious imagery into the service of amorous devotion. Marvell balances the equation of love and religion in such poems, in order to render an apocalyptic love.

The second of the exegetical traditions upon which the poem bases itself is that which regarded antichristianism as idolatry, imaged as "spiritual fornication" with the Scarlet Whore.[10] Hence the imagistic logic that, if the unconverted and unregenerate soul is a 'foolish virgin', as therefore essentially antichristian, it is equally a spiritual fornicator: physical virginity is spiritual unchastity. That is the witty paradox that lies at the heart of Marvell's poem. While she remains unseduced by the speaker, the 'Coy Mistress' is rejecting the spiritual election of a converted love and hence she is, as it were, his personal Scarlet Whore: only by their sexual union can she save herself and him too, by sharing conversion. Hence that sexual union is at once conversion and the renovation that conversion attains. Hereby the Mistress' values of 'Honour' (29) or chastity are wittily reversed by the poet, for they turn her into a whore in the only real sense of the word—the spiritual sense.

This poem of elect love therefore implements the moral of Christ's parable: sexual union is conversion, the activism in which conversion is made actual, and the renovation which activism is bringing into being within history. That activism is required of the poem's lovers because they inhabit the Latter Days, the ambience which the poem emphasizes because temporal urgency impels love-as-activism. The conventional *carpe diem* emphasis on time's brevity thus becomes an eschatological emphasis upon the imminence of the End, intensifying the urgency of seduction. Therefore the poem is unusually emphatic in its reference to Time: 'World enough, and Time' (1), 'our long Loves Day' (4), 'ten years' (8), 'An hundred years', 'two hundred', 'thirty thousand' (13–16), 'An Age' (17); climaxing in Time's invasion of the poem as 'Times winged Charriot hurrying near' (22), which becomes the chariot of Phoebus Apollo, of the Sun-as-Time (45)[11] and the limit of personal existence ('our Sun'); and other temporal references.[12] For this poem the sun as time and the sun as personal duration are almost identical because Latter Day time is itself swift, exerting upon Marvell's lovers a more intense temporal pressure than the conventional *carpe diem* evocation of *telos* alone: 'in this latter scene of time. . .The great mutations of the world are acted, our time. may be too short for our designes'.[13] Thus the poem has a specifically chiliastic sense of time; the lovers lack 'World enough, and Time' (1) because soon Time itself will stop and the world be destroyed. This establishment of the eschatological context at the beginning of the poem is seconded by the notion of personal *telos*—that the lover's 'little world' of the self[13] is mortal and brief, imitating the world's own death. Thus specific reference is made to the Flood which is a type of the final deluge (8), fulfilled in the anti-type of the 'Conversion of the *Jews*' at the End (10). In compressing that fulfilment within three lines the poem as it were enacts its sensitivity to Latter Day atmosphere, that this is 'the last Age' (18).

It is in the light of chiliastic expectation of the End that we should understand the movement of the poem. The first paragraph is a "false" vision of history-as-courtship, the second envisages the consequences of an unconverted love, and the third provides an instructive vision of the course of a converted love. We can understand this movement by examining each of the problematic's two narratives in turn. In the conventional *carpe diem* narrative level, the first paragraph suggests that, were it not for time's transience, the speaker would willingly devote himself to the extended and patient wooing that his Mistress' 'coyness' seems to require and expect. However, in the second paragraph he reiterates with force that the brevity of life prevents such a lengthy wooing, for death will end the possibility of love. Therefore, says the third paragraph, we must take our opportunity to love now, before death prevents us. Hence even on the *carpe diem* level the narrative begins, climaxes, and ends with time and death. This temporal theme is even more insistent than at first appears, since the first paragraph's vision of what a long courtship would be like is in fact ironic, in the sense that the speaker wants the Mistress now rather than later: the vision will be abandoned as soon as he can press the image of death to imply a speedy submission by the Mistress as necessary in time. Therefore we can immediately see an instance of the way in which the eschatological narrative intensifies the effects of the *carpe diem* narrative: the eschatological pressure begins, fills and then ends the "false" vision of endless time and endless courtship. We will see this process in detail in a moment, but first we must specify the characters of the protagonists. If the Mistress as unconverted virgin is in that sense like the Scarlet Whore, so the speaker as converted lover is like Christ the Spouse, recalling that the archetypal godly union is a foretaste of that with Christ at the End. In these images the conventional *carpe diem* protagonists have a newly intense and witty "history" or courtship:

> Had we but World enough, and Time,
> This coyness Lady were no crime.
> We would sit down, and think which way
> To walk, and pass our long Loves Day.
> Thou by the *Indian Ganges* side
> Should'st Rubies find: I by the Tide
> Of *Humber* would complain. I would
> Love you ten years before the Flood:
> And you should if you please refuse
> Till the Conversion of the *Jews*.
> My vegetable Love should grow
> Vaster then Empires, and more slow.
> An hundred years should go to praise
> Thine Eyes, and on thy Forehead Gaze.
> Two hundred to adore each Breast:
> But thirty thousand to the rest.
> An Age at least to every part,
> And the last Age should show your Heart.
> For Lady you deserve this State;
> Nor would I love at lower rate.
>
> (1–20)

This vision of lengthy courtship is the unavailable, and also undesired, model of their future (or "prophecy"). The *memento mori* of the second paragraph is the necessary and equally undesired future—inevitable death. The third is the desired future, in which love would be immediately consummated, achieving a true eschatology and hence being a "true prophecy". The whole movement of the poem is from false interpretation of love's history to true interpretation and instruction for elect love. The first act of this futurist projection in the poem is the first paragraph's mocking vision, here, of a hypothetical courtship which pretends to deference of the lady's self-importance, her need to be wooed devotedly and long: 'For Lady you deserve this State', or pomp. The insinuation that the lady is proud and vain—hence her coldness to him—is the basis of Marvell's subversion of this "courtship" vision. The Mistress is at once virginal and the Scarlet Whore, female symbol of antichristian pride. (This activates the meaning of "sin" in her 'crime' [2].) This characterization begins in the second line, with her 'coyness'. The word 'coy' is ambiguous, for although it seems appropriate to chastity, it is often the initial strategy of a woman who wants to be seduced (as in 'love's coy touch'); Spenser's Scarlet Whore Duessa seduces men by 'coy lookes' which lead to spiritual fornication.[14] We will see the further development of the whore/virgin paradox in a moment.

Then the speaker envisages what their courtship would be like if time were elastic to their needs—as elastic as prophetic time, that is. Many 'Ages' could be spent in the wooing, but first, as a good saint, the speaker would have to contemplate the signs of history and plot the appropriate strategy of action, for courtship here is a version of history, extending over 'Ages'. This is a witty transformation of the Catullan motif of fancied 'Impossibles', envisaging a courtship as long as history itself. Hence the chiliastic lover's "interpretation", precedent to courting action: 'We would sit down, and think which way/To walk, and pass our long Loves Day.' In the latter phrase is a reminiscence of the 'everlasting day' which follows the End of time—'day of life, of light, of love'[15]—because in the Millennium is the endless marriage of saints to Christ. In the period when this poem is set, the Latter Days, 'It is the time between the Contract and the Marriage', in which activist saints 'labour to be fitted and prepared for that time';[16] so, here, the lovers would contemplate the fitting course of a courtship which would end in endless union. The end of the courtship is as it were the end of time, and the consummation is the lovely renovation. They need to consider which 'way' to take to their New Jerusalem of love because there are two spiritual 'ways'. As Puritan preachers constantly reiterated, there is the 'broad way' which leads to destruction and the 'narrow way' to salvation and renovation (that taken by Marvell's Fairfaxes; Matthew 7:13–14). To 'walk' in the true way is to walk in the way of God's will towards the End He has decreed.[17] Obviously, the lovers' effort is to reach that consummatory renovation, and they do what they are told, which is to choose 'this day which [way] you will walk in',[18] preferring the 'sure but rugged way,/That leads to everlasting day' (*A Dialogue Between Thyrsis and Dorinda*, 11–12).

The New Jerusalem they are aiming for is, as it were, 'another country' for which saints set out.[19] However, since their vision of courtship is false (ironic on the speaker's part) as a result of the Mistress' unconverted state, she takes the wrong 'way' by understanding the notion of 'another country' literally. The speaker would be left behind in England (the 'Humber' of Marvell's home, Hull) while she found herself in India (5–7). Since the confluence of rivers was an image of consummation or marriage (as in *Last Instructions*),[21] their separation by vastly distant rivers implies the lovers' frustration and the delaying courtship. However, it becomes apparent that it is the speaker who suffers by this, 'complain[ing]' at home in the traditional love-lorn manner of poets; on the eschatological level, this implies that he has taken the true 'way', by abiding in England the Elect Nation and thus ratifying his trueness in the religion of love. In contrast, the unconverted Mistress is translated to the quasi-paradisal India, famed for its gems:[21] in this exotic location she is offered effortless riches—the 'Rubies' are stumbled upon rather than mined for. But this is a false paradise, for India is in the East whereas the true paradisal location is Western. The East is a geographical symbol of backward time and therefore redolent of antichristian reversion; the apparent and material paradise there is an antichristian deluding image (as is this whole "false prophecy" in the first paragraph, in fact). In that respect its rubies and riches signify its worldliness, that it is of this world rather than the desired future world. As usual, female allure is metonymic for antichristian seduction, and that is the Mistress' characterization here. Like the Scarlet Whore in Revelation, she is located by a river (5), the Ganges, which in this period carried associations of luxury and exotica such as those which the Whore enjoys in her Eastern Babylon (Revelation 17), where in addition to the riches of her city she is herself 'decked with precious stones' (4). The Mistress' jewels here are 'Rubies' to suggest at once the scarlet of the Whore and her materialism. Therefore this becomes another ironic inversion of the Mistress' chastity into whoredom, for the price of a 'virtuous woman is *far above* rubies' (Proverbs 21:10), but in this courtship she can be bought by them. The notion of a price (as in the 'rate' of her love; line 20) is apt because exegetes compared the Whore to human prostitutes in the classical antichristian Rome which Revelation calls Babylon.[22] The implication for this courtship is that the Mistress requires of the speaker not only lengthy devotion but material gifts—inverting, again, the traditional image of virginity as a jewel[23] into an image of whoredom. While the 'Rubies' thus become metonymic for antichristian greed, their colour recalls not only the Whore's redness but also its exegetical explanation: that it was symbolic of popish ecclesiastical robes and of the blood of saints martyred by the Whore, hence emblematizing her cruelty to the faithful.[24] Such is also the nature of the Mistress' cruelty in frustrating her faithful lover's desires; to withhold her favours from him is antichristian pride torturing a converted lover. Her antichristian pride is hence contrasted to his converted and humble "Protestantism" in love—the concealed pun in 'complain' (7) is his religious "protest" against her cruelty. The English true religion and humility are emphasized by his location on the Humber, wonderfully plain and English in contrast to the Ganges. These resonances of the progressively Protestant city of Hull juxtapose the Puritan saint-lover with his unregenerate Mistress; that he abides in his home—spiritual, as well as literal—and she abroad, is eschatologically significant. (We saw the same contrast of 'Forrain' antichristian pride and domestic elect humility in *Appleton House* [1]; and the chiliast activist 'prevents the East', locale of antichristianism in *First Anniversary* [123]). In effect, in her unconverted-to-love and therefore antichristian guise the Mistress tempts the lover with false delights and a negative image of the "true paradise" of love. The red which is traditionally the colour of love is here rendered in its antichristian guise. For the long courtship would be an antichristian retardation of love's progress, effected by the Mistress' Whore-like frustration of the speaker's converted love. In this manner the speaker under-cuts the notion of a lengthy courtship which he does not want, in the very process of imagining it.

The antichristian pride which motivates the Mistress' cruelty—her demand for 'State' in wooing—recalls the political metaphor whereby traditional love-lyrics see the lover as enslaved to the beloved, 'my soules soueraigne'.[25] In amatory terms this merges with the Whore's pride, for 'she saith in her heart, I sit a queen.' (Revelation 18:7). So here the Mistress' 'Heart' is evoked just before the speaker makes his obeisance to her: 'For Lady you deserve this *State*' or dominion over him. It is a personal version of the Whore's antichristian 'Power and Empire'.[26]

But the speaker knows that his Mistress is unconverted, otherwise she would requite him, therefore here there is also a threat which motivates the slightly sarcastic edge to the last couplet. If we return to the first image of her Whoredom, we can see that the speaker's sojourn at Hull also alludes to that port's mercantile prosperity.[27] If the lover in courtship were to become a subject of the Whore's 'State', he would be spiritually seduced (just as her chastity is spiritual fornication) and thus comparable to those seamen who depended upon the Whore in Revelation: 'every shipmaster. . .and sailors. . .and as many as trade by sea' who 'cried' at the Whore's destruction (18:17–18), just as the speaker here 'complain[s]' at their separation. Equally, this separation imitates the way in which the seamen 'stood afar off' (17) from her. The speaker here is also like the kings who are under the Whore's power, as he is in thrall to her 'State', and they too 'bewail. . .and lament' (9) for the woman with whom they spiritually fornicate. His own experience of the antichristian bondage is similarly amorous in kind. The mercantile relationship between the Whore and her seamen links also with the materialism of the Mistress' 'Rubies', such jewels being imported from India in the seventeenth century,[28] and this mercantile reference further emphasizes rapacity on her part. In sum, a lengthy courtship is in effect antichristian fornication, with all its attendant dangers.

If, then, the lover were to implement such a courtship, he would become an antichristian fornicator or idolater, like the kings who are his counterparts here, who 'adore' the Whore (*First Anniversary*). This prospect is envisaged:

> An hundred years should go to praise
> Thine Eyes, and on thy Forehead Gaze.
> Two hundred to adore each Breast:
> But thirty thousand to the rest.
> An Age at least to every part,
> And the last Age should show your Heart.
> For Lady you deserve this State;

Here the convention whereby the love-poet 'adores' his mistress in religiose fashion is given an eschatological pointing, that the speaker is drawn by the Mistress-Whore's beauty into idolatry. Thus Marvell's speaker imitates St John's own wondering 'Gaze' at the Whore: 'When I saw her, I wondered with great admiration'. There is a covert joke in the notion of "Marvell's" imitating St John in this, for the latter was rebuked for it: 'Why didst thou *marvel*?' (Revelation 17:6–7). In this false vision the speaker will pay particular attention to her 'Forehead' because it was there that the mark indicated an individual's spiritual status, and in particular upon the Whore's 'forehead was a name written' identifying her (Revelation 17:5). Exegetes had explained that this image associated the Whore with Roman prostitutes, whose abilities were thus signified for their customers' perusal.[29] So at the amatory level this notion aptly underwrites the speaker's earlier uncertainty about his Mistress' 'coyness', which could be genuine or an amatory strategy, in which latter case she would really be as willing as he for consummation. In that sense, 'the last Age should show your Heart' because, if consummation is the *eschaton* or 'last Age' of courtship's "history", it will reveal in act whether she does love him or not. This notion makes use of the fact that at the End's full revelation all hearts/souls[30] will be revealed in their true spiritual colours, and those who love God will be saved. This is the first occasion on which the speaker characterizes himself as like the divine Bridegroom in his converted love, for while envisaging his potential idolatry, he reminds his Mistress that 'the Lord seeth not as man seeth; for man looketh on the outward appearance'—the Mistress' beauty— 'but the Lord looketh on the heart' (I Samuel 16:7); that is, the End of consummation will allow the speaker, too, to judge of her 'Heart'. Meanwhile she is as mysterious as the Whore (named 'Mystery' upon her forehead; Revelation 17:5) in her ambivalent coyness. If she is revealed as unloving—unconverted—by ultimate refusal of consummation after this long courtship, then she can expect to 'deserve this State' in another sense: to merit the condition of damnation. For it is said of the unconverted that 'though they live long'—as the Mistress would, in this vision of extended time—'their *last age* shall be without honour' (Wisdom of Solomon 3:17). Hence the ambiguity in 'State' encompasses both antichristian pomp and its deserved fate. This is the coda to the speaker's false prophecy of an antichristian courtship, setting the seal on his undercutting ironies.

These have included, by this point, various imitations of the true eschatological vision of history/courtship. The extended false prophecy can only "stretch" the time available for courtship by an antichristian reversion to the Old Testament period ('Flood' [8]), then tracing history to the current time, when the 'Conversion of the Jews' is imminent, recapitulating the various 'Ages' of history. Several sexual jokes intrude into this vision, anticipating the consummation which is supposedly delayed to its end, and they are intensified by the eschatological imagery. If the courtship is to be expanded into the prophetic dimension of time, so in fact is the act of love: 'I would love you ten years before the Flood' puts an antediluvian date on his wooing which extends to the Latter Day 'Conversion'-as-consummation. Both images, of flood, and 'Jews'/juice, imply an equally superhuman control of ejaculation. The ribald play on the identification of conversion with sexual consummation is an instance of the way in which eschatological ideas in this vision become ways of subverting antichristian chastity. Thus the reference to 'Flood' recalls that the first 'Deluge. . .wash'd the World clean from that Filth of Luxury [lust] and Impiety that it had in so long a time been' (*RT*, 239),[31] a purging *desolatio* which is fulfilled typologically by the final Deluge: as retribution for spiritual fornication the Flood signifies the nemesis of antichristianism, and in that sense 'ten years before the Flood' and the Jews' Conversion are almost coeval events. So, far from indulging the notion of lengthy courtship, the lover here is allowing a very short time before Conversion/consummation must come. He is right in his subversion of the apparent topic of his "vision" here, since as he has already stated these are the Latter Days; that is why the antichristian vision is imagistically undermined by sexual chiliasm.

A similar strategy affects the speaker's vision of his idolatrous courtship. His anatomization of his Mistress recalls that of the great Idol of the similar dream-vision of eschatological history in Daniel 2:31f.. The idol's head, breast, arms, belly and thighs, legs and feet are particularized to signify the four World Empires which precede the Fifth Kingdom, of which the fourth is the antichristian 'State' of the Whore. In this manner Marvell prepares for that closing image of this paragraph's vision:

> My vegetable Love should grow
> Vaster then Empires, and more slow.
> An hundred years should go to praise
> Thine Eyes. . .Forehead. . .
>   each Breast:
> But thirty thousand to the rest.
> An Age at least to every part,

—just as each section of Daniel's idol signifies an 'Age' of history. (The meaning of this dream is revealed to man because God is 'a revealer of secrets' [2:47], the capacity which the speaker will later appropriate to his last revelation of his Mistress' heart.) Christ smashes these empires to bring into being the last Kingdom, which begins as a seed, 'but when it is grown, it is the greatest among herbs', 'like a tree/Spreading and overshadowing all the Earth' (Matthew 13:31–2; *PR* IV. 146–51). Like Milton in the latter passage, Marvell here conflates Daniel's vision with that of the Kingdom-Tree, when 'My vegetable Love should grow/ Vaster then Empires, and more slow'. On the conventional level, by reference to the "growth" which is the faculty of vegetative existence, the speaker compares his sexual potency ('My. . .Love' here implying the tumescent penis) to the absolute power of the final Kingdom over all other Empires: 'slow' but sure is its victory, as we know. Another Christological image appropriated by the speaker, this sexual joke picks up the pun on 'juice' in the previous line, and is a wittily literal rendering of 'flesh is grass' (penis as plant), of Daniel's prophecy that the clay feet of the Idol/Empires shall 'mingle. . .with *the seed of men*' (2:43), and of Christ as the victorious 'seed' of man (Genesis 3:15)—semen is Christ-like, generative and therefore vegetative, too. In other words, consummation is the planting of the seed of the Kingdom-tree; it is the desired End. Here again the fake vision of a lengthy "antichristian" courtship is undermined by the intrusion of sex-as-chiliasm. By this point of the poem the speaker has in fact established that he should get what he wants from the Mistress because he is a godly lover, and sex is at once conversion and the Kingdom that conversion wins. Therefore Marvell has wittily transformed the Catullan Impossibles. At first it appears that Catullus' vision of gained love—'thousands of kisses', '*Mille. . .mille. . .*cum *milia*'[32] has been applied in this poem to the vision of what the speaker cannot have, but also *does not want*; a lengthy courtship. In fact, his vision of a 'Millennium' of potency rather implies what he cannot have but does want, the true Kingdom of love. The first paragraph has appeared to defer to antichristian delay of love, in fanciful vision at least, but its images constantly reiterate the need for swift consummation.

So the opening of the second paragraph, in which the speaker is conventionally to fright the Mistress with death, is already well prepared by the eschatological resonances of the first paragraph, which have reiterated the *eschaton* even as the fake prophecy appeared to envisage an extension to time. Imagistically, if not tonally, then, the next lines are not such a surprise as some critics have taken them to be.[33]

> But at my back I alwaies hear
> Times winged Charriot hurrying near:
> And yonder all before us lye
> Desarts of vast Eternity.
>
> (21–4)

Time-as-Death chases men into the 'Grave' (31) and thence into 'Eternity'; equally, eschatological time is driving men fast to the End, and to the eternal life or death that ensues upon it. We know already that it may overtake the lovers if they do not hasten into consummation. This Latter Day intensification of the conventional *memento mori* is further emphasized by image. Although Time is traditionally winged,[34] here the epithet is transferred to his 'Charriot' because Christ's chariot is that of the winged beasts in Ezekiel 1:4–24; equally, the chariot is that of Time as Phoebus Apollo (as in line 45), and hence of Christ the Sun of Righteousness (Apollo is the Sun is Christ, in a classical image suited to the *carpe diem* format).[35] Especially the chariot of the-Sun-as-Time figures Christ as agent of time's ending, that which is envisaged here: His chariot 'right onward drove' His enemies.[36] Similarly chased, if this speaker remains in bondage to an unconverted Mistress, both will fall under His wheels at the End: the 'Deserts of vast Eternity' is the endless desolation of the damned after the End,[37] like the desolated 'Deserts' of *Appleton House*'s foretaste of Ending. Hence 'Desarts' puns on the merited "deserts" of souls at that time; like 'State' earlier, which also implied that eternal damnation would be the 'rate' or price of loving an antichristian Mistress. It would be deserved because the 'rate' of the courtship required would be antichristian slowness; con-trasted here by the tempo of Christ's chariot driving to the End. The speaker is saying that "if, as you seem to desire, we are slow in approaching the consummation of our love, the End will prevent our design and our dilatoriness will be punished, too". Thus Marvell's speaker manages to fright his Mistress not only with the conventional *carpe diem* image of death, but with the divine Death-bringer, the End, and damnation too. Such are the wages of an antichristian, because unconsummated love. Just as the Old Israel wandered the 'desert', excluded from the Promised Land because of their sin of idolatry (Ezekiel 20:15ff.), so if they indulge in the antichristian spiritual fornication, these lovers, too, will be forever excluded from the Kingdom of Love.[38]

It is, of course, the speaker who is a converted soul and therefore can foresee the consequences of antichristian courtship and delay, who 'Heare[s]' Christ Coming. His warning to the unconverted Mistress follows, showing her that her death and desolation will be that of the Whore. At the End the Whore is made 'desolate'—driven into the 'desert'—and 'naked'; her flesh shall be eaten and she will be burned (Revelation 17:16):

> Thy Beauty shall no more be found;
> Nor, in thy marble Vault, shall sound
> My ecchoing Song: then Worms shall try
> That long preserv'd Virginity:
> And your quaint Honour turn to dust;
> And into ashes all my Lust.
>
> (25–30)

The conventional *memento mori*, threatening the loss of beauty and of life, is here grotesquely intensified to imitate the ravaged beauty and destruction of the Whore.[39] The amatory level is equally grotesque, for the speaker implies that the Mistress' recalcitrant virginity will (by rejecting his pleasant lovemaking) remain intact only to suffer inevitable rape by the worms who feed on carcasses, which Donne had described in sexual terms.[40] Marvell intensifies the idea to signify that chastity or spiritual fornication is sex with Satan: 'the diuel [is] a *worme*. . .he slippeth. . .into the verie bowells or entrals of our heart'.[41] The infernal Worm's rape is the reward of spiritual fornication, of course; thus, while the chariot signified Christ as Death-bringer, the worms figure the infernal death of the soul, which suffers the 'worm [that] dieth not' and the everlasting 'fire' (Mark 9:43–4). The Mistress will merit this fate because her chastity is spiritual whoredom; hence the sexual quibbles of this passage, which have long been understood as puns although not as significant. 'Virginity' is what is penetrated by the worms, and the 'quaint Honour' is cunt/chastity/pudenda; thus once again the words denoting chastity reveal that it is, eschatologically speaking, prurient and antichristian. So 'quaint' also implies "proud or haughty"[42] chastity, echoing the first paragraph's diagnosis of her coldness to the speaker as antichristian pride. That, of course, is the ultimate instigator of her damnation as envisaged here: antichristians 'Death weds, and beds. . .first in grave, and then in hell'.[43] By such eschatological means the speaker intensifies his *memento mori*, and the eschatological narrative is the source of its peculiarly grim horror as well as of Marvell's witty application of Latter Day love.

In contrast to his Mistress, the speaker will be saved, for an imminent Coming prevents the antichristian courtship and its ill effects, as he made clear in the first line of the poem. The lover is therefore seen as "outliving" his Mistress, since he will attain everlasting life. Her fate, everlasting death, will thus be for them a more decisive separation than either her coldness to him or her export to the Ganges in the first paragraph. By gradually intensifying the images of separation in this manner, the speaker is redoubling his pressure upon his Mistress, to convert. This extravagant image of the speaker's devotion beyond the grave and into eternity is eschatologically specific also. His fate as a converted saint is to be one of those who 'sung as it were a new song [before God]. . .These were they which were not defiled with women: for they are virgins' (Revelation 14:1, 3–4)—virgins in the spiritual sense, that is.[44] Thus the speaker's 'ecchoing Song' (this poem, in effect) is the new song of the saved, which in *Bermudas* 'may/Eccho' in the harmony peculiar to the Chosen. Thus his converted loving makes him a spiritual virgin, while his Mistress' chastity makes her a spiritual Whore. His song symbolizes the saint-singers' election to resurrection,[45] which releases them from the 'Grave' in which the poor unconverted Mistress must remain. The image has its poignancy, particularly as the speaker is here seen in fact to try to resurrect her. By singing to her tomb he assumes yet another Christological attribute, that at the End 'the dead shall hear the voice of the Son of God; and they that hear shall live' (John 5:25–6).[46] If the speaker can make her dead ears hear his song, she too will be resurrected; that is, in one sense, if the Mistress responds appropriately to this poem-song, she will understand that consummation will give her salvation, too. If she does not, the other sense of the image becomes operative: that in the Whore's destruction 'the voice of the bridegroom and of the bride shall be heard no more at all in thee' (Revelation 18:23), the tomb becoming her City of

Death. This vision of the speaker's possibly endless deprivation underlies the final couplet of this paragraph: 'The Grave's a fine and private place,/But none I think do there embrace' (31–2). Traditionally, the grave is like a bed, but it is a bed without sexual delight (apart from the worms', that is). It is at once 'private' like the bridal bed but also, in the pun, "deprived"—of life, consummation, and salvation. It is 'fine', not so much like a richly furnished bed as like a "finite" state—the ending of death and the exclusion from immortality. This vision of antichristian death (death without love) is furthered by the notion that no one 'embrace[s]' in this grave because the Mistress' antichristian soul is denied the last embrace of Christ the Bridegroom.[47] As the poem has already indicated, that embrace is the Christ-like speaker's too. This is the eschatological edge that sharpens this couplet's mordancy, giving a more specific point to its conventional level—that carcasses cannot make love. We should remember, if we are to appreciate its wit, that resurrected bodies can and do: the saints as Christ's 'members' have union in and with Him, which means that elect lovers embrace beyond the grave, and for them alone it is 'bridall bed'.[48] It is in this sense that Marvell transforms the classical poetic motif of 'Love in a Grave',[49] implicating it with eschatological wit.

So, if time's Ending is suggested in the first line of the poem, the End and its consequences are imported into the second paragraph, and by its close the Mistress should be convinced that to delay consummation would be unthinkable. The only escape from antichristian punishment—let alone anything less horrible—is to give in to the speaker forthwith. That contingency is the subject of the subsequent paragraph, which envisions the consummation of love and hence its Kingdom. This is the true prophecy of their love, supplanting the fake antichristian courtship envisaged in the first paragraph. The Mistress' conversion to love would be effected thus:

> Now therefore, while the youthful hew
> Sits on thy skin like morning dew,
> And while thy willing Soul transpires
> At every pore with instant Fires,
> Now let us sport us while we may;
> (33–7)

'Now. . .now': seize the moment for love's activism by converting, by consummating. On the conventional level of the poem, the Mistress' 'willing' heart/soul responds to her lover. This is imaged as the 'Soul's' conversion because 'we. . .have it in our power to obtain salvation if *willing*':[50] so, by making the choice of free will to convert to love's "true religion", the Mistress achieves "salvation" or consummation. This pattern of salvatory willingness was emphasized in Puritan reflections upon the duty of wives to husbands, recalling the Pauline 'similitude of a marriage' as image for conversion into the renovated soul.[51] This compounding of consummation with salvation and renovation continues the poem's imagistic logic, merging conventional motifs with eschatological ideas. The Mistress' 'instant Fires' are of desire for the speaker: 'at every pore' she perspires with desire. If we take the variant reading for 'hew' here, the 'glue'[52] of perspiration figures both clamminess and the union of bodies in consummation. In the eschatological narrative this idea is stressed by comparison to the desire felt for the Spouse Christ by the 'Soul' which 'with wider pores [can]/Inlarge thy flaming-brested Lovers/More freely to transpire/That impatient Fire';[53] the analogous wording here signifies that the Mistress' desire is a godly sexual desire for her Christ-like lover, the speaker. The image in the analogue is intended to represent chastity, in fact, which is holy desire:[54] here, however, converted desire is the saint's true chastity.

The witty identification of sex with conversion and salvation by Christ sublimates love even as it implies the most earthly coupling, in "sweat". This intensifying tension is maintained by other Christological attributes assumed by the speaker here. The sweat of passion is on the Mistress' skin 'like morning dew', recalling that Christ as 'dew' of grace falls upon the faithful, and in the Immaculate Conception had descended upon His own mother as a fall of dew.[55] That union was the first and typical 'embrace' of Christ, and the speaker's Christ-like, because saintly, embrace of his own partner is of a similarly salvatory type: like all godly unions, it replicates Christ's. Similarly, the converted soul is like the world itself in that it is purged by Christ as 'the refiner's fire', and the Mistress' 'instant. . .Fires' of desire for her Christ-like lover imitate that conversion.

Conversion is always expressed in activism, here rendered as sexual activity. Conversion is renovation of the soul, 'Mortifying and Vivifying', dying to live. In this period it was customary to regard sex as a "death" (in orgasm), and so here sexual activity becomes the "dying to live" of conversion. This godly and intense death, by guaranteeing eternal life to the souls converted, is the mode whereby these lovers will defeat time. They therefore bring on their death rather than waiting for it; they are activist rather than quiet in Time's power:

> Now let us sport us while we may;
> And now, like am'rous birds of prey,
> Rather at once our Time devour,
> Than languish in his slow-chapt pow'r.
> (37–40)

The further insistence upon 'Now' emphasizes that this sexual union is their mode of defeating time: the *carpe diem* "take the day" has become here the grasp of timeliness by activism, rendered as the violence of these lines and the subsequent couplets:

> Let us roll all our Strength, and all
> Our sweetness, up into one Ball:
> And tear our Pleasures with rough strife,
> Thorough the Iron gates of Life.
> (38–44)

Time's 'slow-chapt pow'r' makes of normal lives a slow death and decay. By the 'willing' choice of sexual activism and death the lovers acknowledge the Latter Day urgency implied at the beginning of the poem, consuming their own time and thus accelerating Time. This is the activist acceleration of time, for the lovers here 'devour' time, ending it. This is not merely a witty revenge upon *Tempus Edax*, a purely rhetorical victory; on the contrary, the lovers can *really* eat up time by making it go faster, hence (like Cromwell) bringing its End. This is the reverse of the first paragraph's vision of antichristian dilatoriness in courtship: sexual activity or love-as-activism, because godly, has ability to accelerate time. In so doing it ends the rule of the temporal antichristian 'pow'r', whose 'slow[ness]' prevents the End and thus prevents also the Kingdom of Love from coming into being. To attain that Kingdom of everlasting love is the project of the lovers here, as we shall see.

First, the activist character of this love is stressed by an image which recalls the current civil war. Love was conventionally regarded as a battle:[56] here the 'Ball' of the lovers' union is like a cannonball[57] exploding 'Thorough the Iron gates' of a stronghold, as in contemporary sieges. While the war, as a sign of the End, is pertinent to the poem's chiliastic mood, it is also an occasion for violent activism which aptly characterizes the lovers' amatory activism here. Theirs is an amatory counterpart ('*at once* our Time devour') to the military activism whereby Cromwell 'Time. . .contracts'. Similarly, their activist characterization as 'am'rous Birds of Prey' makes them, like Cromwell the Falcon in the *Ode*, avatars of God's scourgers in the Last Battle, who feed upon the carcasses there: 'all the fowls. . .Come. . .unto the supper of the great God, That ye may eat. . .the flesh of all men' (Revelation 19:12). As such Latter Day predators, these lovers feed upon the flesh of all men, too, in the form of Time who has devoured all men himself. Thus the lovers not merely accelerate Time to its destruction, but also enact their godly election to do so. The controlling idea of the final paragraph is to bring love-as-activism to its crisis in apocalyptic consummation, thereby making Time itself the agent of love's fulfilment rather than its enemy.

In this poem, Time's dominant thematic role is realized in all of its eschatological aspects: as Death, as Christ's final omnipotence, and as that antichristian mortality which—contrasting His resurrecting power—signifies endless Death in damnation. We must keep in mind Time's threefold character—antichristian, Christological, and mortal—if we are to understand the images of the last paragraph. Time is at the centre of a problematic in which a pagan poetic genre is merged with an eschatological narrative; the genre is Roman, as is antichristianism. In classical or pagan poetry, and most especially of course in *carpe diem* poems, death is regarded as final, an afterlife unavailable, and in this sense the genre itself figures the power of Time as Death and, here, as the everlasting death of antichristianism. On the other hand, Christian Time allows of an afterlife because of Christ's victory over Death, guaranteeing resurrection. In this poem, the *carpe diem* genre itself underpins the notion of time as antichristian Death, while in the eschatological narrative Christological Time is signified, as in the 'Charriot' of Christ (22). The obverse aspect of Time was signified in the vision of an "unconverted" Mistress' everlasting death. The ambiguity of Time in spiritual terms is signified in the problematic of the poem by the appropriate ambiguity of the 'Charriot'. For Satan, too, had his chariot (*FQ* I. iv. 36), and his power over worldliness was emblematized by the popular Francis Quarles as Satan's driving a chariot in which the world itself was the cargo.[58] In origin this image is classical, recalling the chariot of Santa Roman equivalent, Pluto, and hence implementing Marvell's identification of his classical genre's Death with the Antichrist. In apocalyptic terms, Marvell's image of the 'winged Charriot' in its Satanic aspect recalls the Locusts of the Apocalypse, winged for speed, 'the sound whereof was as the sound of chariots of many horses running. . .This setteth out the great feare they wrought in al places where they came, for the noise of chariots. . .is terrible.'[59] Hence the fear of the speaker here in hearing that pursuit, for Antichrist's agents 'pursue those that flye', a damnatory 'Death [that] preacheth hard at your heeles'.[60] These images of mortal and antichristian pursuit by Time's chariot in its damnatory form balance Time's Christological aspect, the ambiguous image of the chariot signifying both potential issues of the spiritual life. The damnatory potential of Time was indicated in the Mistress' 'Grave', its salvatory potential in the speaker's new Song.

The threefold aspect of Time is maintained in this final paragraph. In devouring Time as Death the lovers take an apt revenge upon Death the Devourer.[61] But Death is only truly a Devourer in its antichristian aspect, as the everlasting death: signified by Satan the Devourer.[62] The latter, a traditional image especially emphasized by chiliasts as the archetype of antichristian devouring, was figured in *Tom May* as a

devouring bird. Thus, here, *Tempus Edax,* or Time
the Devourer, is specifically Satan the Devourer as bird of
prey, and in devouring him as 'Birds of Prey' the lovers are
enacting a revenge upon antichristian damnatory power; that
is, in simple terms, they are saving themselves from antichristian damnation by means of love-as-activism, a godly
devouring. By activism they can achieve resurrection, a defeat
of death which was described in precisely the terms implied
here: 'So shalt thou feed on Death, that feeds on men',[63]
achieving eternal life. Thus the lovers' devouring or "consumption" of Time, both as eating and as "accelerating", is
not merely a revenge upon antichristian power but a victory
over it. By this means *both* lovers—now the Mistress is
converted too—assume the Christological power of salvation, for by Him, too, 'Death is *swallowed up* in victory' (I
Corinthians 15:54). Christ the Spouse's 'love is strong as
death' (Song of Solomon 8:6), and by means of love-as-
activism they similarly can defeat Death and Antichrist.

It is only by recognizing this eschatological narrative in the
image of Time's devouring that we can comprehend the next
section, which has proved the most difficult for critics
attempting to explain this baffling poem. The difficulty of line
44 especially, which has evoked numerous singularly irrelevant explanations, is compound by a variant reading provided
by the insertion of an 'r' in the *Miscellaneous Poems* text:[64]

> Rather at once our Time devour,
> Than languish in his slow-chapt pow'r.
> . . .
> And tear our Pleasures with rough strife,
> Thorough the Iron gates/grates of Life.

The 'rough strife' of sex-as-activism prevents a negligent and
damnatory 'languish[ing]' in Time. The lovers lie in Time's
mouth, and thus their victory is snatched 'in the teeth of
time', defiantly and bravely that is.[65] Essentially, the subsequent image recapitulates this idea, amplifying its implications. The 'gates/grates of Life' are the teeth and mouth of
Time, the devouring agents implied in his 'slow-*chapt* pow'r'.
So in one sense 'Life' here means "existence" or the temporal
duration of the lovers. Poets had described the mouth as a

'gate', like the other sensory orifices, and the teeth as 'grates'.[66] The lovers thus 'tear' their pleasures out of his mouth and power; since their 'Pleasures' are the bodily delights of love, they are—metonymically—tearing their mortal bodies out of his power, too. In this sense sexual activity is agent of immortality, for in escaping the mouth of Time-as-Antichrist they are specifically escaping from the Beast, whose 'iron teeth. . .devoured and brake in pieces' the godly (Daniel 7:7):[67] such are the 'Iron grates' from which love-as-activism delivers them.

This is an escape from the antichristian bondage, or 'pow'r' in Time. In death that bondage is figured by the 'mouth of Hell',[68] that to which any devouring antichristian mouth itself consigns its victims; so the 'deepe-deuouring iawes' of Spenser's Dragon-Beast 'Wide gaped, like the griesly mouth of hell,/Through which into his dark abisse all rauin fell.'[69] For the lovers to emancipate themselves from the Devourer's antichristian mouth is also to escape the hell of damnation that lies within it. Hereby they enact their salvation, and the enactment is consummation as conversion—'our Pleasures', in which sexual activity becomes sainted activism, implying resurrection.

The source of antichristian power over man is the frailty and mortality of his body, the mortality which is endless if Antichrist devours him. In that sense the body, here, becomes a paradoxical instrument of escape from its own mortality, for the bodily activity of sex is here made agent of immortality. That paradox is possible for Marvell because the body's traditional characterization underlies the 'gates of Life'. If the physical senses were 'gates', the body was regarded as a 'city' under siege by demonic forces of temptation.[70] That traditional iconography informs the recollection of Civil War sieges here, in which the lovers' union in a "cannonball" smashes 'Thorough' the city 'gates'; that is, in their sexual union they implement a mutual bodily "invasion", each a body-city with sensual 'gates' for access. Both are cities, and both are invaders, but the mutuality of invasion allows that they are a unanimous (as it were) "cannonball" of assault. The doubleness both of 'Ball' and of "city" implies their 'willing' (35) mutual choice of sexual "death". Hence the voluntary choice of godly activism as well as its violent energy are the sources of this violent image of copulation. The sexual "death" imitates the effect of Death upon the godly, which is the release of the immortal soul from its bodily prison of mortality—the 'body of this death'[71] which *A Dialogue Between the Soul and Body* described in conventional terms as a 'Dungeon'. As the effect of sin and as susceptible to sin, the body is a foretaste of hell, escapable only by godly resurrection after death. Here the body as a prison of sin is figured as the 'grates' or bars and grilles of sensible existence ('of Life'), and by escape into each other through sex the lovers are imitating release from mortal 'Life'. The release of the soul effected by death is here effected by the sexual "death".

By this emancipation from the prison of body, sin, and hell, the lovers once more are implementing the Christological power given to godly activists. At the End Christ would activate the general resurrection by unlocking hell's prison and emptying its mouth,[72] forcing 'death and hell [to give up] the dead that were in them' (Revelation 20:12–13), and it is that emancipation which the lovers anticipate here. Of Christ's harrowing of hell the Old Testament type was Samson's destruction of the gates of Gaza, the antichristian city. Samson's power as divine agent was implied in his riddle, that 'Out of the eater came forth meat, and out of the strong came forth sweetness' (Judges 14:14), which foretold Christ, He who combines strength for victory over death with sweetness of grace for salvation. Already the lovers have imitated the first part of the riddle, by eating the Eater Time (39), as Christ Himself does in His similar resurrection. The lovers' imitation of its second element is achieved when, in their assault upon the mortal prison, they 'roll all our Strength, and all/Our sweetness, up into one Ball'. Literally, in sexual union they combine masculine 'strength' with feminine 'sweetness';[73] on the eschatological level, they unite their own peculiar powers in the sexually activist effort to achieve a Christological energy against death. Not only should activism make use of the individual's particular abilities, as we know, but here union also as it were redresses the sexual division in humankind, the "hermaphroditism" of sex figuring the Christological power at the End to 'bring all [doubleness] into one againe'. His 'sweetness' is essentially His love for mankind, imitated in theirs for each other; by love they as it were "save" each other.

Conversion through sex achieves salvation: in conversion, a psychological crisis here imitated by the sexual one, Christ entered the soul violently just as He would enter the world on the Last Day—the soul/heart being the analogous 'little world', as in this poem. The unconverted heart is a fortress, fortified by sin, which Christ invades. He takes the 'doore of entrance into you', the moment of crisis being 'the Petard, that broke open thy *Iron gate*, that was the *Chariot*, by which he entred into thee'.[74] In the moment of conversion Christ's chariot breaks through the 'Iron gate' of the unconverted soul-city, just as He will break through that of hell-prison at the End. So, here, by sexual conversion the lovers will 'make our [chariot of the] Sun. . .run' (45–6), bringing Him into their hearts. Equally, in their mutual "invasion" of each other's bodily prisons they imitate in their sexual conversion Christ's violent entrance into the individual during conversion.

In the first paragraph we saw that they were faced with the spiritual choice between the activist 'way' to salvation and the 'broad' way which, by dilatoriness, would lead to antichristian damnation for the Mistress if she remained unconverted and went "abroad". Here they have made their choice of activism—avoiding the choice to 'languish' in Time. Therefore they escape the mouth of Time-as-hell and achieve resurrection—entry into the New Jerusalem. That simultaneous escape and entrance is implied in the 'gates of Life' which they tear through, 'Thorough' allowing the ambiguity of a going-out which is equally a going-in, since it specifies neither. The gated city of 'Life' is at once the gated New Jerusalem of everlasting life, to which they gain access by their "death" here, and the gated City of Hell and Death,[75] from which souls are released by resurrection. The latter is explicitly present in 'Iron', which was the chthonic metal[76] signifying evil and hence the antichristian 'iron teeth' too. Similarly, in the formulation 'gates of Life' is a deviation from the traditional formula 'gates of death', which it implicitly recalls.[77] The ambiguity of these 'gates of Life', as at once the gates of duration/death/damnation and of eternal life, rests upon the orthodox theological notion that the gates of death are the only access to eternal life: 'our *issue* in death shall be an *entrance* into everlasting life'; a going out which is also a coming in, to the Kingdom. When 'the gate of my prison [of death and sin] be opened, a gate into Heaven I shall have'.[78]

Given this complex of imagistic implication, in which both 'gates' and 'grates' have useful connotations, it is no wonder that we have two versions of this line, for the textual insertion that makes for 'grates' may reflect Marvell's own indecision in the original manuscript of the poem. Both hell and the New Jerusalem, like the devourer's mouth, have gates and grates, since 'grates' could figure the portcullis[79] within the gates of a stronghold. That the lovers' egress out of Hell City should be violent is understandable, but that ingress into the New Jerusalem should be by the same degree of violence may at first appear strange. In fact, while the New Jerusalem was in any case a fortified city (as we have seen), from scripture it was stressed—especially in the Puritan myth of constant spiritual warfare—that activist saints should be 'those violent ones which force the Kingdom of Heaven'.[80] It is this militant attitude—against Antichrist and for salvation—that the lovers' violent copulative "assault" enacts here; love-as-activism can force entrance to the Kingdom of Love, Christ the Spouse's New Jerusalem. That reward is the ultimate victory over what had seemed to be Time's proscription of love, for in that Kingdom love will be endless. The lovers' sexual 'Pleasures' hence signify those renovatory 'Pleasures' which the activist Hastings also enjoyed after death (*Hastings*, 30). By this means the lovers' sexual union is rendered as not only 'Conversion', but also the activism in which conversion is expressed, and the resurrection and renovation which reward converted action. Hereby sex itself, for these godly lovers, becomes victory over time in a way that was not possible for the pagan genre of *carpe diem*.

In the last paragraph of the poem the intensity of sexual activity becomes the most striking figure of activism's consumption of time, personalizing that mode whereby Cromwell's 'Vigour' could 'contract' it. Activism consumes time, accelerates it, in order to bring on the End. Since that is what the lovers are envisioning in sexual activism, the Final Image ratifies their victory over time by accelerating the Coming: 'Thus, though we cannot make our Sun/Stand still, yet we will make him run.' (45—6). On the literal level, this implies that although they cannot extend time (in the manner envisaged in the first paragraph), thus extending their lives and courtship, yet they can shorten time. That idea has been a great critical problem, explanations for which have consisted in the assertion that sexual intensity makes time fast, "as it were": a remarkably rhetorical victory for the lovers, if that is all this means. But, as we have seen, their victory is, far from rhetorical, eschatological and therefore real. In eschatology only the spiritual reality matters. The godly lovers' activism is like all other species of activism in that it speeds time; thus 'make him run' is very specific. They not only consume their own lives ("make our sun of personal duration travel faster"), but accelerate the Coming of Christ the Sun of Righteousness. Thus they implement the desire of the godly (in literal fashion) that He should hasten to come. That desire is for the consummation of time, which is also the consummation of the Last Marriage to Christ the Bridegroom, invoked here as 'the sun. . .like a bridegroom' in His vigour, who 'rejoiceth. . .to run a race.' (Psalm 19:4–5). His vigour and haste as Bridegroom is replicated and anticipated by theirs as violent lover-activists. In their hasting of time they properly match themselves to His hasting and His desire, and thus their sexual version of activism is Christologically conceived. They are like Cromwell in matching the divine tempo; so, chiliastically timely, this Final Image contradicts the antichristian extension of time which the first paragraph manifested as the antichristian version of love.

Hence the logic whereby the play on speeding up (46) and prolonging time (46) also compares with the Cromwellian poems. Like him, in *First Anniversary*, the lovers here do not 'make our Sun stand still'. In terms of *carpe diem* convention, of course, they cannot do this and thereby extend existence; in terms of the eschatological narrative, the speaker has from the first indicated that it cannot be done in the Latter Days and that anyway, as converted saint, he would not want to extend time and courtship. Rather they will chiliastically make the sun run as Cromwell does, by opposing his haste to the antichristian forces which make time stand 'still'; and like Hastings the lovers will 'out*run* [their] age'. While, in *Death of O.C.*, Joshua's miracle of making the sun stand still in the heavens is recalled as an image of the divine favour vouchsafed to Cromwell (191—2), here that allusion is more successfully used to imply that that Old Testament miracle is inappropriate and unavailable in the new dispensation of Christ. He must be made to 'run' if He is to bring their Kingdom of Love, for haste is the Latter Day mode.

This Final Image implements the greatest irony of the poem. The *carpe diem* genre is redirected from pagan defeat of love by death to Christian victory by death as the *eschaton*; virginity is antichristian fornication and godly union is chiliastic activism. Therefore, if the lengthy courtship envisaged in the first paragraph is antichristian, immediate consummation is chiliasm in action, and by bringing on the Coming it brings endless consummation—the Kingdom inaugurated by the Coming. By that process the Kingdom of Love suddenly renders all the pagan/antichristian 'Impossibles' of the first paragraph possible. The lovers will have, not endless courtship (as there), but endless consummation (much better, naturally). Union as members of Christ in the Kingdom will endow the speaker with the Christ-like potency envisaged in the first paragraph as impossible; the Mistress will experience not antichristian riches, but the true effortless plenitude of the New Jerusalem paradise; and there she will find rather the 'Rubies' of *Christ*'s blood (salvation) and Christ's redemption, the 'jewel' of His ransom of mankind.[81] Equally, the 'long Loves Day' that was unavailable to the lovers in time is what the Kingdom will give them in its 'everlasting day' of Love. That Kingdom replaces the antichristian 'State' of bondage and the 'pow'r' of mortal time with the lovers' own rule, the reign of the saints in the Millennium. In this manner the Final Image's reversal of the initial 'Impossibles' is the poem's greatest irony, an irony at once eschatological and affirmative. The affirmation of the lovers' victory is an effect of God's irony, whereby time as eschatology is emancipation from time. Similarly, Marvell's reversal of the Catullan 'Impossibles'—elements proscribed by time and mortal existence—overturns the essentially defeatist character of the *carpe diem* genre, which "ratifies" time's power by making it the persuasion to love now; by making time the agent of *love's* power and endlessness, Marvell turns the pagan-antichristian genre upside down in a sort of literary act of eschatological 'overturning'. Catullus saw the sun's diurnal resurrection as something he could not have (*To Lesbia*, 4—6), but the Final Image's 'Sun' is chiliastically made 'our Sun' too. The 'rate' of love is no longer its "price", but the "tempo" which brings love's endless "rewards".

Apocalyptic union identifies the lovers with Christ: as the Christological 'Ball' of union they achieve His perfection, which was traditionally imaged by the geometrical perfection of a sphere.[82] In that sense, too, He is 'our Sun' the divine globe—the goldenness of which counteracts the 'Iron' of death, war, and hell. The apocalyptic solution of the lovers' temporal problem enacts that which is denied in the geometrics of *The Definition of Love*. In that poem, because time is linear, each lover's life is a line, and as "parallel lines" they are condemned to "infinite extension" and thus endless separation. This is the condition of all mortal loves: as Thomas Browne wrote, 'United soules are not satisfied with embraces, but desire each to be truly the other, which being impossible, *their desires are infinite*, and must proceed without a possibility of satisfaction.'[83] Marvell's *Definition* renders that frustration in formal mathematical terms, which imply the rigid conditions of existence, that 'Fate does Iron wedges drive' between the lovers (III). The Iron Age Fate is antichristian tyranny, forbidding elect union because such union is only possible in the final Kingdom, and hence would signify that the Fourth Empire of Antichrist had been destroyed:

> For Fate with jealous Eye does see
> Two perfect Loves; nor lets them close:
> Their union would her ruine be,
> And her Tyrannick pow'r depose.
>
> (IV)

If Iron Age Fate is the Whore's time and age, her Fourth

Empire is signified by the fourth stanza. To let the lovers 'close' in union would be to have let time 'close' in its Ending, the Kingdom effecting their union. The time-bound frustration of 'As Lines so Loves. . .so truly *Paralel*' (original italics) is that their very "truth" in love and compatibility impels their frustration at the impossibility of parallels uniting; this is love under the conditions of doubleness. Like the lovers of *Coy Mistress*, the only solution to their frustration is apocalypse, for at His Coming Christ 'brings all into one againe'. If 'Loves whole World on us does wheel' (V), then the world itself must be crushed from globe into wheel—in geometric terms a '*Planisphere*'—and this must be effected by apocalypse. Union is therefore impossible

> Unless the giddy Heaven fall,
> And Earth some new Convulsion tear;
> And, us to joyn, the World should all
> Be cramp'd into a *Planisphere*.
>
> (VI)

The *Definition*'s wistful image of the apocalyptic solution recalls in 'giddy Heaven fall' Virgil's Sign of the End, 'aspice convexo nutantem pondere mundum. . .caelumque profundum' (Eclogue IV, 50–1). But the End is not yet. The Final Image sums up temporal frustration:

> Therefore the Love which us doth bind,
> But Fate so enviously debarrs,
> Is the Conjunction of the Mind,
> And Opposition of the Stars.
>
> (VIII)

The *stars* should conjoin, of course, that being an astrological function; instead, the 'Conjunction' is mental compatibility between the lovers, frustrated by the parallel extensions of mortal doubleness. To redress that, the 'Conjuncton of the Stars', implicit in the paradox here, is required, because this would signify destiny's conjunction of apocalypse with their love, rendering that love timely. Equally, as unifying their doubleness, that would be the personal 'Conjunction' effected by the apocalyptic Coming. But, because the time of apocalypse is not yet fulfilled, the lovers are subject to the

'Opposition of the Stars': destiny and the current time oppose the fulfilment of union. If *Definition of Love* formalizes the despair of lovers whose apocalyptic solution is as yet denied, *Coy Mistress* celebrates the conjunction of love through timeliness and its apocalyptic issue.

If *Coy Mistress* and *Definition* are therefore oppositional variants on the theme of love in history, *Coy Mistress* extends and wittily dramatizes the devotional emblem-poem *On a Drop of Dew*. Unhappily exiled from its heavenly home, nervous of its fragile embodiment on earth, the dewdrop of the soul is enfranchised from earthly chill (the cold of death and sin) when "evaporated" at the rising of the Sun of Righteousness, by the warmth of His love. Hence it achieves reunion with the heavenly Bridegroom:

> Congeal'd on Earth: but does, dissolving, run
> Into the Glories of th'Almighty Sun.
>
> (39–40)

Here, too, to 'run' is essentially to die, 'dissolving' from the body but finding thereby the 'Glories' of immortal life in Christ's Kingdom, which is His glorification, too. The exile is ended by this *telos* in the Final Image, for as the fortieth line it signifies numerologically the fulfilment of the forty years of exile from their own Kingdom which was undergone by the Old Israel. (Similarly, line 40 of *Coy Mistress* marked the duration of Time's 'pow'r' to exile the lovers from their Kingdom.) The poem *Dew* ends not just with death-unto-resurrection, but with the vision of the final resurrection in glory; for that is the true history of the soul, extending beyond time, and this emblem of the soul's experience would be incomplete without it. Like *Coy Mistress*, this poem, too, is a love story. Like her counterpart in the Latin version of this poem, *Ros*, the soul on earth is a virgin fearful of spiritual fornication: 'it the purple flow'r does slight' of carnality, avoiding its tempting bed, 'Scarce touching where it lyes' (9–10); therefore it is 'In how *coy* a Figure wound. . .the World excluding' (27–9). The dewdrop soul is like a young virgin fearful of assault (*Ros*, 17–20), 'Trembling lest it grow impure' (*Dew*, 17). The dewdrop's spherical character recalls its heavenly origin and signifies its purity (5–8). It 'Frames as it can its native Element' in this form because it strives to remain the perfect sphere or *virgo intacta* for the heavenly Bridegroom's final embrace: that which the Final Image effects, 'dissolving' that intactness for union. Joy dissolves the dewdrop's earthly grief of exile—the dewdrop then 'its own Tear' (13)—into consummating warmth. While this poem implicitly recalls Christ as Himself the dew of grace, foreshadowed in the type of 'Manna' (37), because the dewdrop-soul is that manna (Christ's grace living as a promise within) it too is "unfulfilled" until He comes, putting grace into effect. The covert narrative of sexual fulfilment in this devotional poem makes it complementary to *Coy Mistress*, where the witty love-lyric becomes at once wittier and more profound by means of its eschatological narrative. It is no accident that their Final Images should be so similar.

However, unlike *Dew*, this poem acknowledges the violence, pain and cataclysm of apocalypse as well as its promise and fulfilment, and gives the intensity of that compound to the personal experience of love. Without recognizing this apocalyptic dimension, we cannot begin to understand the peculiar tone and power of *To His Coy Mistress*. There is no sense in trying (as so many have) to deny the essential grimness of this poem, for its grotesqueries, seen in their true—eschatological—light, are the very condition of its celebration and affirmation. The poem's putative dating at 1646[84]—which I would suggest is confirmed by its forty-six lines, formalizing the temporal theme—would indeed place it in the Latter Day War and hence topicalize its urgent sense of imminent Ending. The poem's mood is apocalyptic and dangerous, but thereby extravagant and witty, too; eschatology is at once temporal pressure and liberating too. This poem is Marvell's finest achievement in the joco-serious mode: love and eschatology live more vividly in each other's presence.

(ii) RENOVATION OF THE DESOLATOR: *THE MOWERS SONG*

A similar transformation and revivification of a classical genre is effected in *The Mowers Song*, where the traditional Pastoral

'Complaint' of the unrequited lover is re-intensified by its Latter Day ambience. As usual, the lover reproaches the natural landscape around him for its luxuriance, as if indifferent to his misery.[85] But this conventional pattern is, in the poem's problematic, merged with a parabolic tale of Latter Day love. In contrast to the elect lovers of *Coy Mistress*, the tragi-comic Mower and his Juliana are unregenerate or 'natural' beings—a spiritual value denoted here partly by their rusticity or "naturalness". Thus the Mower's frustrated love is magnified by images of desolation: in the psychological crisis of the poem, "natural" love and its antichristian bondage goad the Mower into his naïve salvation.

Marvell's ubiquitous figure of the Mower has long been recognized as a departure from the central tradition of Pastoral, which tended to concentrate upon the Shepherd[86]—a tradition reflected in some slighter Marvellian Pastoral lyrics.[87] No one has provided a convincing explanation for this new departure in Pastoral; whereas, in fact, Marvell's frequent return to the Mower figure reflects his chiliastic cast upon Pastoral, as the figure represents Death, desolation, and—foreshadowing Christ the Mower—desolating harvest in the service of renovation.[88] His peculiarly desolatory characteristics (in contrast to the Shepherd) are evident especially in his representation of man's need to toil for sustenance after the Fall (Genesis 3:17–19). In *Paradise Lost* Abel is a shepherd whereas the sinful Cain is a 'sweaty reaper' like Marvell's (XI. 434–7). The issue of sin is introduced immediately in the *Song*:

> My Mind was once the true survey
> Of all these Medows fresh and gay;
> And in the greenness of the Grass
> Did see its Hopes as in a Glass;
>
> (I)

From this innocence the Mower has "fallen".[89] As the 'Grass' is mortal man, the 'Hopes' reflected in its greenness are those of bodily *renovatio*: 'the verdant state of things is the symbol of the Resurrection'.[90] He has lost his chance of salvation and resurrection, he thinks, because his fall was

When *Juliana* came, and She
What I do to the Grass, does to my Thoughts and Me.
(I)

This is the refrain of the poem, its meaning slightly modified
at each recurrence. In the literal sense, she "reduces" the
Mower in the same way that he reduces the field to
stubble—at once "reduces" him and causes him to "fall" like
the grass ('the Grasses fall', *The Mower to the Glowworms*
[II]), "reduces" to and by lust. That is, like the biblical grass,
this lust is the biblical fornication of "idolatry": as lover, he
idolizes her, and as soul his idolatry enslaves him to her
soi-disant antichristian dominance. The latter is indicated by
Juliana's nomenclature: as Maria-Astraea is the renovating
August of Time, so the Mower's inamorata is the antichristian
July of Latter Day *desolatio*. In *Damon the Mower*, her
influence scorches the earth and deranges the Mower; in *The
Mower to the Glowworms* her 'foolish fires' of lust mislead
him (III), and as a result he loses his way "home"—to
Heaven.[91] That is, like *Tom May*, and Marvell visiting
Fleckno, he has wandered from the true spiritual way.

'Not *July* causeth these Extremes,/But *Juliana's* scorching
beams' (*Damon*, III): her desolating effect upon the landscape, imaged as heat and fire,[92] signifies her antichristian
linkage with the earth's last conflagration. Her scorching of
fields to stubble is implicit in the refrain here, where the
Mower's reduction of the fields to stubble by reaping is
imitated in her psychological effect upon him: the result of his
fall before her will be not merely antichristian enslavement
but its burning damnatory issue. Her Coming—'When
Juliana came'—is a profane Coming, in contradistinction to
Maria-Astraea's, ending the Mower's 'Hopes' of salvation. By
such means this tragi-comic Pastoral lyric takes a blackly
comic intensity from its transformation into a Pastoral
comedy of Latter Day love.

If Juliana is the Mower's personal Scarlet Whore, the
Mower is an appropriate foil, since mowers had long been
associated with concupiscence and frequently featured in
bawdy ballads. Indeed, the word 'mow' was colloquial for
copulation.[93] As a faintly comic lyric protagonist, the Mower

personalizes apocalyptic psychology, while his resonances as a type universalize the experience of the poem, as a sort of witty parable for individual experience of the Latter Days. (Indeed, this tragi-comic parabolic quality is probably the source of critics' difficulties with the *Mower* poems).

Naturally, Juliana drives a wedge between the Mower and Creation (II–III), and while the grass 'Grew more luxuriant', the Mower 'pine[d]' (II). While on one level this signifies that like all poetic lovers he is consumed by his unrequited love, on another it signifies that he is "devoured" by this antichristian lust. Like all mankind, the Mower depends upon the growth of the grass for survival: it is his sustenance, just as spiritually he is her food because she is antichristian. That grim little joke underlies the refrain in the second stanza. In the following stanza that image is developed as antichristian subjection. The Mower reproaches the meadows for their luxuriance 'While I lay trodden under feet?/When *Juliana* came . . .'; that is, she treads upon him as he was used to tread upon the grass. The latter signifies his once (as it were) erect stance and upwardly mobile soul, with its 'Hopes' of resurrection; quondam Lord of Creation like Adam— subjecting both Nature and mortality, as two elements of the 'Grass' symbolism. However, he has had an equally Adamic Fall, also through his love for a woman (the traditionally chauvinistic notion that woman caused the Fall). Thus he is now subjected, his unhappiness making him less than the luxuriant Creation of which he was once "overlord" and 'survey[or]'; and his subjection to Juliana's "treading" is the antichristian obverse of Christ's treading the serpent at the End, the Mower's personal experience of the antichristian dominance which precedes that final victory. This antichristian success in further alienating the Mower from his natural environment is an implementation of the sinful potential of postlapsarian division. Man's doubleness is his division from the Creation, his internal division between soul and body, the war within between good and evil, and the war without which is the sexual division. Since only Christ's Coming will repair man's divisions, what the Mower requires to repair Juliana's ill effects is the solution at once to antichristianism and to doubleness—to precipitate the apocalypse. For this comically diminutive account of the eschatological trope, it should be remembered that in one sense the Mower treads 'Grass' as "flesh"—mortality or mankind, as does Juliana when she treads on him: she has subjected his flesh to lust, while generally she has subjected mankind to her antichristian government. In this comic image the pair are representative of the universal psychological experience of antichristianism. The solution is, equally, at once universal and personal. A voluntary provocation of the *eschaton* is, as in *Coy Mistress*, a suicide:

> But what you [the fields] in Compassion ought,
> Shall now by my Revenge be wrought:
> And Flow'rs, and Grass, and I and all,
> Will in one common Ruine fall.
>
> (IV)

The 'one common Ruine' with which the Mower threatens his little world imitates the universal ruin. Specifically, it brings him into 'one' again with Nature, which instead of denying 'fellowship' (III) with his desolating pain will share with him the *desolatio*. Just as the final 'Ruine' is ultimately fortunate, so this is a fortunate 'fall', recalling Adam's own Fortunate Fall into the realm of free will: the Mower's wilful suicide does in fact save him from Juliana and damnation, a contrast to the desolating fall of the first stanza. This is because the true 'Grasses Fall' or harvest is not the Mower's annual reaping but the Harvest of the End:

> We talk of harvests; there are no such things,
> But when we leave our corn and hay [of flesh]:
> There is no fruitefull yeare, but that which brings
> The last and lov'd, though dreadful day.[94]

Thus, by sublimating his office—effecting a miniature apocalyptic harvest—the Mower asserts identification with Christ, and partakes of His victory over antichristianism and mortality. In the eschatological logic of the poem, he revenges himself not only on his environment—ending the pain of alienation—but upon Juliana too, thus aborting unrequited

and tormenting love. The Mower is not such a fool as he
seems, since by instinct (his professional instinct, as it were)
he has done the right thing, effecting at once escape and
victory. Identity, or singleness, is restored to him by a
paradoxical suicide. (In which, of course, there is an echo of
conversion's annihilation of the "natural man" or concupis-
cent Mower-type).

By relieving Juliana of the initiative of desolation, the
Mower's self-annihilation brings renovation by means of
personal Ending or conversion:

> And thus, ye Meadows, which have been
> Companions of my thoughts more green,
> Shall now the Heraldry become
> With which I shall adorn my Tomb;
>
> (V)

In this Final Image the *telos* is envisaged, with consequent
renovation of the self and ultimate resurrection. The fields
that were once the 'Heraldry' of his 'Hopes' of renovation are
returned to that function on his tomb: the Mower effects a
restoration of his renovatory capacity, just as the End itself is
'the restoration of all things'. The final articulation of the
refrain after these lines indicates that what Juliana did to him
was to make him conscious of sin and alienation (as the first
stanza indicated), thereby in fact supplying the prerequisite of
conversion. By taking 'Revenge' upon the landscape's sin of
indifference (Nature is fallen too),[95] the Mower as it were kills
and converts Nature too—into the 'Heraldry' of renovation.
As Juliana destroys him, so he destroys all, and thereby
restores it. In that sense 'Heraldry' implies memorial and
familial symbolism, signifying the Mower's new-won immortality and regeneration/generation.

By means of its curious but logical play with eschatological
tropes of individual psychology, this poem wittily encapsulates the biblical reminder that 'If therefore that which is
sown be not turned upside down . . . then cannot it come that
is sown with good'. (II Esdras 4: 28–9). In that light the
Mower's experiences are not merely vaguely comic and
almost antipastoral (as they seem), but rather wittily clever

exploitations of psycho-spiritual realities. Marvell has found yet another method of bending Pastoral to chiliastic purposes.

(iii) RENOVATION AND CREATION: *THE GARDEN*

The topic of *The Garden* is essentially what seems to have been the only love of Marvell's life: poetry itself. Recalling the tradition of solitudinous reflection in an enclosed garden, it is animated by that element in the Puritan spirit of 'rural simplicity and plainness, of the countryman's dislike for the wicked city, England's Babylon';[96] a plainness analogous to that of the 'true religion' itself. This attitude is distinctly different from the Stoic-hermetic-Sabine-Roman Catholic (etc.) atmospheres in which the poem is usually placed by critics wrestling with its images and argument.[97] The joco-serious mode of *The Garden* is similar to that of *Appleton House* in its playfully stringent intensities. There Marvell underwent a sylvan interval which proved to be negligent, while here he experiences a true interval of quietism, that in which the private poem of apocalypse is made: an interval, that is, fully conscious of the true purposes of quietism, and of remembrance of activism as its necessary context.

The first stanza withdraws from that world with a characteristic extravagance, which acknowledges that quietism must (as, at the end of the poem, it will) ultimately give way to activism:

> How vainly men themselves amaze
> To win the Palm, the Oke, or Bayes;
> And their uncessant Labours see
> Crown'd from some single Herb or Tree.

The 'uncessant Labours' 'To win' life's race implicitly recall a cardinal text of activism, 'I have finished my *course . . .* Henceforth there is laid up for me *a crown* of righteousness'.[98] Such a recollection of activism's race to the End—to be 'Crown'd' in sainthood—remains of covert significance within the purely metaphorical logic of the argument, and is to be borne in mind for a re-emergence later. It is supported precisely by the terms of its "alternative"; for the 'prudent' tree, the 'sacred Plants' of 'quiet . . . And Innocence', reflect the biblical characterization of godly men: 'called trees of righteousness, the planting of the Lord'.[99] Such 'sacred Plants' are in their own way, like the race of activism, conducive that 'the Lord . . . might be glorified'.[100] Like the trees 'that to Heaven shooting are' (the Fairfaxes in their legitimate quietism), such plants are symbolic of an interval. The metaphor of man as righteous tree colludes with the sanctified *locus amoenus* of a garden in Marvell's description of his quietist interval here.

Thus the 'Inverted Tree' of "Marvell's" negligence in *Appleton House* is replaced by the righteous Tree in its integrity: 'where s'eer your barkes I wound,/No Name shall but *your own* be found' (III). The joco-serious argument of the first four stanzas, with its dependence upon paradox, in fact establishes the antinomy of quietism and activism. Forsaking 'busie Companies of Men', Marvell finds that 'Society is all but rude,/To this delicious Solitude' (II). There is a quibble on 'Companies' as amorous relations,[101] which the next stanza develops by envisaging trees as 'Fair[er]' alternatives to women: 'How far these Beauties Hers exceed!', 'am'rous . . . this lovely green'. Thus, whereas in *Appleton House*'s withdrawal, 'Beauty, aiming at the Heart,/Bends in some Tree its useless Dart', in the true quietism of *The Garden* trees actually substitute for women. The association between amorous relationship and the world of action, evident in both poems, here provides an identification of love and activism (as in *Coy Mistress*). The wit of that counterpoint to 'delicious Solitude' is the more evident when we recall Thomas Browne's desire to 'procreate like trees',[102] without a mate: asexual trees thus recalling original innocence in 'that happy Garden-state,/While Man there walk'd without a Mate' (VIII). More significant is the biblical 'tree' as a metaphor not merely for 'righteousness' but for renovation. The paradox of trees' 'green Age' in *Appleton House* figured that of renovation; the trees' 'lovely green' is appropriate to *The Garden* because such an interval properly refreshes and renovates the self. Equally, the insistent paradoxes of these stanzas reflect the paradoxes of renovation itself.

Here such renovatory paradoxes spring from the Pauline comparison of resurrection to a seed's germination: 'a diuersitie both in one and the self same thing which hath now one forme and then another. . .[like] the resurrection. . . or . . . changing . . .into a better state'.[103] The renovatory significance of trees, emblematizing resurrection, implies that renovation is metamorphosis by ending: 'We shall all be changed . . . in the twinkling of an eye, at the last . . . this corruptible must put on incorruption' (I Corinthians 15:51–3). This sudden metamorphosis[104] is anticipated by that of conversion into 'New Creature'.[105] As recapitulated in the quietist interval, personal renovation is signified by the further paradoxes of stanza four:

> When we have run our Passions heat,
> Love hither makes his best retreat.
> The *Gods*, that mortal Beauty chase,
> Still in a Tree did end their race.
> *Apollo* hunted *Daphne* so,
> Only that She might Laurel grow.
> And *Pan* did after *Syrinx* speed,
> Not as a Nymph, but for a Reed.

The withdrawal from action is here explicitly also 'Love . . . his best retreat'. The wilful inversion of the mythic allusions here—Apollo and Pan were in the active race for love, not trees—also maintains the poem's withdrawal from love-as-activism. Equally, these myths of metamorphosis recall the nature of renovation. In the Christianization of pagan myth, Apollo and Pan were figures for Christ,[106] and the pursuit of Daphne was understood as the Bridegroom's pursuit of the soul, His bride; so Daphne's transformation itself became a metaphor for the pursuit of the soul's perfection.[107] This condition was attained by the transformation into the 'new creature'. That metamorphosis, electing the soul to final resurrection, was prefigured and promised by Christ's Passion and resurrection. Hence the Christological puns of 'The *Gods*, that mortal Beauty chase,/Still in a Tree did end their race'. This witty formulation, introducing Apollo/

Christ's pursuit, also allows to 'chase' the ambiguity of "delineate, create": the Creator of 'mortal Beauty' Himself died, for God the Father and His son 'in a Tree did end their race' or "family". Wrapped in the classical formula of '*Gods*', this introduction to the classical myths of metamorphosis thus underpins the Christological reference of 'Apollo' and 'Pan', and signifies the redeeming paradoxes of the Passion— the Creator killed, the death that promises resurrection. The 'Tree' of the Passion is symbol equally of man's sin and of its ransoming promise of renovation. The 'end' of Christ's active 'race' was a beginning also, because a transformation. The 'Still' quality of death is yet a mutation, for Christ and His saints: the alteration, which is also a stillness, itself implies the death/renovation implicit in the 'end' of time itself—the 'end' of the *human* 'race' which the Lord created and 'chase[d]'.

These ambiguities make of Marvell's wilfully extravagant paradoxes and inversions witty formulations for renovation. Similarly, the 'Reed' of Pastoral poetry and the 'Laurel', signifying here especially Apollo's metonymy for prophetic poetry and healing (or renovation),[108] characterize this poem itself, as a Pastoral of quietist renovation for the poet. It contrasts with the 'Bayes' of the first stanza, which was identified as activist poetry by its associaton with the race of activism, warlike ('the Palm') and civic ('the Oke'). Here, the preferred 'race' (28) is the pursuit of the soul's private perfection, in the renovatory interval. Properly, then, the poem espouses the poetic 'Garlands of repose' (8; in distinction to the poetic '*wreaths* of Fame and Interest' in *The Coronet*).

This evocation of renovation introduces Marvell's experience of a 'wond'rous Life' in which the garden anticipates the last state of renovation:

> What wond'rous Life in this I lead!
> Ripe Apples drop about my head;
> The Luscious Clusters of the Vine
> Upon my Mouth do crush their Wine;
> The Nectaren, and curious Peach,
> Into my hands themselves do reach;
> (V)

The fifth stanza evokes the Fifth Kingdom, Marvell's interval anticipating the pleasures of that final renovation. As in *Bermudas'* vision of the same effortless plenitude of the New Jerusalem, the saint is the patient of Nature's service: 'He makes the Figs our mouths to meet' or, here, 'Vine/Upon my Mouth do crush their Wine'. The wine's self-induced pressing is to recall Christ as the Winepress at the End (Revelation 14:19; 19:15), an image of apocalyptic judgment which, here, is conflated with the redemptive wine of His blood (prepared for by His Passion in stanza IV). In receiving the draught Marvell is envisaged as one of those redeemed at the final judging. That image participates in the general allusion, both here and in *Bermudas*, to the banquet of the saved at the End, where God "serves" the redeeming food to the elect (Revelation 19:9).[109] The banquet's dishes are drawn from the fruits of the Tree of Life, including the 'Apples'. The 'wondrous' nature of the New Jerusalem pleasures is anticipated by the wondrous object, the '*curious* peach', which implies God's natural workmanship, and the 'Nectaren' hybrid signifies that 'grafting' whereby New and Old Israel are matched in God's election (Romans 11:16ff.), as His spiritual 'fruits'. But the final couplet, while misread and overread—like the rest of this poem—by commentators, is neither positive nor negative in implication. The Latter Day War raging outside this garden (as glanced at in the first stanza's activist symbols) recapitulates that whereby the Old Israel was scourged, and their desolation is 'A Lodge in a Garden of Cucumbers' or melons.[110] That image is reflected in the 'Melons' here because Marvell's retreat from the desolated Garden of England into this internal garden of renovation is only temporary; and he must share the mortality of which war is the contemporary agent. Because this is only a brief foretaste of future immortality, the end of this stanza acknowledges his mortality still: 'Stumbling on Melons, as I pass,/Insnar'd with Flow'rs, I fall on Grass' (V.39–40). The line 40 is numerologically recalling Israel's period of exile from the Kingdom/Canaan, the 'Flow'rs' are again those of corporality, and the 'Grass' that of flesh. Falling, as man always falls, by the flesh, Marvell's 'Stumbling' recalls the difficulty of the true 'way' to this Kingdom and his 'pass'-age recalls that this mortal world is 'only for waftage' to that destination, and beset with snares for the saint's feet. On a more literal level, Marvell's harmless landing on soft turf intimates that this stumbling is merely the necessary recollection of mortality that must penetrate the renovation available in this world.

At this point, while the senses anticipate their final delights, 'the Mind' effects a further 'withdraw[al]' in the garden. In the 'Mind' the renovation of the spirit takes its full effect,[111] and thus the interval *properly* begins. With, of course, 'Mean while':

> Mean while the Mind, from pleasure less,
> Withdraws into its happiness:
> The Mind, that Ocean where each kind
> Does streight its own resemblance find;
> Yet it creates, transcending these,
> Far other Worlds, and other Seas;
> Annihilating all that's made
> To a green Thought in a green Shade.
>
> (VI)

This is not only the mind in *renovatio* ('happiness') but also the imagination in poetic creation: taking flight from the characterization of renovatory poetry in stanza IV. The burden of this stanza is that the poet's imagination, renovated in this interval, recreates the external world and thus anticipates the recreation in *renovatio* of the end: 'creates, transcending these,/Far other Worlds'. Thus the self's anticipation of its renovation provides a similar anticipation to the poetic imagination.

Springing from the notion of the poet's creative activity as analogous to that of God the Creator, the mind's ability to comprehend 'each kind' reflects its equally analogous "omniscience". 'All things are subject to the Mind . . . The seas, the air, the fire, all things . . . And this liberty is the excellence of the mind'.[112] Compared thus to the 'Ocean', the mind is taken to imitate the sea's capacity to reproduce all the 'kind[s]' of life which are found on land;[113] more particularly, the reflective 'sea of glass' in Revelation itself could represent *Contemplative* men'.[114] Therein they imitate the divine meaning of the 'sea of glass', that 'this globe . . . is in the view of God as crystal' and clear.[115] Hence, in renovation, the mind's capacities imitate the divine perception of the world. Similarly, 'it creates, transcending these,/Far other Worlds', for in poetic creation it imitates not only God as Creator, but also as re-Creator of the world. Like Hastings in *his* interval, it 're-creates', both in terms of its own refreshing recreation (the mind at joco-serious play) and in its renovation of the actual world into 'other Worlds'. Poetry provides a metamorphosis which is analogous to that of *renovatio* itself.

By this means his imagination mimics Marvell's personal renovation in his 'little world of man':[116] microcosmic echoing the macrocosmic renovations, in the poet-saint's 'renovation or renewing of the mind'.[117] Marvell recalls Sidney's description of poetic invention, that:

> The poet . . . doth grow in effect another Nature, in making things either better than Nature bringeth forth, or, quite anew . . . . Her world is brazen, the poets only deliver a golden.[118]

—'each kind/Does *streight* its own resemblance find' in the poetic mind because, like the 'streightness' which Maria-Astraea bestowed upon Nature, the poetic mind 'better[s]' or reforms Nature's realities, and pictures instead nature as it will be in the 'golden' renovation of the End. The poet can do this because in imitating God's divine apprehension of the World-Sea he sees beyond phenomena to the providential beauty behind them, the sea of glass.[119] In this sense the "sea of reality" is annihilated/desolated so that the 'sea of glass' becomes visible: the poet is 'Annihilating all that's made/To a green Thought' of renovation. In this annihilation the mind's 'Ocean' anticipates the final Deluge.

The 'green Shade' in which this is achieved is the 'umbra' of poetic life, which retires from time and activism; 'green' again because renovating by quietism. Because of the poetic mirroring of the world in renovation, this is also a 'green Shade' or shadow/"image" of that renovation. Equally, the poem's constant recollection of Christ's agency in that renovation is recalled in that biblically He was the 'Shade' or refuge and protector of His elect,[120] as this garden's 'verged Shade' is to Marvell. In its combination of artificial green darkness with renovatory verdancy, this image is equivalent to *Bermudas'* 'green Night' in the New Jerusalem.

The Ending metamorphosis effected by poetic imagination is as swift as the world's; equally, the Six Days of Creation were understood as ideas rather than temporal units, the Creation being as swift as the End.[121] Just so is the poet's own creation-as-annihilation 'streight' or instant. Numerological-ly, this sixth stanza recalls the days of Creation, and also that the present Latter Days are the 'sixth age' before the seventh millennium, or world's sabbath.[122] In the sixth age will be effected the transformation anticipated by the poet's here. Poetry is properly eschatology, an activity miming both the process and the product of God's plan.

In the sixth or Last Age, time itself is a tree,[123] the Chosen are the branches of Christ and live in the promise of the Cross-tree[122]—images which inform the seventh stanza. As the seventh is the Millennium Age, so this stanza anticipates the renovation then of 'My Soul'. Having pursued perfection (IV) and envisioned the renovation (V-VI), his soul antici-pates its emancipation by death into life:

> Here at the Fountains sliding foot,
> Or at some Fruit-trees mossy root,
> Casting the Bodies Vest aside,
> My Soul into the boughs does glide:
> There like a Bird it sits, and sings,
> Then whets, and combs its silver Wings;
> And, till prepar'd for longer flight,
> Waves in its Plumes the various Light.
>
> (VII)

As, at one level, man is a 'tree', so is his 'Soul' 'like a Bird':

> Mankinde . . . is like the Birds of Paradice . . . born without legs . . . they hover in the air: so are we birds of Paradice; but cast out from thence, and born without legs, without strength to walk in the ways of God, or go to heaven; but by a power from above, we are adopted in our new birth to a celestial conversation.[125]

Thus, while in his mortality Marvell is 'Stumbling' (V), unable 'to walk' perfectly spiritually, so here he feels the 'sliding foot': 'This is the true perfection of them that are borne anew, to confesse that they are imperfite'.[126] But, equally, his 'Soul' can, in its 'new birth' by a renovatory experience, achieve a 'celestial conversation' with the 'Light'. For this is the 'Light' of revelation,[127] as distinct from the 'Shade' of vision in the previous stanza. For, according to Augustine:

> the knowledge of the creature is a kind of twilight, compared with the knowledge of the Creator; and then comes the daylight and the morning, when that knowledge is linked with the praise and love of the Creator.[128]

The full light of revelation appears only in man's perfected union of 'praise and love' with God. Till that union we see the light 'in faded colours', says Augustine[129]—in 'various light', like the refractions on the bird-soul's 'silver Wings'. Revelation is 'various', refracted and fragmented to our apprehensions, until the End, 'when the bright truth discovers all things in their proper colours'.[130] Therefore the soul's ecstasy, feeding upon the promises of revelation, can be fully achieved only by the 'longer flight' of the soul to heaven after death[131] (and, ultimately, to the new heaven). With that acknowledgment of the necessary proscription of the ecstatic experience, Marvell's *'various'* Light' comprehends also the significance of the 'Hoopebird' in Ovid's *Metamorphoses* (appropriately enough for this poem's metamorphic motif)— that its 'order and *variety* of Colours' was 'an Emblem of the *varieties* of the World, the succession of Times and Seasons, and signal *mutations* in them'.[132] Thereby the rainbow of 'various Light' reflects also the revelation in historical events, and their own "metamorphoses". In a sense this means that God's will plays through the radiated being of the saint in his renovatory moment, in the same way as His will plays through the mirror-glass of history; the saint is thus like history just as his poetry was like eschatology. The soul's renovation is his union with God and the purposes of God.

This level of meaning is appropriate to the prophetic character of Marvell's 'Soul', a faculty in which it recalls his characterization of Milton:

Thou singst with so much gravity and ease;
And above humane flight dost soar aloft,
With Plume so strong, so equal, and so soft.
The *Bird* nam'd from that *Paradise* you sing
So never Flags, but alwaies keeps on Wing.
. . .
Just Heav'n Thee, like Tiresias, to requite,
Rewards with *Prophesie* thy loss of Sight.

(*On Mr Milton's "Paradise Lost"*, 36–44)

As we saw, the disability of the Bird of Paradise is 'requite[d]' by its communion with the divine. Extrapolating from Milton's own description of his muse as a bird, Marvell's use of the bird of paradise to characterize prophetic poetry (44) is replicated in *The Garden's* 'Bird'.[133] It mediates revelation 'in its Plumes', its poetry; for, like Milton's 'Plume', this is at once the bird's wing and the quill with which the poet writes, identifying the prophetic muse with its servant, the writer, and its medium, the poem which is written. For the poetry of renovation, to which the fourth and sixth stanzas lay claim, is properly that of prophecy. So, here, the prophetic soul directs the renovated imagination.

For similarly prophetic reasons, the metaphor of the 'Tree' achieves its apotheosis here. 'My Soul into the boughs does glide' because this is the Kingdom-tree, 'so that the birds of the air come and lodge in the branches of it' (Matthew 13:32). That evocation of the Kingdom as the goal of prophetic poetry seals the seventh stanza's numerological reference to the Seventh or Kingdom Age. Similarly, seven is the number—and that age the consummation—of sanctification;[134] then the soul-bird will take its 'longer flight' to sainthood. This interval, and the prophetic poetry which is born of such renovation, are appropriate modes of 'prepar[a-tion]' for that time.

By such means the classical image of the poet as a bird,[135] and the commonplace that 'The Muses rejoice in the fountain and the grove',[136] are brought to refer to the renovatory poet's experience. In the new earth 'They shall not hunger nor thirst; neither shall the heat nor sun smite them . . . even by the springs of water shall he guide them'.[137] So Marvell is fed (V) and 'Shade[d]' (VI), and has access to 'the Fountain'—the 'water of life', which regenerates.[138] Similarly, here the 'Fruit-tree' (like that of stanza V) recalls 'the Tree of Life' and of the righteous man, which 'bringeth forth good fruit'.[139] Thus are encompassed both the renovated man's 'good fruit' and those fruits of the Kingdom which reward his fruity goodness. Similarly, in the 'Fountain' of the "paradise within" there is reference also to the soul's own nature: as 'that Ray/Of the clear Fountain of Eternal Day' (*Dew*, 19–20). Himself both a 'Fountain' and a 'Light' from God, the saint's soul is itself revelatory.[140] Neighbour to that thought is the recollection of the corporal: 'the Fountains sliding foot' is like an oxymoron, reflecting at once the soul's 'Fountain' and the 'sliding foot' of the flesh (wet earth, the earth from which Adam was made). That dichotomous unity encapsulates the stanza, for while it remains on earth and in the body, the soul may only anticipate the ultimate renovation. The 'Fountain', the 'washing of regeneration' in conversion, is grant of access to the Kingdom: 'except a man be born of water', 'he cannot see the kingdom of God'.[141] Seeing what it can in 'the . . . Light' allowed, the soul must therefore content itself with poetic vision of *renovatio*.

The 'enlightened' vision that succeeds renovatory conversion is an 'answer' to divine pressure, 'sometimes spoken of under the metaphor . . . of tasting':[142] thus Marvell was pressed to taste the divine fruits and wine. The metaphor applies equally to the renovation of his self and of his poetry, for here another of Marvell's jokes recalls that (as Aubrey tells us) 'He kept bottles of wine at his lodgeing, and many times he would drinke liberally by himselfe to refresh his spirits, and exalt his muse'.[143] In this comically actual manner a covert joke oils the transition from the renovation of the senses (V) to that of poetry itself (VI). It is, one might say, Marvell's personal signature to the experience of *The Garden*, a joco-serious verification.

As that witty verification introduced the experience of renovation, so an outrageous moment in the eighth stanza marks his exit from the experience of ecstatic *renovatio*:

> Such was that happy Garden-state,
> While Man there walk'd without a Mate:

After a Place so pure, and sweet,
What other Help could yet be meet!
But 'twas beyond a Mortal's share
To wander solitary there:
Two Paradises 'twere in one
To live in Paradise alone.

(VIII)

Since the soul cannot permanently 'Cast . . . the Bodies Vest aside', it returns to an intensified sense that what it desires is 'beyond a *Mortal*'s share'. Recalling the loss of the original 'Garden-state'—from which mortality ensued—Marvell remembers that the Fall was the fault of the woman, Eve. In wishing that he had not been created to share Eden, Marvell flouts God's will, that 'It is not good that the man should be alone: I will make him an *help meet*' (Genesis 2:18). This blasphemy maintains the poem's extravagant rejection of love-as-activism. But *qua* blasphemy, it measures the impossibility of 'Two Paradises . . . in one': it characterizes *itself* as frustrated by the given order of things. This determines both mating and mortality, man's flesh and his love of the flesh. A protest which recognizes this necessity (as itself the thing protested), Marvell's outrageousness here intensifies the moment of loss, when the renovatory experience must be acknowledged as temporary. On earth it is a momentary internal 'Paradise alone'; between the 'Two Paradises' of the first Eden and the last Kingdom, recollecting the innocence of the former and fore-'tasting' the perfection of the latter. In that sense, it is indeed 'Two Paradises . . . in one', but on earth one simply cannot 'live' there.

The necessity for a return to the world is acknowledged in the last stanza, following upon its outrageous "recognition":

How well the skilful Gardner drew
Of flow'rs and herbes this Dial new;
Where from above the milder Sun
Does through a fragrant Zodiack run;
And, as it works, th' industrious Bee
Computes its time as well as we.
How could such sweet and wholsome Hours
Be reckon'd but with herbs and flow'rs!

(IX)

Here the Final Image ends the quietist interval by an assertion of the activist principle. A necessity of 'time', that principle is asserted by a revocation of the time from which this interval has provided an interlude ('Dial', 'Sun . . . through' 'Zodiack run', 'Computes its time', 'Hours . . . reckon's'). Thus the way 'the . . . Sun/Does . . . run' recalls us to diurnal time, its 'run' also recollecting the active race of men's 'Labours' in time, from which the first stanza withdrew. It is 'the milder Sun' because it is setting, marking an end to this day's interval. Enacting, as it did in *Appleton House*, the eclogic-pastoral convention whereby the poem's experience ended with the sunset, this image again invokes the "sunset" of time itself: 'the milder Sun' is that of Christ, who, as the Son, represents God's grace and therefore His mercy; 'milder', also, because 'nor yet angry' (*First Anniversary*, 106). Yet the sunset adumbrates the Coming, when men will be called to account and their activist roles assessed. Then He will indeed be 'angry'.

The 'Dial new' through which the sun/Son takes his course is not only the "new dispensation' of mercy guaranteed by Christ, but 'the new benefit at His coming granted to none of the former ages of the world, but onely to these last times';[144] that is, the 'Dail new' is the nature of Latter Day time specifically, the time of activism, in which Christ too speeds the tempo, like the sun that rejoices to run a race.[145] His running to the Coming here denotes Marvell's recall to His purposes in the world. That activist moral is reinforced by 'th' industrious Bee', traditionally symbolic of constructive activity[146] and, for Marvell especially, of godly readiness. 'Each Bee as Sentinel . . . if once stir'd,/She runs you through, or askes *the Word.' (Appleton House*, XL.) The pun on "watchword" and "watch the Word of God"[147] emphasizes the bee's symbolism of a vigilant activism which answers His instructions with timeliness: as Marvell now must, it appears. 'The Bee through these known Allies hums,/Beating the *Dian* with its *Drumms*' (XXXVII) in Fairfax's warlike garden. That implication of militant activism in the 'Bee' recalls the warlike world of *The Garden*'s first stanza, giving lesson to the poet. 'th' industrious Bee/Computes its time as well as we': that is, it "reckons, takes account of, and judges"[148] its time, just as the activist must be timely. In that sense it provides a timely reminder to the quietist poet: 'Computes . . . time as well as we', not only equalling activist humankind, but providing a reckoning against which 'we' must be measured. For chiliasts must be, like the bee, 'faithfull workemen'.[149] Moreover, 'the Commonwealth of Bees' was frequently adduced, in the mid-century crisis, as a model for human governments, as it had been in Virgil's *Georgics*.[150] The bee's significance as a metaphor for the political world thus emphasises its reference to the world of action and time.[151] Its allusion to the *national* 'Garden'—England 'The Garden of the World'—is a reminder that the national counterpart of individual renovation requires the saint's active effort, a renovatory implication which recalls that, like *renovatio* itself, 'The Bee of al others makes his vintage in the Spring'.[152]

Further, the Bee's husbandry here reflects in little that of 'the skilful Gardner', God the Husbandman: who plants the "righteous trees" of men, and "waters" them with renovation.[153] Both He and Adam, the 'Gardner' of Eden, are workmen, 'skilful' (as He was in the delineation of 'mortal Beauty', 27). History, like poetry, is workmanship.

The bee's husbandry refers to 'time' (70)—a pun on thyme,[154] which makes Time itself a plant. Also, 'a fragrant Zodiack', Marvell's image of a horologue,[155] is an emblem of time which the bee 'works', just as the activist saint works in and on time. Hereby he must bring the *universal* renovation into being. The 'Zodiack' of destiny forms 'this Dial new', the 'melioris ab ortu' of Christ's dispensation of mercy[156] ('milder'), and "foretaste" of the 'new' age which will be men's renovation after the Coming.

The suitability of the horologue to this 'Dial new' is particularly that the mortal 'flow'rs' of men thereby signify the time. They have their destined roles in the universal course, or 'Zodiack'. Similarly, the bee was supposed to possess 'a greater sense of foresight' than most of the creatures;[157] reflecting the necessity for the saint to be 'looking for' as well as 'hasting unto' the End (as II Peter enjoins).

And if we recall this poem's indentification of activism with love, it is pertinent that 'th' industrious Bee' (as distinct from the drone) is female,[158] as she was in *Appleton House*. Just as bees provided a governmental model, so:

> Marriage is . . . *the Seminary of the Common-wealth, seed-plot
> of the Church . . . right-hand of providence . . . the foundation of
> Countries . . . and Kingdomes.*[159]

This view, which saw in the marital relationship a microcosmic model for political and religious order, took the 'helpmeet' text as cardinal.[160] The family 'is as a Bee-hive . . . out of which are sent many swarms of Bees . . . into the Church and Common-wealth'.[161] So the feminine bee and her commonwealth complete this figuration for the world of action and relationship, to which Marvell must now return— prompted, that is, by the "sign" or "particular revelation" of the bee, which indicates a necessity for activism.

The main source for the final stanza is Quarles, who described the Apostles (and saints) as those 'through which the Sun/Of Righteousnesse should as his Zodiack run'.[162] So, here, as God's light had played through his soul (VII), Christ's will must be expressed in Marvell's use of his own time. As an interval, this has been a 'sweet and wholsome' refreshment for activism, reckoned or timed by the 'herbs and flow'rs' because herbs are often medicinal, especially as Christ, who in Quarles' 'wholesome' spiritual garden was described as 'that rich herbe of grace'.[163] As the Redeemer and as healers, herbs signify the restorative effect upon Marvell of his interval. While, recalling mortality, the 'flow'rs' indicate that this healing is time-bound, they also signify the poetic flowers produced therein, the 'Garlands of repose'. Equally, the allusion in 'Zodiack' again evokes Sidney's renovating poet, 'freely ranging only within the zodiac of his own wit', scenting golden 'flowers' of expression.[164] So finally, as throughout the poem, poetry and eschatology are rendered identical.

Similarly, the issue from the interval implies an issue from the short lyric form, just as the poet's exit from the 'shadows' in the *Ode* committed him to a political poem. In this poem, the prophetic bird-muse took a short flight, 'till prepar'd for longer flight'; in contrast to Milton's sustained flight in epic, which 'With Plume so strong. . .So never Flags, but alwaies keeps on Wing'. Marvell's similar desire for 'graver Accents' of prophecy, in *First Anniversary*, recalled Virgil's foretelling of his epic. That fulfilment by Milton and Spenser of the prophetic muse in epic, Marvell's 'longer flight' glances at,[165] and intimates the poetic activism which must succeed his exit from the quietist poem. If we are to follow the notional dating of this poem to the mid-century,[166] we may see in it something of Marvell's decision to enter public life: both as Cromwell's polemical poet (after 1652) and as (later in the 1650s) MP for Hull. Polemics, both in the later poetic satires and the controversial tracts, were symptoms of a commitment to activism—an activism never fulfilled, like Milton's, in the poetic form of epic:

> Behold, I make all things new. And he said unto me, Write: for these things are faithful and true.
>
> (Revelation 21:5)

Upon the vision of 'all things new'—of renovation—follows the necessity of witness: 'Write'. Such writing is necessary during times of crises, for the sain't work is 'Redeeming the time, because the days are evil . . . understanding what the will of the Lord is' (Ephesians 5:16–17). That imperative is what links together all the writings of Marvell's life.

In *The Garden* that witness is private. Its adaptation of the Christianized classicism of the *hortus conclusus* is a sort of generic pun on the sense of 'conclusus': "enclosed" in that this is an interval in time; "concluded", because this is an interval in the times of "Ending". This is the 'garden' of the Church of Saints: 'Thou who dwellest in the gardens, the companions hearken to thy voice', meaning that 'Christ dwelleth in his Church, whose voyce the faithfull heare'.[167] So Marvell, like Hastings, here 'recreates his active Minde'.

The poem's privacy adopts, as usual, a joco-serious mode. Indeed, just as the poem's paradoxes imitate the great paradox of renovation—'Annihilating' to make 'green'—so it is precisely the poem's extravagance which allows poetry to aspire to the renovatory process here. That aspiration, which by extravagance understands itself very well, subserves Marvell's characteristic effort in poetics. In *The Garden's* problematic, a classical *Beatus Ille* format colludes with the beatitudes of a renovatory interval—evoking another Marvellian Final Image of dissolution and resolution. Thus the problematic's usual effort—to 'redeem the times' in poetic structure—here contains the assertion of poetry as itself a form of the redeeming *renovatio*.

7

A Revelation Revealed

The public themes of Marvell's "maritime" poems utilize images and motifs which are equally vital to that apparently "private" lyric, *The Unfortunate Lover*. In this chapter I am concerned to explicate that poem, in the light of Marvell's maritime images, as a parabolic expression of his reaction to the fall and regicide of Charles I. Thus it transpires that this poem can be grouped, along with the *Horatian Ode* and the *First Anniversary*, within that core of Marvell's *oeuvre*—the poems which actively engage with the process of history. It is "private" rather in the sense that it was intended to conceal its real subject from all but a very small audience.

(i) PRIVATE REVELATIONS OF POWER

To all critics this poem has represented a puzzle, and attempts at its explication have to date been so unconvincing that at least one critic has honestly admitted: 'I have no idea what *The Unfortunate Lover* means . . . and I have been unable to discover anyone else who can give a convincing reading of the poem'.[1] It seems, therefore, that 'this obscure and private'[2] lyric is deliberately cryptic (as many critics have concluded), and my account of it is intended to explain Marvell's motives for his cryptic procedure here, as well as the meaning of the poem. In fact, that meaning is itself the source of Marvell's cryptic treatment, which is fundamentally self-protective, as in so many other Marvellian lyrics. The subsequent section will analyse the poem itself: here I want to approach both the meaning and the motives of Marvell's poem by way of the sources and images which inform the lyric.

In this relation the various attempts of critics to explicate the poem are instructive. The poem provides a series of so-called 'emblem-like' scenes,[3] portraying the tribulations

257

of an 'Unfortunate Lover', and uses the traditional amatory motif of the Ship of the Lover,[4] which here undergoes a shipwreck. Therefore 'the passion in this poem is love, and just as obviously frustrated love'.[5] Several critics have placed the poem in the Petrarchan tradition of love-poetry, most of them concentrating upon its similarity to emblems of lovers and the trials of love, such as those of Otto Van Veen.[6] These tend to view the poem as a biography of a "typical" and fictional lover, one without a specific identity. But two critics have taken a quite different approach. R. H. Syfret suggested that the poem might be an allegorical account of a voyage by the then Prince of Wales;[7] Annabel Patterson proffered the idea that the poem was connected with Charles I.[8]

Before Patterson's account of the poem came into my hands, I had concluded that the poem was connected with Charles I, and the fact that we each arrived at this conclusion independently seems itself significant. However, the nature and scope of our analyses are fundamentally different, despite some points on which we agree; in particular, I see *The Unfortunate Lover* as an eschatological poem, on Marvell's customary model of the problematic.

This problematic is in fact the origin of the two divergent critical approaches to the poem, for it juxtaposes a "Petrarchan" narrative with the political narrative. Marvell's procedure causes the traditional image of the Petrarchan lover to cohere with a political image of Charles I as 'Philogenes', the lover of his people—an image which Marvell obtained from the Caroline masque. In this manner the poem records Marvell's evaluation of Charles I's fall; a topical subject, since the poem has long been dated to 1648–9,[9] the years of defeat and regicide. The poem's account of civil war and the king's "tragedy" thus answers E. E. Duncan-Jones' observation that 'some substratum of fact remains to be detected in *The Unfortunate Lover*'.[10]

Similarly, it has been observed that this poem appears to be written for some 'coterie',[11] which would have understood its recondite subject. In fact, Marvell's audience would have been that circle of court-poets amongst whom he moved at the time,[12] and to one of whose poems he alludes in the course of the lyric,[13] presumably as a compliment to that audience.

This group would have been at once, as royalists, sympathetic to his subject, responsive to his use of the Petrarchan tradition, and familiar with the court-masques from which Marvell derives the character of his political narrative.

Indeed, Marvell explicitly alludes to the masque in the fourth stanza of his poem, describing the scenes there portrayed as 'This masque of quarrelling Elements'. This reference is amplified by other theatrical metaphors in the poem, which twice puns on 'play' and remarks the 'spectacle' (I, VI). It has been observed that the poem as a whole has a 'stridently theatrical' quality, which has evoked derogatory comment.[14] In fact, this theatrical format is, as in *Appleton House*, an enaction of the metaphor of history as theatre. By means of this format Charles' history is placed within its proper context, as an act within the great drama of history.

As in the *Horatian Ode*, Charles is a destined 'Actor' in the historical drama. His portrayal as such in the 'masque' of *The Unfortunate Lover* is particularly apt, because of his notorious fondness for—and participation in—the masques presented at his own court.[15] Princes were anyway regarded as 'Players' who acted for a national audience[16], a fact recalled by Marvell in his *Upon the Death of O.C.*:

> The People . . .
>   blame the last *Act*, like *Spectators* vain,
> Unless the *Prince* whom they applaud be slain.
>   (7–10)

The 'spectacle' of Charles as *The Unfortunate Lover* gives the 'People' what they want. Here Charles even declaims, just as an actor should ('all he saies' [VII]); he is both seen and "heard".

The theatrical presentation of Charles in this poem is even more apt than these ideas suggest. For it is especially pertinent that a poem concerning his fall from power should imitate his own masques, which were themselves expressions and justifications of his rule. The masques presented at Charles' court were favourable images of absolutism, and propaganda for his central policies, animated symbols of royal power.[17] Self-confirming versions of Charles' fondest delusions,[18] the masques (as recalled by Marvell's poem) thus reveal the causes of Charles' fall; the king who was a successful ruler only on the stage of his own court[19] is appropriately portrayed as *merely* a masquer: 'he in Story only rules' (VIII). The 'masque' of the poem at once delineates Charles in his own terms and represents the fallacies fostered by those terms.

In this theatrical form, the poem's veiled allusions to its royal subject achieve their particular resonance. The 'Unfortunate Lover' is one who acts in history, destined 'to make impression upon Time', and whose birth and death are attended by the portents proper to such royal events (I-III). He is an 'Heir' (IV) and 'rules' (VIII). The less perceptible allusions of the poem to its royal subject can only be understood after some attention to the Caroline masques which provide sources for Marvell's poem.

First, it is necessary to understand that these masques were regarded not as mythic formulations but as idealizations of current realities. The monarchical claims asserted therein were believed to be accurate representations of the power that the monarchy actually possessed, and the masque was an abstract version of politics and power.[20] Thus art was itself power, and power a form of art.[21] It is therefore appropriate that Marvell's masque-poem should be an image of political reality; his irony here being that Charles' ruin is portrayed in the mode which had been used to idealize his power.

The political assertiveness of the Caroline masques had not been lost upon Charles' Puritan antagonists. They recognised that the self-congratulatory politics of the masque provided 'the monarchy . . . with an impenetrable insulation against the attitudes of the governed'.[22] To condemn court masques—as William Prynne had done in *Histrio-Mastix*—was correctly seen as an act of rebellion.[23] The masque was symbolic of everything that such Puritans most disliked about Stuart rule, an example of decadence and an assertion of absolutism.[24] Such views were shared even by the monarchist Marvell, an implacable enemy of absolutism; that he too condemned the *mores* of the court is evident from his satires of courtly *amours* and affectation in *Daphnis and Chloë* and *Mourning*.

It was recognized that such court arts as the masque were 'an index to a deep malaise',[25] something which Marvell's evocation of 'masque' in this poem recalls. Moreover, Prynne had declared that watching plays was 'the cause of untimely ends in Princes'[26]—an ironic prophecy of Charles' ruin that is, no doubt, pertinent to Marvell's poem.

The ironies of Marvell's use of the masque-form in his lyric are mitigated by the other level of the image—its ability to place Charles within the historical drama. As we have seen, Marvell's view of Charles was a complex one, since he regarded this king as at once the rightful ruler and as too weak to retain those 'ancient Rights' —as the dupe of the bishops, betrayed into absolutism. The portrait of Charles in this poem reflects the complexity of that view. Charles as masquer is seen in the terms he himself chose, and those terms are to that degree respectful as well as ironic. The masque-form was itself regarded as an expression of loyalty because of its identification with the monarch,[27] and Marvell's use of it here is a confirmation of his royalist sympathy. As we shall see, the key to Charles' portrait in this poem is that he is there—as perhaps he was in reality—a "noble idiot", a righteous man in error. *The Unfortunate Lover* is at once a memorial and an evaluation of this failed monarch. In this manner the poem reflects the nature of the masque itself, which was understood to be instructive.[28]

Thus it is not surprising that there was a precedent for Marvell's combination, in his 'masque', of loyalty and criticism. In 1634 the legal profession had attempted to persuade Charles to alter his policies, by embodying their advice in the loyal form of a masque: to speak to him in his own terms.[29] Marvell may intend in his poem a similar communication with his courtly audience, to moralize their king's fall. For this purpose the "generalizing", exemplary character of the poem—and its "typing" of Charles as *The Unfortunate Lover*—is an appropriate mode.[30] It is a heightening or idealization of reality, as the masque itself was.

Similarly, while the poem's "emblematic" quality maintains its Petrarchan fiction, it also recalls the character of masque as a series of animated emblems. The scenic succession of the poem's incidents, and its cryptic images, are equally representative of masques. One critic, indeed, has asserted that 'In this poem, Marvell . . . is attempting a mediation between verbal and visual arts';[31] the true model for this 'mediation' is in fact the masque, which was the form that most readily combined these arts.[32]

Moreover, the masque-form was especially appropriate to Marvell's use here of the "theatre of history". The fall and ruin of Charles was a catastrophe of the kind that challenged the chiliast to reconcile it with the fortunate character of history. That fortunate design was usefully reflected by the masque-form; for masques, opening with an 'antimasque' of some unfortunate character, then proceeded to expel the antimasque—the main masque celebrating that expulsion. In this manner masque-form provided an ineluctably fortunate pattern, which in Marvell's poem could intimate the ultimately happy issue of the historical drama. The masque-form therefore implies that the tragedy of Charles is part of a larger "comedic" movement, an implication of great importance to the chiliastic view. And, as we shall see, the poem deliberately recalls the antimasque-masque pattern, in a significant way.

Just as the masque-form could intimate the great design of the historical drama, it was also appropriate to a particular "moment" of crisis in that design. For court masques were always topical, reflecting some current political subject;[33] accordingly, in this poem the 'masque' treats the current crisis of Charles' ruin.

In this manner the poem's masque-form is condign to its subject, on several levels. Its mixture of positive and negative connotations for Charles is seconded by the poem's peculiar tone. The oddity of that tone has been a puzzle to critics: it has been described as at once hyperbolical and compassionate, ridiculous and poignant in the portrait of its central figure.[34] In fact, as I have suggested, Marvell's view of Charles was such as to produce this mixture—an individuated instance of his joco-serious mode. Moreover, that mixed tone is particularly appropriate to the poem's "masque", since masques were themselves mixtures of comedy and higher emotions (the comedy usually being provided by the antimasque).[35] In Marvell's poem, as in the masque, poignancy is stronger than comedy; also as in masque, the "ceremo-

nial" content of the poem implies its fundamental seriousness. The pathos here reflects Charles the "noble", the
comedy pertains to his "idiocy"; the mixture, however, is
extremely delicate.

This "double" attitude to Charles is reflected by the
problematic which portrays him as, on one level, a faintly
ridiculous version of the Petrarchan lover. On the other, he is
Philogenes, the lover of his people. This latter narrative, and
its association with masque, are illuminated by two particular
Caroline masques. In the next section I shall be discussing
some parallels between these masques and Marvell's poem;
here, it is necessary to show how these parallels came about.
The narratives and images of these masques represent the
background of thought which informs Marvell's lyric.

The first of these masques was *Love's Triumph through
Callipolis*, one of Charles' assertions of his 'divine kingship'.[36]
Published in the 1616 Folio edition of Jonson's *Works*, the
text of this masque would have been available to Marvell—
who was, of course, an admirer of Jonson (as *Tom May*
testifies). In this as in 'all masques the celebration of virtue
and love is also an assertion of divine power';[37] the monarch's
embodiment of Love *is* his power.[38] The masques' identification of 'Love' with power—their sanctification of the king as
'Lover'—is what informs Marvell's portrait of Charles as a
typical 'Lover'. In *Love's Triumph* Charles is celebrated as an
'heroical' lover—the "highest" sort[39]—just as, in Marvell's
poem, the lover is an heroical figure who 'nak'd and fierce
does stand/Cuffing the Thunder with one hand' (VII). *Love's
Triumph* portrays Charles' court as 'Callipolis', the home of
true and virtuous love: 'Love, who was wont to be respected
as a special deity in court, and tutelar god of the place'
(20–21). The court's 'true' love is contrasted with those
vicious types of love represented by the antimasquers, who
are seen 'expressing their confused affections in the scenical
persons and habits of the four prime European nations.'[40] In
this manner England's love-power is contrasted to the false
forms of love-power manifested in other kingdoms. This
political moral lies behind the 'depraved lovers' of the
antimasque, amongst whom are 'An adventurous romance
lover', 'a fantastic umbrageous lover', 'An angry quarrelling

lover' and 'A melancholic despairing lover'.[41] In the masque
these vicious "types" are dispelled by Charles, the 'heroical
Lover'.

In Marvell's poem, the 'Unfortunate Lover' quite evidently
displays—at one time or another—all these 'depraved'
characteristics. He is both 'adventurous' and 'romantic', as
well as 'fantastic'; he is certainly 'umbrageous': 'No Day he
saw' (III). He is also 'melancholic' and 'despairing': 'at his
Eyes he alwaies bears' 'bitter Tears', and 'Sighs' (III). His
capacity for 'angry quarrelling' is displayed in the 'fierce'
lover in the seventh stanza. All these 'depraved' characteristics co-exist with his 'heroical' nature; Marvell has conflated
the "types" of both masque and antimasque in his portrait of
Charles, revealing his "weakness" as a lover, and thereby also
his weakness as a king. (In the terms of the masques, king and
lover are the same.) In this manner Marvell's 'Lover' is an
ironic adaptation of the ideal 'heroic' Charles of *Love's
Triumph*, and of comparable masques.

Similarly, Marvell's backdrop of the sea (II – VII) imitates
that of many masques, and the same backdrop appears in
Love's Triumph. There the triumph of Love takes place in
'The prospect of a sea', and the royal lover arrives by boat,
images which reflect the usual associations of sea-power.[42]
Equally, in Marvell's poem the lover is carried by a ship, from
which he is 'brought forth': an adaptation of the masque's
"coming of Love" by ship. There Charles meets with
Henrietta Maria as 'Queen of Love', and their 'perfect love' is
celebrated as a symbol of ideal government.[43] In relation to
this concept of love-as-government, the 'sea' here represents
both vicissitudes and passions, which that love-as-
government controls. The sea is thus at once a metaphor for
political unrest and for violent passion.[44] The same combination in the metaphor appears, as we shall see, in *The
Unfortunate Lover*. Equally significant for Marvell's poem is
the masques' general equation of love and power.

This equation takes, in the masque of *Salmacida Spolia*
(1640),[45] a rather different characterization of Charles the
lover from that of the earlier masque: here he is 'Philogenes,'
"lover of his people". This, the very last of the Caroline
masques, anticipates the posthumous hagiography of Charles

by portraying him as a king patient of his subjects' fury;[46] it is full of ironic premonitions of his fate in the Civil War. Moreover, the imagery and the narrative of this masque, which was printed in a quarto edition in 1640, are very similar to those of Marvell's poem.

The proscenium arch of the masque—which traditionally defined the dramatic action[47]—displays symbols of Charles' royal virtues,[48] some of which, like the imagery of the masque itself, hint at martyrdom, anticipating the popular image of Charles as martyr. Here are represented the figures of Reason, Intellectual Appetite, Counsel, Resolution, Fame, Prudence, and Affection to the Country. Also present in the frieze is Prosperous Success, 'with the rudder of a ship' (i.e. that of the Ship of State). Other virtues present in the frieze are specifically Christian, including 'Doctrine', 'Innocence', and 'Forgetfulness of Injuries'.[49] These qualities are the means by which Charles is seen to resolve the disturbances of the state, the *moralitas* of the masque being that he 'seeks . . . to reduce tempestuous and turbulent natures into a sweet calm of civil concord'.[50] These political disorders are represented by the antimasque: 'Discord' appears in a storm and, 'having already put most of the world into disorder, endeavours to disturb these parts'.[51] Britain is thus a Fortunate Isle where the ungrateful people raise needless discontents,[52] the latter signified by the 'Storms' and 'Winds' of Discord. The antimasque is dispersed by the 'secret power' and 'sacred wisdom' of the king, 'under the name of Philogenes or Lover of his People'.[53] These 'secret' powers are intended at once to represent that "love of the *gens*" and the beneficent absolutism of the king; as in other masques, his power over nature—and especially over the unruly sea—is in fact an assertion of absolutism. The rewards of that protective power are similarly stated in terms of 'Love': in return for the king's 'prudence for reducing the threatening storm', Pallas sends down from heaven his queen, Henrietta Maria.[54]

Although Charles-Philogenes is victorious in the masque, his characterization is quite different from the 'heroical' lover of *Love's Triumph*. The pre-eminent qualities of this Philogenes are patience and endurance,[55] a victim's rather than a victor's virtues. As such they presage posthumous portraits of

Charles, such as that in *Eikon Basilike* of Charles the Martyr. Yet Philogenes is still seen as a "higher" version of love, counterpointed by the 'mad lovers' and 'amorous courtier' of the antimasque:[56] they represent rebellious political passions, curbed by Philogenes' order-inspiring love. He brings peace to the land, the allusion of the title being to the 'spoils of peace'.[57]

The apotheosis of 'peace' in the masque is ironic in view of the real 'Discord' which broke out in England only a year later and which the king did not manage to suppress. That irony is the key to Marvell's use of the theme and imagery that appear in this masque: *The Unfortunate Lover* is an ironic inversion of the narrative of *Salmacida Spolia*. With hindsight, Marvell's Philogenes becomes the 'Unfortunate' lover of his people. The 'frustrated love' of Marvell's protagonist is that of Charles as Philogenes, repudiated by his people. Thus, as we shall see, the poem imports and adapts the imagery of this masque, providing an ironic historical gloss upon Charles' self-portrait there.

To Charles-as-Philogenes Marvell adds some echoes of Josiah, the 'righteous king' who ruled Israel in the Old Testament. An allusion to Josiah was discovered in the last stanza, by E. E. Duncan-Jones;[58] Annabel Patterson related to this some sermons for the king which explicitly compared him to Josiah.[59] Neither of these commentators, however, has seen that there is a recollection of Josiah in the central section of the poem, and that recollection is specifically Puritan, reflecting Marvell's diagnosis of Charles' fall. This reference will be discussed in the following section.

For the moment it is sufficient to recall that Marvell understood power to be a providential dispensation: 'I take the magistrate's power to be from God, only in a providential constitution',[60] which may by the same token remove or transfer that power when necessary. When the magistrate could not effect the reformation of the state—a perennial necessity—'this work . . . falls to the Peoples share, from which God defend every good Government' (*RT*, 239–40). This "reformation by rebellion" had been the case in the Civil War, as Marvell saw it, and *The Unfortunate Lover* is a masque-like account of that process. As in the *Horatian Ode*,

Marvell here portrays providence at work in the destruction of a king.

(ii) REVELATION OF A ROYAL TRAGEDY: *THE UNFORTUNATE LOVER*

As I have indicated, the problematic of *The Unfortunate Lover* involves, on the one hand, a "Petrarchan narrative" of the traditional type of the disappointed lover; on the other hand, a "political narrative" in which that disappointed lover is Charles, the frustrated Philogenes. The generalized Petrarchan type of the 'Unfortunate Lover' is a means whereby Charles' fall may also be universalized, absorbed into the universal pattern of history. For Marvell thus to "place" his defeated monarch is in some ways a consolatory procedure as well as, chiliastically, a necessary one.

The manner in which the poem's narrative is historicized and universalized becomes evident in the first stanza:

> Alas, how pleasant are their dayes
> With whom the Infant Love yet playes!
> Sorted by pairs, they still are seen
> By Fountains cool, and Shadows green.
> But soon these Flames do lose their light,
> Like Meteors of a Summers night:
> Nor can they to that Region climb,
> To make impression upon Time.
>
> (I)

The poem thus opens with a generalization. Some lovers are destined for a tranquil *amour*, which cannot raise them to a level where they might make an historical 'impression'; the Unfortunate Lover, however, can make such an historical impression. The meteoric 'Region' was understood to be that of Time,[61] and it is assumed that the Unfortunate Lover can 'climb' thereto because his love is of a somewhat grander sort than that of those 'With whom the Infant Love yet playes'. Their 'Infant Love'—although in one sense Cupid—is also 'Infant' in time: it has not "grown up" to time in the way that the Unfortunate Lover's has. Thus the comparison of the two loves is a temporal one, the Unfortunate Lover alone being "adult". This difference in the scale of the two loves is proper to that between personal love—'Sorted by pairs'—and Charles' "national" love as Philogenes: a monarch's love for his people necessarily touches history, 'make[s] impression upon Time'.

This establishment, in the first stanza, of the context of 'Time' and history is the setting for the poem as a whole. Private loves are 'Like Meteors of a Summers night', transient as their lives. A monarchical love makes more enduring meteoric 'impressions' because it participates in the general destiny. 'To make impression' can mean "to attack",[62] and this pun reflects a king's engagement with history. The first stanza's suggestion of a relationship between 'Time' and 'Love' implies that time overtakes sublunary lovers, whereas the Unfortunate Lover catches up with time—'climb(s)' to it.

A similar relationship between Time and Love is suggested in *Salmacida Spolia*:

> Time never knew the mischiefs of his haste!
> Nor can you force him stay
> To keep off day.
> Make then fit use of triumphs here!
> . . .
> Move then like Time, for Love as well as he
> Hath got a calendar,
> Where must appear
> How ev'nly you these measures tread.[63]

Here the initial lines suggest the transience of love in time, urging the *carpe diem* idea, while the latter lines require that the masquers' dance must 'Move. . .like Time', be in step with time. Only then can it express the enduring power of love-as-order, which the masque's triumph celebrates. That reasoning informs the similar distinction made in Marvell's first stanza.

The temporal motif, initiated here, remains operative throughout the poem and assumes a specifically eschatological character. The first stanza indicates that this lover engages with time, and in the last stanza his tribulations are traced to the fact that he was 'by the Malignant Starrs,/Forced to live in

Storms and Warrs'. Thus the lover's sufferings are caused by his living at an 'Unfortunate' time, a moment of time distinguished by 'Storms and Warrs'. This link between time and the lover is reinforced by the implication of destiny: the lover 'Forced' to live thus by the 'Starrs' of fate. These—time (history) and fate—are the elements of eschatology, the destined pattern of history, and this is the context of the lover's tragedy. This eschatological context reveals the poem's title in its true sense: the Un-fortunate lover is fortune's victim, a casualty of the eschatological process. History is the proper context of Charles' tragedy.

This temporal and eschatological context is developed at several levels. The diurnal and seasonal pattern is evoked by references to 'dayes' and 'night' (I, III, VI), and to 'Summers' (I). The narrative of the poem is made insistently temporal: 'yet', 'still', 'soon' (I); 'when', 'e're', 'at the last' (II); 'alwaies', 'While' (III); 'While' (IV); 'soon', 'still', 'while' (V); moving to the dramatic moment, 'And now. . .' (VI). This insistence on the temporal process of the lover's history is reinforced by evocations of the general pattern of life and death: which at once generalize his situation, and also reflect the tendency of life towards the *telos*—towards the individual's parallel version of the universal *eschaton*. That parallel is made quite explicit.

First, the pattern of generation is established, springing from the first stanza's reference to an 'Infant'; the second stanza evokes the 'Mother' and birth of the lover. The fourth stanza recalls the 'Birth', and the fifth relates it to the teleological pattern, by referring to 'Life and Death'. The eschatological counterpart of this pattern is invoked in the third stanza, which alludes to 'the Fun'ral of the World', the Last Day. To characterize the universal *eschaton* as a 'Fun'ral' is to relate individual ends—for which 'Fun'rals' are usual—to the general End. Similarly, since the poem records the biography of the lover, it moves from his 'Birth' in stanza II to his 'dying' in stanza VIII; the end of the poem is also his end. In this manner the whole poem is built upon the teleological pattern.

Moreover, the time in which the lover is 'Forced' to live is characterized as the Latter Days. He lives in an age of 'Storms and Warrs', the Latter Day *desolatio*, and the scene of his sufferings is marked by apocalyptic imagery:

> No Day he saw but that which breaks,
> Through frighted Clouds in forked streaks.
> While round the ratling Thunder hurl'd,
> As at the Fun'ral of the World.
>
> (III)

Within this Latter Day setting the lover is, like the fishers of *Appleton House*, portrayed as an 'Amphibium' (V), an inhabitant of the confusion of land and sea that prefaces the End: he is caught between the 'Rock' and the 'Waves' in a landscape of desolation (VII). This Latter Day locale is framed by the metaphor of 'masque', which places it within the theatre of history. Thus the scenic progress of the lover's narrative becomes itself an eschatological drama, of which the arbiters are 'Time' (I), 'Heaven', 'Fortune' (VI), and the 'Starrs' (VIII).

The universalization of the lover's tragedy is, as we have seen, indicated in the first stanza. There also the "tragic" mood is established by the opening word of the poem, 'Alas . . .'. In later stanzas the anatomization of the lover—'Eyes', 'Breast' (III), 'Heart' (V), 'Breath' (V), 'Blood' (VI, VII), 'brest' (VI), 'hand' (VII), 'Wounds' (VII), 'Ear' (VIII)—has a similarly generalizing effect, and the apothegmic description of him as 'Th' *Amphibium* of Life and Death' (V) implies that he is a figure of universal relevance. Again, the psychomachia of his conflict is formalized by abstractions—'Hopes' and 'Despair' (V)—which also contribute to the depersonalization of his situation, as well as imitating the psychomachias common in masque. The lover's narrative assumes a sharply "existential" character, especially due to the 'masque of quarrelling Elements' (IV) that are detailed throughout the poem in an undescriptive, universalized manner. Thus, in addition to such general concepts as 'Nature' and 'Heaven', Marvell introduces 'Flames' (I, VI), 'Waves' (II, VI, VII), 'Seas' (II), 'Winds' (II), 'Rock' (II), 'Stone' (II), 'Clouds' (III), 'Thunder' (III), 'Hurricane' (IV), and so on. Similarly, the lover's existence consists solely of conflict and subsistence: 'fed. . .digested. . .fed. . .famish. . .feast' (V). This existential and universalized narrative characterizes the lover as a "type", but he is a masquer, not an emblem. Thus the poem is given dramatic movement by the disturbed language of conflict ('frighted', 'quarrelling', 'insulting', 'cruel', 'doubtful' [III–V]), and especially by the violence of the verbs: 'drave', 'split', 'surging', 'roar', 'breaks', 'forked', 'ratling', 'hurl'd', 'cuffing' (II–VII). In this manner Marvell's central figure is made at once "typical" and dynamic.

In the light of this universalized and eschatological context, it is possible to understand the narrative of the poem. Stanza I, as I have indicated, treats the fortunate lovers with whom this lover contrasts: they reside in a pastoral locale of 'Fountains cool, and Shadows green', which counterpoints the stormy landscape of the rest of the poem—the world of the lover. In fact, this first stanza stands, in relation to the rest, as antimasque to masque: this calm antimasque is dispelled by the stormy masque itself, of 'quarrelling Elements'. Marvell's structure here represents an ironic inversion of the normal masque movement. For, normally, the antimasque provides an image of disorder which is dispersed by a masque representing the triumph of order. (And in many masques one of these elements involved a pastoral scene.)[64]Similarly, there was an hierarchy of players in the masque, the antimasquers being professional actors, while the masquers were courtiers.[65] Here the antimasque becomes an image of order, the masque a narrative of disorder, reversing their usual roles. But the masque movement is preserved by the hierarchical difference between the sublunary lovers of stanza I's antimasque, and the transcendent royal lover of the masque.

Marvell's inversion of the natures of masque and antimasque is, as I have said, an ironic one. In the Caroline masque the dramatic movement is from conflict to calm; in *Salmacida* it represents the resolution of political unrest. In Marvell's poem, the movement is from peace to political turbulence, imitating England's descent into civil war. As we shall see, stanzas II and III are images of that war. In this fashion Marvell intimates that history has reversed the optimistic moral of the Caroline masque: whereas in his own court Charles was able to imagine that he could suppress rebellion, the recent history of England had proved him mistaken. By imitating this historical fact in the reversal of masque-structure, Marvell makes an ironic comment upon the delusions of the Caroline masque.

The masque had portrayed absolutist power as a 'secret wisdom' which could tame the natural world: political power was seen as a magical control of such phenomena as sea and wind.[66] Such abstract images of power anodised its less pleasant aspects, even as they sanctified that power. In Marvell's poem that motif undergoes a reversal, similar to his reversal of masque-structure itself. Whereas Charles in the court-masques—and especially in *Salmacida*—controlled and calmed the political 'Sea', as Marvell's Unfortunate Lover he becomes its victim:

> 'Twas in a Shipwrack, when the Seas
> Rul'd, and the Winds did what they please,
> That my poor Lover floting lay,
> And, e're brought forth, was cast away:
> Till at the last the master-Wave
> Upon the Rock his Mother drave;
> And there she split against the Stone,
> In a *Cesarian Section*.
>
> (II)

From this 'Birth' (IV) here to his death in stanza VIII, Charles is a victim, whether of 'Sea', 'Cormorants', or 'Flames'. Such a characterization is an ironic reversal of his dominance in Caroline masques: whereas, there, he ruled the political 'Seas', here 'the Seas/Rul'd', usurping his monarchical function. The cause of this reversal is the Civil War, which the stanza portrays in symbolic terms.

In the masques—especially in *Salmacida* and *Love's Triumph*—the 'Sea' had been at once an image of mutability and a symbol of the passions, over which Charles had exercised control.[67] Here the Petrarchan narrative is supported by the traditional image of the lover's passions as 'seas' which torment his Ship of Love and subject him to the vicissitudes of fortune.[68] On the level of the political narrative, those 'seas' are—as in the masques—symbolic of the turbulent state. Thus the combination of narratives in stanza II imitates the dual function of the sea-image in the masques themselves, where it had signified both personal and political "passions".

The plot of this stanza is a symbolic rendition of the Civil War, in terms which allow the conflation of Petrarchan and political metaphors. Thus the 'Sea' is, in this sense, that of the political world; the ship is at once the Ship of Love and the Ship of State; and the 'Shipwrack' is the Civil War, the foundering of that Ship of State. Once these symbols are understood, the images in the stanza that have so puzzled critics—the 'Mother', the 'Rock', and the 'Cesarian Section'—reveal themselves as coherent elements of the narrative.

First, as I have indicated, Marvell was accustomed to use 'Sea' or 'Waters' as an image of the state—as the masques had done. So, here, the 'Seas' that usurp the "ruler's" function intimate Charles' people in rebellion. Recalled here is the source of that metaphor, in Revelation 17:1, 'The waters . . . are peoples, and multitudes, and nations'; 'that is, as vnconstant and variable as are the waters'.[69] Thus the stormy sea of political unrest here imitates that of *Salmacida*, where 'These storms the people's giddy fury raise' (361). The storm—further described in the next stanza of the poem— was a common metaphor for war, and Marvell had used it in this sense in *Ingelo* (111). In *Eikon Basilike*, the frontispiece showed the martyrdom of Charles I against a background of stormclouds and a turbulent sea, and there too that background signifies the rebellion of the Civil War.

The 'storm' of the Civil War effected, as Marvell saw it, a necessary reformation—albeit in a precipitate manner. The necessity of reformation in the state was compared by him to a ship's need for propulsion by 'disturbance':

How should [politicians]. . .arrive at their design'd port, but by disturbance? for if there were a dead calm always, and the Wind blew from no corner, there would be no Navigation.

(*RT*, 232)

Here Marvell suggests that the Ship of State requires reformatory 'disturbance' if it is to progress. In *The Unfortunate Lover* such a stormy disturbance drives the Ship of State to its 'shipwreck'; the Civil War was an extreme form of reformation which has a necessarily "wrecking" issue. The 'Seas' and 'Winds' of the people's rebellion are the agents of this ruin. In this stanza Marvell intimates what he reiterated in his later works, that the Civil War was an unfortunately extreme version of a necessary reformation. He indicates this thought by means of the Ship of State metaphor whereby the reformers themselves had justified rebellion.

Moreover, the erring Ship of State in this stanza reflects also Stuart misgovernment, signified by the helpless course of the Ship of State here. This 'steerless' metaphor was used elsewhere by Marvell as an image of confusion: 'no man knows whither away [it]. . .may be driven, or what port It is bound to, and whether it do not sail without steerage, compass, or anchor' (*Howe*, 188). The application of this "wandering ship" to the idea of misgovernment is made clear by another chiliast's account of incompetent monarchs:

> some of these mightie ones shew themselves but little better than the [low]. . .When as they that ought to gouerne the sterne of the Commonwealth, let all go at random. . .letting themselves be carried headlong by the tempest of their owne strong and furious passions, into imminent danger of shipwrecks: when as their carefull watchfulnesse. . .ought to serue them for sailscables, ankrs, masts, and skuttles, whereby to gouerne and direct the vessel whose steersman they are appointed. . .so this ship being depriued of her gouernor, is let loose and laid open to the mercie of the waues, violence of windes, and rage of tempests, without any direction or gouernement.[70]

Similarly, in Marvell's poem the king, who was understood to be the 'steersman' of the Ship of State, lies helpless: 'my poor Lover floting lay', unable or unwilling to steady the course of the state. The formulation here—'my poor Lover'—mixes criticism with pathos, for Charles-Philogenes as the victim of his people. Charles was both a 'poor' steersman and a pathetic figure; he is here, as always for Marvell, both a rightful and a fatally weak king.

To formulate Charles' fall, the notion of a 'Shipwrack' is especially pertinent because one of his most provocative acts had been the imposition of "ship-money", and of this fact Marvell here makes ironic use. The issue of ship-money had been a part of Charles' generally absolutist mode of government:[71]

> For [the bishops] having gained this Ascendent upon him, resolv'd whatever became on't to make their best of him; and having made the whole business of State their Arminian Jangles, and the persecution for Ceremonies, did for recompence assign him that *imaginary absolute Government, upon which Rock we all ruined.*

(RT, 134; my italics)

Absolutist illusions were thus the 'Rock' upon which the state foundered; so, in stanza II, the Ship of State is driven 'Upon the Rock' of absolutism. Here and in *RT* that metaphor expresses the occurrence of civil war.

Another of the stanza's metaphors, the lover's 'Mother', has proved as difficult for critics to explain as the 'Rock'. It is evident from the stanza itself that the 'Mother' is the ship, and so it has been understood;[72] however, that in itself does not explain the maternal metaphor. Rather, if the ship is the Ship of State, then the 'Mother' is also the state—England. Marvell did indeed call her 'our *mother* of England', of whom Englishmen are 'sons' (*Smirke*, 10). So, here, Charles is the royal "son" of England.

A similarly political idea informs the equally difficult metaphor, of his birth by 'Cesarian Section'. This metaphor is linked to that of the 'Mother' 'split against the Stone'. This split is that of the mother—of her womb—and thus reflects a 'split' in the English nation. It is, in effect, an image of divisive civil war. (Cf. a similarly "divisive" image for the War in the *Horatian Ode*, where Cromwell 'Did thorough his own Side/His fiery way divide'; see above p.76.)

This meaning is developed in the metaphor of 'Cesarian Section'. On the level of the Petrarchan narrative, this recalls Lucretius' description of the normal child's birth, as E. E. Duncan-Jones noted, and 'is the effect of an accident in which nature copies the accoucheur's art'.[73] On the level of the political narrative it is an image of the Civil War, elaborating the 'split'. As in the *Horatian Ode*, Marvell is here recalling a Roman parallel for the Civil War, for the Roman civil war between Caesar and Pompey began when Caesar crossed the Rubicon, effecting a 'section' of the Roman state into civil war. This is the political significance of the 'Cesarian Section', evoking both Caesar's "crossing" ('section') and its issue of civil division. Moreover, it recalls also Caesar's own "unnatural birth"—the source of this natal term—as a portent of his political destiny. Civil war is an "unnatural birth" in the mother-state, which does violence to the national mother herself.

One may compare to this "birth" of faction Marvell's analogous image in *The Character of Holland*, where the Ship of the Church was 'split', spawning a multitude of sects:

> when *Religion* did it self imbark,
> And from the *East* would *Westward* steer its Ark,
> It struck, and splitting on this unknown ground,
> Each one thence pillag'd the first piece he found:
> Hence *Amsterdam*, *Turk-Christian-Pagan-Jew*,
> Staple of Sects and Mint of Schisme grew.
>
> (67–72)

Here the implicit idea of an unnatural birth—its progeny displaying incongruous or mongrel characteristics—is analogous to that in *The Unfortunate Lover's* national "birth".

By the sectioning of the Ship of State, Charles is 'cast away': repudiated by the nation, as the pun here indicates. This event occurs 'e're [he is] brought forth', before, that is, his reign is 'brought forth'—fully revealed—in the theatre of history. Charles has had no chance to prove himself by the issue of his policies, by what he "brings forth". In this manner Marvell condenses his idea—expressed, as we saw, in *RT*—that Charles would eventually have effected reformation, and that therefore the Civil War was precipitate.

By means of the 'Cesarian Section' of civil war, Charles is "delivered" to the waters; to, that is, the mercy of his people. Thus 'my poor Lover floting lay', at the mercy of those "waters". In this fashion Marvell reverses the motifs of Caroline masque, in which Charles controlled the waters/people. There he possessed a power over all natural phenomena; in this poem he remains throughout their victim, tortured 'betwixt the Flames and Waves' (VI). By this reversal Marvell dramatizes the ruin of royal power and provides an ironic comment upon the delusions of the court masques. In those masques Charles had been, year after year, the 'heroic Lover': here he is reduced to 'my poor Lover'.

This narrative of royal ruin explicates the critical problem of this "birth", which is simultaneously a "death". Commenting on the 'shipwrack', one critic has remarked that 'What the poet so wittily figures as a birth is a moment which is usually, of course, that of death. If a birth, it is on all counts a most perverse and unnatural one'.[74] I have indicated why the birth is "unnatural", and it is a 'death' for similarly political reasons. Until the defeat of civil war, Charles was the monarch; civil war transforms him into a more doubtful figure. It is at once the "death" of his power, and the "birth" of his character as the Unfortunate Lover, the death of the masques' 'heroical' lover and birth of his 'Unfortunate' counterpart. This "death" of his power is complemented by the people's usurpation: 'the Seas/Rul'd', the birth of an *unnatural* power.

The close relationship of the metaphors, in this stanza, with those of the masques is particularly evident by comparison with *Salmacida Spolia,* which provides analogues for stanzas II–IV. Marvell's stanzas create an image of storm and discord:

> 'Twas in a Shipwrack, when the Seas
> Rul'd, and the Winds did what they please,
> That my poor Lover floting lay
> . . .

> The Sea him lent these bitter Tears
> Which at his Eyes he alwaies bears.
> And from the Winds the Sighs he bore,
> Which through his surging Breast do roar.
> No Day he saw but that which breaks,

Through frighted Clouds in forked streaks.
While round the ratling Thunder hurl'd,
As at the Fun'ral of the World.

While Nature to his Birth presents
This masque of quarrelling Elements.
                                        (II–IV)

Masques often included such 'quarrelling Elements';[75] here
the 'masque of quarrelling Elements' provides natural symbols for the discord of civil war (as the masque had done in
Appleton House also). In *Salmacida Spolia*, the rebellious
discord of the English people was represented in a similar
manner. The antimasque opens, as 'A curtain flying up, a
horrid scene appeared of storm and tempest' (111), and these
were due to 'the people's giddy fury' (361). Similarly, in
stanza III the Unfortunate Lover, Charles, is subjected to an
apocalyptic scene of 'Thunder' and 'Lightning' and a 'mad
Tempest' (VI), all of which represent the Latter-Day
Revolution in England. This scene is amplified in the masque
thus:

> a horrid scene appeared of storm and tempest. No glimpse of the
> sun was seen, as if darkness, confusion, and deformity had
> possessed the world and driven light to heaven. . .Afar off was a
> dark wrought sea, with rolling billows breaking against the
> rocks, with rain, lightning and thunder. In the midst was a globe
> of the earth, which. . .falling on fire, was turned into a Fury.
>   (111–18)

This, *Salmacida Spolia*'s image of rebellious discord, is
matched by Marvell's 'masque' of the English Revolution.
The masque's 'storm and tempest' appears not only in the
scene of stanza III but also in the 'mad tempest' of stanza VI.
The identification of 'storms' and civil war is made evident in
the hendiadys of stanza VIII, 'Storms and Warrs'. Equally,
the masque's direction that 'No glimpse of the sun was seen,
as if darkness. . .had possessed the world', is echoed in stanza
III: 'No Day he saw but that which breaks' as lightning. This
stanza also imitates the masque's 'rain, lightning, and
thunder'. In stanza II the 'master-Wave' of war drives onto

the 'Rock', recalling the 'rolling billows breaking against the rocks'. Similarly, the masque's admixture of 'sea' and 'fire' informs stanzas VI–VII, with their 'quarrelling Elements' of 'Flames and Waves' (47), 'Wave' and 'Flames' (53–4). The masque's metamorphosis of 'earth' by fire is imitated in stanza VII, where the Unfortunate Lover is 'Torn into Flames' (54). Even the poem's "unnatural birth" finds an analogue in *Salmacida Spolia*. There the Fury instigates the natural-political disorders:

> Blow winds! and from the troubled womb of earth,
> Where you receive your undiscovered birth,
> Break out in wild disorders.
>
> (128–31)

In the Fury's apostrophe the discord of the state is given 'birth', as it is in Marvell's second stanza.

In the third stanza, the 'quarrelling Elements' are— initially—'Sea' and 'Winds'. As we have seen, the 'Sea' is the people, and the 'Winds' are their noisy disturbances. Thus Charles' subjects become a sorrow to him: 'The Sea him lent these bitter Tears', 'And from the Winds the Sighs he bore/Which through his surging Breast do roar.' Thus their passions stimulate his, disturbing his own internal 'sea' of passions. People and king are mutually provoked in civil war. This is the victimization of Charles-Philogenes by the people he loves, whereby that love becomes 'bitter' and 'unfortunate'.

Charles' patient suffering of the 'Winds' aroused by his people appears also in *Salmacida*. There their disturbances are 'Those quarrelling winds, that deafened unto death' (356); here they are 'quarrelling' as at a 'Fun'ral'. In the masque, Charles-Philogenes is praised for his patient endurance of those 'Winds':

> If it be kingly patience to outlast
> Those storms the people's giddy fury raise
> Till like fantastic Winds themselves they waste,
> The wisdom of that patience is thy praise.
>
> (360–3)

Similarly, the 'Seas' that become the Lover's 'Tears' (III) are anticipated in the masque:

> Blow winds! until you raise the seas so high
> That waves may hang like tears in the sun's eye,
> That we, when in vast cataracts they fall,
> May think he weeps at nature's funeral.
>
> (124–7)

Here the 'waves' that become 'Tears' are associated with 'nature's funeral' at the Last Day; just as, in Marvell's stanza, the lover weeps 'as at the Fun'ral of the World'. Both here and in the masque the images of desolation invoke the *eschaton*, the ultimate *desolatio*.

Such an invocation is proper to the poem's image of one of the Latter Day wars. The eschatological mood here is supported by the Petrarchan narrative of the problematic. For in the terms of that narrative the 'Sea' is an image of fortune's vicissitudes, of which the Un-fortunate Lover is a victim; such imagery is commonplace in the love-poems of that type.[76] This Petrarchan metaphor figures, here, the equally traditional image of the sea as providence,[77] that pattern which leads to the 'port' of the *eschaton*.[78] Related to this providential metaphor was the masques' treatment of 'Neptune', 'as a figure for the divine power existing through the waters' and thus 'the governance of divine providence'.[79] The sea, in this sense, represents the flux whereby providence achieves its ultimately fortunate issue. Thus its disorders create health, are desolations for the sake of renovation. (As they were in *Character of Holland* and *First Anniversary*.) In this manner of the "Petrarchan" meaning, the 'Sea' evokes the providential context of civil war. This war is part of the Latter Day desolation; so Marvell contextualizes it, as a desolation like that 'at the Fun'ral of the World'. It is eschatological providence which decrees that Charles should be unfortunate, and Marvell saw it thus in the *Horatian Ode* also.

Hence Charles' ruin is pictured, in the third stanza, as part of the general Latter Day *desolatio*. On one level, the portents of 'Thunder' and lightning here intimate the fall of a monarch—Charles' fall. Such portents are described in the

Death of O.C.: 'A secret Cause does sure those Signs ordain/Fore boding Princes falls' (101–2). On another level, these are signs of the End, as the eschatological allusion demonstrates. The biblical prophecies of the End describe precisely such darkening and disturbance in the heavens: 'the sun [shall] be darkened, and the moon shall not give her light, and the stars shall fall from heaven, and the powers of the heavens shall be shaken' (Matthew 24:29). Such portents were adopted in many descriptions of the End, and Milton, in particular, suggests an End analogous to that in Marvell's poem:

> there shall be signs in the sun and in the moon, and in the stars, and upon the earth distress of nations, and perplexity, the sea and the waves roaring, men's hearts failing them for fear.[80]

Marvell's stanza evokes this desolation of the End as the context for the national *desolatio*, the Civil War being itself a constituent of the Latter Days' 'distress of nations'.

The desolations of the End were necessary elements of the providential plan, and the consequent paradox of fortunate desolation informs Marvell's linkage between this stanza and the next. The scene described in stanza III as like the universal 'Fun'ral' is characterized in stanza IV as a 'Birth'. The critical problem represented by this linkage has been expressed thus: 'The juxtaposition of funeral and birth in successive lines [provides an]. . .ambiguous relationship between life and death'.[81] In fact, this 'ambiguous' linkage conveys several evaluations of Charles' place in history. He was indeed "born" in the shadow of the 'Fun'ral of the World', since he is a Latter Day ruler; his reign must be seen, from its inception, within that context. Second, as a Latter Day monarch he is subject to that political 'distress of nations' which characterizes those times. His political 'Life' is conducted within the period of universal 'Death'; for this reason he is 'Th'*Amphibium* of Life and Death' (V). As such an amphibium, he is a typically eschatological creature. Moreover, the political desolation which overtakes both himself and his nation is part of the fortunate process which leads to the *renovatio*: a compound of 'Life and Death'—of 'Birth' and 'Fun'ral'—

which imitates the paradox of revivifying desolation. Thus the 'Fun'ral' of stanza III is succeeded by the 'Birth' of stanza IV, implying the revivifying movement of history. Charles is a casualty of the Latter Days, himself an 'Amphibium' inhabiting that paradoxical period. By these oxymorons Marvell implies the ultimately fortunate process which requires that Charles be unfortunate.

In the light of this pattern of providential *desolatio et renovatio*, it is not surprising that the imagery of these stanzas recalls a passage in *RT*, where Marvell described the providential sanction of such desolations:

> So that God has hitherto, in stead of an Eternal Spring, a standing serenity, and perpetual Sunshine, subjected Mankind to the dismal influence of Comets from above, to Thunder, and Lightning, and Tempests from the middle Region, and from the lower Surface, to the raging of the Seas, and the tottering of Earth quakes, beside all other the innumerable calamities to which humane life is exposed, he has in like manner distinguish'd the Government of the World by the intermitting seasons of Discord, War, and publick Disturbance. Neither has he so order'd it only (as men endeavour to express it) by meer permission, but sometimes out of Complacency.
>
> (*RT*, 231–2)

Here Marvell discusses the natural desolations that overtake 'humane life', suggesting that they possess an analogy in the political desolations of states. Just as nature reveals God's "common providence", so political history is arbitrated by His "special providence". The same natural symbols of *desolatio* appear in *The Unfortunate Lover*: the 'Comets' appear in stanza I, the 'Thunder, and Lightning', in stanza III, the 'Tempests' in stanzas II and VI, and 'the raging of the Seas' dominates most of the poem. Here, as in *RT*, these natural desolations figure forth the political desolations of the 1640s.

From the rest of the passage in *RT* it is evident that Marvell is speaking of the Civil War. He defends such 'publick Disturbance' by asserting that it is necessary to the reformation of states. By means of such reforming agitations the Ship of State achieves its 'Navigation' (232). In this poem the

'Shipwrack' figures the actual ruin of that political ship during the Civil War, its extreme and destructive *desolatio*, representing Marvell's royalist dismay at its outcome. But, as a chiliast, he must intimate here (as he does later in *RT*) that such political desolations fall within the providential pattern, and are appropriate to the current Latter Days. Marvell's portrait of that providential context balances, although it does not eradicate, the pathos of Charles' victimization.

The poignant portrait of Charles-Philogenes as Unfortunate Lover is maintained throughout these stanzas; the scene of destruction and tribulation here embodies the effects of Charles' 'Malignant Starrs'. In stanza III Charles personifies the "distress of the nation" in civil war; his 'Tears' and 'Sighs' are caused by the people's tumults. Similarly Josiah, to whom Charles was so often compared, was portrayed in the Bible as the personification of Israel's sorrow. He took upon himself the sins of his nation, and the consequent wrath of the Lord:

> Because thine heart was tender. . .when thou heardest. . .that [the] inhabitants [of Jerusalem] should become a desolation and a curse, and [thou] hast. . .wept before me.
>
> (II Kings 22:19)

Josiah's grief reflects the desolation of the Old Israel: Charles' grief, here, reflects the desolation of the New Israel, England. So, in Marvell's poem, the 'Sea' and 'Winds' of the people's unrest are transformed into the 'Tears' and 'Sighs' of their king: like his precursor Josiah, Charles takes upon himself the nation's desolation. This thought, figured by the imagery of stanza III, introduces Charles' further sufferings in the following stanzas, culminating in his "martyrdom" in stanza VII.

The beginning of this movement to 'martyrdom' in stanzas IV–V intimates also the causes of the nation's desolation, which is also the destruction of Charles himself. The political meaning of these stanzas retains the implicit comparison of Charles-Philogenes to Josiah. Before examining these stanzas in detail, it is necessary to explain the background to this comparison.

Royalist sermons which identified Charles with Josiah

compared them as righteous kings suffering for the sins of their subjects. However, in his sermon to Parliament, *Reformation and Desolation* (1642), Stephen Marshall put forward a Puritan view: that England required 'Reformation', and that if this reformation was not effected by king and Parliament, God would purge and punish the nation by 'Desolation'. He insists that Charles is a righteous king who could reform the New Israel as Josiah had reformed the Old, but is prevented by the antichristian bishops, the source of the national sin.[82] In effect, Marshall's sermon is a warning to Charles that he must repudiate the bishops, and if he is not willing to do so, Parliament must compel him. Charles will become another Josiah only by this means, and the alternative to this 'Reformation' is the 'Desolation' of civil war. A similar moral, made tragic by dint of hindsight, informs Marvell's stanzas (IV–V). These clarify the poem's reference to civil war and diagnose its causation: the antichristianity of the bishops, and their corruption of Charles' monarchy. In the light of this diagnosis it is possible to explicate the imagery of these stanzas, and expecially the 'Cormorants' that appear here, the identification of which has been, hitherto, a critical problem.

First, it is necessary to understand that the 'quarrelling Elements' (IV) are the conflicting parties of the Civil War. Marvell had used the same image for the Civil War in *Hastings*, who from heaven 'views the *Turnaments*/Of all these Sublunary *Elements*' (35–6) in the 1640s.[83] Within this context, 'Cormorants' appear to torture the lover:

> A num'rous fleet of Corm'rants black,
> That sail'd insulting o're the Wrack,
> Received into their cruel Care,
> Th' unfortunate and abject Heir:
> Guardians most fit to entertain
> The Orphan of the *Hurricane*.

> They fed him up with Hopes and Air,
> Which soon digested to Despair.
> And as one Corm'rant fed him, still
> Another on his Heart did bill.
> Thus while they famish him, and feast,

He both consumed, and increast:
And languished with doubtful Breath,
Th' *Amphibium* of Life and Death.
(IV–V)

These cormorants are the agents of the lover's victimization
here, and they figure Charles' ruin at the hands of the clergy.
To feed upon his heart/soul[84] is an antichristian devouring,
signified by the notorious voracity of cormorants, which
traditionally signified gluttony.[85] Not only are evil men 'the
hugest Cormorants, whose gorges have bene long ingurgi-
tated with the *World*',[86] but Milton made Satan himself a
cormorant in a passage in which he is compared to
antichristian clerics (*PL*. IV. 190ff.). Similarly, apart from his
image of Satan as vulture (in *Tom May*), Marvell was
accustomed to revile antichristian elements and especially
clerics by comparison to evil birds like the crane and the
jackdaw.[87] Here the clerical cormorants are 'black' because of
their clerical garb, and their 'cruel Care' intimates the
damnatory nature of their "ministry". Implementing at once
political and religious antichristianism—for both aspects
Marvell used the symbolism of predatory birds—they preside
over the 'Wrack' of the Ship of State, against the 'Rock' (II):
the antichristian elements which delighted in England's ruin,
they 'sail'd insulting o're the Wrack'. Marvell notes, sarcasti-
cally, that the cormorants are 'fit Guardians' for the Stuart
'Heir'. Their spiritual guardianship is, because antichristian, a
betrayal of souls in their keeping; Charles is 'Th' unfortunate
and abject Heir' because he submits to their domination. This
implication echoes that moment in *RT* when
Marvell explains Charles' ruin as due to episcopal domination: he did 'the Clergyes drudgery', a fact recalled in his
'abject' character here. That passage in *RT* also provides a
gloss for the next stanza, in that the bishops 'having gained
this Ascendent upon him. . .did for recompence assign him
that imaginary absolute Government, upon which Rock we
all ruined' (134); that is, Charles' relationship with the
bishops was doubly foolish. On the one hand, he made over
to them such power that they could make 'the whole business
of State' their own province (134). On the other, he received

in return a purely 'imaginary' absolutism, by which Marvell refers to the *Dei Gratia* status accorded Charles: his delusions of absolute power, fostered by the episcopal establishment, were the cause of the Civil War. This account of the Civil War accords—as we have seen—with Marvell's insistent thesis that princes are misled by episcopal pressure; absolutism or "false government" is traceable to episcopal ambitions. In Marvell's view, Charles' ruin was provoked by Laud and his Arminian colleagues.

Thus, in *The Unfortunate Lover*, we see Charles dominated by clerical 'Cormorants', whose 'cruel care' is at once his sustenance and his bane. 'They fed him up with Hopes and Air'; that is, they foster in him 'Hopes' of absolutist government. The 'Air' is the false pomp of such delusions. At another level it is the breath of life itself, sustaining the lover—an ironic reflection that absolutism was as the "breath of life" to Charles, sustaining him in his folly. It merely prolongs his agony:

> They fed him up with Hopes and Air,
> Which soon digested to Despair.
> And as one Corm'rant fed him, still
> Another on his Heart did bill.
> Thus while they famish him, and feast,
> He both consumed, and increast.

These lines imply that relationship with the bishops which Marvell described in *RT*. Charles is 'feast[ed]' and 'increast' by his absolutist 'Hopes', yet 'famish[ed]' and 'consumed' because he has relinquished real power to the bishops. As the bishops-cormorants 'feed' his absolutism, so they simultaneously 'famish' him of his true dominion. As an absolutist, Charles 'both consumed, and increast'—grew in delusion, but ruined his own monarchy. In this stanza Marvell shows how episcopacy drove the Ship of State on to the 'Rock' of absolutism, causing its 'Shipwreck' (II). The 'Birth' of Charles in his guise as Philogenes the absolutist delivered him to these clerical 'Guardians'. Since Marvell's diagnosis of the causes of the Civil War was by no means unusual, we may instructively compare that of a pamphleteer in 1644: 'Our...

Satanicall instruments [the bishops] persuade the King if he will but taste the fruit of this illegal prerogative tree, he shall be an absolute monarch, while indeed he becomes a very slave to them and their devilish devices.'[88] This observer echoes Marvell's notions even in the metaphor of feeding, and the irony that in aspiring to absolute dominion Charles made a drastic submission informs Marvell's stanza; but it also portrays Charles as the victim of antichristian episcopacy, in which the Civil War finds its real origin. In this manner Marvell, without absolving Charles of blame, ascribes the ultimate responsibility for war to the bishops. Thus, as throughout the poem, Charles is portrayed as both pathetic victim and active participant in his own ruin.

Marvell's use of malignant birds as images of antichristian agents of desolation originates, of course, in Revelation 19:17–18, where 'all the fowls. . .may eat the flesh of kings' during the last battle of the Latter Days;[89] so Charles is one of the royal victims of this scourge, that 'did bill' upon him at the time of England's own Latter Day conflict. It may be that this line provides a clue to specific identities, 'bill' containing a hidden eponym of a kind consistent with Marvell's cryptic procedure. The most prominent clerical figure in Charles' downfall was, of course, William Laud, Archbishop of Canterbury, executed in 1645 but possibly "present" in the prophetic timetable of the poem because he 'deform'd the whole reign of the best Prince that ever wielded the *English* Scepter' (*RT*, 134). The eponym "Bill" might well, by a species of paronomasia, include reference also to John Williams, Archbishop of York, thus encapsulating an allusion to the two highest clerical offices in the land. Both men are appropriate to Marvell's thesis here. Laud was the "evil angel" of Arminianism and of ecclesiastical interference in politics. Seen by many as Charles' antichristian arbiter, he was a prominent example of overweening clerical ambition— 'Happy had it been for the King, happy for the Nation. . . had he never climbed that Pinacle', even to become 'chief Minister' of state (*RT*, 133–4). Williams had held the office of Lord Keeper, was a pluralist and notorious intriguer and was reported as author of the dubious notion of 'the King's two consciences';[90] Marvell noted 'Th'Ambition of [this] *Prelate* great' (*Appleton House*, XLVI). Thus the two archbishops fittingly represent Marvell's brief against episcopacy: antichristian ambition, political interference, Arminian imposition, corruption, and crucial influence upon the king. Williams' opposition to Arminianism evidently did not excuse his other defects, either to Marvell or to Fairfax.[91] Equally, the ecclesiastico-political wrangling between Williams and Laud would, far from undermining their coexistence in this stanza, rather have illustrated Marvell's perennial contention that episcopal squabbles are conducted at the expense of the political order. Indeed, the two cormorant-clerics are here endowed with suitably contrary modes of "ministry": 'one. . .fed him. . .Another' ate him. This image simultaneously conveys both clerical in-fighting and political meddling, compounding the paradoxes of Charles' situation here.

Marvell deliberately emphasizes the centrality of these stanzas (IV and V), which occur at the half-way mark in the poem. For, as Maren-Sophie Røstvig has noted, significant nouns form a pattern in stanzas I–IV, which is then reversed in stanzas V–VIII.[92] This circular semantic structure pivots on 'Corm'rants':

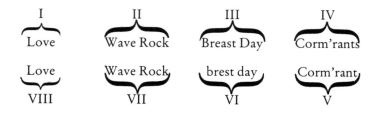

I	II	III	IV
Love	Wave Rock	Breast Day	Corm'rants
Love	Wave Rock	brest day	Corm'rant
VIII	VII	VI	V

In this manner the 'Corm'rants' become the highlighted central element of the poem. This structure reflects, in fact, the causal nature of the bishops in Charles' 'unfortunate' history. Both structurally and thematically they are the critical factor in the poem, the arbiters of Charles' fall. In this fashion Marvell accords a central place to the source of the national conflict. From this point stanzas VI–VII proceed to demonstrate the conflict of the Civil War.

Before explicating those stanzas, it is necessary to show

how Marvell supports his political narrative here, by means of the Petrarchan and personal narrative. On this level, the 'Hopes and Air' are the vain ambitions of the lover, who, hoping to gain his beloved, is thus more readily vulnerable to 'Despair' when he is rejected. This Petrirchan motif is an ironic reflection of Philogenes' absolutist 'love' for his people: the aspirations of Charles-Philogenes are precisely the reason for his rejection by his "beloved" people. Similarly, Charles is the dupe of the bishops not only in government but also on the personal level. His 'Heart' is at once his lover's heart, seat of passion, and his soul.[93] At that level, his soul is in the keeping of the 'Guardian' bishops: they pretend so to guard it but in fact 'bill' upon it. That devouring of Charles' soul intimates the damnatory motive of this antichristian "ministry". The ambiguity of 'Heart'—at once the Petrarchan 'Heart' and the royal "soul"—allows this implication in the lines.

The true Christian ministry is here seen as reversed. For Christian redemptive ministry is symbolized by the "Pelican", which draws blood from its own heart.[94] Signifying Christ's redemptive power, the 'Sad Pelican' was used by Marvell to counterpoint the antichristian ministry of the papist Flecknoe, in *Fleckno, an English Priest at Rome*;[95] the clerical cormorants reverse that ministry by feeding off Charles' 'Heart', in an antichristian inversion of true spiritual 'Care'.[96]

Marvell's procedure and imagery in these stanzas find analogues in *Salmacida*. In that masque the king's careful love of his people is contrasted with 'o'erweening priests' (336). And Marvell's 'Hopes' that 'increast' echo those of Charles' people in the masque, who complain of his 'delay' in rescuing them, that 'whilst our hopes increase our time doth waste' (329). In Marvell's poem that paradox of 'increase'/'waste' becomes 'consumed'/'increast', and Charles himself is the victim of the paradox. So here, as throughout the poem, Marvell implements an ironic reversal of the masque's imagery and of its absolutist assertions. It is Charles, not the 'beloved people' (301), who requires rescue here.

The 'doubtful' struggle of 'Life and Death' within Charles-Philogenes is that between the vigour and the destruction of monarchy itself. In this respect the monarch's divided nature reflects the division in his country, just as his body has imitated—in 'Tears' and 'Sighs'—the turbulence of the body politic (III). That traditional metaphor in which the state is a body, the king its head, informs the relationship between Charles' 'doubtful Breath' and the nation's own 'Life and Death' struggle. His psychomachia—as an 'Amphibium'— imitates at this level 'Devision that taile-headed Amphisbaena',[97] as a contemporary expressed it, and what I have called the Civil War's effect of "doubleness". Throughout the poem, both Charles and his nation are suffering the effects of desolation. As Philogenes, Charles personifies the "tragedy" of civil war.

Of this civil war, the many antitheses and paradoxes of the poem are *figurae*. War is an antithetical state, and civil war a paradoxical one. These images of conflict are elaborated in the next two stanzas, which develop from the psychomachia of stanza V, and from the causal diagnosis given in that stanza, proceed to the effects of civil war.

In the stanza VI this characterization of civil war founds itself upon a Petrarchan idea. The lover is caught 'betwixt the Flames and Waves': in the Petrarchan narrative, he is caught between passion ('Flames') and the vicissitudes of fortune:[98]

> And now, when angry Heaven wou'd
> Behold a spectacle of Blood,
> Fortune and He are call'd to play
> At sharp before it all the day:
> And Tyrant Love his brest does ply
> With all his wing'd Artillery.
> Whilst he, betwixt the Flames and Waves,
> Like *Ajax*, the mad Tempest braves.
>
> (VI)

The conflict takes place because 'angry Heaven' decrees the Civil War. Just as Marvell characterized the war in the *Horatian Ode* as 'angry Heavens flame', so here 'angry Heaven wou'd/Behold a spectacle of Blood', the war. The reason for heaven's anger has been explained in the previous stanza: the bishops' antichristianism was the national sin, fostering also false government. As in the *Ode*, heaven's wrath is a 'flame'—the 'Flames' of divine retribution combine with the 'Waves' of rebellion to torment Charles.

Also as in the *Ode*, heaven's anger calls for Charles 'to play' his tragic scene in the historical drama. Here the military metaphors ('At sharp', 'Artillery') emphasize Marvell's subject, the Civil War; this political level of meaning is supported by the Petrarchan image, of the lover assaulted by the "batteries" of Cupid's armoury. Here that Petrarchan motif is made literal in its reference to the Civil War.

Here, also, heaven's anger is retribution for Charles' clerically inspired absolutism, represented in the 'Tyrant Love'. On the Petrarchan level, this is Cupid, who victimizes the Unfortunate Lover. On the political level, the 'Tyrant Love' is Charles' own tyrannical conception of Philogenes, the absolutist lover of his people. In this sense, Charles becomes a victim of his own absolutist aspirations: his 'Tyrant Love' becomes his own enemy. This political psychomachia has an ironic implication, that Charles the tyrant-lover is himself tyrannized by love. Perhaps this irony is intended to imply that Charles-Philogenes loved his people too much to suppress them bloodily in war—that, in a sense, he allowed himself to be defeated. This pathetic notion would have accorded well with the popular hagiographical image of Charles as martyr. By such an implication the stanza maintains the poem's ambivalent attitude: Charles is here both the mistaken absolutist and the martial hero who 'braves' 'the mad Tempest' of war.

In its portrait of Charles-Philogenes as warrior, the poem recalls *Salmacida*. That masque insists upon the 'valour' of Charles-Philogenes (322, 372), eulogising the king as a martial hero (esp. 732-3). In the poem he is compared especially to Ajax, son of Oileus. This has been recognized as an allusion to Virgil's *Aeneid* (I. 45f.),[99] which tells of the manner in which the goddess Minerva revenged herself upon that warrior for his 'mad sin'. This reminiscence is especially appropriate to Marvell's subject in the stanza. That subject—the retribution of heaven for Charles' absolutist folly—is reinforced by this allusion to a warrior punished by the gods for his madness. Moreover, the 'Flames and Waves' of

Charles' punishment recall Minerva's persecution of Ajax, who was tortured by a 'flame' and tossed by 'waves', and he, like Charles, was driven upon a 'Rock'. In this manner the Virgilian reminiscence provides one of Marvell's cherished Roman parallels for the Civil War.

This stanza also maintains the implicit Josian comparison. Here England is seen to be punished by heaven's anger; in Kings Josiah explains that Israel labours under 'the wrath of the Lord' (II Kings 22:13), for the same reason—the national sin of idolatry. Moreover, in stanza IV Charles is seen as an 'Orphan', like Josiah, whose father was assassinated (II Kings 21:20–4). In this manner the central stanzas maintain Charles' identification with Josiah, the righteous king of a corrupt Israel: an identification which seems to imply Charles' own religious innocence—recalled in *RT*, where Marvell asserts that he was a 'pious' king. Thus Marvell's central stanzas imply that the bishops are the true villains of the Civil War, and Charles is their victim.

In the next stanza, the image of Charles as a victim is amplified by his characterization as a martyr, a characterization fostered by royalist propaganda at this time.

> See how he nak'd and fierce does stand,
> Cuffing the Thunder with one hand;
> While with the other he does lock,
> And grapple, with the stubborn Rock:
> From which he with each Wave rebounds,
> Torn into Flames, and ragg'd with Wounds.
> And all he saies, a Lover drest
> In his own Blood does relish best.
>
> (VII)

Here, in the initial lines, Charles is seen in conflict with the 'Rock' of episcopally determined absolutism, a development of his conflict with his own "tyrannical love" in the previous stanza. Charles as martial hero is here seen to be engaged in a vain struggle in which, nevertheless, he is courageous and resolute. The 'Waves' of the rebellion constantly pull him away from the 'Rock', symbol of absolutism—a symbolic narrative, in fact, of the rebellion's success. Charles' defeat is represented as physical wounding, 'Torn into Flames, and ragg'd with Wounds'. In this fashion the stanza culminates the poem's portrait of Charles as victim, casualty of the Latter Day war.

It is the final couplet which transforms the victim into a martyr:

> And all he saies, a Lover drest
> In his own Blood does relish best.

Here 'saies' is a pun: Charles, the actor in history, declaims ('says') as an actor should. On another level, 'saies' is a contraction of "assays",[100] his attempts and assaults in the war. In the Petrarchan narrative those "assays" are the lover's attempts at his desires, supporting the political meaning, in which the war was—in all respects—the crucial "assay" of Charles' reign. These words and attempts are 'best relish[ed]' by 'a Lover drest/In his own Blood'. This is an allusion to Christ, the bridegroom or lover of the soul, who expressed His love by His bloody ransom of man; traditionally, He was represented as 'drest/In his own Blood'.[101] Thus the lines suggest that only Christ—the transcendent "victim" of His own "love"—can 'best' appreciate ('relish') the sufferings of Charles as lover. Moreover, Christ as Judge evaluates, at the End, the actions and motives of men; it is proper that He should be Charles' Judge. The implication that His evaluation is favourable absolves Charles of religious guilt.

On another level, it is the 'Unfortunate Lover' himself who is 'drest/In his own Blood': the manner in which he 'relish[es]' his own wounds indicates that his is the martyr's attitude, in which victimization becomes transcendence. This double level of meaning rests on the word 'Lover': Christ and Charles are both 'unfortunate Lovers'. Moreover, the ambiguity which embraces both Charles and his Lord is especially appropriate, since Christ was Himself a king,[102] and Charles' kingship is His precursor. The Christological implications of this stanza are all associated with Revelation 19 (the locus also of the last conflict and its birds of prey, evoked earlier in the poem). There Christ at the Coming is 'clothed with a vesture dipped in blood' (19:13). Here, too, He is a warrior, on 'a white horse' (19:11), leading 'the armies that were in heaven' (19:14), with 'a sharp sword' (19:15). With Christ as warrior comes the fulfilment of Christ as lover too, at 'the marriage of the Lamb' (19:7). Moreover, this is Christ in His capacities as Judge and King: 'He [shall] smite the nations, and he shall rule them', 'King of Kings' (19:15–16).

This evocation of the Kingdom Age is pertinent to Marvell's Latter Day "tragedy": human kings may fall, but such desolations merely preface the renovated Kingdom. Here the divine king 'relishes' the human king's martyrdom, which was indeed required of him by 'angry Heaven' (VI). Charles is thus seen to submit to his doomed role in the eschatological plan; as, equally, he submitted to his own tragedy in the *Ode*.

The seventh stanza's portrait of Charles-martyr should be seen in the context of royalist propaganda at this time, which urged that image with much popular success. In royalist literature there was a constant 'drawing of parallels. . . between Charles' fate and that of Christ', of which Charles was himself conscious and which are reiterated in *Eikon Basilike*.[103] There Charles regards the 'Essays' (or assays, as in this poem) of his subjects' perfidy as a Christ-like burden, and states 'I care not much *to be reckoned among the Unfortunate*, if I be not in the black list of irreligious. . . Princes' (23). Marvell's Unfortunate Lover takes Charles' persona at his word. This procedure is at once complimentary—praising by imitation—and ironic, for nothing remains of Charles' monarchy but its self-generated images of delusion. To portray Charles in his own images is at once to allow him the grace of those aspirations and to judge their insubstantiality.

The scene here, as elsewhere in the poem, recalls the frontispiece of *Eikon Basilke*, where surrounded by images of martyrdom Charles is seen against the background of a turbulent sea. This hagiography was issued in the year of his execution, when this poem too was written. (It was rumoured that Marvell had aided Milton in the writing of *Eikonoklastes.*)[104] In its frontispiece Milton recognizes both the popish idolatries of martyr-cults, and their most recent source:

In one thing I must commend his openness, who gave the title to this book [*Eikon Basilike*] The King's Image; and by the shrine he dresses out for him, certainly would have the people come and worship him. [105]

In this spirit he diagnoses the nature and aims of the frontispiece. It is, in effect, a distillation of the Caroline masque:

[There is] the conceited portraiture before his book, drawn out of the full measure of a masking scene, and set there to catch fools and silly gazers. . .

The picture set in front would martyr him and saint him to befool the people. . .But quaint emblems and devices, begged from the old pageantry of some twelfthnight's entertainment at Whitehall, will do but ill to make a saint or martyr. [106]

Milton recognised the drift of absolutist images in the Caroline masques, where monarchy was "sanctified" in a manner which justified the worst excesses of prerogative rule. Here he sees that the hagiography of Charles in defeat was merely the obverse of his *Dei Gratia* kingship in the masques: the images assimilated to both are equally false, and Milton indicates this especially by his derogatory use of 'masking' as "delusion". In Marvell's poem it has a similar resonance: it is at once the masure of Charles' ruinous fallacies, and—on the "positive" side—a symbol of the historical "masque" in which Charles is a tragic actor.

Milton's attribution of masque-concepts to *Eikon Basilike* is particularly pertinent to *Salmacida*, in which Charles-Philogenes strikingly anticipates Charles-martyr. Commenting on *Salmacida*, Stephen Orgel and Roy Strong have noted this anticipation in the proscenium-frieze, which grants to Philogenes 'attributes of the suffering Christ'. [107] Thus in *Salmacida* Charles as lover of his people figures forth Christ, the divine lover of mankind. That figural relationship informs Marvell's 'Lover drest/In his own Blood', where both Charles and Christ are evoked.

This image is given an original twist by a Marvellian irony; the image is based upon conflicting personae accorded to Charles during the Civil War. To royalists Charles' persona became that of the "Man of Sorrows",[108] imitating that of Christ Himself. The tradition of Christ as "Man of Sorrows" has its biblical origin in Isaiah 53:3, and its Messianic prophecy portrays Christ as the one who will assume the sins of His people, redeeming them by His sacrifice (53:4–5):

> Surely he hath borne our griefs, and carried our sorrows; yet we did esteem him stricken, smitten of God, and afflicted.

This Christological type, taken up by royalist propagandists, is recalled by Marvell in his poem. In stanza III Charles-Philogenes is a "man of sorrows":

> The Sea him lent these bitter Tears
> Which at his Eyes he alwaies bears.
> And from the Winds the Sighs he bore,
> Which through his surging Breast do roar.

Here, as I remarked, the logic of the imagery indicates that Charles takes upon himself the tumults of his people ('Winds', 'Sea'), so that they become his own internal psychomachia. The 'Seas' of rebellion become 'his surging Breast'. Thus Charles is here the royalist "Man of Sorrows", and like Christ in Isaiah, he takes upon himself the griefs of his people. Both are un-fortunate, 'smitten of God. . . afflicted'. In both cases this process is motivated by love—in Christ's case, divine love that redeems; in Charles', the love of his people proper to Philogenes. In both cases that love issues in sacrifice. Christ was sacrificed in order to redeem men's sins; Charles atones for that national sin which evoked the wrath of 'angry Heaven'. This thought provides the narrative from stanzas III to VII, where Charles is the "Man of Sorrows", and victim of the bishops' antichristian machinations; then he is the victim of heaven's *desolatio* against that antichristianism; and finally, in stanza VII, the martyr to that sin. In this manner Marvell reveals Charles' ruin as the price of England's sins, and a function of her desolation.

This, Marvell's ratification of Charles in defeat, is under-scored by this stanza's political allusion. Whereas Charles'

royalist persona was "the Man of Sorrows", to parliamentarian propagandists he was 'the Man of Blood', an agent of
Antichrist who wreaked death in the nation.[109] That parliamentarian tag is twisted by Marvell into the 'Lover drest/In
his own Blood'; Charles is here not a man spilling others'
blood but a martyr whose own blood is spilt. By his
transformation of the derogatory 'Man of Blood' Marvell
enacts a revenge upon the parliamentarian cliché and declares
his own royalist sympathy. In the seventh stanza Charles'
portrait is at its most favourable.

This stronger emphasis upon Charles' nobility (as opposed
to his idiocies) prepares for the last stanza. In the Final Image
Charles' death is portrayed as the assumption of a martyr.
This stanza provides a memorial to his tragedy, synthesizing
both its ironies and its poignancy:

> This is the only *Banneret*
> That ever Love created yet:
> Who though, by the Malignant Starrs,
> Forced to live in Storms and Warrs;
> Yet dying leaves a Perfume here,
> And Musick within every Ear:
> And he in Story only rules,
> In a Field *Stable* a Lover *Gules.*
>
> (VIII)

In the Petrarchan narrative, this stanza suggests the
"apotheosis" of the lover. But the stanza's details, and
especially the last line, have puzzled critics;[110] in fact, this is a
characteristic Final Image, synthesizing the poem's narratives. It involves a complex admixture of the major elements
of the poem.

'This is the only *Banneret*/That ever Love created yet': in
the Petrarchan sense, this lover has been distinguished in
love's 'Warrs', the love-war portrayed in stanza VI. 'Tyrant
Love' has conferred knighthood upon him: a 'Banneret' is a
knighthood created on the battlefield, and conferred by the
king. This notion is an ironic reflection upon Charles, for as
Philogenes he receives a knighthood which displaces the
monarchy to which he is 'Heir' (IV). Defeated and executed,

he is no longer a king; rather he attains the merit of a martial hero. In this sense the Civil War has "made" Charles, transformed his function. This idea carries a positive connotation, that Charles' tragic achievement is indeed an achievement of a kind, a martyrdom; but it also carries an irony, that Charles the tyrannous Philogenes is himself subordinated to the favours of 'Tyrant Love'. He is both the victim and the martyr of his absolutism. This loss of monarchical function underpins the penultimate line, that 'he in Story only rules'. The martyrdom that embraces this loss is indicated by another Christological reference, for Christ was 'God's bannerite';[111] as in Revelation 19:11, where he 'in righteousness. . .doth. . .make war' as the Knight 'called Faithful and True'.[112] This reiteration of Charles' comparison to Christ provides the sympathetic resonance in this couplet, balanced by the ironic portrait of Charles as king-turned-knight. This tension of sympathy and irony is, as we have seen, characteristic of the poem as a whole, and it is maintained throughout this final stanza.

The first couplet's allusion to a 'Banneret' recalls the historical scene which is the true context of the poem, for at Edgehill in 1642 Charles had created a banneret, the first such creation for a long time.[113] That contemporaneous resonance of the Civil War is amplified in the next couplet. Philogenes is 'by the Malignant Starrs,/Forced to live in Storms and Warrs': Charles' tragedy is to be the victim and martyr of this Latter Day ethos, of which the national effect was civil war. The 'Malignant Starrs' shadow forth the eschatological destiny which decrees the time of desolation, but they have also a quite specific reference to the Civil War. It will be recalled that, in *Hastings*, Marvell vilifies the parliamentarians as the 'Democratick Stars', who are held responsible for the hero's death. Similarly, here, the 'Malignant Starrs' are the parliamentarians who effected the regicide.

This allusion is, therefore, suitably succeeded by Charles' death in the next line. 'Yet dying leaves a Perfume here,/And Musick within every Ear'. This has long been recognized as a reference to Josiah the righteous king: of whom Ecclesiasticus (49:1) had remarked that 'The remembrance of Josias is like . . .perfume. . .it is sweet. . .as musick at a banquet of wine'.[114] In this manner Marvell concludes the Josian comparison, and this conclusion is pertinent to the foregoing portrait of Charles as martial hero. For Josiah was slain in battle, and greatly mourned (II Kings 23:29); moreover, like Charles (in Marvell's analysis) a righteous man in error, 'he consulted not with the Lord, and therefore was slaine'.[115] This allusion occurs in the eighth stanza of a poem in which each stanza has eight lines, which may be a numerological reference to the fact that Josiah became king at the age of eight.[116] By means of this comparison with Charles, Marvell portrays the latter as a righteous king, no less righteous because misled.

Charles's apotheosis in 'Perfume. . .And Musick' recalls the characterization of Philogenes in *Salmacida*, and of Charles the 'heroical Lover' in *Love's Triumph*. In *Salmacida* Charles' triumph as Philogenes is celebrated by a 'Triumph of Music' (458ff.), an image of the concord achieved by the "power" of love. Here too Charles achieves apotheosis, attaining 'heavenly graces' (390–1); he will inevitably reach heaven, 'Where, we are taught, the heroës are gone' (340). In *Salmacida*, as in Marvell's poem, Charles' heroism demands apotheosis.

Such a 'musical' effect is of course characteristic of masques. Moreover, Marvell's 'Perfume. . .And Musick' finds a close analogue in *Love's Triumph*; they may both be indebted to the Josian source in this respect. In *Love's Triumph* Euphemus, the spirit of true and virtuous love, prophesies the triumph of perfect love—Charles—in Callipolis:

> Then will he flow forth like a rich perfume
> Into your nostrils, or some sweeter sound
> Of melting music.

(78–80)

The triumph of Charles, here, evokes that 'music and perfume' by which Marvell indicates Charles' apotheosis in this poem.

In *Salmacida* there appears also an analogue of the lines in which the lover is 'Forced to live in Storms and Warrs'. There the Spirit of Concord repines the fate of Philogenes:

> though the best
> Of kingly science harbours in his breast,
> Yet '*tis his fate to rule in adverse times*,
> When wisdom must awhile give place to crimes.
>
> (188–91; my italics)

The same 'fate' is bestowed upon Marvell's own Charles-Philogenes, and something of the same regret informs his lines. But if Charles is a Latter Day martyr, 'Yet dying he leaves' music 'within every Ear': his memory is perhaps his best achievement, and makes of him a symbolic personage to 'every' one. (The same was true of Josiah's memorial music: 'all the singing men and the singing women spoke of Josiah in their lamentations to this day, and made them an ordinance in Israel'. The Geneva Bible comments that 'The people so lamented the losse of this good king, that after when there was any great lamentation, this was spoken of as a prouerbe'.)[117] This thought is both ironic—Charles is greater in death than in life—and sympathetic, that this too is an achievement.

That ironic balance informs the final couplet, in which Marvell anticipates Charles' significance as an historical personage:

> And he in Story only rules,
> In a Field *Sable* a Lover *Gules*.

In the penultimate line there is an ambiguity: on the one hand, the lover is supreme 'only' in 'Story', since his actual life was 'unfortunate'; on the other, he "alone" attains this supremacy. Both of these meanings are relevant to the Petrarchan narrative. In 'Story' the ambiguity has proved more difficult: a 'Story' can be a fiction, a chronicle (history) or a picture,[118] and critics have tended to opt for one of these meanings. In fact, this is a characteristic Marvellian ambiguity, all three meanings of which are crucial to the Final Image. The suggestion that the Unfortunate Lover is pre-eminent in "fiction" provides the culmination of the Petrarchan narrative in the poem. Indeed, tragic loves were always the most celebrated, and by intimating this fact Marvell makes a parting gesture at the generic tradtion that he has chosen for his poem.

The significance of 'Story' as "history" completes the eschatological and political narrative of the poem. Since Charles is now dead, he 'rules' only in the history of the past. Deprived of his monarchical power by rebellion, he 'rules' only in the delusory history or "fiction" of masque. In a sense he was Philogenes the absolutist only in the masques, and Marvell returns Charles to that imaginary kingdom. In this manner the meanings of "fiction" and "history" are made to interrelate. It is a judgment upon Charles that he in fiction merely—in 'Story only'—ruled as he thought fit.

That evaluative judgement is counterpointed by the ambiguity in 'only rules': *supremely* rules. In the masques' 'Story' Charles did indeed rule supreme. And in "history" too he has a unique quality. His was the only formalized regicide in English history, a fact of which the regicides were rather proud. In that sense Charles is, therefore, unique in '[hi]Story'. This fact is supported, in this stanza, by Marvell's celebration of his martyrdom; that 'leaves a Perfume here', an exemplum of Charles' acquiescence in his destiny. As an exemplum it is proper that he should take a pre-eminent place in the chronicles of history: his tragic fate is a lesson in 'Heaven's anger' and the cost of the providential plan. On this level the Final Image summarizes the relationship between 'Fortune and He' (VI), redirecting us to the 'Unfortunate' of the title.

That summary informs the pictorialized Unfortunate Lover of the last line. Much speculation has raged over this line: is the image heraldic, a device, or a picture? It is indeed a *figura*, in the sense that it emblematizes his 'Story', and it recalls the first stanza, where we are told of his 'impression upon Time'. This line manifests that 'impression' as if on a seal; just as it summarizes his significance in history, in 'Time'. This seal-like impression is especially appropriate to the portrait of a king, which traditionally formed part of royal seals. Moreover, its pictorial or emblematic quality recalls the memorials of Charles I (on pendants and the like) which were cherished by many royalists. Such a recollection is appropriate to the Final Image, which is itself a summatory memorial to Charles.

The lover is 'Gules' because, as the seventh stanza indicated, he is 'drest/In his own Blood'. In this manner the 'Gules' of the Final Image recalls the Christological reference there and emblematizes his martyrdom—that which caused him to 'rule' 'in Story', at every level. The 'Field Sable' is at once the dark background of the poem, and the battle-'Field' of the Civil War; the colour black is a memorial of Charles' death and tragedy, which were decided in that 'Field'. In this fashion the Final Image crystallizes the narrative of the poem, containing within it the Civil War and eschatological martyrdom. Charles, as both martial hero and sacrifice, is summarized in the colour 'Gules'.

This summarizing image is carefully reconciled with the Petrarchan narrative: the bloody lover and his tragedy— 'Sable' and 'Gules'—are equally central to that narrative, and red had been paired with black before, as 'ensigns of death and ruth' in love.[119]

As I have indicated, there is in this final stanza a recollection of the Caroline masque, and its "fictions". In the last line the clash of two primary colours is a symbolic version of the poem's conflict of 'Flames and Waves', the warring antitheses of bright and dark; it provides a pictorial equivalent of the earlier 'masque of quarrelling Elements'. The Final Image, by stabilizing that conflict into the stillness of picture, calls a halt to the "moving pictures" of the poem and thus gives a sense of rest and resolution. This "stilling of conflict" is especially significant as an image of the cessation of the Civil War: these events have passed into '[hi]Story', like Charles himself. He, being dead, is necessarily now still.

This combination of arrest and death in the Final Image connotes the fact that, with Charles' martyrdom, the desolation also ends. His sacrifice is thus "restful" in historical terms. The arrival of peace is here symbolized by the containment of Charles within a picture; his assimilation into "history" is also an assimilation into art. That assimilation occurs not only by means of his pictorialization but also by his placing in 'Story', "fiction". On one level, the poem itself effects that assimilation into art.

The transformation of Charles into "art" effected by the

Final Image imitates the transformation that is usual at the end of a masque. For at the close of a Caroline masque the real world and the world of art mix, as the courtiers themselves become masquers. In one sense the royal and courtly personages are assimilated into the artistic form of the masque, just as here Charles-Philogenes undergoes transformation into art. In the masques, as I have indicated, art (the "power" of the imagination) was used as an analogue of political power: to achieve an imaginative order was to create a political harmony. In Marvell's poem Charles himself is shown to be lacking—in reality—that magical imaginative power which controlled the sea in the masques. But in the Final Image, Charles-Philogenes is returned to the realm of art; the images fashioned for him in the masques have become truly relevant only in his death, when the human Charles has been extracted, and only the perfected art of the image remains. His 'Blood[iness]' becomes 'Gules', art rather than an 'Unfortunate' life. In this manner Marvell finally allows Charles his persona in masque-art; untrue to his life—at least in terms of power—it is a fitting memorial to the power of his posthumous persona. By this means Marvell strikingly anticipates the compulsive quality of Charles' image in history, as the martyr of the English Revolution.

The form of the Final Image may even have been suggested by *Salmacida*. There the 'Good Genius of Great Britain' is 'a young man in a carnation garment', a warrior with 'an antique sword' (164–5). This may have suggested the English lover 'Gules', who is also a martial hero—a conversion, with hindsight, of the 'carnation' Englishman into the 'Lover drest/In his own Blood'. Moreover, Marvell's suggestion that his is a king proper to fable and chronicle is reminiscent of *Salmacida's* similar conclusion:

> Who this King and Queen would well historify
> Need only speak their names; those them will glorify:
> Mary and Charles, Charles with his Mary namèd are,
> And all the rest of loves or princes famèd are.
>
> (204–7)

Salmacida's suggestion that Charles is pre-eminent in

kingship and love anticipates the supremacy that Marvell accords to his Philogenes in the Final Image. His treatment provides an ironic twist upon *Salmacida*'s formulation, since *Salmacida* relegates all other lover-princes to 'fame', whereas Marvell attributes only fame to Charles himself. For only Charles' fame remains after his death, and only in repute does he achieve the perfection that *Salmacida* claims for him. The Final Image places him in the 'Field' of art—of colours and images—and that location is timeless, redeeming Charles from the unfortunate 'Field' of his history. It is, then, appropriate that this artistic 'impression' should represent his 'impression upon Time'. Marvell has (as it were) granted his king a true dominion in art.

The so-called "heraldic" quality of the Final Image may have been suggested by memorials of Charles, which would be pertinent to the memorial character of the Final Image itself. One such royalist relic of Charles illustrates the kind of design favoured: it is a locket in heart shape, done on hair of a funereal hue, and containing a piece of linen stained with blood—presumably, Charles' blood. The pendant carries a skull and crossbones, identifying it as a memorial, and also a portrait of the king.[120] Many such pendants were made both before and after the regicide, and no doubt anyone with royalist contacts would have seen at least one example. One can see how the colours of red and black would be readily associated with them, and that their designs might suggest Marvell's Final Image.

Many of these memorials conceal the king's portrait. Doubtless the same political discretion informed the arcane portrait of Charles in Marvell's poem; fundamentally royalist sympathies were not to be advertised at such a time, as Lovelace's recent history had demonstrated. Marvell's poem *To Lovelace* manifests his sense of the instability of the political situation, in a poem written at much the same time as *The Unfortunate Lover*. And the reminiscence, in this poem, of Lovelace's *Lucasta* (1.57) seems to connect *The Unfortunate Lover* with that insecure political mood, while, like *To Lovelace*, it compliments his fellow royalist. That political sensitivity is more than sufficient reason for Marvell to have framed his poem in images that have puzzled critics ever since, images which, however, were readily recognizable to a courtly royalist audience familiar with the masques.

The other major critical difficulty of this poem has been its peculiar tone, with its mixtures of the extravagant and pathetic. In fact, this tone is a symptom of Marvell's attitude to his defeated monarch; it arises from the problematic, in which Charles is seen in his own extravagant mask, at the same time as his pathetic history is recounted. That ironic admixture reflects Marvell's own recognition both of Charles' folly and of his qualities. Such an ambivalent attitude was often the Stuarts' legacy to their adherents: 1649 was no time to be a *complacent* monarchist.

The problematic of this poem reveals Marvell's attitudes in defeat, in a manner similar to that in the *Horatian Ode* of the following year. As in that poem, Charles is both judged and celebrated. The 'tragic Actor' of the *Ode* is here seen in full masking-dress, and there is the same reconcilement to Charles' 'unfortunate' role in the eschatological drama. The heightened tone and the imagery of conflict in this poem manifest its proximity to the regicide; in this respect, the formalized "masque" element allows Marvell to distance the tragedy. Like other poems that he wrote in this period, *The Unfortunate Lover* shows Marvell in engagement with the current crises in history, and its problematic reveals—as so often—a poetic structure designed to formalize his reconcilement with the demands of the eschatological process. While the later poems and prose work also implement an eschatological vision, it is especially in the poems addressing the mid-century crisis that the whole range of Marvell's resources—spiritual, intellectual, eclectic and witty—is brought to bear upon the pressing need for a personal and national integration into the will of God in history. It is the depth of Marvell's commitment to apocalypse that impels his effort to make of poetry itself an eschatology.

Notes

Books are published in London unless otherwise specified.

Note on Terminology

1. My definitions of these terms, and preference for 'eschatology', are derived with some slight modifications from those of Brian W. Ball, *A Great Expectation: Eschatological Thought in English Protestantism to 1660* (Leiden, 1975), 13. He gives 'chiliasm' a different connotation.

Introduction

1. This approach is particularly popular in criticism of *An Horatian Ode* (see Ch.3). An example of this approach in a more general relation is Balachandra Rajan, 'Andrew Marvell: The Aesthetics of Inconclusiveness', *Approaches to Marvell: The York Tercentenary Lectures*, ed. C. A. Patrides (1978), 155–73.

2. For accounts of Marvell criticism *see*, for instance, John Carey, *Andrew Marvell: A Critical Anthology* (Harmondsworth, 1969), Introduction; Donal Smith, 'Marvell', *English Poetry: Select Bibliographical Guides*, ed. A. E. Dyson (1971), notes 'the contradictions and confusions in Marvell criticism', 'a criticism [often] turgid, ingenious, and perverse' (104, 100); Anne E. Berthoff, *The Resolved Soul: A Study of Marvell's Major Poems* (Princeton, NJ, 1970), ix, finds that Marvell criticism has espoused methods which 'are, if not destructive, often faulty or irrelevant'.

3. *See* Ch.2.ii.

4. *See*, for instance, the discussion of critical accounts in Bruce King, 'In Search of Andrew Marvell', *REL* VIII (1967), 31–41; and Pierre Legouis, 'Marvell and the New Critics', *RES*, n.s., VIII 32 (1957), 382–9.

5. *See* French Fogle's analysis of critics' accounts of the poem, and their defectiveness (not to say their resort to paraphrase and evasion): 'Marvell's "Tough Reasonableness" and the Coy Mistress', *Tercentenary Essays in Honor of Andrew Marvell*, ed. Kenneth Friedenreich (Hamden, Conn., 1977), 121–39.

6. *See* introduction to Ch.7.

1: A Revelation for the Times

1. For the account of Reformation eschatology and its Protestant version of history which is given here, the most relevant sources are: William M. Lamont, *Godly Rule: Politics and Religion 1603–1660* (1969), who analyses the evolution of conflicting political creeds from eschatological bases; Christopher Hill, *Antichrist in Seventeenth-Century England* (1971), for a general survey and *The World Turned Upside Down: Radical Ideas During the English Revolution* (Harmondsworth, 1975) for sectarian millenarianism; Peter Toon (ed.), *Puritans, the Millenium and The Future of Israel: Puritan Eschatology 1600–1660* (Cambridge, 1970); for the theology of eschatological speculation, Brian W. Ball, *A Great Expectation*; E. L. Tuveson, *Millenium and Utopia: A Study in the Background of the Idea of Progress* (1964). For a more detailed summary of the ubiquity and effects of eschatology at this period, *see* M. C. Stocker, 'Poet of the Latter Days:

Andrew Marvell', D.Phil. dissertation, University of York (1981), Ch.2, *et passim*.

2. Stephen Marshall, *An Answer to a Booke Entituled An Humble Remonstrance* (1641), 78–9, quoted in G. W. Whiting, *Milton's Literary Milieu* (New York, 1964), 224.

3. Stephen Marshall, *(Reformation and Desolation: Or, a Sermon tending to the Discovery of the Symptomes of a People to whom God will by no meanes be reconciled* (1642), 42–3. Cf. Michael Walzer, *The Revolution of the Saints: A Study in the Origins of Radical Politics* (1966), 178–9. Cf. Thomas Temple, *Christ's Government in and over his People* (1642), repr. in facsim., *The English Revolution: I: Fast Sermons to Parliament*, ed. R. Jeffs, 34 vols. (1970–71), IV, 32–3; Ball, 98; Lamont, 94.

4. For example, Marshall, *Reformation*, 51.

5. Walzer, 179.

6. Appended to *Mr Smirke: or, the Divine in Mode* (1676).

7. For a detailed demonstration of these features, *see* Stocker, 'Poet of the Latter Days', Ch.3, ii.

8. *See* Ch.2.

9. Lamont, *Godly Rule* and Hill, *Antichrist* both confirm this conclusion, in their different ways.

10. Eschatological ideas in *The Rehearsal Transpros'd* (1672; and Part II, 1673), *Mr Smirke* and *An Account of the Growth of Popery and Arbitrary Government in England* (1677) are examined in Stocker, 'Poet of the Latter Days', Chs.3 and 4.

11. *See* the account of such Lectureships by Claire Cross, 'Parochial Structure and the Dissemination of Protestantism in Sixteenth–Century England', *Studies in Church History* 16 (1978), 269–78. Cf. her *Church and People 1450–1660* (Glasgow, 1976), 231. Samuel Parker, quoted by Marvell in *RT*, 306, confirms the Puritan cast of the Lectureships and episcopal hostility to them. For my working definition of Puritanism, *see* Stocker, 'From Faith to Faith in Reason', *Contexts of English Literature 1630–1700*, ed. T. G. S. Cain and K. Robinson (forthcoming).

12. Marvell describes his father's religious inclinations, *RT*, 203–4.

13. The colleges particularly distinguished for Puritan learning were Christ's, St John's, and Emmanuel. *See* Charles Webster, *The Great Instauration: Science, Medicine and Reform, 1626–1660* (1975), 37; Toon, 23, on Hebraist Studies for millenarian purposes.

14. Godfrey Davies, *The Early Stuarts, 1603–1660* (Oxford, 1959), 355–6.

15. Cross, 'Protestantism', 6.

16. *See* Josephine Waters-Bennett, *The Evolution of "The Faerie Queene"* (New York, 1960), 111.

17. *RT*, 89; a similar occasion arises in *Smirke*, 87–8, and in both cases Marvell is issuing a reproof to 'Popish' opponents, on eschatological grounds.

18. Webster, 32; Toon, 56. Mede's influence is discussed by Ball, Lamont, and Hill, *Antichrist*, 26–7; cf. Walzer, 292; Tuveson, ix. Another influential *Revelation* exegete, John Stoughton, was at Emmanuel (Webster, 35).

19. Accounts of this incident are given by W. Hilton Kelliher, *Andrew Marvell: Poet and Politician, 1621–78* (British Library, 1978), 25; John Dixon Hunt, *Andrew Marvell: His Life and Writings* (1978), 32.

20. M. A. Breslow, *A Mirror of England: English Puritan Views of Foreign Nations, 1618–1640* (Camb., Mass., 1970), discusses such fears.

21. An association reflected, for instance, in the Parliamentary Protestation which Marvell signed on 17 February 1641 (for the circumstances, *see* Kelliher, 31). The background to ideas of 'godly government' in this period is given by Lamont's *Godly Rule.* For the alliance of constitutionalism and Protestantism in the eschatological struggle, *see* A. S. P. Woodhouse (ed.), *Puritanism and Liberty: Being the Army Debates (1647–9) from the Clarke Manuscripts with supplementary documents* (1938), 43; Robin Clifton, 'Fear of Popery', *Origins of the English Civil War*, ed. Conrad Russell (1973), 156.

22. *The Prose Works of John Milton*, ed. J. A. St. John *et al.*, 5 vols. (1848–53), II. 513.

23. *Ibid*, 514.

24. Preface to *Eikonoklastes*, Bohn edn, I. 313: cf. also Marvell's *Smirke*, 21. Lucy Hutchinson, *Memoirs of the Life of Colonel Hutchinson* (Everyman, 1908), 6, is an illustrative allusion to the antichristian 'bondage'.

25. 'A Letter from Amsterdam to a Friend in England' (1678), *Somers Tracts*, ed. Walter Scott, VIII. 88: quoted in M. C. Bradbrook and M. G. Lloyd-Thomas, *Andrew Marvell* (Cambridge, 1961), 8n. Cf. Anon., 'On his Excellent Friend Mr Andrew Marvell' (1678), cited in Kelliher, 119–20, for similar sentiments.

26. Sir George Clark, *The Later Stuarts 1660–1714* (2nd edn, Oxford, 1956), 78–80, 92; echoing similar fears in the 1640s–50s (Clifton, 'Fear of Popery', 150–53). Marvell himself cites such fears in the Commons, *GP*, 295–7. Cf. Milton on national alarms, *Of True Religion*, II. 509; and 'A Dedication of the Legacy of. . .Herbert Lord Bishop of Hereford, to his Diocess' (1678–9), repr. in Grosart, IV. 160ff.

27. Clark, 66.

28. Marvell, *Letters*, 42–3 and the note thereon (362).

29. *See* Kelliher, 90.

30. John Aubrey, *Brief Lives*, ed. Andrew Clark, 2 vols. (Oxford, 1898), 54. Cf. Kelliher, 119–20, who notes another reference to this rumour.

31. Hunt, 183.

32. Hill, *Antichrist*, 158. For an account of the vested interests motivating the Church settlements, *see* K. A. Beddard, 'The Restoration Church', *The Restored Monarchy 1660–1688*, ed. J. R. Jones (1979), 155–75; cf. Clark, 18–19, 21–4.

33. For Marvell's London connections, *see* Kelliher, 29—although we fundamentally disagree about Marvell's political views, since Kelliher believes that Marvell was a republican or Cromwellian throughout the 1640s and 50s. (His thesis leads him to the canard so often found in such 'republican' accounts of Marvell: the unjustified contention that *Tom May* is apocryphal. On *May*'s authenticity, *see* the notes to Ch.3, below.) John

M. Wallace, *Destiny His Choice: The Loyalism of Andrew Marvell* (Cambridge, 1968), 202, ratifies the evidenced and more popular view that Marvell was loyal 'to the Crown until 1649'. I take it to last longer than that. Although some have doubted that *Villiers* is by Marvell, it is printed both in Margoliouth's edition and in E. S. Donno's: Andrew Marvell, *The Complete Poems* (Harmondsworth, 1972). Donno prints it as part of the canon, Margoliouth as an appendix. In Margoliouth, 435, E. E. Duncan-Jones suggests points in favour of Marvell's authorship. Wallace, 30n, accepts it as authentic; Bradbrook and Lloyd-Thomas rightly note that 'It has Marvell's tone and accent' (32n.). Biographical information on its authenticity is provided by P. H. Burdon, 'Andrew Marvell and Richard Flecknoe in Rome', (*N&Q* XIX (Jan. 1972), 16–18, 18.

34. Dennis Davison, 'Marvell and Politics', *N&Q* n.s. II. 5 (1955), 201–2, provides a succinct summary of critics' attitudes to Marvell's allegiance. Donal Smith, 'The Political Beliefs of Andrew Marvell', *UTQ* 36 (1966–7), 55–67, takes Marvell to be a 'Trimmer' on the Halifax model; a view developed and linked to 'Loyalism' by Wallace's *Destiny His Choice*. In so far as Wallace stresses Marvell's constitutionalism, he is accurate and helpful.

35. Godfrey Davies, 147f. On respect for the king's office, cf. 138–9.

36. William M. Lamont and Sybil Oldfield, *Politics, Religion and Literature in the Seventeenth Century* (1975), x.

37. Godfrey Davies, 126.

38. On such divisions *see* Lamont and Oldfield, xx,x; on the inherent tendency of Puritanism to sectarian fragmentation Howard Shaw, *The Levellers* (1968), 7, is particularly instructive. Cf. P. W. Thomas, 'Two Cultures? Court and Country under Charles I', *Origins*, ed. Russell, 169. The eschatological bias of the parliamentarian cause gave rise to democratic impulses which were ultimately inimical to the parliamentarian regime; *see* Lamont, 139–40.

39. Lamont and Oldfield, x.

40. Davies, 108, 128. The close association of Charles' cause with the episcopacy exacerbated fears of his 'Papist' tendencies; *see:* Clifton, 161–2; *Mercurius Britannicus*, no. 89 (30 June to 7 July 1645) 40–40ʸ; Whiting, 330; Halifax, 'The Character of a Trimmer', *Complete Works*, ed. J. P. Kenyon (Harmondsworth, 1969), 78; Hill, *Antichrist*, 157.

41. J. P. Kenyon, *The Stuart Constitution* (1966), 147; Lamont, 95. Foxe's ideas were particularly important in this respect; *see* Lamont, 23–4; Clifton, 149–50. For contemporary examples, *see* Milton, *The Reason of Church Government*, Bohn edn, II. 508; Henry Vaughan's poem, *White Sunday*, 30–2; Lucy Hutchinson, 6; Hill, *Antichrist*, 82, quoting Nathaniel Homes' sermon to Parliament. The chiliasm and the militancy (especially in this respect), and the political utility, of such preachers is studied in detail by John F. Wilson, *Pulpit in Parliament: Puritanism during the English Civil Wars 1640–48* (Princeton, 1969). Cf. also H. R. Trevor-Roper, 'The Fast Sermons of the Long Parliament', *Essays in British History*, ed. Trevor-Roper (1965), 85–138.

42. These were *A Letter to Dr Ingelo, In Effigiem Oliveri Cromwell*, and

In eandem Reginae Sueciae transmissam.

43. Breslow, 55 *et passim;* Toon, 37; Hill, *Antichrist,* 99, Temple, 27; Samuel Hartlib, *A Government of the Famous Kingdom of Macaria, shewing its excellent Government* (1641), 13.

44. Thomas Goodwin, 'A Brief History of the Kingdom of Christ, Extracted out of the Book of Revelation', *Works,* Nichol's Series of Standard Divines: Puritan Period (Edinburgh, 1861), III. 207.

45. The major texts for this position were Acts 1:7 and Matthew 24:36—'But of that day and hour knoweth no man. . .but my Father only', and 'It is not for you to know the times or the seasons, which the Father hath put in his own power'. Like Marvell, Milton uses this unrevealed "timing" of the Last Day to rebuke those impatient for the Last Day: thus in *PR* Christ, answering Satan's temptation that He should create the Kingdom at once, avers:

> All things are best fulfilled in their due time
> . . .
> If of my reign prophetic writ hath told
> That it shall never end, so when begin
> The Father in his purpose hath decreed,
> He in whose hand all times and seasons roll.
> (*PR,* III. 182–7)

Here Christ is echoing *Acts* 2:7, as a caveat against 'impatience' for the Coming. (Cf. Fixler's thesis on *PR* as a counterblast to this zeal, as described in Ch.2 below.) For the importance of such texts in the eyes of chiliasts, *see* Toon, 53. Owen repudiated all attempts to fix the date of the Last Day (Toon, 38), as did the Westminster Assembly of Divines of 1643—8 (Toon, 113). So did John Wilkins, *A Discourse Concerning the Beauty of Providence in all the rugged passages of it* (1649), 84 (citing Acts 1:7); Marshall, *Reformation,* 28; Temple, 50; Thomas Goodwin, 'An Exposition of the Book of Revelation' [1639], *Works,* III. xxvii-viii; Halifax, 66. Cf. II Peter 3:3–9, a salient eschatological text.

46. Cf. Ball, 181. To this view the Fifth Monarchists were the major exception. Richard Sibbes, *The Brides Longing for her Bride-groomes second Comming. . .* (1638), explains that patience is necessary because the number of the elect must be fulfilled before Christ can establish the Kingdom (46–7). That diligence and patience must be combined is emphasized by Wilkins, 66. A close analogue to Marvell's attitude here in the *RT* can be found in the statements of Goffe in the Putney debates, on this topic (Woodhouse, 135).

47. *See* Ch.4. i and ii, below.

48. Cf. the opening proposition of *General Councils,* 91.

49. See the remarks of Cromwell and Ireton, opposing Army radicals, in the Putney Debates (repr. in Woodhouse); analysis of these is given in Stocker, 'Poet of the Latter Days', Ch.8.i.

50. *PL* I.1; Marvell, *Letters,* 312.

51. On contemporary belief that one could interpret history by means of the scriptures, prayer and a study of the relation between events and biblical prophecies, *see* Lamont, 129f.

52. The Putney Debates thrash out the question: *see* Ch.4.iv, below, and Stocker, 'Poet of the Latter Days', Ch.8.i.

53. J. P. Kenyon discusses Marvell's indigence, in 'Andrew Marvell: His Life and Times', *Andrew Marvell: Essays on the Tercentenary of His Death*, ed. R. L. Brett (Oxford, 1979), 7–8, 27–8.

54. Prynne quoted in Lamont, 181.

55. For the circumstances of publication, *see* Kelliher, 60–1. The most interesting critical discussions of the poem are those of Wallace, who sees it as 'a deliberative oration' (137); and Joseph A. Mazzeo, 'Cromwell as Davidic King', *Reason and the Imaginaton*, ed. Mazzeo (1962), 29–55.

56. Mazzeo considers the passage irrelevant, an attitude which suggests that Marvell did not know what was relevant to his own poem. James F. Carens, 'Andrew Marvell's Cromwell Poems', *BuR* 7 (1957), 41–70, describes this passage as reflecting the views of the Fifth Monarchy Men. Since they are roundly condemned in the poem, this seems illogical. He also states that 'The "latter days" was a slogan of the Fifth Monarchy Men, a Millenerian [sic] sect' (62), an astonishing observation. Wallace, 139, only reluctantly acknowledges the millenarian moment here, and finds the poem 'unique' (eccentric?) in Marvell's works.

57. *See*, for example, Wallace, 109.

58. Richard Sibbes, *Light from Heaven. . .in Four Treatises* (1638), 253.

59. Milton, *Areopagitica*, Bohn edn, II. 92–3. Behind this passage—and Marvell's—is the idea that God Himself is an 'Architect' (e.g. *PL*, VIII. 72).

60. *Areopagitica*, 90.

61. For the importance of II Peter as a chiliast text, *see*, for example, John Evelyn, *The History of Religion: A rational account of the true religion*, 2 vols., ed. R. M. Evanson (1850), I. 162–3. Cf. also the various applications of this text noted in Ch.4 below.

62. *See*, for example, Temple, speaking of Parliament's responsibilities,30.

63. *A Poem Upon the Death of O[liver] C[romwell]*, 142.

64. For the interpretation of *Revelation*'s 'day', *see* Ch.4.i, below.

65. Here, in the *First Anniversary*, Marvell echoes the similarly orthodox utterance of Wilkins in 1649: 'Let no man presume to censure the several vicissitudes and changes of things. . .Remember we are but short-sighted, and cannot discern the various references, and dependancies, amongst the great affairs in the world. . .we do in this world. . .see onely the *dark side* of Providence.' (72).

66. Cf. *Areopagitica*, 90 (cf. n. 60, *supra*).

67. For example, Temple, 50; Putney Debates, Woodhouse, 21, 38–9.

68. Cf. Hutchinson, 6; Temple is basing his sermon on this text.

69. Cf. Temple, 34–5, detailing these powers.

70. *At a Vacation Exercise in the College*, 11. 29–30.

71. These characteristics are recorded in the art depicting the universal Last Things: pertinent examples may be found in the paintings of Hieronymus

Bosch; in C. M. Kaufmann, *An Altar-piece of the Apocalypse* (1968); Heinrich Wöfflin, *The Art of Albrech Dürer*, trans. A. & H. Grieve (1971) and Richard Cavendish, *Visions of Heaven and Hell* (1977). For contemporary literal examples, *see*, for example, Baillie, quoted in Whiting, 234; Bernard Gilpin, 'Antichrists of the Reformation', *In God's Name: Examples of Preaching in England 1534–1662* (1971), ed. J. Chandos, 30, 38; Evelyn; *History of Religion*, I. 161; all which are indebted to I Peter 5:8: 'the devil as a roaring lion walketh about, seeking whom he may devour'. The Beasts and Dragon of the Book of Revelation were portrayed accordingly. Cf. also Milton's *Lycidas*, 128–9, and *PL*, XI. 508 on antichristian clergy. Cf. Spenser's *Shepheardes Calender*, 'May' (37–54) and 'July' (53–6). The notion that false clerics were 'devouring wolves' was indebted to Matthew 7:15. To Marvell's in *First Anniversary* one can compare a very similar thought in Thomas Adams, *The Black Devill. . .The Wolfe worrying the Lambes and The Spirituall Navigator Bound for the Holy Land* (1615), *Spiritual Navigator*, 15: where the 'Sea of Rome' (antichristianism) is said to 'deuoure' souls, like 'the World, [which] as the Sea, is a swallowing Gulfe'. Cf. *First Anniversary* II. 71–2, quoted below.
72. Marvell's attitude to 'presumption'—in particular, that presumption and pride were bases of antichristian error— is fully treated in Stocker, 'Poet of the Latter Days', Appendix I. *See* his *Defence of Howe*, 167–8, and the discussions of *Appleton House* and *Blake*, below.
73. *On Mr Milton's "Paradise Lost"*, II. 31ff.
74. Cf. Chapter 4.iv, below.
75. Cf. Daniel 7:13–14: 'I saw in the night visions. . .one like the Son of Man came with the clouds of heaven'; and Revelation 1:7, 'Behold, he cometh with clouds'.
76. Cf. Milton, *PL*. XIII. 45–6, where Michael prophesies that Christ until the Coming is 'Lost in the Clouds from Heav'n to be revealed/In glory of the Father.' And cf. also Milton's *De Doctrina*, Bohn edn, IV. 485: where he quotes Daniel 7:13–14, and comments that this Kingdom is 'given [Christ]. . .from the time when he came with the clouds of heaven (in which manner his final advent is uniformly described)'. Cf. Joseph Mede, *The Key of the Revelation [Clavis Apocalyptica]* (1643), II. 102; the gloss on Revelations 1:7 in Geneva Bible (1599); the use of the motif in the very title of the sermon to Parliament by Peter Sterry, *The Clouds in Which Christ Comes* (1647). Cf. also the examples cited by Ball, 34–5.
77. *See* Ch.4.i., below, for the doctrine of progressive revelation.
78. *See* II Peter 3:10–12.
79. For Mohammedanism as antichristian, *see* Lamont and Oldfield, 8. For the theology of Fifth Monarchists, *see* Ball, 181ff.; Toon, 66ff; B. S. Capp, *The Fifth Monarchy Men* (1972).
80. Mede, I. 99. Cf. Richard Bernard, *A Key of Knowledge. . .of St. John's mysticall Revelation* (1617), 177, who regards them as Catholic clerical heretics; as does the Geneva Bible (1560) in its gloss on Revelation 9:7ff. Cf. Toon, 58–9. Thus the Locusts were usually regarded as heretics, and in Mede's case as Muslims in particular.
81. For this fear *see* Toon, 82.

82. Wallace, 89, 185–6. Margoliouth considers that Marvell was 'a royalist in the first place', and cites *Lovelace* and *Villiers* on this point (303); he sees Marvell as essentially a constitutional monarchist. Bradbrook and Lloyd-Thomas suggest that he was 'Trimmer' in a sense close to Wallace's constitutionalist/'Loyalist' picture of Marvell (2). For the 'republican' view of Marvell, *see*, for example, Annabel Patterson, *Marvell and The Civic Crown* (Princeton, NJ, 1978). With Christopher Hill I disagree mainly on the degree of Marvell's "radicalism"; *see* his 'Andrew Marvell and the Good Old Cause', *Mainstream*, 12 (1959), 1–27; and 'Milton and Marvell', *Approaches to Marvell*, ed. C. A. Patrides (1978), 1–30. Warren Chernaik, *The Poet's Time: Politics and Religion in the work of Andrew Marvell* (Cambridge, 1983) thinks him a 'libertarian'.

83. Note that 'the Puritans' Royalism before 1641 was Messianic', (Lamont, 94), a pertinent reminder. *See*, for instance, the account of Fairfax's retreat from the regicide given in C. V. Wedgwood, *The Trial of Charles I* (1967): esp. 35–6, 80–83, 101–4, 120–2, 211–13. Fairfax wrote on regicide ('On the Fatal day, Jan:30 1648'): 'Oh lett that Day from time be blotted quitt/And let beliefe of't in next Age be waued. . .' (Bodleian MS. *Fairfax*, 40, 600).

84. *Villiers*, 13–16.

85. *Ibid.*, 14.

86. *See*, for example, *An Honest Discourse Between Three Neighbours* (1655), 4–5, 15 and esp. 13. (This tract is discussed in Ch.3, below); *see also* Christopher Hill, *God's Englishman: Oliver Cromwell and the English Revolution* (Harmondsworth, 1972), 171.

87. *Ibid.*, 171–3.

88. Wallace thinks that the *First Anniversary* is 'an argument that Cromwell should accept the. . .crown' (108; 111–2). However, Kelliher would argue that here the poet 'stops short of kingship. . .if only for the time being' (61), in accordance with his 'republican' approach to Marvell.

89. *See* his letter to George Downing, 11 Feb. 1658, *Letters*, 307–8.

90. Marvell's "middle way" in politics and religion, as well as his expressed views, seem to me to indicate that he was an Independent: most of all in his proponence of (Protestant) religious toleration; his probable espousal of a loosely organized state Church, while opposing episcopacy; and his constitutional monarchism. His friend John Owen was an Independent (he is defended in *RT*). (For the friendship, *see* Bradbrook and Lloyd-Thomas, 15, 91, 95, 118.) For Owen's influence in religion, *see* Toon, 37. The close relationship between Owen and Cromwell is discussed in Hill, *Antichrist*, 105, and *God's Englishman*, 175, 189. Howard Schulz, 'Christ and Antichrist in *Paradise Regained*', *PMLA* LXVII (1952), 790–808, suggests that Milton was an Independent (795).

91. A detailed account of these views is given in Stocker, 'Poet of the Latter Days', Ch.4.

92. Clark, 81, 3.

93. For Marvell's involvement, *see* K. H. D. Haley, *William of Orange and the English Opposition* (Oxford, 1953), Ch.4: 'The Fifth Column', esp.57–9. For the informer's report of 1671, *see* Kelliher, 103. An account

of Buckingham's acquaintance with Marvell is given in Kelliher, 90–91; cf. Burdon, 17–18 who suggests that it may have begun as early as 1646.
94. Haley, 59, 58.
95. Dean Morgan Schmitter, 'The Occasion for Marvell's "Growth of Popery"', *JHI* XXI (1960), 568–70.
96. *Ibid.*, 569. The veiled reference is in *GP*, 374.
97. Clark, 88.
98. His personal Dutch contacts are described by Bradbrook and Lloyd-Thomas, 115; Hunt, Ch.4, treats Marvell's acquaintance with Holland.
99. *See* his letter to the Hull Corporation, no. 36 (37–8); and to Trinity House, nos. 5–6. Cf. also Bradbrook and Lloyd-Thomas, 5–6.
100. Kelliher, 120.
101. Haley, 65ff: I conclude that Blood's agency was *fully* 'double' because that sorts with his career and Marvell's admiration.
102. Clark, 90.

2: A Revelation for the Poet

1. For examples of the interpretation of features of Revelation in Spenser, *see*, for example, Waters-Bennett, *Evolution of the Faerie Queene*, esp. Ch.9; John E. Hankins, 'Spenser and the Revelation of St. John', *PMLA* LX (1945), 364–81; Stocker, 'Poet of the Latter Days', Ch.5.ii; articles by Joseph Wittreich on 'Apocalypse' and by Margarita Stocker on 'Eschatology' in the *Spenser Encyclopaedia* (forthcoming: Cleveland, 1986). On Milton's millenarianism, etc., *see* Schulz; Michael Fixler, *Milton and the Kingdoms of God* (1964); Joseph A. Wittreich, *Visionary Poetics: Milton's Tradition and His Legacy* (San Marino, Calif., 1979); Austin Dobbins, *Milton and the Book of Revelation* (Alabama, 1975).
2. For instance, Raymond A. Anselment, '"Betwixt Jest and Earnest": Ironic Reversal in Andrew Marvell's "The Rehearsal Transpos'd"', *MLR* 66 (1971), 282–93, finds him 'demanding' (293); cf. Bruce King, 'In Search of Andrew Marvell', *REL* 8 (1967), 31–41, 32; Joseph Summers (ed.), *Selected Poems of Marvell*, The Laurel Poetry Series (New York, 1961), 7. Anselment finds that Marvell rarely provides 'any resolution of issues' in the poetry (293); cf. Balachandra Rajan, 'Inconclusiveness', *Approaches*, ed. Patrides, 155–73.
3. *See*, for example, Smith, 'Andrew Marvell', *English Poetry*, ed. Dyson, 96–110, 97; E. S. Donno (ed.), *Andrew Marvell: The Critical Heritage* (1978), 5.
4. A lengthy example of such a response is a poem, written probably by a Yorkshire connection of Marvell's, which has been printed by L. A. Davies, 'An Unpublished Poem About Andrew Marvell', *YES* 1 (1971), 100–1; he dates the poem between 1689–97. Lines 7–10 esp. imply Marvell's "prophetic" role, I think. Anthony à Wood notes that the *Poems* 'were then taken into the hands of many persons of his persuasion ['fanaticks'], and by them cried up as excellent' (*Athenae Oxonienses* (1691–2)), repr. in Donno, *Critical Heritage*, 102. Cf. also John Ayloffe's poem, *Marvell's Ghost* (c. 1678), which makes Marvell a prophet of doom.

The poem is part of a tradition in which Raleigh especially (because of his *History of the World*) returns to warn England of error: cf. *Britannia and Ralegh*, which is printed in Margoliouth (*see* Ch.5 below).

5. *See*, for example, Sibbes, *Bride*, sig. A5, 34; Hill, *Antichrist*, 103–4.

6. Shaw, 4–5; Cf. Ch.4.iv., below.

7. Hill, *God's Englishman*, 219. Cf. Hill, *Antichrist*, 127; Walzer, 290.

8. Cf. Ch.2, 2, *supra*.

9. Aubrey, II. 54.

10. This was a frequent practice, and—as we saw—Marvell had his secrets.

11. Aubrey, II. 53; cf. Anthony à Wood's similar observation, quoted in Donno, *Critical Heritage*, 54.

12. *See* Ch.2, 2, *supra*.

13. This probability is enhanced by the discovery of a different "version" of *To His Coy Mistress* in Haward's manuscript collection. For this version, *see* Kelliher, 53.

14. For other speculations upon the effect of the Civil War on his poetry, *see* Christopher Ricks, '"Its own resemblance"', *Approaches to Marvell*, 108–35; Patrick Cruttwell, *The Shakespearean Moment: and its place in the Poetry of the Seventeenth Century* (New York, 1960), Ch.7.

15. Abraham Cowley, *The Civil War*, ed. Allan Pritchard (Toronto, 1978), ll.143–3.

16. In this line I follow an emendation suggested by R. G. Howarth, 'Marvell: An Emendation', *N&Q*, Aug. 1953, 330.

17. Sibbes, *Light from Heaven*, 255.

18. Thomas Browne, *Religio Medici, Selected Writings*, ed. Geoffrey Keynes (1970), II. 7.

19. For such traditions, *see* Michael West, 'The Internal Dialogue of Shakespeare's Sonnet 146', *SQ* 25. 1 (Winter, 1974), 109–23.

20. Cf. Ch.3 below.

21. Marvell is probably conflating two traditional images here: the Renaissance metaphor of the Army as a 'Body' (discussed by Thomas P. Roche, with reference to Tasso, in *Literary Uses of Typology: from the Late Middle Ages to the Present*, ed. Earl Miner (Guildford, 1977), 57); and the metaphor for the church in I Corinthians 12:12–27: 'For as the body is one, and hath many members. . .so also is Christ. . .there should be no schism in the body. . .[if] one member suffer, all the members suffer with it'. To Marvell's metaphor of 'Architects' who square and hew' one may compare Milton's metaphor for sectarian differences (quoted, *supra*): 'some squaring the marble, others hewing the cedars' while they are 'building' the Church. To Marvell's statement about 'squaring' governments with religion, cf. Joshua Sprigge's similar contention in 1647, in Woodhouse, 134–5.

22. Cf. esp. Ch.2.ii, below.

23. Browne, *Religio*, I. 34.

24. *Ibid.*, I. 46.

25. St Augustine, *The City of God*, ed. and tr. D. Knowles and H. Bettenson (Harmondsworth, 1972), XI. 18. 449.

26. T. S. Eliot, 'Andrew Marvell', *Selected Essays* (1951), 68. Donno, *Critical Heritage*, 16–18, shows that this 'alliance' had already been noted

by Eliot's predecessors.

27. E.g. Kitty [Scoular] Datta, 'Marvell's Prose and Poetry: More Notes', *MP* 63 (1965–6), 319–21, 319.

28. Bishop Burnet, quoted in Kelliher, 107.

29. V. A. Kolve, *The Play Called Corpus Christi* (1966), 129–30, 139.

30. *Selected Essays*, 45; cf. 421.

31. See Grosart, III. 367–8. Cf. *RT*, 231.

32. *Selected Essays*, 45.

33. The phrase is from Edgar Wind, *Pagan Mysteries in the Renaissance*, rev. edn. (1968), 200; for *serio ludere*, see 200–36. As for the critics: in a glancing reference, Warren L. Chernaik suggests that there is a 'Christian wit' in Marvell ('Marvell's Satires: The Artist as Puritan', *Tercentenary Essays*, ed. Friedenreich, 268–96, but considers that this is his oddity; Leo Spitzer, 'Marvell's *Nymph Complaining*. . .Sources versus Meaning', *MLQ* 19 (1958), 231–43, suggests a relationship between 'comic spirit' in hagiography and metaphysical wit, but sees this as secularized.

34. Lamont and Oldfield, xiv.

35. Quoted in Pierre Legouis, *Andrew Marvell: Poet, Puritan, Patriot* (Oxford, 1968), 2.

36. Bradbrook and Lloyd-Thomas, 18, 21.

37. 'Unpublished Poem', printed by L. A. Davies (*op. cit.*), l.6.

38. *Mr Smirke*, 84–5; cf. *Last Instructions to a Painter*, 762. Cf. Lucy Hutchinson, who comments on the history of reformation in England that 'God in comparison with other countries hath made this as a paradise', so, to complete the parallel, the serpent hath in all times been busy to seduce' (5).

39. The most prominent amongst them being D. C. Allen, *Image and Meaning: Metaphoric Traditions in Renaissance Poetry* (Baltimore, 1960), 115–53, who also discusses Roman 'garden' poetry in relation to this poem; and cf. Maren-Sophie Røstvig, '"Upon Appleton House" and the Universal History of Man', *ES* 42 (1961), 337–51, who accepts Allen's point but herself expounds a typological and hermetic reading of the poem which is often somewhat strained, and gives no sense of a coherent aim in the poem. Cf. also her '"In ordine di ruota": Circular Structure in. . ."Upon Appleton House"' *Tercentenary Essays*, ed. Friedenreich. Another typological reading is provided by Charles Molesworth in 'Marvell's "Upon Appleton House": The Poet as Historian, Philosopher and Priest', *SEL* 13 (1973), 149–62, who claims that 'the *persona* [of Marvell in the poem] dramatises all the virtues of Appleton House and its owner'. Kitty Scoular explicates the 'emblems' of nature in the poem in *Natural Magic: Studies in the Presentation of Nature in English Poetry from Spenser to Marvell* (Oxford, 1965), 120–90. Berthoff, *Resolved Soul*, 197, briskly rejects "hermetic" readings but also applies a resolutely anti-historical interpretation of the poem as a 'masque of nature'. Too much criticism of this poem is either "hermetic" or "impressionistic" in kind and "typological" readings tend to misapprehend the meaning of such images. Better than most such "typological" readings is that of Barbara Lewalski, 'Typology and Poetry: A Consideration of Herbert, Vaughan and Marvell', *Illustrious Evidence:*

Approaches to English Literature of the Early Seventeenth Century, ed. Earl Miner (London, 1975), 41–69, J. B. Leishman explicates Maria's progress by the "praise of the mistress" in contemporary poetry, in *The Art of Marvell's Poetry* (London, 1966), Ch.5. D. C. Evett discusses the poem as an ideal landscape in '"Paradice's Only Map": The *Topos* of the *Locus Amoenus* and the Structure of Marvell's "Upon Appleton House"', *PMLA* LXXXV (1970), 504–13, making one or two mistakes of mere fact.

40. Few, if any, Marvell scholars would agree with William Empson's insistence that Mary Palmer's claim to have married Marvell was genuine: I heard his assertion—though not his evidence, which is no doubt to appear in some form soon—when he gave the Clark Lectures at Cambridge. For an account of Mary Palmer's case, *see* Bradbrook and Lloyd-Thomas, Appendix A.

41. The idea that in some way (and for whichever purpose) the Red Sea is a type here, is accepted by many commenters on the poem; *see*, for example, Røstvig, '"Upon Appleton House" and the Universal. . .', 339.

42. In this relation it is useful to recall that 'European gardens. . .offered a whole abstract of the world outside', according to Hunt, 91, who notes that this poem evokes the world's whole natural order.

43. Samuel Hartlib, *The Reformed Husband-Man; or a Brief Treatise of the Errors, Defects, and Inconveniences of our English Husbandry. . .* (1651), 5.

44. Most critics are agreed that the Nunnery is not favourably presented, but Douglas Bush took a peculiar course in suggesting that Marvell celebrates the nuns' devoutness, *English Literature in the Earlier Seventeenth Century, 1600–1660* (Oxford, 1945), 160: contrast Evett, 508; Allen, 119; Røstvig, '"Upon Appleton House". . .', 342; Berthoff, 196; Hunt, 97.

45. II Thessolonians 2:9; cf. Marvell on the popish 'Imposture', Ch. 1, above, and the description of this idea in C. H. and K. George, *The Protestant Mind of the English Reformation 1570–1640* (Princeton, 1961), 382.

46. For witches as antichristian, *see* H. R. Trevor-Roper, 'Witches and Witchcraft', *Encounter* (May, 1967), 15.

47. The source of the traditional characterization of Christ as the Bridegroom was Psalm 19:1–5. He "married" His Bride—the Church—only at the Second Coming; *see*, for example, Sibbes, *Bride*, 50–51. The wedding occurs in the marriage 'of the Lamb', Revelation 19:7.

48. Apparently, Fairfax had observed Williams' fall with some satisfaction (Margoliouth, I. 285).

49. Fairfax's anticatholic attitudes are evinced in Bodleian MS. *Fairfax 40*, a manuscript collection which contains varioius antipapist materials, especially in the latter half of the volume. *See* esp. 602–10, and e.g. 604ff.,a translation of "A Carracter of the Romish Church by Francisco Petrarca—Laura. Can: 106", which describes the Roman Church as 'a shameles strumpet' (606). (This is taken to be an autograph collection; *see* Leishman, 252n.) Eschatological rhetoric was familiar to Fairfax, who had spent the Civil War years not only himself engaged in the 'Holy War' but also

subjected (especially by Army representatives and by Cromwell) to the various degrees of chiliastic oratory employed at this time. He would readily have understood the drift of Marvell's poem.

50. The *type* is taken as the meaning of this stanza by Røstvig, '"Upon Appleton House" and the Universal. . .', 340. For the typological terms used here, *see* Joseph A. Galdon, *Typology and Seventeenth-Century Literature* (The Hague, 1975), 30–1: 'the type signifies the anti-type, and the anti-type fulfils the type'. Adams, *Spirituall Navigator*, 9, says that in crossing the *'redde sea. . .*the old *Israelites* [are types] of the new and true Israelites'.

51. For the Red Sea as traditionally a figure of baptism, *see* Galdon, 21–2; Thomas Browne, *Pseudodoxia*, II. vi. ix. 178. Arnold Whittick, *Symbols: Signs and their meaning and Uses in design*, 2nd edn (1971), 348, notes that it is a prophetic symbol both of baptism and of entry to the promised land.

52. Jeremy Taylor, *The Golden Grove: Selected Passages from the Sermons and Writings*, ed. L. Pearsall Smith (Oxford, 1930), 278. Marvell was familiar with Taylor's works; he cites the latter as a worthy authority in *Smirke*, 85.

53. *See*, for example, Browne, *Pseudodoxia*, II. v. iii. 7–8; the Geneva Bible's gloss on this passage of Revelation (1560): 'The elect for a certaine space. . .are in troubles: for the greshoppers [namely locusts] endure but from April to September, which is fiue moneths'. Note that harvest-time (the season appropriate to this section of the poem) falls within the period stipulated here. For the identification of Locusts and grasshoppers, cf. also the *OED*.

54. In the verses quoted, Marvell is referring to two distinct types of scene-change used by Inigo Jones. Hunt discusses the relationship between masques and gardens, 104–6.

55. For the importance of Beard's book, *see* Lamont, 122–3. Cromwell admired it: Maurice Ashley, *The Greatness of Oliver Cromwell* (1958), 43. Thomas Browne uses the image more than once: for example, 'this latter scene of time' (*Hydriotaphia, Selected Writings*, V. 150). Marvell also uses the image in *GP*, 412. Cf. Jan van der Noodt, *Theatre for Worldlings* (1569): Spenser's epigrams and Sonnets from which are repr. in *Poetical Works of Edmund Spenser*, 3 vols., ed. E. de Selincourt (Oxford, 1910), 1, Appendix, 484–504.

56. Browne, *Religio*, I. 47; and cf. C. A. Patrides, *The Grand Design of God* (London, 1972), 83.

57. Similarly, Marvell describes a later attempt 'to have raised a Civil War' as aiming to make of England a *'rase champagne* of religion, government, and propriety' (*GP*, 304). Fairfax himself had been involved in the Grandees' negotiations with the Leveller leader, John Lilburne, and with the gradual suppression of his party in 1649; the Army was, of course, a reservoir of Leveller support at that time.

58. The Digger movement's aspirations are best represented by the works of Gerrard Winstanley, especially his 'manifesto', *The Law of Freedom* (1652): repro. in Winstanley, *The Law of Freedom and other Writings*, ed. Christopher Hill (Harmondsworth, 1973). Winstanley did not flinch from

warning both Fairfax and Cromwell that they had no right to appropriate
the powers wrested from the king, and that they must attend to the wishes
of the 'people'; for an example, see *Selections from the Works of Gerrard
Winstanley*, ed. L. Hamilton (1944), 275–7.

59. On the literal level, Marvell is recalling the picture of the creation of the
animals in Davenant's Temple of Praise (Scoular, 188). Cf. *Gondibert* II.
vi; cf. *RT*, 47.

60. In this relation I would re-evaluate the attention paid to optical
perspectives (e.g. in LXIII) by Frederick H. Roth, Jr, 'Marvell's "Upon
Appleton House": A Study in Perspective', *TSLL* XIV. 2 (1972), 269–81,
amongst others; such studies miss the point by elevating (precisely) an
effect to an argument. In fact, the fundamental function of such effects is to
enact the micro/macrocosmic relationships in the poem, and to make us
aware of the larger contexts or 'perspectives' implied by the poem. This
function is most readily related to the imagery of masques, which
themselves often involve changes of scenery or 'perspective' (in both
physical and thematic senses); and in this fashion such effects contribute to
the scale and the 'history' of the poem.

61. Jeremy Taylor, 280–1.

62. Adams, *Spiritual Navigator*, 47.

63. This image is usually read by critics as referring in some way to the first
Flood (Evett, 510; Lewalksi, 66; Allen, 132). As in the case of the Red Sea
motif, critics fail to recognise that these images have a peculiar contemporary relevance (like the rest of the poem) which is based upon the *anti*-types
that distinguish the Last Days.

64. The relationship between the Denton estate and the regular floodings at
Nunappleton is revealed by a sequence of letters in the *TLS*: R. Wilson,
'Marvell's Denton' (26 Nov. 1971, 1481), John Newman, 'Marvell's
Appleton House' (28 Jan. 1972, 99), A. A. Tait, 'Marvell's Appleton
House' (11 Feb. 1972, 157), James Turner, 'Marvell' (31 Mar. 1972, 367).
See also Hunt's description of the Nunappleton estates and their
topography, 83–5.

65. Hebrews 10:37, 'For yet a little while, and he that shall come will
come, and will not tarry'; cf. Revelation 22:20 'He [Christ] who
testifieth these things saith, Surely, I come quickly. Amen. Even so, come,
Lord Jesus'.

66. For the contemporary re-echoing of Revelation 22:20, *see* Toon, 113.

67. *See*, for example, Jeremy Taylor, 278, who refers to 'the first day of
Judgement. . .that (I mean) of the universall deluge of waters upon the old
World'.

68. *See* Lewalski, 53, who explicates Noah's Ark and the Ark of the
Covenant in Herbert's *The Church Militant* as types of that Church. The
typology of the Ark could also refer to the individual Christian; *see*
Galdon, 134–5. Marvell himself uses the image of the Ark of the Church in
The Character of Holland, 67–8.

69. Scoular, 143n., notes that '"Propheticke trees" were not uncommon in
contemporary poems'. For yet another view of the 'mosaic' pun *see* Allen,
146 and Røstvic, 347, who both see here a reference to the burning bush.

70. The "Book of Fate" was a traditional image; cf. Shakespeare, 2 *Henry IV*, III. i. 45–6: 'O God, that one might read the book of fate,/And see the revolutions of the times'.

71. Wilkins, 63. Cf. Toon, 52, and cf. Marvell's statement of a belief in the "natural signs" of providence in *General Councils*, 148. The Scriptures were believed to explicate such natural 'signs': *see*, for example, Thomas Burnet, *The Sacred Theory of the Earth*, ed. Basil Willey (1965), III. 240. Hence Marvell's is a specialized use of the idea that nature is God's 'Book' (as in, e.g., Browne, *Religio*, I. 16).

72. Jeremy Taylor, 280.

73. This was the '*mare vitreum*'. *See*: Browne, *Religio*, I. 50; Burnet, *Sacred Theory*, III. 239; Adams, *Spiritual Navigator*, 38. The reference to Revelation is 4:6, 'Before the throne there was a sea of glass like unto crystal'.

74. The appellation , 'Paradice's only Map' is applied initially to the estate itself, but as the estate reflects Maria's nature (11. 750–2), it describes her too by implication.

75. Cf. the second stanza of the poem: 'The low-roof'd Tortoises do dwell/In cases fit. . .Their bodies measure out their place'. In this fashion the last stanza recalls the beginning of the poem.

76. Critical comment on the last stanza (of which T. S. Eliot disapproved) tends to be impressionistic or evasive: for some examples of the kind, *see* Evett, 512; Allen, 153; Roth, 280; Berthoff, 193. Leishman, 221–2, and Bradbrook and Lloyd-Thomas, 33n., think that Marvell's notion of 'Shoes-Canoos' may have been suggested by a Cleveland poem.

77. *See* Hill, *World Turned Upside Down*, 19; Toon, 67.

78. Toon, *ibid*.

79. Acts 17:5–6.

80. Hill, *World*, 19.

81. George Gillespie, 'A Sermon Preached before the House of Commons', 27 March 1644, quoted in Hill, *Antichrist*, 86.

82. *The Character of Holland*, 58; cf. William Symonds, *Virginia* (1609) A2ᵛ: Christianity has caused 'the surprising and conquering of great Nations, by *Fisher-men*'.

83. *Historical Essay on General Counsils*, 92; cf. too *ibid.*, 142, where he reminds his readers that 'humility' is 'the lowliest but the highest of all Christian qualifications'. A similar thought is expressed by Stephen Marshall in a sermon to the House of Commons, *The Song of Moses. . .and the Song of the Lambe* (1643), 15: 'Who were they but the *poorer*, and *meaner sort* of people, that at the first joyned with the Ministers, to raise the building of Reformation: few, of the *Princes*, & *Nobles*, putting their necks to the work of the Lord;. . .the *greatest things* have been done by them, from whom *least* could be expected'. Marshall is expressing the contemporary moral for those parliamentarians engaged in the effort for reformation. Beard, 6–7, sees the "high and mighty" of the world as those who are most culpable in their actions, and who therefore stand in most need of his lesson in God's 'judgements'. Isaiah 2:12–17 informed the proud that the Last Day involved their destruction in particular. All these

instances manifest the tendency of chiliasm towards radicalism in this period.

84. The passage appears in *Smirke*, 22: answering Turner's accusation that Croft is 'turning all upside down', Marvell comments; 'wherein does he "turn all upside down"? This hath been a common topick of ecclesiastical accusation. Our saviour was accused [thus]. . .And Saint Paul. . .was made odious upon the same crimination. . .Acts xvii. 5, 6. For, "certain lewd fellows, of the baser sort, set all the city in an uproar, crying, those that have turned the world upside down are come hither also"'.

85. For example, Roth, 277; Allen, 146–7; Lewalski, 65.

86. Wilkins, 34: 'the hearts and affections of men do follow the guidance of his decrees; men may do after their own counsels and inclinations, but they are still suitable to his Providence'; thus they 'still accomplish his counsell in prosecuting their own designes' (56). Cf. Browne, *Religio*, I. 43: 'all the creatures of God in a secret and disputed way doe execute his will'.

87. For example, for Bush, 160, the poem is 'relatively formal and uneven and overlong'; Legouis finds it 'composite rather than composed', a 'long, too long, poem', *Andrew Marvell*, 63, 82); Bradbrook and Lloyd-Thomas find it 'uneven, muddled' (38); Robin Grove, 'Marvell', *Melbourne Critical Review* 6 (1963), is even more damning. It is worth noting that even those critics who do admire the poem rarely succeed in portraying it as coherent, or in suggesting a major thematic objective within it.

88. *See* n.39, *supra*, for Allen and Leishman; Summers provided an account of the poem in the Introduction to *Selected Poems*, in which he emphasized the ideas of action versus the retired life in the poem, and its "perspectives"; the essay to which I refer here is Joseph Summers, 'Some Apocalyptic Strains in Marvell's Poetry', *Tercentenary Essays*, ed. Friedenreich. Leishman had already noted that Maria's 'vitrifying' activity referred to the vitrefaction of the world at its End, although this point is isolated in his general account.

89. For accounts of the genre of the country-house poem in this period, *see* G. R. Hibbard, 'The Country-House Poem of the Seventeenth Century', *JWCI* XIX (1956), 159–74; and Charles Molesworth, 'Property and Virtue: The Genre of the Country-House Poem in the Seventeenth Century', *Genre* I (1968), 141–57. Leishman, 253ff., discusses this poem as 'formally related' to the genre.

3: The Revelation in Action

1. *See*, for instance, Margoliouth, I. 295; Brooks and Bush, repro. in Michael Wilding (ed.) *Marvell: Modern Judgements* (1969); Bradbrook and Lloyd-Thomas, 72–6; L. W. Hyman, 'Politics and Poetry in Andrew Marvell', *PMLA* LXXIII (1958), 475–9; J. A. Mazzeo, 'Cromwell as Machiavellian Prince in Marvell's *An Horatian Ode*', *JHI* 20, I (1960), 1–17.

2. *City of God*, XI. 32. 465.

3. Cf. Wilkins' injunctions, 72, 83; that this attitude is especially necessary at a time of civil war, 69–71. Cf. also Matthew Newcomen, *A Sermon of the Right Use of Disasters* (1644), which has a similar moral.

4. Cf. Wilkins, 72.

5. Although *May* was written in 1650, it may have undergone a slight topical adaptation in 1661, when May's body was transferred from Westminster Abbey (*see* Margoliouth, I. 303; cf. Summers, *Selected Poems*, 150n.); the lines involved (89–90) have no bearing on my discussion, however, as they consist merely of a joke on the removal. As Kelliher notes, 63, Marvell had a habit of continuously revising some of his poems. This poem, which is no more vulnerable to attacks upon its authenticity than the *Ode*, has recently suffered from critical attempts to exclude it from the canon. George de F. Lord, editor of *Andrew Marvell: Complete Poetry* (New York, 1968) was the first to attack its genuineness. For a survey of Lord's policy and decisions on authenticity, *see* Michael Wilding's review in *MLR* 66 (1971), 664–5. Both Smith ('Andrew Marvell', 96) and Legouis (Margoliouth, I. 304) have recognized that such attacks on the poem's authenticity seem to be motivated by the fact that (for critics taking a 'republican' line on Marvell) it is an 'invonveniently royalist poem' (Smith, 96; Margoliouth, I. 304). For instance, Patterson rejects *May*'s authenticity in the service of her 'republican' thesis (*Marvell and the Civic Crown*, 119n.). It does not seem to have occurred to critics taking this approach that perhaps they should rather question their 'republican' account of Marvell. Those who accept the poem as authentic are, not surprisingly, in the majority (e.g., Margoliouth, I. 303; Donno, *Complete Poems*, prints it as such; Summers, *Selected Poems*, 150n.; Frank Kermode, *Selected Poetry* (1967), xii; Laurence W. Hyman, *Andrew Marvell* (New York, 1964), 75. Legouis (Margoliouth, I. 304) and I agree not only in finding it authentic but also in associating it with the voices of *Fleckno* and *Character of Holland*, both of which are close to it in dates of composition.

6. This belief followed upon the idea that men's own inclinations were utilized by God for His purposes. Thus Marvell noted in *General Councils* that the bishop's contumely was utilized by providence for their own chastisement: cf. *ibid.*, 136, where Marvell notes God's supervision of Julian's persecution as a scourge for the bishops, and the subsequent 'remarkable stroke of God's judgement' suffered by Julian himself. Cf. Beard, 379: 'God busieth sometime the most wicked about his will, and maketh. . .the diuell himselfe serue. . .to bring to passe his fearefull judgements'; and Wilkins, 55–6: many self-interested men 'stil accomplish his counsell in prosecuting their owne designes'.

7. Some critics have considered the use of Roman tropes important to our understanding of the poem: for instance, J. S. Coolidge, 'Marvell and Horace', *MP* 63 (1965), III–20; L. Proudfoot, 'Marvell: Sallust and the Horatian Ode', *N&Q* (29 Sept. 1951), 434; A. J. N. Wilson, 'An Horatian Ode. . .the thread of the poem and its use of classical allusion', *CQ II* (1969), 325–41.

8. The only critic who seems to have discussed the 'Roman colour' in *May* is Hunt, who suggests a view different from mine (131).

9. Cf. Margoliouth's remarks on Marvell's use of Lucan's *Pharsalia* (as he thinks) in the *Ode*: he recognizes that Marvell's dispraise of Lucan here makes any *republican* use of Lucan in the Ode unlikely (Margoliouth, I.

305). R. H. Syfret had suggested parallels between Lucan's poem and the *Ode*, in 'Marvell's "Horatian Ode"', *RES* n.s., XII (1961), 160–72; I do not find such parallels either particularly convincing or structurally significant.

10. Marvell disliked equally Parker's use of Roman analogies (*RT*, 64 *et passim*); like May, Parker used such parallels for a purpose distasteful to Marvell.

11. Dante, *The Divine Comedy*, ed. D. L. Sayers and B. Reynolds, 3 vols. (Harmondsworth, 1973–5): *Inferno* xxxiv. 286–7.

12. Cf., for example, Horace's *Odes* IV. 15, where the poet characterizes himself as a private man extolling a public theme.

13. Kermode suggests that the poem did circulate privately, amongst royalists (*Selected Poetry*, xii).

14. I refer to the poem *Epistle to Augustus*. An article which illuminates the legal situation in Pope's time is C. R. Kropf, 'Libel and Satire in the Eighteenth Century', *Eighteenth-Century Studies*, VIII (1974–5), 153–68.

15. See esp. Jean Seznec, *The Survival of the Pagan Gods* (New York, 1961), a study of the Christianization of the classical pantheon. *See also* Lawrence A. Sasek, *The Literary Temper of the English Puritans* (New York, 1961), which discusses Puritan use of classical authors and motifs. Cf. other studies of classicism of that kind by Davis P. Harding, *The Club of Hercules: Studies in the Classical Background of "Paradise Lost"* (Urbana, 1962), and his *Milton and the Renaissance Ovid* (Urbana, 1946).

16. Cf. his elegy on *Hastings*, where the Christian heaven is inhabited by 'The gods themselves' (41), amongst them 'Hymeneus' (43).

17. See, Ch.4, below.

18. Cf. Horace's analogous move from private to public themes in *Odes* I. 32. i. A similar exodus from the poetic concerns of the young man is described in Spenser's *FQ Proem* (i), where the poet abandons pastoral for public themes: 'Lo, I the man, whose Muse whilome did maske,/As time her taught, in lowly Shepheards weeds,/Am now enforct a far unfitter taske. . .'.

19. Margoliouth reads this to mean that 'To shut in and cramp a man of high courage is worse (less tolerable for him) than to oppose him' (I.298). This seems to ignore the fact that no one 'incloses' Cromwell: they 'inclose' '*with*' him, which is rather different, since it carries the notion of engagement.

20. *See* Chandos, plates (not numbered) between 128 and 129.

21. *See*, for example, Godfrey Davies, 127.

22. Cf. A. J. N. Wilson, 331.

23. W. R. Orwen, 'Marvell's bergamot', *N&Q* (Aug. 1955), 340–1.

24. One example of the use of this libel against Cromwell is a passage in the spurious 'Sermon of Cromwell' repro. in Chandos, 464: 'it was I that juggled the late King into the Isle of Wight'. Milton denies the accusation in *Second Defence*, Bohn edn, I. 283–4.

25. The italics are present in all the reliable editions of the poem—*see* Margoliouth's, for example—but are not *necessarily* Marvell's.

26. Cf. the similar construction in *First Anniversary*, 106: there the 'nor yet angry Son' will eventually *become* 'angry'.

27. The administration was conducted by the Council of State (namely, the Grandees), which was chosen annually. For the tendentious relationship between Cromwell (and the Army) and Parliament, *see* Godfrey Davies, 146–9; and Richard Overton's diatribe against the new dictatorship (1649), in Shaw, 120.

28. For these niceties of the Roman 'principate', *see* Jane F. Gardner, *Leadership and the Cult of the Personality* (1974), Introduction, and Chs. 8–11.

29. At his home in Velitrae.

30. In line 101 of the *Ode.*

31. Milton, *First Defence*, Bohn edn, I. 129–30.

32. According to Puritan thought, God executed strokes of judgment upon a nation by any of several means: 'he used the whip of a conquering nation. . .or he stirred up ambitious men to wage civil war'; and this was the reasoning which was applied to the Civil War in England (Walzer, 178–9). Cf. Marshall, *Reformation*, who tells the Commons that 'Gods wrath is kindled' against England, and that Marshall will enlighten them as to 'what kinde of flame it is'; 'a devouring fire' and a 'flame' of wrath (10, 9–12). Marvell's images of 'flame' and fire are of the same ilk.

33. Cf. Marvell's *Death of O.C.*, 265–6: 'When angry Jove darts lightning through the aire,/At mortalls sins.' Cf. also Spenser, *FQ* I. viii. 9; Milton, *PL* II. 173f.; VI. 491; Virgil, *Georgics* I. 328f.; Horace, *Odes* III. 4; I. 2; I. 3.

34. Suetonius, *Divus Augustus*, 94. 6 (Loeb edn, 1913).

35. He quotes Suetonius' life of Augustus in *RT*, 308–9.

36. *Ibid.*, 94. 2. Cf. Horace, *Odes* II. 5; Virgil, *Georgics* IV. 560f.; Ovid, *Metamorphoses*, 758–60.

37. Suetonius, 91. 2.

38. Cf., for example, John Napier, *Napier's Narration* (1641), Sig. C3; Hill, *Antichrist*, 145.

39. Marshall, *Reformation*, 52.

40. Revelation 16; Matthew Henry, *Commentary: Acts to Revelation*, ed. David Winter (1975), 532.

41. Marshall, *Reformation*, 44. The seven vials of Revelation were understood as tribulations which would damage the power of Antichrist (e.g. *ibid.*, 44–5); cf. Goodwin, *Brief History*, 209; Tuveson, 27. Marshall, 44, avers that 'all Protestant writers do agree' on this point. Ball, 100–1. Cf. also II Esdras 15:5–42; Marshall, *Reformation*, 13.

42. The 'course of empires on earth was always subordinated to the ultimate conquest of all by [Christ's] kingdom' (Ball, 129; cf. Daniel 2:21). Thus it was observed during the Army's Putney Debates of 1647 that 'Jesus Christ his work in the last days is to destroy [Antichrist]. . .there must be great alterations of states' (Goffe: repro. in Woodhouse, 40). Here Cromwell effects such a political 'alteration'. Remarks like Goffe's were used to justify the revision of the English state. Similarly, later the Fifth Monarchists justified their own revolutionary aims by the text, Jeremiah 51:20, 'Thou art my. . .weapons. . .for with thee will I. . .destroy kingdoms'. (*See* Toon, 68.).

43. *RT*, 135.
44. Cf. Thomas Fairfax, Bodleian MS. *Fairfax* 40, 582: 'As Natur's rule by prouidence deuine/Soe Fortune, too, in an obstrucer line'.
45. These lines were misread as bespeaking a *political* acquiescence by Laurence Lerner, 'Andrew Marvell: An Horatian Ode. . .', *Interpretations*, ed. John Wain (1955), 68; cf. Wallace, 80. Legouis rightly disagrees with both of them, Margoliouth, 1. 300; although for a reason different from mine.
46. Cf. Fairfax's poem on Charles' execution, 'On the Fatal Day' (Bodleian MS. *Fairfax* 40, 600): 'But if the Power deuine permited this/His Will's the Law and ours must acquiesse'.
47. E. E. Duncan-Jones has rightly emphasized that there is no derogation here (Margoliouth, I. 299).
48. For a succinct statement of this doctrine as Charles liked to hear it, *see* Roger Manwaring's 'Sermon before the King' (1627), repro. in Chandos, 313.
49. *See*, for instance, Godfrey Davies, 157–8; Hill, *God's Englishman*, 225; Milton, *Works*, ed. Bush, 188. The texts upon which justification for the regicide was largely based were Psalms 144:10; 149:6–9.
50. *See* Christopher Hibbert, *Charles I* (1968), 277.
51. *See* the detailed discussion of this belief in Ch.4 below.
52. Thomas Brightman, *A Revelation of the Revelation* (1615), in Lamont, 50. Cf. Goodwin, *Brief History*, 209, who states that the seven vials constitute 'the last act of this long *tragi-comedy*' of eschatology. Contemporary writers often described the Civil War in particular as a 'tragedy' (see Cruttwell, 123). Characterizations of the Latter Day tragedy were part of the eschatological metaphor of 'theatre'.
53. Marvell uses the 'tragic' aspect of the metaphor again in *GP*, 412, where he notes that the popish conspiracy prospers: 'It has now come to the fourth Act, and the next scene that opens may be Rome or Paris, yet men sit by, like idle spectators, and still give money towards their own tragedy'.
54. Cf. Ch.4. ii., below.
55. Varro, *De Lingua Latina*, V. 41; Pliny, *Natural History*, 28. 15; Plutarch, *Camillus*, 31. 4.
56. Wallace had suggested that the 'Architects' were the regicides themselves; Claude J. Summers pointed out the fallacy in his interpretation and suggested the 'Architects' to be the parliamentarians who disapproved of the regicide: 'The frightened Architects of Marvell's "Horatian Ode"', *Seventeenth-Century News*, 28 (1970), 4.
57. I am referring, of course, to the native Irish (as is Marvell). The quotation is from Edmund Calamy (1641), in Hill, *Antichrist*, 78. Cf. Clifton, 'Fear of Popery', 144, 158–60; Russell, 13; Jeremy Taylor, 'A Disuasive from Popery' (1664), Preface, *The Golden Grove*, 35–8; Temple, 44–5.
58. *See* Godfrey Davies, 135. Cf. G. E. Aylmer (ed.), *The Interregnum: The Quest for Settlement 1646–1660* (1974), 114; John Goodwin, *Anti-Cavalierisme: Or, Truth Pleading As well the Necessity, as the*

Lawfulness of this present War [against those]. . .who are now hammering England, to make an Ireland Of It (1642); cf. Temple, 44–5, and Marshall, *Reformation*, 47, who both urge that Parliament should succour the fellow-saints persecuted in Ireland by the 'Papists.'

59. Clifton, 'Fear of Popeye', 150, notes that the Irish rebellion was believed by Englishmen to be a product of 'deep popish conspiracy'.

60. Godfrey Davies, 108, 112, 162–3, 116–7. Temple, 25–6, and Marshall, *Reformation*, 47, both express the contemporary hysteria about the 'massacre'. Cf. Marvell, *GP*, 259.

61. Both Temple (29) and Marshall (*Reformation*, 47) urged Parliament to rescue their fellow-saints in Ireland, and thus to reclaim a part of Britain herself from Antichrist.

62. *See*, for instance, Sir Thomas Elyot, *The Book Named The Governor* (1531), ed. S. E. Lehmberg (1962), 82; 'Caesar. . .is a noble example of industry, for in his incomparable wars and business incredible. . .*he did not only excogitate* most excellent policies and devices to vanquish or subdue his enemies, *but also prosecuted* them with such celerity and effect'.

63. *See*, for example, Sallust, *Bellum Catilinae*, Loeb edn (1931), VIII. 5: 'prudentissumus quisque maxume negotiosus erat; ingenium nemo sine corpore exercebat'.

64. Cf, for example, Milton, *PL*, XII. 581–2, where Adam is admonished that he should 'add/*Deeds* to thy *knowledge* answerable'. *See* Lamont, 94, 117.

65. Legouis rightly notes that Marvell was 'consistently hostile to the native Irish all through his political career' (Margoliouth, I. 301). But Mazzeo accepts this section at its face value; Toliver, 190, thinks that 'The reaction to the Irish campaign. . .is. . .purely eulogistic'; Carens, 50, finds that 'the Irish tribute is, at the least, an imperfection in the poem'; Hyman, 'Politics', 476, says that 'The passage on Ireland is, of course,. . .grossly partisan'.

66. A. J. N. Wilson, 335.

67. *See*, for example, Napier, Sig. C3. Cf. also Ch.5 below.

68. Cf. Herbert's poem, *Providence*, where he cites as an example of God's providential care 'A servile hawk', 'tall without height' (103–4).

69. Horace, *Odes* IV. 4. i.

70. Seznec, 263. Wind, 96, describes the eagle's association with *Jupiter Tonans* in particular.

71. Horace, *Odes* I. 37. v.

72. For the European struggle, *see* Hill, *Antichrist*, 105; Lamont, 144–5.

73. Cf. Marvell's use of the 'horns' of the Beast in *First Anniversary*. Revelation 17:12, 'the ten horns which thou sawest are ten kings'; cf. Revelation 17:13–15. According to Mede, the ten-horned beast represented the secular power of the Pope, while the two-horned beast of Revelation represented his religious power (Toon, 59). Cf. Goodwin, *Brief History*, 213; 'The Declaration of the Army in Scotland' (1 Aug. 1650), repro. in Woodhouse, 474–8, 477.

74. Cf. Temple's assertion that 'where we see the false Religion hath received some blowes, we may assure our selves, a further ruine will

certainely follow', because Revelation says so (46–7).
75. See *OED*, A. I, A. I. 6, B. 2.
76. For the full implications of this comparison, *see* Ch.4 below.
77. Virgil, *Aeneid* VI. 789–806.
78. *See* Godfrey Davies, 166.
79. 'On the New Forcers of Conscience Under the Long Parliament' (c. 1646), 20. Milton expressed the same antipathy to Presbyterian intolerance as to prelatical impositions (cf. *Areopagitica*), for reasons similar to Marvell's impatience of intolerance; and the English Presbyterians were at this time doing their best to replace the established episcopal church with their own (to Milton and other liberal Puritans) equally repressive establishment. There was hostility amongst many English Puritans to the imposition of Presbyterianism on the Scottish model, and also to alliance with the Scots (*see* Woodhouse, 15–16).
80. For the religious and political rifts between Independents and Presbyterians, see *ibid.*, 16–17; Lamont, Chs. 4–5. Cromwell (an Independent) and the Army (largely anti-Presbyterian) had been engaged for some time in a power-struggle with the political arm of Presbyterianism that existed within Parliament.
81. Marvell expresses his distaste for the Presbytery' in *Lovelace* (24). It follows from his other views, and is part of the common ground between himself and Milton.
82. Cf. Godfrey Davies, 155–6, on 1648.
83. Cf. Vaughan, *The King Disguis'd*: 'O strengthen not/With too much trust the treason of a Scot!' Also cf. Marvell's contempt for the 'Pict' in *First Anniversary*, 318.
84. It was quite customary to use the word 'Fortune' for "Providence": for example, Browne, *Religio*, I. 18.
85. Sallust, *Bellum Catilinae*, II. 4–5: 'Nam imperium facile eis artibus retinetur quibus initio partum est'. Proudfoot (*op. cit.*) seems to have been the first to notice this source. There is a parallel in *RT*, where Marvell says of respect for the clergy that 'things are best preserved by the same means they were at first attained' (139).
86. *See*, for example, Horace, *Odes* I. 4.
87. This idea of a struggle with Antichrist at once spiritual and temporal was constantly reiterated throughout the 1640s and 50s, as a context for England's troubles both within and without. Thus one Puritan: 'more terrible than all flesh and blood [enemies], we have to do with Principalities and Powers, who act and guide. . .our humane adversaries. . .for [Satan]. . .is the spirit that stirres up all opposites both in Church and State' (Robert Baillie, cit. in Whiting, 234; cf. 239). cf. Walzer, 290.
88. This context for the line was suggested by E. E. Duncan-Jones, 'The erect sword in Marvell's "Horatian Ode"', *EA* 15 (1962), 172–4.
89. *See* esp. *PL* VI. 44: 'Michael, of celestial armies prince'. He is also the Archangel who, in *PL* XI–XII, is chosen to prophesy the eschatological design of history.
90. The quotation is recorded in Whiting, 241. The saints' side were, during the Civil War, understood to be 'Michael the Arch-Angel and his

followers' (quoted *ibid.*, 233; cf. 235). Michael was, in the struggle recorded in Revelation 12f., understood to represent the power of Christ over Antichrist (*see* Hankins, 364–5).

91. See Whittick, 207; Daniel 12:1, 10:13; Jude 9; Revelation 12:7. Cf. *PL* VI. 278, where Michael's is 'this avenging sword'. For further information on the iconography of Michael's sword, and its significance especially for the Last Day, *see* Philip Rollinson, 'The Traditional Contexts of Milton's "Two-Handed Engine"', *ELN* 9 (1971–2), 28–35. And cf. the illustrations of the Archangel reproduced in R. M. Frye, *Milton's Imagery and the Visual Arts: Iconographic Tradition in the Epic Poems* (Princeton, NJ, 1978).

92. A reproduction of the emblem can be found in Maurice Ashley, *Oliver Cromwell and His World* (1972), 89. Faithorne was a prominent artist at this time.

93. Michael was frequently portrayed as treading the Beast, signifying his victory over the latter in Revelation. (*See*, e.g., Rollinson's example of Michael 'standing triumphant over the Beast of the Apocalypse' [31n].).

94. Hibbert, 275. For the idea of 'providential' government by the sword, *see* Sprigge's remarks in Woodhouse, 135.

95. *See*, for example, the comments of R. G. M. Nisbet and Margaret Hubbard, *A Commentary on Horace: Odes Book I* (Oxford, 1970), 20.

96. 2, 22.

97. 7.

98. 7, 15; cf. 4–5.

99. 10. He is quoting Romans 8:28, a salient text for chiliasts; cf., for example, Wilkins, 73, 85.

100. 15.

101. Francis Bacon, *The Advancement of Learning*, ed. G. W. Kitchin (1915).

4: Revelation and Renovation

1. Barbara Herrnstein Smith, *Poetic Closure: A Study of How Poems End* (1968), 4–5.

2. Thomas Browne, was perhaps another writer structurally affected by the historical design: *see* Patrides, *Grand Design*, 83, who asserts this notion, without demonstration.

3. Augustine, *The Confessions*, trans. E. B. Pusey (1907), xxviii. 38. 274–5.

4. Fast Sermons to Parliament are particularly apt examples. Helpful studies are Roper's essay in *Essays in British History*, and Wilson, *Pulpit*.

5. Bacon, *Advancement*, 80.

6. Cf. Ch.1 above, for Marvell's use of this idea in *First Anniversary*. Schulz, 795, notes the 'indeterminate' lengths of times denoted by such words as 'day' in biblical usage. Cf. Augustine, *City of God*, XX. 7. 908.

7. Milton, *Areopagitica*, Bohn edn, II.98; cf. Bacon, *Advancement*, 80–1; Wilkins, 72.

8. Milton, *Areopagitica*, II. 89. Cf. Augustine, *City of God* XX. 5. 902.

9. *Smirke*, 49–50, is an example of this principle at work. For the doctrine,

see I Corinthians 13:9–12; Woodhouse, 45–6.

10. Augustine, *City of God* XX. 2. 898.

11. Milton uses this text to explain why the hour of the Coming is unknown to men: *De Doctrina*, IV. xxxiii. 476.

12. Augustine, *Confessions*, xxxi. 41. 276.

13. Wilkins, 52; cf. Augustine, Epistle 137, 'To Volusian', *Letters* (Fathers of the Church Series, New York, 1953), III. 31: 'the impressive order of creation from the beginning. . .the interlocking of time, giving credibility to the past by the present, giving authenticity to earlier happenings by later ones, and to ancient events by those more recent'.

14. B. H. Smith, 36.

15. I Corinthians 14:5, 13.

16. The way in which prophecy 'veil[s] the meaning' is discussed by Augustine, *City of God*, XX. 16. 927–8. Cf. Daniel 12:9; II Esdras 12:37–8.

17. Thomas, 'Two Cultures?', 172.

18. *See* Ch.1 72n, above.

19. *On Mr Milton. . .*, 53–4: an allusion to the Wisdom of Solomon 11:20, and refers to this idea that the poet imitates God as Creator. (As Margoliouth, I. 338, confirms.) Moreover, Wisdom 11:20 celebrates God's providential care for man, which is Milton's subject in *PL*.

20. Tuveson, 4.

21. Isaiah is the biblical book that most fully manifests the *desolatio/renovatio* pattern, since the greater part of it is a diapason of blessing and punishment for the Chosen People. Cf. Adams, *Spiritual Navigator*, 47–8.

22. Luther, quoted in Tuveson, 28; cf. Ball, 100.

23. Cf. Webster, xvi. Milton, *De Doctrina*, IV. 477; he cites also the traditional texts, *Matthew* 24:3–27 and II Timothy 3:1.

24. For example, 'Declaration of the English Army in Scotland' (Aug. 1650), repro. in Woodhouse, 474–7.

25. Cf. Ch.3 above; for Marshall's importance *see* Walzer, 182.

26. *Ibid.*: Ball, 186.

27. Marshall, *Reformation*, 44; Ball, 100–1; Wilkins, 63–6.

28. Thomas Burnet, *Sacred Theory*, 239–40.

29. *See* Donno, *Complete Poems*, note to line. 402 (p.273).

30. Henry Robinson, *Liberty of Conscience* (1644), quoted in Woodhouse, 47.

31. The Geneva Bible glossing Revelation 21. For these various levels of 'renovation', *see*, for example, Thomas Collier, 'A Discovery of the New Creation', a sermon preached to the Army at Putney on 29 Sept. 1647, on the text Isaiah 65:17, which is the *OT* prophecy of Revelation 21; repro. in Woodhouse, 390–6. For the remaking of the world and nature, *see also* Tuveson, 6, 17.

32. *See*, for example, Collier, Woodhouse, 394–6. Cf. Walzer, 182.

33. For Marvell's statements of man's corrupted nature see *Smirke*, 81–2; *Howe*, 167–8; *General Councils*, 122; *RT*, 231, 268; *Appleton House*, LXX. For the 'new creature', see *Howe*, 168.

34. For the description of this process of 'Conversion' from the 'natural' man, *see* Alan Simpson, *Puritanism in Old and New England* (Chigaco,

1961), 2, 4–5; cf. Woodhouse, 39–40.

35. Milton, *PL* XII. 586–7; Hartlib, *Macaria,* 14. Augustine, too, had made an analogy between the soul's emparadisement and that of the earth: *City of God,* XII. xiv. And cf. Ball, 180.

36. From the title of a tract on the subject of inner Conversion: Thomas Goodwin, *The Trial of a Christian's Growth: in Mortification, or purging our corruption; and Vivification, or bringing forth more fruit* (1643), repro. in *Works,* III., *see* esp. 457ff.

37. For Puritan self-monitoring, *see* Woodhouse, 21 and Walzer, 301. This is a process consequent upon Calvinist tenets. For Marvell's statements of it see *General Councils,* 125: 'Every man is bound to "work out his own salvation with fear and trembling" [Philip ii. 12]—and therefore to use all helps possible. . .hearing, conferring, reading, praying for the assistance of God's Spirit; but when he hath done this, he is his own expositor, his own both minister and people, bishop and diocess, his own Council; and his conscience excusing or condeming him, accordingly he escapes or incurs his own internal anathema'. Cf. also *RT,* 246: 'Christianity has obliged men to very hard duty, and ransacks their very thoughts'.

38. *Dew,* lines 19–26.

39. Marvell also refers to this passage when describing contemporary clerical 'false prophets', in *Howe,* 168.

40. Just as His Second Coming is necessary to the universal renovation, so His Passion and Resurrection is a prerequisite for each individual's resurrection at the End.

41. Leishman (cit. Margoliouth I. 245n.) saw the allusion but not its antichristian import.

42. Genesis 3:13–19 prophesied that Christ would 'bruise' the head of the Serpent (Satan). This became an eschatological image, in which Christ trampled the Dragon/Serpent—symbolizing His victory at the End. *See,* for example, Milton, *PL* X. 189–91.

43. *See* M. R. James, The *Apocalypse in Art* (London, 1931), 31–2; cf. Revelation 4–5.

44. Temple, 30; Ball. 180; Collier, 390.

45. *See,* for example, Temple, 50, echoing and citing this text. Cf. Symonds, 53.

46. Temple, 5. Here he cites Hebrews 2:7, that in the Kingdon 'Thou has put all things in subjection under his feet'.

47. Geneva Bible gloss on I Corinthians 15:20–5.

48. John Clarke, Putney Debates (Woodhouse, 39).

49. Temple, 30. Christ assumes His 'Crown' at the Last Day; cf. Ball, 185.

50. Milton, *De Doctrina,* IV. 484–5.

51. Sibbes, *Bride,* 43–4; Milton, *De Doctrina,* 484. Fixler, 9, rightly notes that 'the *regnum Christi* was for Milton the ultimate justification of the ways of God'.

52. Fixler, 13.

53. *See,* for example, Augustine, *Epistle 137,* 27–8; Arthur Golding, *Shakespeare's Ovid: Arthur Golding's Translation of the Metamorphoses* (1567), ed. W. H. D. Rouse (1961), Epistle to Leicester, 11.

54. Sibbes, *Bride*, 45–6; cf. Toon, 76.

55. Augustine, *Selected Letters*, Loeb edn (1953), *Epistle 258*; 499.

56. Lactantius, *The Divine Institutes I-VII*, trans. Sister M. F. McDonald, O.P., Fathers of the Church (Washington, 1964), VII. xxiv. Rosemond Tuve, *Images and Themes in Five Poems by Milton* (Camb., Mass., 1957), 61 and n.; Tuveson, 12, discusses Lactantius' influence upon millenarianism. *See also* Frances Yates, *Astraea: The Imperial Theme in the Sixteenth Century* (Harmondsworth, 1977) 4, 35–6. For example, Augustine, *Epistle 137*, 28–9; *The Letters of Abelard and Heloise*, trans. Betty Radice (Harmondsworth, 1974), Letter 6; Abelard to Heloise, 181; Evelyn, *History of Religion*, I. 92n. And cf. Domenico Comparetti, *Vergil in the Middle Ages*, trans. E. F. M. Benecke (1966), 97–101.

57. *See*, for example, Francis Charles, *Hosanna* (1647), repro. in facsim. *Hosanna and Threnodes*, ed. John Horden, English Reprints Series (Liverpool, 1960), sig. B2-B2ᵛ: ' 'Borne in Augustus time': 'And now the milde Augustus sate above/The sphere of Rome like a Propitious love. . ./And when the Olive branch of Peace was showne/Then, not before, the Prince of Peace came downe!' Cf. Evelyn, *History of Religion*, I. 98; Phineas Fletcher, *The Purple Island*, I. xxviii. The biblical text for Christ as 'Prince of Peace' was Isaiah 9:6.

58. Yates, 3–4; 10.

59. *Ibid.*, 39; 61.

60. Yates, 'Queen Elizabeth I as Astraea', 29–87.

61. *Ibid.*, esp. 42ff.

62. Lactantius, VII. xxiv. 530. Cf. Browne, *Religio*, I.47, 53.

63. *See*, for example, Tuve's interpretation of the Ode, *op. cit.*

64. Tuve, 61.

65. E. K. Rand, 'Milton in Rustication', *SP* XIX (1922), 109–35. Cf. also Tuve, 37–72. The influence of Virgil on Milton's works in general is considered by Harding *(op. cit)*, and John R. Knott, Jr, *Milton's Pastoral Vision: An Approach to "Paradise Lost"* (Chicago, 1971). Cf. note 106, below; and Patrides, *Grand Design*, who also confirms Milton's eschatological emphasis in this poem (85; and cf. 97, note 65).

66. Lawrence A. Saseck, *The Literary Temper of the English Puritans* (New York, 1961), 78–80, 87–8, 91; Camparetti, 97–8; Tuveson, 4.

67. As in the Ovidian *locus classicus* for Astraea (*Metamorphoses* I. 150), which Marvell quotes in *RT* 305-6, twisting its Elizabethan reference in sarcastic deference to Parker's "antichristian" proclivities, to make it refer to Mary Tudor; thus the papist 'usurpation' of the image implied here gives extra impetus to his rebuke to Parker's episcopal pretensions. The passage as a whole is an ironic antichristian inversion of Reformation history in England, calculated to reveal Parker's ideas in their true colours.

68. J. N. Browne, 'A Note on Symbolic Numbers in Spenser's "Aprill"', *N&Q* CCXXV (1980), 301–4; J. M. Richardson, 'More Symbolic Numbers in Spenser's "Aprill", *N&Q (Oct. 1982), 411–12*. For a general account of Astraean motifs in Spenser, *see* Margarita Stocker, 'Astraea', in the forthcoming *Spenser Encyclopedia* (Cleveland, 1986). Patrick Cullen's uninspiring attempt to make Marvell's *Little T.C.* a 'Golden-Age Eclogue'

in comparison with Spenser's *Aprill* and Milton's *Ode* received an effective riposte from Pierre Legouis (Cullen, 'Imitation and Metamorphosis', *PMLA* LXXXIV [1969], 1559–70; Legouis, *PMLA* LXXVI [1971], 275–7). Cullen's soi-disant 'Golden-Age Eclogue' is quite different from the Revelatory Eclogue I indicate, comprising especially libertine motifs and an indifference to the sex and age of the Virgilian model; significant since Astraea is not a boy.

69. Margarita Stocker, 'Remodelling Virgil: Marvell's New Astraea' (forthcoming).

70. For example, Woodhouse, 41–5; Burnet, *Sacred Theory*, 240; Wilkins, 61; cf. Milton, *De Doctrina*, IV. 438, citing, for example, I Corinthians 10:11, Revelation 1:19.

71. Walzer, 290.

72. *See* Stocker, 'Poet of the Latter Days', VIII. i.

73. Woodhouse, 38–9; cf. Temple, 50.

74. Putney Debates, Woodhouse, 41–2.

75. Woodhouse, 38–9.

76. Cf. II Peter 3:10; I Thessalonians 5:1–3; Revelation 16:15.

77. The poem is dated by its publication in *Lachrymae Musarum* (1649), a volume of elegies by divers hands upon the death of Henry Hastings, son of Ferdinand Earl of Huntingdon, from smallpox on 24 June 1649, at the age of nineteen. (Cf. Margoliouth, I. 240; Kelliher, 39.) Marvell's poem has little relevance to the intrinsic importance of Hastings; rather, Hastings as a skilled linguist and well-favoured young man presents an instance of a common phenomenon, that 'the good die young'. Thus Marvell has managed to express his own preoccupations within the format of a conventional elegy written rather as a commission than out of personal feeling; the same thing occurs in Milton's *Lycidas*, and is not uncommon with conventional elegies in this period. Dryden's elegy in the volume is much more specific about Hastings' valuable attributes, as well as about the cause of death, *etc.* Legouis notes the royalism of the deceased's parent (*Andrew Marvell*, 13), and rightly sees the poem as an expression of royalist sympathies (14). The *DNB* entries on Hastings' family in this period evidence a largely royalist commitment, as well as developments of allegiance and religious concerns comparable with Marvell's own.

78. Wilkins, 63–6, discourses upon the necessity for the saint to diagnose the actions of providence in the 'strange commotions' and oddities of the Civil War and the Latter Days: 'observable passages' must be examined and understood.

79. S. K. Heninger, Jr, 'Marvell's "Geometrick Yeer": A Topos for Occasional Poetry', *Approaches to Marvell*, ed. Patrides, 87–107.

80. Richard Crashaw, 'In the Glorious Epiphanie of our Lord God, a Hymn', 26–27.

81. Thomas Goodwin, *The Trial, Works*, III. 463. Cf. Thomas Browne, *A Letter to a Friend, Selected Writings*, ed. Keynes, 105, stating that the duration of a life should be computed by its virtue.

82. Cf. Ch.2 above on Lovelace; compare the War as Fall in *Appleton House*.

83. Thomas Goodwin, *Brief History*, 217.
84. Hill, *God's Englishman*, 219.
85. Cf., for example, Browne, *Religio*, I. 43; 49.
86. For the variety of critical views, see *The Poems of John Milton*, ed. John Carey and Alastair Fowler (1968), 410–11n.
87. For example, 304, 312, *et passim*.
88. Sibbes, *Bride*, 101.
89. For example, Wilkins, 66.
90. *Areopagitica*, Bohn edn, II. 98.
91. Woodhouse, 136.
92. For a wide range of critical analyses of the poem, of varying degrees of interest, see Friedenreich's anthology; Cullen, *op. cit.*; J. L. Simmons, 'Marvell's "The Picture of Little T.C. . . ."', *Explicator* 22 (1964), Item 62.
93. Bodleian MS. *Fairfax* 40: the 'Egloge' extends from 647 to 656 in the manuscript-book. The author, Edward Fairfax, was the son of the first Sir Thomas Fairfax of Denton, and died in 1635. He was famed as the translator of Tasso's *Gerusalemme Liberata*, pub. 1600. Apparently his twelve eclogues were written in the first year of James' accession: the Fairfax family possessed a manuscript of these (*DNB* VI. 995–6). The couple of surviving eclogues have recently been printed in the Oxford edition of Fairfax's *Works*, but the transcription there is not always reliable. I quote from MS. *Fairfax* 40. Marvell refers to Edward Fairfax's *Godfrey of Bulloigne* in his *Ingelo*.
94. Letter to Edward Harley, 3 May 1673, *Letters*, 328.
95. Letter to the Hull Corporation, *ibid.*, 166.
96. *RT.* 159–60. Marvell also asks, with a combination of asperity and humour and self-gratulation (after the reception of *General Councils*), 'Who would write?' (*Letters*, 346).
97. Marvell uses this classical motif for the purpose in his translation of *Senec. Trad. ex. Thyeste Chor.* 2: 'All I seek is to lye still/Settled in some secret Nest. . .And far of the publick Stage/Pass away my silent Age' (3–7).
98. For such critical accounts *see*, for example, Hyman, 'Politics', 477; Patterson, 16; Harold E. Toliver, *Marvell's Ironic Vision* (1965), that in Marvell's poetry there is a constant concern with 'withdrawal' and 'emergence' (esp. 88); George de. F. Lord, 'From Contemplation to Action: Marvell's Poetical Career', *Andrew Marvell: A Collection of Critical Essays*, ed. G. de. F. Lord (Englewood Cliffs, NJ, 1968), 55–73.
99. Margoliouth, I. 369n.
100. For computations of the Last Day, *see* Ball, *A Great Expectation* Ch.3, esp. 124.
101. For Astraea's combination of virginity and piety, *see* Yates, 33–4. Marvell uses the same linkage as in *Appleton House* in *Ingelo* (*see* Stocker, 'Remodelling Virgil').
102. Scoular saw some resonance of the Virgin Mary in Maria but does not see the Astraean source for this resemblance (*Natural*, 173).
103. For Astraean wisdom and mastery of 'secret mysteries', *see* Yates, 34.
104. For Virgo's mastery of speech, etc., *see* Yates, 34.

105. A suggestion made by Duncan-Jones (Margoliouth, I. 292).
106. *De Doctrina Christiana*, XVII. Bohn edn, IV. 319.
107. *See* Margoliouth, I. 290, where Legouis invokes Grosart, but himself rejects any but a "literal" interpretation of the 'Serpent'; a characteristic example of Legouis' attitude to the interpretation of Marvell.
108. Jeremy Taylor, 280.
109. *Ibid.*
110. He knew *Lycidas* when it was first published, which implies that he knew the *Ode* then, too, since they were in the same volume (1645). For his knowledge of *Lydicas*, see Margoliouth, I. 290. Other reminiscences of Milton can be found in *Fleckno* (1646/8), *First Anniversary* (1654; cf. Margoliouth, I. 324); the Ode is invoked, ll. 151–2 (Margoliouth, I. 323). Duncan-Jones (Margoliouth, I. 291) rightly recognized a similarity between lines 657–64 of Marvell's poem and lines 32, 64, and 229–30 of Milton's Ode, but does not offer any explanation of their similarity. She does not see the larger parallels, either. For the friendship, *see* Marvell's letter to Milton, 2 June 1654 (*Letters*, 305–6). The terms of Milton's recommendation imply an acquaintance aready established: Kelliher dates it to c. 1650/2 (86–7). Edward Phillips and John Aubrey testify to the friendship; Marvell defended Milton at the Restoration, and in *RT*, 311–13; other symptoms of close friendship are recorded by Donno, *Critical Heritage*, 54.
111. I have since seen an article by Dolores Palomo, 'The Halcyon Moment of Stillness in Royalist Poetry', *HLQ* 44 (1981), 205–21, which lists halcyon references as a royalist/conservative tic. In Fanshawe and Milton and, of course, in my account of Marvell here, the halycon is but a small unit in a much larger idea, which is generic, and in fact eschatological in theme.
112. *Egloge*, 656; in 'Orpheus' recalling the 55th line of Virgil's Eclogue.
113. *Egloge*, 647.
114. Several of Virgil's Eclogues utilize this convention; for example, I, II, VI, IX, X. Many *beatus ille* poems also adopt the convention; see Maren-Sophie Røstvig, *The Happy Man: Studies in the Metamorphoses of a Classical Ideal, 1600–1700*, 2 vols. (Oslo, 1962), I, *passim*. Milton adopts it from Virgil: Knott, 90f. Cf. Spenser's *Calendar*, eclogues 5, 6, 8.
115. *See,* for example, the poem quoted in Hill, *Antichrist*, 144, which demonstrates the antichristian reference of Babel.
116. *Areopagitica*, II. 90.
117. Cf. the fine literary-critical analysis of Virgil's Fourth Eclogue by Michael C. J. Putnam, *Virgil's Pastoral Art: Studies in the "Eclogues"* (Princeton, NJ, 1970): he rightly explains Virgil's 'sceleris. . .nostri' (IV. 13) as referring to the sin of civil war amongst the Romans (143–4).
118. D. C. Allen thinks that the rail 'is Charles I', to which Margoliouth ripostes 'To me the rail is just a rail' (I. 285).
119. Legouis in Margoliouth, I. 286, 'The name probably comes from Virgil's Thestylis, who, in *Eclogues* ii. 11–12, brought garlic and wild thyme to the reapers'. There is another reminiscence (of *Eclogue* I. 58) in the 1.526 (cf. Margoliouth, I. 289).

120. In the masque, the spectators become actors by joining in the dance: the masque's action absorbs the audience into itself. Cf. Ch.7, below.
121. Duncan-Jones noted the echo (Margoliouth, I. 290) but did not elaborate. A similar contrast is implied in *On Mr Milton*, where the literal and irreverent 'Play' of a plagiarist is condemned, in contrast to the true "drama" of the 'vast Design' ('Might hence presume the whole Creations day/To change in Scenes, and show it in a Play', 21–2).
122. *An Apology for Smectymnuus* (1642), Bohn edn, III. 151.
123. Duncan-Jones noted the same Miltonic origin of this phrase (Margoliouth, I. 292), but, again, does not elaborate.
124. For example, Scoular, *Natural*, 183, 186–7; D. C. Allen, 143; Bush, 161.
125. *See*, for example, M. C. Bradbrook, 'Marvell and the Poetry of Rural Solitude', *RES* XVII, 65 (1941), 37–46.
126. Patterson, *Marvell and the Civic Crown*, 107n.
127. Marvell implies a similar mistaking of the Sybilline leaves in their disarray, in his *Illustrissimo Viro*, ll. 31–2. For the use of Eclogue IV in that poem, *see* Stocker, 'Remodelling Virgil'.
128. William Empson, *Some Versions of Pastoral: A Study of the Pastoral Form in Literature* (Harmondsworth, 1966), 102.
129. *Ingelo*, line 21.
130. *The Constitutional Documents of the Puritan Revolution 1625–1660*, ed. S. R. Gardiner (3rd edn, Oxford, 1906), 137–44, reprints the Petition.
131. *See* Ch.5, n. 124, below.
132. Scoular, *Natural*, 171, noted that here the fishes stole Marvell's calling but, in keeping with hermetic readings of the poem, saw this as 'an act of voluntary humility'.
133. Wallace recognized that Maria now is Marvell's master of languages, 255.
134. For this stanza D. C. Allen uses Marvell's *Bilboro* as a gloss, for the notion of trees as 'pedigree', and as implements of war.
135. For example, Deuteronomy 20:19; Isaiah 56:3; Matthew 7:17, etc. On Marvell's image, in st. LXXI, of himself as an 'Inverted Tree', *see* the history of the idea provided by A. B. Chambers, '"I was but an Inverted Tree": Notes toward the History of an Idea', *Studies in the Renaissance*, 8 (1961), 291–9; again, this imAge is too seriously understood.
136. Cf. *Death of O.C.*, 261ff.
137. *See* Margoliouth, I. 288 (citing Davison and Wallerstein): the lines are from *La Solitude*, 6–10.
138. I intend to publish a full-length treatment of the seventeenth-century redirection of Pastoral, and its consequences.
139. *See*, for example, the account of the genre given by Peter V. Marinelli, *Pastoral* (The Critical Idiom series, 1971).

5: A Revelation for the Revolution

1. Wallace, 110, notes this fact in relation to *First Anniversary*.
2. The friendship between Marvell and Harrington is recorded by Aubrey, 'Life of Harrington', *Brief Lives*, I. 293; cf. II. 54. The enigmatic

connexion between Marvell and Harrington's Rota Club is discussed by Kelliher, 77.

3. As in, of course, *Appleton House* and *Smirke* (cf. Ch.2 above).

4. *See* Josephine Waters-Bennett, 'Britain Among the Fortunate Isles', *SP* 53 (1956), 114–40, who discusses some of the sources and features of this idea.

5. Pliny *Naturalis Historia*, IV. xxii; translation, Loeb edn, II. 119.

6. DeWitt T. Starnes and E. W. Talbert, *Classical Myth and Legend in Renaissance Dictionaries* (Chapel Hill, NC, 1955), 160ff. For other descriptions of the Fortunate Isles, *see*, for example, Lucian's parody (*Works*, Loeb edn (1913), I, *Verae Historiae*, I. 247–357, which also parodies the New Jerusalem); *Sir Thomas North's Translation of Plutarch's Lives*, 8 vols. (Oxford, 1928), IV. 369–70 (Marvell was familiar with this example, echoing North's 'Sertorius' (the location) in his *Nymph*—an echo spotted by Muir, 115, commenting on the latter poem); Edward Fairfax's translation of Tasso, *Godfrey of Bulloigne* (1600), xv. 35–6, xvi. 11; cf. also Pliny, *Naturalis*, VI. xxxvii, on the location of the Fortunate Isles in the Canaries.

7. *See* Starnes, 159–61, 309–31; esp. 310–11.

8. Starnes (*ibid.*) gives detailed discussion of Milton's use of such motifs.

9. Pliny, *Naturals*, II. xcvi (Loeb edn, I. 209).

10. Starnes, 160–1.

11. Johnathan Swift, *Gulliver's Travels* (Harmondsworth, 1967), 198–200; 'The word, which I interpret the *Flying* or *Floating* Island, is in the original *Laputa*' (203).

12. Starnes, 161. Waters-Bennett, 'Britain', also refers to the influence of Comes, 124.

13. Starnes, 159–61, 309–31.

14. *Ibid.*, 309, 311.

15. Waters-Bennett, 'Britain', 117.

16. *Ibid.*, 114, 118–19,124, 139.

17. *Ibid.*, 128–9.

18. Cf. also Stephen Orgel and Roy Strong (eds.), *Inigo Jones: The Theatre of the Stuart Court*, 2 vols. (Berkeley, 1973), 71.

19. Margoliouth, II. 369.

20. Cf. Orgel and Strong on Neptune's significance in England, 54; 71.

21. *See* the confused remarks in Margoliouth, I. 366, for example.

22. *See* Margoliouth, I. 400–1 on the poem's authorship. For Ralegh as a Protestant hero, *see* Breslow, 46–7, who also notes the use of Ralegh by Protestant writers at various dates as 'England's Forewarner' against papist conspiracies (47). Patrides, *Grand Design*, 81f., notes the influence of, and veneration for, Ralegh's *History of the World* (1614) throughout the century. Cf. Whiting, 39; Webster, 2–3.

23. *See* Ovid, *Metamorphoses*, XV for the assumption of Julius Caesar into the heavens. Cf. *Aeneid* VII. 785ff.

24. Ben Jonson, *The Fortunate Isles, and their Union: Celebrated in a Masque Design'd for the Court on the Twelfth Night, 1626, Works* (1716), VI. 54–75. The masque was designed by Inigo Jones. Cf. Allan H. Gilbert,

The Symbolic Persons in the Masques of Ben Jonson (New York, 1969), 38, 169.

25. Jonson, *Fortunate Isles*, 68–9.

26. *Ibid.*

27. *Ibid.*, 68–9; Starnes, 161.

28. Jonson, *Fortunate Isles*, 69–70.

29. Johnson, *Fortunate Isles*, 74. Cf. Stephen Orgel, *The Illusion of Power: Political Theater in the English Renaissance* (Berkeley and London, 1975), 75.

30. *Neptune's Triumph for the Return of Albion* (1623), Ben Jonson and Inigo Jones. Cf. Orgel, *Illusion*, 70ff.

31. *See* Orgel's account of the imagery of Jones' design (with the plates thereto), *ibid.*, 73–4.

32. *Ibid.*, 72–3.

33. Cf. Orgel, *ibid.*, 73.

34. Temple, 22. The source of this 'Isles' motif, which he is quoting, is Psalm 91:1.

35. A pertinent example is Thomas Fairfax's poem, *The Christian War-fare*, MS. *Fairfax*, 40, 583ff., which uses, *passim*, the traditional metaphor of the Ship of the Soul. Cf., for example, Donne, 'A Hymne to Christ, at the author's last going into Germany', st. I; Browne, *Letter to a Friend, Selected Writings*, ed. Keynes, 106; Herbert, 'Miserie', 76–7; Roger Edgeworth, *Of Idolls and Images* (1557), repro. in Chandos, 5.

36. Sig. A3–A3v. Cf. Adams, *Navigator,* 11. For other examples of the sea as an emblem of the world, *see* Kathleen Williams, 'Spenser: Some Uses of the Sea and the Storm-tossed Ship', *Research Opportunities in Renaissance Drama*, XIII-IV (1970–71), 135–42, esp. 140. Many examples can be found in such collections as Quarles' *Emblems* and Ripa's *Iconologia*.

37. Robert Purnell, quoted in Ball, 92.

38. *See*, for instance, Plutarch's *Lives*, 'Caesar', xxiv (Loeb edn, 1919 VII. 527), and Horace, *Odes*, I. 14; for the allegory of which *see* Nisbet and Hubbard, Commentary, 179.

39. Walzer, 179–82. For an example of the kind of political rhetoric involved, *see* Col. Rainborough's animadversion on the topic during the Putney Debates (Woodhouse, 33); Marshall, *Song of Moses*, 37.

40. Marvell's use of the Ship of State metaphor here has been discussed by John M. Wallace, 'Marvell's "lusty Mate" and the Ship of the Commonwealth', *MLN* 76 (1961), 106–10.

41. Collier, 395–6; cf. Sprigge, also in Woodhouse, 134–5. Temple, 49.

42. Herbert, 'The Church Militant'; *see* esp. 259–60, 275–7: 'Yet as the Church shall thither westward flie,/So Sinne shall trace and dog her instantly. . .the Church by going west/. . . drew more neare/To time and place, where judgement shall appeare'. It owes something to the flight of the Woman Clothed with the Sun from persecution in the Revelation.

43. *See*, for example, Marshall, *Song of Moses*, 43: Parliament must 'sink and swim with the Church'. For the absolute interinvolvement of Church and state, cf. also Temple, 23–4; Walzer, 179–80.

44. 'A Vindication of the Late Vow and Covenant' (1643), 12: cited in

Whiting, 229.

45. This imagery is taken directly from Revelation 17:1, 15. Cf. John Mayer, *Ecclesiastica Interpretatio* (1627), 483; Richard Bernard, *A Key of Knowledge. . .of St John's mysticall Revelation* (1617), 158.

46. For an account of the interpenetration of Utopianism and Puritan millenarianism of chiliasm, see A. L. Morton, *The English Utopia* (1978); Ch.3, 'Revolution and Counter-Revolution', discusses the seventeenth century in particular; 95–7 put Macaria—and Harrington's *Oceana*—in the context of such Utopianism. Cf. also Woodhouse, 47–8. The topic of Puritan reformist science is treated in detail by Webster, *op. cit*; *see* esp. xvi; the text from Daniel was 12:4 (cf. Webster 2). Webster, 16; Tuveson, 87–90; Walzer, 297–8.

47. Thomas, 'Two Cultures?', 191. Webster, Ch.1, gives an extended account of Bacon's influence; cf. Woodhouse, 47.

48. Francis Bacon, *New Atlantis* (1626), *Works*, 14 vols., ed. J. Spedding, R. L. Ellis, D. D. Heath (London, 1857–74), III. 129–66.

49. The quotation is from Temple, 14. Morton discusses the influence of this work, 80–6. *See also*, the Geneva Bible (1599), 'The Argument' of the Song of Solomon ('Iesus Christ the true Salomon & King of peace'), and gloss on 6:12, 'Ierusalem was called Shalem, which signifieth peace'.

50. Hartlib, *Macaria*, Preface, sig. A2. For discussion of Hartlib's reforming activities, *see* Morton, 92, 95–7, 86; Woodhouse, 48; Toon, 62. For more extended treatment of Hartlib and other reforming "scientists", *see* Nell P. Eurich, *Science In Utopia: A Mighty Design* (Camb., Mass., 1967). Hartlib's exposition of Revelation (probably merely masquerading as a "translation" of someone else's) was *Clavis Apocalyptica* (1651). For an asseveration of the renovatory character of Puritan science, *see*, for example, his 'To the Reader', *Husbandman*, sig. A2.

51. *Macaria*, 2, 4–5, 7, 12.

52. *Ibid.*, 9.

53. Thomas Blenerhasset, 'Revelation of the True Minerva' (1582), quoted by Waters-Bennett, 'Britain', 124; cf. 116. A similar Golden Age description of Elect England appears in Fanshawe's 'Ode': the 'Island' of Britain is 'A world without the world', 'one blest Isle' to which Astraea returns (9, 11).

54. Bacon, *Advancement*, 79–80.

55. Ball, 108–9 and n.; Woodhouse, 45–6; Browne, *Hydriotaphia*, ed. Keynes, 119.

56. Yates, 23, 54.

57. *Ibid.*, 49–50.

58. Breslow, 3, 139; Temple, 31; Ball, 106.

59. Toon, 46; Breslow, 55.

60. Breslow, 50, 73f.; Clifton, 'Fear of Popery'; L. B. Wright, *Religion and Empire: The Alliance Between Piety and Commerce in English Expansion 1558–1625* (Chapel Hill, 1943), 118–9, 151, 156; Samuel Purchas, *Hakluytus Posthumus; or, Purchas His Pilgrimes*, 20 vols. (Glasgow, 1905–7), XIX. 249.

61. Wright, 112–4; cf. Purchas, XIX, 'Virginia's Verger', 260, 266.

62. Hughes, *A Letter, sent into England from the Summer Ilands* (1615), quoted in Wright, 113. Cf. Alexander Whitaker, *Good Newes From Virginia* (1613), Epistle Dedicatorie by William Crashaw, sig. A3v., B; and 21.

63. Purchas, XIX, 'Virginia's Verger', 239, 260, 229. Cf. Wright, 106; William Symonds, *Virginia: Virginea Britannia* (1609), Epistle Dedicatorie, sig. A3v.

64. *See* the discussions of this belief in Walzer, 232; Toon, 36; Wright, 157; Webster, 36–40, demonstrates the part played by Puritan divines and academics in the promulgation of this idea. Examples of the pamphlet literature, apart from those cited *supra*, are Robert Johnson, *Nova Britannia. Offring Most Excellent fruites by Planting in Virginia* (1609); John Smith, *The True Travels, Adventures, and Observations of Captain John Smith*, repro. in *Works*, 2 vols., ed. Edward Arber (1895). The motives and character of New England theocracy are discussed by Simpson and by Perry Miller, *Errand into the Wilderness* (Camb., Mass., 1954). Cf. Herbert, 'Church Militant', 247; Hartlib, *Macaria*, 5.

65. Wright, 91. Cf. Symonds, 9; Purchas, XIX. 267.

66. Purchas, XIX. 237.

67. Purchas, Dedication to Prince Charles; Wright, 132.

68. The phrase is Wright's; his fourth chapter is 'A Western Canaan Reserved For England'.

69. For example, *Andrew Marvell*, 102; Wallace, *Destiny*, 141 calls it 'a failure'.

70. Breslow, 56.

71. Margoliouth, I. 329.

72. Wallace recognized the connexion between this poem and the offer to Cromwell of the Crown (142), but he thinks that is the sole subject of the poem.

73. *See*, for example, Wallace, *Destiny*, 142.

74. Hyman, *Andrew Marvell*, 102.

75. Cf. the similar implications of Herbert's remark on the New World in 'Church Militant' (247–51), the pith of which is that 'gold and grace did never yet agree'. That notion is a common one in Pastoral, and in classical ideas of the 'Golden Age' in particular; that age actually involves the exclusion of material gold, as Ovidian and other accounts of it make clear.

76. Pliny, *Naturalis*, VI. xxxvii.

77. Line 34: for interpretation of the poem, *see* Stocker, 'Remodelling Virgil'.

78. *See*, for example, Margoliouth I. 245–6.

79. The article that appears to have stimulated such views is the brief and somewhat perfunctory exposition of Rosalie L. Colie, 'Marvell's "Bermudas" and the Puritan Paradise', *Renaissance News* X (1957), 75–9. Articles providing variations on and developments of her views are Toshihiko Kawasaki, 'Marvell's "Bermudas"—A Little World, or a New World?', *ELH* 43 (1976), 38–52; Annabel Patterson, '"Bermudas" and "The Coronet": Marvell's Protestant Poetics', *ELH* 44 (1977), 478–99, who considers that these poems reflect Protestant views on literary aesthetics

(from Psalms, etc.); Summers, 'Some Apocalyptic Strains', gave a brief discussion of this poem which is generally similar to Colie's (199–201).
80. Such views are represented by Tay Fizdale, 'Irony in Marvell's "Bermudas"', *ELH* 42 (1975), 203–13; and R. M. Cummings, 'The Difficulty of Marvell's "Bermudas"', *MP* 67 (1970), 331–40. Philip Brockbank, 'The Politics of Paradise: "Bermudas"', *Approaches to Marvell*, ed. Patrides, 174–93, gives an account of modified ironies in the poem.
81. For various seventeenth-century accounts, the best compilation is Purchas, XIX. ix, esp. Chs. 16–20. Some interesting commentary on these tracts is provided by Frank Kermode, (ed.), *The Arden Shakespeare: The Tempest* 1964), Introduction. The most interesting of the tracts are Lewis Hughes, *A Letter* (1615) and *A Plaine and True Relation of the Goodnes of God towards the Sommer Ilands* (1621); William Strachey, *The True Repertory of the Wracke* (1610).
82. Cummings and Brockbank both remark on these dissensions at some length; cf. Hunt, 117. As early as 1610, Strachey is recording disagreements, mutiny, and an execution.
83. Sibbes, *Bride*, 3,
84. Cf. Ch. IV. ii, above. Cf. for example Tertullian, 'Adversus Marcionem', iii. 24, cit. in *The Early Christian Fathers*, ed. and tr. H. Bettenson, 164. (Marvell was familiar with Tertullian: see *General Councils*, 149.) Cf. Also Fixler, 17; Revelation 9:15; Temple, 4–5.
85. Jeremy Taylor, 268.
86. For example, Berthoff, 55, assumes that they have already landed; Brockbank that they have not, 189; Summers, 200, says that they have lived in the islands for some time already and 'know them well'. Ironic readings of the poem tend to make much of the confusion.
87. Cf. *First Anniversary*, where Marvell provides a complicated conceit whereby the English Fleet 'sink the Earth that does at Anchor ride' (364).
88. One of many remarks on their flatness is that of Anthony Trollope, *The West Indies and The Spanish Main* (1968), 375.
89. Cf. Revelation 21:10; Edward Fairfax, *Egloge*, MS *Fairfax* 40, 655; Marshall, *Reformation*, 44 (the Last Day is when Christ will 'bow the heavens'). Cf. Tertullian, 'Adversus', 164. Cf. PL. X. 647–8.
90. Beard, 2.
91. MS *Fairfax* 40, 536. For Leviathan as Antichrist in Christian lore, see John Block Friedman, 'Antichrist and the Iconography of Dante's Geryon', *JWCI* 35 (1972), 108–22; esp. 118. This conflation was of Job 40:20 with the Beast from the Sea in Revelation 13.
92. For the liturgical and exegetical relationship between the Leviathan of Isaiah 27:1 and the Beast from the Sea in Revelation, see Tuve, 63 and n.; she notes that the consequent reference in Isaiah to the Second Coming also specifically invokes the advent of Justice.
93. Adams, *Spiritual Navigator*, 24; 25, identifies this leviathan with the Red Dragon of Revelation 12.
94. Adams, *Blacke Devill*, 32; Strachey, *Purchas*, 15 provides the "Bermudan" or literal level of this statement, remarking that 'These Ilands are often afflicted and rent with tempests, great strokes of thunder,

lightning and raine in the extremity of violence'.

95. Beard, Preface, sig. A4. For 'stern' here see *OED*, I.

96. Thus Wilkins, 52, cites this text as the definition of God's providence. Cf. Browne, *Religio*, I. 17: God's secret work of providence is a 'way full of meanders and Labyrinths', a maze.

97. Pliny, *Naturalis*, I. 235–7, in Whiting, 81; to which the latter compares Milton, *PL* VII. 412–16.

98. Starnes, 309–12 treat the identification of Hesperides and Fortunate Isles in Renaissance literature.

99. *Ibid.*, 309.

100. Hughes, quoted in Wright, 114; cf. Strachey, *Purchase*, 17; Trollope, 368. Strachey, *ibid.*, remarks that if it had not 'pleased God to bring us, wee had not come one man of us else a shoare', and similar remarks can be found in the other tracts.

101. Wright, 113.

102. Purchas, 'Virginia's Verger', 257.

103. Matthew Henry, *Acts to Revelation*, 538, glossing Revelation 21:9f. on the New Jerusalem: 'The wall for security. Heaven is a safe state. . .secure[d]. . .from all evils and enemies'.

104. Adams, *Spiritual Navigator*, 23, 24.

105. Trollope, 368.

106. Milton, *De Doctrina*, IV. 479.

107. Adams, *Spiritual Navigator*, 8–9.

108. *Purchas*, XIX. ix. xvi. 173.

109. Revelation 4:10–11; 5:9–10; 7:10.

110. Comes' *Mytholigiae*, quoted in Starnes, 311.

111. Geneva Bible (1560), gloss on Revelation 21:11. Cf. Milton, *PL*. X. 678–9. *See also* Starnes, 311; the *ver aeternam* was a typical constituent of the Golden Age: *see*, for example, Ovid, *Metamorphoses*, I. 107. *See also* Upton, *Variorum Spenser*, 258, on *FQ* III. vi. 42; to which, for eschatological and Fortunate Isle motifs, compare Tasso, *Gerusalemme*, trans. Fairfax, 54.

112. See OED *1.4 and 2. 1c*.

113. Mirelli Levi D'Ancona, *The Garden of the Renaissance: Botanical Symbolism in Italian Paiting* (Florence, 1977), 315. Bruce King, *Marvell's Allegorical Poetry* (Cambridge, 1977), 43, notes that the pomegranate is 'among the fruits of the Promised Land', and 'a common symbol for the Church': the point is that it symbolizes esp. Church *unity*. Cf. Exodus 28:33 and I Chronicles 3:16.

114. Commenting on *Appleton House*, LXIII–IV, Scoular, *Natural*, 182, notes the ubiquity of the motif in contemporary poetry.

115. Bacon, *New Atlantis*, 132–4: his sailors are battered by tempest, rescued by providence (129), and landed on the "New Jerusalem" island of New Atlantis, 'this happy island' (139). It, too, has remained 'unrevealed' for many ages, 'a land unknown' (139) and 'remote' (139), like Marvell's Bermudas. The "New Jerusalem" resonances are constant and insistent in Bacon's piece. In the New Atlantis they 'are beyond both the old world and the new' (134); cf. also 133, 136, 158: where it is said to possess 'Water of

Paradise'.

116. For example, Margoliouth, I. 246; Hyman, *Andrew Marvell*, 40.

117. A full exposition of the tradition of the three Trees, including many iconographical examples, is given by Stanley Stewart, *The Enclosed Garden: The Tradition and the Image in Seventeenth-Century Poetry* (1966).

118. More, Account of Voyage, and 'Articles which Master R. More, Governour Deputie of the Sommer Ilands, propounded to the Company that were there with him. . .1612', repro. *Purchas*, XIX. ix. xvi. 172ff.: the latter propounds 'godly' colonization.

119. More, *Purchas*, 174; cf. Strachey, *ibid.*, 22–3.

120. *Ibid.*, 175.

121. *Ibid.*, 174.

122. *Ibid.*, Strachey, *Purchas*, 18; Trollope, 372.

123. I Kings 5:6.

124. *See* Lewalski, 'Typology', 45–6. The internal 'walled' temple is that propounded to Parliament by Thomas Wilson, *Jerichoes Down-Fall* (1643), 36: 'prepare God an habitation. . .'.

125. Jereby Taylor, 268.

126. More, *Purchas*, 176.

127. Pliny, *Naturalis*, VI. xxxvii. Brockbank, 184, noted this source for the line, but he gives it a derogatory implication.

128. More, *Purchas*, 176: cf. Strachey, *Purchas*, 17.

129. *See* the various explanations proffered by, for example, E. B. Benjamin, 'Marvell's "Bermudas"', *CEA Critic* 29 (1967),10–12, 12; Toliver, 102–3; Fizdale, 210, reads it ironically.

130. Sibes, *Bride*, 20. Cf. Charles Herle, *Davids Song of Three Parts* (1643), where, explicating the paradisal Psalm 95:1, he explains the spiritual Canaan of rest which is here greeted by a song of praise on entry, and continues: 'there we shall always delight to see, and seeing to love, and loving to praise, and praising to sing, and singing to praise and so backe againe' (15).

131. Temple, 44.

132. Colie, 'Marvell's "Bermudas"', 78.

133. Temple, 46.

134. Breslow, 60.

135. Bradbrook and Lloyd-Thomas, 65.

136. Temple, 36–8.

6: *Revelations of Love*

1. The tradition is described in Røstvig, *Happy Man*, who discusses *The Garden* in that light.

2. Thomas Clayton, in Friedenreich, 61.

3. Fogle, 137. King, *Allegorical Poetry*, simply ransacks the Bible for possible sources, as usual, in order to make *Coy Mistress* an unlikely parody of its genre; Stewart (see below) also sees the poem as a parody of asceticism; a similar augument animates Bruce E. Miller, 'Logic in Marvell's "To His Coy Mistress"', *NDQ* 30 (1962), 48–9: all these are

simplistic in their attitude to their findings of Christian-Platonic features in the poem, and make it a muddle rather than a great poem, despite their intention to enhance its reputation. Like Miller, others have discussed the apparent logical fallacy in the poem's syllogism (B. H. Smith, 134–5; J. C. Maxwell, 'Marvell and Logic', *N&Q*, July 1970, 256; J. V. Cunningham, 'Logic and Lyric', *MP* 51 (1953), 33–42): however, in fact Marvell is unconcerned to maintain more than the generic convention of syllogism, and he explodes it only in so far as (as I indicate below) he wants to subvert the intitial proposition—not for parody but for its eschatalogical significance; in other words, the initial proposition is reworked in the course of the poem, rather than superficial or repudiated. For another variation on the Christian-Platonic assays on the poem, *see* Anthony E. Farnham, 'Saint Teresa and the Coy Mistress', *BUSE* 2 (1956), 226–39. There are too many other discussions of the poem, of varying degrees of vagueness or irrelevance or local interest, to detail here; but critics may be seen wrestling with the poem's various baffling images in, for example, J. J. Carroll, 'The Sun and the Lovers in *THCM*', MLN 74 (1959), 4–7; Robert Daniel 'Marvell's *THCM*', *Explicator* I. 5 (1943), Item 37; R. A. Day, 'Marvell's "Glew"', *PQ* 32 (1953), 344–6; Frederick L. Gwynn, 'Marvell's *THCM*', 33–46, *Explicator* (May 1953), Item 49; L. W. Hyman, 'Marvell's "Coy Mistress" and Desperate Lover', *MLN* 75 (1960), 8–10; Lawrence A. Sasek, 'Marvell's *THCM*', *Explicator* 14 (April 1956), Item 47; W. A. Sedelow, 'Marvell's *THCM*', MLN 71 (1956), 6–8; L. N. Wall, 'Thomas Randolph and Marvell's "Coy Mistress"', *N&Q* n.s. 15 (1968), 103; John Wheatcroft, 'Andrew Marvell and the Winged Chariot', *BuR* 6 (1956), 22–53. Most readers of the vast range of criticism of this poem may find the process dispiriting. Toliver, 156–7, says usefully that the logical structure of the poem's argument 'does not account for the wit and ambivalence of the poem', and this is the essential problem which must be addressed in analysing this lyric.

4. I used to think this an obvious point, but experience tells me that it is not: for discussion of the morbidity of *carpe diem* poems, *see* Gordon Braden, '"Vivamus, mea Lesbia" in the English Renaissance', *ELR* IX. 2 (1979), 199–224.

5. Stanley Stewart, 'Marvell and the *Ars Moriendi*', *Seventeenth-Century Imagery*, ed. Earl Miner, 133–50.

6. The theological discussion of this parable in this period is usefully discussed by Robert G. Walker, 'Rochester and the Issue of Deathbed Repentance in the Restoration', *South Atlantic Review* 47. 1 (1982), 21–37. *See also* Matthew Henry, 227–8 on this parable and its relation to the Song of Solomon, which enters into the discussion given below; cf. his 230.

7. Thomas, 'Two Cultures', 189.

8. For the eschatological version of this exegetical tradition, *see* Thomas Brightman, *A Commentary on the Canticles* (Amsterdam, 1644.) Brightman was probably the most significant influence on millenarian and similar exegesis in this period: *vide* Lamont's account of his influence, as well as Ball, *passim*.

9. *See* W. and M. Haller, 'The Puritan Art of Love', *HLQ* IV (1941–2),

235–72, esp. 248; R. M. Frye, 'The Teachings of Classical Puritanism on Conjugal Love', *Studies in the Renaissance* 2)1955), 148–59.

10. For example, Clifton, 'Fear of Popery', 146–7; Thomas Case, *Spiritual Whoredom Discovered in a Sermon before the House of Commons* (1647).

11. For Apollo as Christ, *see* notes to *The Garden*, below; Gwynn rightly saw Phoebus Apollo here, but deviates into the unlikely idea of Phaethon, too.

12. 'Tide' (6) also refers to time (OED I. 1, 3, 4); *Tempus Edax* is in lines 39–40; 'Life' (44); 'Now. . .Now. . .now' (33–8); 'instant' (36); 'youthful' '(33); 'morning' (34); 'slow' (40, 12); 'Eternity' (24), etc.

13. Browne, *Hydriotaphia*, V. 150.

14. For 'crime' meaning 'sin, *see*, for example, Spenser, *FQ* II. xii. 75. The first example of 'coy' is Shakespeare, *Rape of Lucrece*, 669; the second is *FQ* I. ii. 27. For the pun on 'coy' there, *see* the comment by Dodge in *The Works of Edmund Spenser: A Variorum Edition*, ed. E. Greenlaw *et al.* (Baltimore, 1961), on this *FQ* stanza (202); cf. *OED* I. 1–3. The Whore appears virginal but shall be revealed as whore (Isaiah 40:1).

15. First quotation from Marvell's *Dialogue Between Thyrsis and Dorinda*, 12; cf. 35–6. Second is from Vaughan, 'The Day of Judgement', 1. Cf. Herbert, 'Sunday' and Spenser, *FQ* VII. viii. 2; *Apocalypse of Peter*, 524; and the discussion of endless day in *Bermudas*, Ch.5 above.

16. Sibbes, *Bride*, 94: the whole place is on the Marriage to Christ *topos*.

17. *Matthew* 7:13–14; Matthew Henry, Acts, 61: 'both the ways, and both the ends: now let the matter be taken entire, and *considered impartially*, and then *choose you this day* which you will walk in'. The 'way' and 'walk' motif is common in the Bible; for example, I Corinthians 7:17; Jeremiah 10;23; Deuteronomy 5:33; Psalm 128:1; Daniel 9:10. Esp. Jeremiah 6:16: 'Stand in the ways. . .and ask. . .where is the good way, and walk in it'. Cf. also II Chronicles 6:27; Job 12:24; Geneva Bible gloss on Romans 8:1; St. Bernard, *A Rule of Good Life* (1633), 160; *PL* XII. 646–9; Evelyn, *History of Religion*, II. 3.

18. Matthew Henry, 61, on the Matthew text.

19. Jeremy Taylor, 268: the alternative to this world which is 'but of a *dayes* abode'.

20. *See*, for example, Shakespeare's image of frustration in Sonnet LVI; Quarles' application of the motif to Christ's love; Daniel's use of a geographical conceit in his Sonnet 18, 'to th 'Orient do they Pearles remoue'.

21. Browne, *Pseudodoxia Epidemica*, VI. vii. 153; Breslow, 55.Cf. *Last Instructions*, 'from the *Ganges* Gems' (719).

22. For example, Geneva Bible gloss on Revelation 17:3–4.

23. For example, *Rape of Lucrece*, 1191. Cf. also Campion, *A Book of Airs*, V (Works, ed. Bullen, 1903, 10–11).

24. For example, John Mayer, *Ecclesiastica Interpretatio* (1627), 446, 483. Cf. Lamont, 42; Breslow, 72.

25. Daniel, Sonnet 21; cf. the same motif in Donne, *First Anniversary*, st. 3, and Cotton, 'To Chloris, Stanzas Irreguliers', 31–8, in both cases playing with the notion.

26. *RT*, 15. Cf. the similar attachment of empire, pride and riches in Fairfax's *Egloge*, 654–5 and 649, where the Whore 'takes [lovers] for her slaues, not for her loues'. Hankins usefully discusses the Whore as Pride in Spenser's Lucifera, 366. Geneva Bible, gloss on Revelation 17:4, notes: her 'beautie onely standeth in outwarde pompe and. . .craft like a strumpet', and on verse 1 explains that Antichrist in this form intimates his capacity to 'seduce' souls, the common image used for his power. For the 'Antichrist-ian Empire', see also Napier, Sig. C3.

27. For Hull's increasing importance as a port, see Cross, and for its prominent role in the Civil War (enforcing Marvell's topicality here), see Davies, 132–3. For the Civil War allusions in this poem, see below.

28. Cf. n. 21, *supra*. The collusion between commerce and the Whore's seamen and riches is reflected in the Geneva Bible's glosses on her worldliness and rapacity, associated with her river the 'riche Euphrates' (Revelation 16:13 gloss); as with the similarly rich Ganges here. In *Blake*, as we saw, 'both Indies gold' was associated with antichristian power.

29. Joseph Mede, *The Key of the Revelation* (1643), II. 111, explicating Revelation 17:5. For Mede's influence, see Ch.1 above; like Marvell, Thomas Fairfax makes love an idolatry in 'Of a Faire Wife to Coregio', MS *Fairfax* 40, 565–6: 'Thy Idoll as thou make's of itt'. Women as agents/embodiments of Antichrist are indicated by George Smith, quoted in Whiting, 229; and Richard Bernard, *A Key of Knowledge. . .of St. John's mysticall Revelation* (1617), 179, 'carnal allurements to spiritual idolatrie, as women doe'.

30. For the interchangeability of 'Heart' and 'Soul' in this period, see Ch.7 below. The relevant text here is I Corinthians 14:24–5: 'the secrets of [each] heart made manifest' at the End. Cf. *Hebrews* iv. 12–13; quoted by Marvell, *Smirke*, 88.

31. For the type of Flood as antichristian nemesis of the End, see the context provided for the notion by Toon, 52; Matthew 24:27–39 is the relevant text. For the origional Flood as punishment for lust see Genesis 6:7–12; Chaucer, *Parson's Tale*, 836–9 (*Works*, ed. F. N. Robinson, second edn (London, 1957); Milton, *PR* II. 178–81.

32. *Carmina* V, 'To Lesbia', 7–10. For comment upon the Catullan 'Impossibles' in the *carpe diem* tradition, see Braden, *op. cit.*, and John Bernard Emperor, *The Catullan Influence in English Lyric Poetry, Circa 1600–1650* (New York, 1973).

33. Following T. S. Eliot's remark on this couplet in his essay on Marvell, *Selected Essays* (1951); more useful is his emphasis on Marvell as a poet of European Latin culture.

34. For the history of Time's iconography, see Erwin Panofsky, *Studies In Iconology: Humanistic Themes in the Art of the Renaissance* (1972), 'Father Time'.

35. For Apollo as Christ, see notes to *The Garden*, below: cf. *FQ* I. xii. 2.

36. *PL*, VI. 829–31; cf. VI. 711–12, III. 394; Ezekiel 1 and 10.; Mede, II. 102.

37. The 'second death': Revelation 2:11, 19:20, 20:14. Bacon *Advancement*, i. 360, similarly uses 'vastity' to signify desolation. Cf. also

Marlowe, *Dr Faustus* (*Complete Plays*, ed. J. B. Steane [Harmondsworth, 1969], V. ii. 181): 'no end is limited to damned souls'.

38. Cf. Bernard, *Rule*, 174: 'Fornication' describes sin and idolatry, 'by which the kingdome of heaven is shut'.

39. Revelation 18:8: she will be visited with 'death, and mourning, and. . .she shall be utterly burned, supplying the mourning and death and ashes here; the type in Isaiah 47:1–15 supplies the dust and nakedness and remembers her pride in her 'kingdoms' too. For his Spenserian motifs (366) of Lucifera the Whore, Hankins cites Isaiah that her 'secret parts' shall be discovered; as, indeed, in my discussion they are by the worms in Marvell's poem (for which the 'burning instead of beauty' is also relevant to the Mistress-Whore's fate in these lines).

40. Donne, 'Death's Duel' (Hayward edn, 748–9): he will beget the worm that 'shall feed. . .sweetly upon me'.

41. Bernard, *Rule*, 445; cf. *Apocalypse of Peter*, 509. The eschatological book of II Esdras is also relevant to the womb image here: 'In the grave the chambers of souls are like the womb of a woman' in that they give birth to souls if resurrected (4:41–2). Note also that in *Rape of Lucrece* rape is the 'mortal sting' of the serpent/worm/penis/devil (362–4).

42. *OED* A. II. 9; cf. 1b., "scheming" too.

43. Phineas Fletcher, *The Purple Island*, Co. I. xxvii.

44. Mede, II. 83, on Revelation 14:2–4; Mayer, 440.

45. Mede, II. 80, citing Psalm 40:2–3.

46. For comment on the biblical text, *see* Toon, 14.

47. Donne, 'Hymne to God My God in My Sicknesse', 25, uses this idea: let Christ 'my soul embrace'.

48. *FQ*, I. x. 42.

49. For the classical necrophiliac *topos* in Renaissance poetry, *see* Braden, 223; D. C. Allen, 'Love in a Grave', MLN 74 (1959), 485–6; *Emperor, 17*. They throw precious little light on Marvell's *denial* of the classical motif here.

50. Milton, 'Of Regeneration', *De Doctrina*, IV. 329. Cf. Marvell's similar ratification of the will in *Howe*, cit. in Ch.4 above.

51. Romans 7; *see* the Geneva Bible's copious glosses. Cf. Haller, 248.

52. For a summary of the variants, *see* Margoliouth, I. 253–4. Donno, *Complete Poems*, 234–5 also favours 'glue/dew', following *Eng. poet. d. 49* and *Bod. MS Don. b. 8.*, the other extant version of the poem. Cf. Kelliher, 'A New Text of Marvell's "To His Coy Mistress"', *N&Q* 17 (1970), 254–6. For 'transpire' as "sweat", see *OED* 1 and 2. For parallels to the notion of love's heat and flame, see *Villiers*, 69–70.

53. Crashaw, 'To the Name above every Name. . .', cit. by Donald M. Friedman, *Marvell's Pastoral Art* (1970), 197n., though he does not elaborate. Cf. Spenser, 'Hymne of Heavenly Love', 267–71, 281.

54. *See*, for example, Bernard, *Rule* 39; Browne, *Religio*, I. 32; Herbert, 'Employment (2)', 6–10. Bernard says that one must '*burne* with the desire of' Christ the Bridegroom.

55. For example, 'I sing of a maiden', *Medieval English Lyrics*, ed. R. T. Davies (1963), 155; Geneva Bible gloss on Psalm 72:6. This links with

Christ as Apollo in the poem, as in *FQ* I. v. 2.
56. See notes to Ch.7 below; cf. Daniel, Sonnet 24, on this *topos*.
57. Cf. the usage in Thomas Carew, 'To Celia, Upon Love's Ubiquity', ll. 7–8.
58. Francis Quarles, *Emblemes* (1696; repro. of 1653), Emblem XI, which covers the 'walk/way' motif in this connection. Cf. *Golding's Ovid*, 111, for the classical format.
59. Bernard, *Key*, 179.
60. Evelyn, *Miscellaneous Writings*, 524; *OED* 'Heel', II. 10, on the latter commonplace. Cf. *FQ* I. ix. 25–6.
61. For death the devourer (here conflated with time the devourer), *see* for example Spenser, the 'The Ruines of Time', 52; *PL.* X. 980–81, 985–6, 991; Herbert, 'Death'. For Time (as Saturn) the devourer, *see* Marlogiouth I. 254; Browne, *Religio*, I. 23, *Selected Writings*, 31; Starnes, 159.
62. Cf. also *May*, 91–4: 'The *Cerberus* and all his Jawes shall gnash. . .Thou. . . .the perpetual Vulture feel'. Cf. esp. Hieronymus Bosch's triptych, *The Garden of Earthly Delights*, right wing, in which Satan is a predatory bird devouring the damned. Cf. the comparison of Satan with 'ravenous fowl' in *PL* X. 267–9; and Ch. 8, below. Hence the witty revenge by 'Birds of prey' here. For Satan as devourer I Peter 5:8 is the most salient text in this period.
63. Shakespeare, *Sonnet* 146, 13.
64. For the textual problem *see* Donno, *Complete Poems*, 235n., who also notes the image's 'problematical basis. . .and [critics'] somewhat desperate search for signification'. *See* Bodleian MS. *Eng. poet.* d. 49, 20.
65. See *OED* on 'teeth' and on 'time' for listings of the commonplace.
66. For example, Shakespeare, *2 Henry IV*, IV. v. 30: 'his gates of breath'; cf. Milton, *Vacation Exercise*, 5. The teeth of Spenser's dragon are on the same model: cf. 'Presse not the two-leaved Rubie *Gates*,/Which fence their Pearl-Portcullis *grates*'; Edwrd Benlowes, 'To My Fancie upon Theophila', *Theophila: or, Love's Sacrifice. A divine poem* (1652). The full theological treatment of the body's sensory 'gates' is that of Chrysostom: *see* 'The Golden Book of St John Chrysostom', trans. John Evelyn, *Miscellaneous Writings*: esp. 116. Cf. *FQ* II. ix. 23–4, and its gloss in *Varorium*, 367; *The Letters of Abelard and Heliose*, trans. Betty Radice (Harmondsworth, 1974), 89.
67. Cf. the 'yron teeth' of Spenser's Blatant Beast, like the mouth of hell (*FQ*, VI. xii. 26).
68. For example, Chaucer, *Parson's Tale*, 856–7: the lustful kiss 'is the mouthe of helle'.
69. *FQ* I. xi. 12.
70. As in Bunyan's long allegory of the motif, *The Holy War*. Cf. n. 66, *supra*.
71. Romans 7:24; cf. e.g. Bernard on 'the prison of this mortalitie', *Rule*, 154. Hell as prison is figured, too; *see* note 72 below.
72. For example, *Gospel of Nicodemus*, 134; *Apocalypse of Peter*, 512; all such *loci* treat Hell as a prison with gates and bars of iron, broken by Christ. The OT type of the Harrowing of Hell, Isaiah 40:1–2, says: 'I will

break in pieces the gates of brass, and cut in sunder the bars of iron' (2). For the 'mouth of death' as antichristian 'thraldome' of hell's 'euer dying paine', *see* Spenser, 'Hymme of Heavenly Love', 120–6; for Harrowing the prison cf. also Milton, *PL* X. 185–8. 'The seuen fold yron gates of grislie Hell' poets can Harrow, like Christ, emancipating souls: Spenser, 'Ruines of Time', 372ff. cf. *PL* II. 645–7. Sin itself is 'a continuall prison. . .fore-feeling the aproch of Hell' (Beard, 538); cf. also Whiting, 234. Cf. the same ironic premonition in the antichristian thraldom of Marvell's nunnery: 'The Walls. . .These Bars. . ./The Cloyster outward shuts its *Gates,*/And, from us, locks on them the *Grates*' (*Appleton House*, XIII). In hell sinners 'are confined as in a prison till the end of the world': Robert Burton, *The Anatomy of Melancholy* [1621], ed. Holbrook Jackson (1972), I. 196 (citing also Augustine). Pictorial representations emphasized this: cf. those in T. S. R. Boase, *Death in the Middle Ages* (1972). The relevant text is Psalm 24:7: 'Lift up your heads, O ye *gates*'.

73. Masculine and feminine properties are noted also by Malekin, 25, 143. Margoliouth, I. 254, sees a pomander, but Donno, *Complete Poems*, 235, is more helpful in noting that a 'Ball' signifies 'concentration of properties'. Friedman, 186, rightly felt that it was a cannonball. The reference to Samson's riddle is noted by Berthoff, *Resolved Soul*, 114, without elaboration. For Samson as type, *see* Temple, 14; and Milton, ed. Carey, 334n.

74. Donne, *Sermons*, ed. G. R. Potter and E. M. Simpson (Berkeley, 1959), no. 10 (1622), 272. Cf. *Rape of Lucrece*, 595, in which the hardened heart is 'an iron gate'.

75. For the gates and mouth of grave and hell, *see* esp. Donne, 'Death's Duel', 739; Psalm 107; hell as the prison present in the body, Beard, 538; Fletcher, xv–vi; *see also* on the literal gates of death, William Day, '*An Exposition of the Book of the Prophet Isaiah*' (1654), 139.

76. *See*, for example, *FQ* I. v. 20; Revelation 9:9. Examples are numerous.

77. Donno notes that the phrase was proverbial, in notes to *Complete Poems*; cf. Starnes, 358.

78. Donne, 'Death's Duel', 740 and 752. Cf. Bernard, *Rule*, 154: Christ will open the gates of heaven if 'we deserve to be freed from the prison of this mortalitie, and attain to the gate of our heavenly countrie'.

79. See note 66 *supra*, on Benlowes: Marvell similarly conflates the 'portcullis' sense of 'grates' with these teeth, in his image of siege here. For hell's portcullis, see *PL*. II. 874. The gates/grates of the hellish mouth further intimate that the Beast itself is 'the city [or stronghold] of the wicked' (Augustine: *see* Toon, 16), contrasting with heaven's stronghold.

80. Browne, *A Letter to a Friend*, ed. Keynes, 110, recalling Matthew 11:12. Heaven is difficult of access, 'strait': *see* Christopher Blackwood, *Expositions and Sermons. Upon. . .Matthew* (1659), 533–4. Effectively, the 'violence' involved is death (Bernard, *Rule*, 33), but prayer could anticipate: hence the 'cannonball' of Marvell's lovers, for prayer is 'Christianorum bombarda, the Christian artillery. . .whereby heaven is said to suffer violence, and by a kind of battery to be taken by force' and the 'fire within' or exploding powder (cf. Marvell's 'Instant Fires'): Charles

Herle, *David's Song of Three Parts* (1643), 15. Saints are 'mighty through God to the pulling down of strongholds' (II Corinthians 10:3–4), whether heaven's or hell's. For the sexual image of invasion that supplies the conventional level here, *see*, for example, *Rape of Lucrece*, 469.

81. For example, Francis Quarles, *Hosanna* (1647), sig. C3; Herbert, 'To All Angels and Saints', 14; 'Ungratefulnesse', 7–12. Red must be the colour of this jewel, for it is the liturgical allusion to His saving blood.

82. Cf. *Dew*; Browne, *Religio*, I. 9.

83. *Ibid.*, II. 6.

84. Margoliouth, I. 253, summarizes the reasoning involved. The controversy between E. E. Duncan-Jones (*TLS* 5 Dec. 1958) and Roger Sharrock (*TLS* 31 Oct. 1958; 16 Jan. 1959) is really a matter of how Flood and Conversion relate. In fact, the relation is Marvell's version of the popular contemporary analogy between the Noachian Age and the Latter Days (for which, *see* Ball, 19, 43): the Flood is analogous to the Deluge. So, in fact, Marvell's lover allows very little time to his *Mistress*, which should not surprise us. For 1656 as the projected date of the Conversion of the Jews, *see*, for example, Toon, 71, and Keith Thomas, *Religion and the Decline of Magic* (Harmondsworth, 1973), 167–8.

85. As, for instance, does Colin Clout in Spenser's *Calender*.

86. Spenser again makes evident the Christlike features of Shepherds as 'The Good Shepherd', of course.

87. The Pastoral dialogues, *Clorinda and Damon*, etc.

88. Cf. *Damon the Mower*, 88: 'Death thou art a Mower too'. For Christ the Desolating Mower—the last one—*see* esp. Mede's comment on Revelation 14:14, who emphasizes that the reaper here is Christ (II. 102); *Geneva Bible* (1599) states on this text that the harvest is the Latter Day desolation, evoked 'by reason of the rage of that sickle which Antichrist calleth for'.

89. Most critics have recognized a 'fall' of some sort here. *See*, for example, Roth, 279. Cf. also the 'Grasses fall' in *The Mower to the Glowworms* (II), and the reference to the Fall in the first couplet of *The Mower Against Gardens*.

90. Thomas Browne, *The Garden of Cyrus*, Dedicatory Epistle, *Selected Writings*, ed. Keynes, 161.

91. 'She my Mind hath so displac'd/That I shall never find my home' (IV). For the sense of 'home' as heaven, cf. Herbert's poem, 'Home'.

92. Cf. also I–IV of Damon (an "internal" version of the Latter Day *desolatio*), and esp. line 20: she 'burns the Fields and Mower both'. Cf. *The Mower to the Glowworms*, 'She my Mind hath so displac'd' (IV). Both in *Mower's Song* and *Damon*, the mental disorder caused by Juliana also involves the loss of spiritual hope: *Mower's Song* (I); *Damon* (I), 'wither'd like his Hopes the Grass'.

93. *See*, for instance, V. de Sola Pinto and A. E. Rodway (eds.), *The Common Muse* Harmondsworth, n.d.), for example, nos. 99 and 100, both from the sixteenth century; Ralegh, 'The Advice', 16–19. See *The Penguin Dictionary of Historical Slang*, 596—this meaning seems to have slipped the net of the *OED*.

94. George Herbert, 'Home', 55–8. That the Revelation harvest is at once a desolation for revenge/vengeance (like the Mower's here), and also a renovatory exercise, Mede, II. 99 makes clear: 'The name of *Harvest* comprehendeth three things: the cutting downe of corne, the gathering it, and the threshing it. Whence it cometh to passe that it frameth a two-fold parable in holy Writ, and of contrary sense; one while of slaughter and destruction, as it were of cutting downe and threshing; another while of restoring and safetie, according to the property of gathering'. The motif *desolatio et renovatio* thus conflates the two. Cf. Mede, II. 102.

95. Cf. *The Mower Against Gardens* 1–2.

96. Walzer, 243.

97. For a survey of critics' myriad responses to *The Garden, see*, for example, Pierre Legouis, 'Marvell and the New Critics', *RES* n.s. III. 32 (1957), 382–9; Bruce King, 'In Search of Andrew Marvell', *REL* VIII. (1967), 31–41. It is a vexed subject.

98. II Timothy 4:7–8.

99. Isaiah 40:3.

100. *Ibid.*

101. See *OED*, 2; cf. I. c.

102. Browne, *Religio*, II. 9, 79.

103. *Geneva Bible* (1599), glossing I Corinthians 15:38ff., which is the Pauline *locus*.

104. *Ibid.*, commenting on verse 51ff.

105. For example, Milton, 'Of regeneration', *DDC*, Bohn edn, IV. 18. 330; citing resurrection, 331.

106. For example, Milton, *Nativity Ode*, st. 8; Marvell, *Clorinda and Damon*, 20f; Starnes, 358–9. (Cf. Friedman on Pan, 4.) Christ is Apollo, esp. as the Sun. Cf. Christine Rees, 'The Metamorphosis of Daphne in Sixteenth- and Seventeenth-Century English Poetry', *MLR* 66 (1971), 251–63, 251.

107. Rees, 251, 263.

108. Starnes, 177–81, 432n; cf. Mirelli Levi D'Ancona, *The Garden of the Renaissance: Botanical Symbolism in Italian Painting* (Florence, 1977), 201–2.

109. Cf. Herbert, 'Love (3)'; Donne *Sermons*, VII. 302–3; Revelation 19:9.

110. William Day, 6, glossing Isaiah 7:8.

111. Milton, *De Doctrina*, Bohn edn, IV. 18. 327–8: 'The intent of SUPERNATURAL RENOVATION is. . .to create afresh, as it were, the inward man, and infuse from above new and supernatural faculties into the minds of the renovated. . .the regenerate are said to be PLANTED IN CHRIST'.

112. Sir John Eliot, quoted in Hill, *The Century of Revolution, 1603–1714* (1974), 89.

113. *See*, for example, Margoliouth, I. 268. Cf. the sea as an emblem of 'fertile. . .generation', Spenser, *FQ*. IV. xii. 1–2. At the End all creatures are 'renewed': Thomas Goodwin, 'Brief History', 217.

114. Adams, *Spiritual Navigator*, 3; Revelation 4:6.

115. Bacon, *Advancement*, 206.

116. Herbert, 'Man'. At the Day of Judgment, Browne, *Religio*, I. 50.
117. Collier, 390: 'an internal and spiritual change' analogous to that of the world. Cf. Milton, *DDC*, Bohn edn, IV. 329. Cf. Thomas Goodwin, 'The Trial of the Christian's Growth', *Works*, III. 466, on 'spiritual ravishment'.
118. Sidney, *A Defence of Poetry*, ed. Jan van Dorsten (Oxford, 1966), 23–4.
119. Geneva Bible on Revelation 15:2, the Sea of Glass 'containing the treasurie of the judgements of God' in history.
120. *See* Steward, *Enclosed Garden*, for the extensive background to this idea.
121. Browne, *Religio*, I. 45, 52.
122. *Ibid.*
123. *See* the Pauline metaphor for the Ingathering of the Nations, Romans 11: cf. Ball, Ch. 1 and, esp., Ch. 19.
124. *Ibid.*
125. Jeremy Taylor, 41.
126. Geneva Bible (1599) gloss on Romans 7:25.
127. Cf. *Blake*, 19; Sibbes, *Light from Heaven*, title; Milton, *PR*. IV. 288–90; 'Of Man's Renovation', *DDC*, Bohn edn, IV. 17. 323.
128. Augustine, *City of God*, XI. 7. 437.
129. *Ibid.*
130. Marvell, *GP*, 309.
131. For example, George Chapman, *Chapman's Homer*, ed. Allardyce Nicoll (1967), 2 vols., II. xi. 278: death is 'when. . .the soule assumes her flight'.
132. Thomas Browne, *Certain Miscellany Tracts* (1684), Tract IV, Item 2: citing Ovid.
133. Marvell remembers the exordium of *PL*. I. Joseph Wittreich, 'Perplexing the Explanation', *Approaches to Marvell*, ed. Patrides, 280–305, cites a comparison between the two poems here, to a different end. For the Bird of Paradise in *On Mr Milton*, cf. Margoliouth, I. 337.
134. For both 'sanctification' and the seventh age, *see* Augustine, *City of God*, XI. 31. 465–6. (He also discusses 6 as the number of Creation.) Cf. Thomas Goodwin, 'Brief History', 213, on the ubiquitous number 7 in Revelation.
135. For example, Horace, *Odes* II. 20. i.
136. Starnes, 24.
137. Isaiah 49:10; Revelation 22:1; cf. Milton, *De Doctrina*, Bohn edn, IV. 18. 328, and *Ephesians* v. 26: 'cleanse. . .with the washing of water by the Word'. Thus the 'water of the *Word*' and the light of *revelation* are similar. On the baptismal implication of this process, *see* Geneva Bible (1599) gloss on I Corinthians 15:29.
138. Revelation 22:2, 'the tree of life' is by the 'river of the water of life' (as here). For the 'fruits' *see* Matthew 7:15–19 (quoted by Marvell at the opening of *Defence of Howe*).
139. Matthew, 7:33; Romans 7:4.
140. Cf. *Dew*, the soul 'recollecting its own Light' and 'receiving in the Day' (24, 30); cf. 'the *fountain* of light', Milton, *PR*. IV. 289; for the

doctrine, *De Doctrina*, Bohn edn, IV. 30. 447.

141. Milton, *De Doctrina*, Bohn edn, IV. 18, 328, citing John 3:3–5.

142. Milton, *De Doctrina*, Bohn edn, IV. 17. 323.

143. Aubrey, II. 54.

144. Mede, II. 82, citing 'all things are become new', II Corinthians 5:17.

145. See *Coy Mistress*, Ch.6.i, above.

146. Whittick, 212–3; George Ferguson, *Signs and Symbols in Christian Art* (1976), 12; *Chapman's Homer*, II. ix, 'Dedication' (32); *Golding's Ovid*, 'To the Reader', 18.

147. Pierre Legouis, 'Marvell's Grasshoppers', *N&Q* n.s. V. 3 (1958), 108–9, 109n., suggested the pun.

148. *OED* records all of these meanings for 'Compute'.

149. For such eternal 'glorie' is laid up: Geneva Bible (1599), gloss on I Corinthians 15:58. Cf. Vaughan's 'The Bee' as God's indefatigable servant (79–82).

150. *Georgics*, IV; Marvell, *Loyall Scot*, 266–73; Henry Hawkins, *Partheneia Sacra (1633)*, (Menston, 1971), 72 (cf. 74–5); for the political crisis, Wilkins, 78; John Daye, *The Parliament of Bees...Being an Allegorical Description of the actions of good and bad men in these our daies* (1641); Gerald de Malynes, *The Commonwealth of Bees* (1655); Samuel Purchas (the Younger), *A Theatre of Politicall Flying-Insects* (1657); cf. Charles Butler, *The Feminine Monarchie: or, a Treatise Concerning Bees, and the due Ordering of them* (Oxford, 1609), and Edmund Southerne, *A Treatise Concerning the Right Use and Ordering of Bees* (1593). The monarchical implications of the bee may be relevant to Marvell's national 'garden' here, given his views. In *Georgics* II. 248–50 bees provide an *exemplum* for rebuilding the state after the Roman Civil War.

151. That bees imply monarchy may also have covert implications for Marvell.

152. Hawkins, 71.

153. Thomas Goodwin, 'The Trial', 438–9; Augustine, *City of God*, XII. 26. 505. Cf. Hebrews 6:7; the activist *moralitas* is drawn by the Geneva Bible (1599) gloss on verse 12.

154. Cf Marvell's *Hortus*, 56 'thymo'; and Virgil, *Eclogue* V. 77: 'dumque thymo pascentur apes'.

155. For the horologue, *see* K. J. Höltgen, 'Floral Horologues prior to Marvell's Garden', *N&Q* n.s. XVI. 10 (1969), 381–2. Cf. Marvell on the heliotrope, *General Councils*, 131.

156. Cf. *Ingelo*, cit. *supra*.

157. Augustine, *Epistle* 137, 23–4. Cf. Herbert, 'Praise(I)', where they 'Sting my delay' (17–20); and 'Providence', 65–8, on bees as an example of the providential order.

158. For example, Milton, *PL*. VII. 489–93; cf. Carey and Fowler, 804n.

159. Daniel Rogers, quoted in Haller, 'Puritan Love', 246–7.

160. *Ibid.*, 245–6; cf. Walzer on marriage and political order, Ch.5.iii.

161. Quoted in Haller, 'Puritan Love', 246.

162. Quarles, *Hosanna*, D2ᵛ–D3.

163. Quarles, *Hosanna*, 'Buried in a Garden', 12–14.

164. Sidney, *Defence*, 24. For this 'Zodiack' as also time (like its flowers of mortality), cf. Shakespeare, *Measure for Measure*, I. ii. 178.
165. Milton, *Vacation Exercise*, 29–30; cf. 33–5. Cf. Spenser, 'Hymne of Heavenly Beautie', st. IV: 'Of the soare faulcon so I learne to fly,/That flags awhile her fluttering wings beneath,/Till she her selfe for *stronger flight* can breath'.
166. Such datings link it with *Appleton House*, in the early 1650s.
167. Song of Solomon, 8:13, and its gloss in the Geneva Bible (1599).

7: A Revelation Revealed

1. Summers, *Selected Poems*, 15.
2. Peter T. Schwenger, 'Marvell's "Unfortunate Lover" as Device', *MLQ* 35 (1974), 364–75, 364; James Reeves and Martin Seymour-Smith, in their selected edition of Marvell's poems, find it 'strange. . .[and] obscure' (166); Maren-Sophie Røstvig, '"In Ordine di Ruota"', 250, remarks its 'riddling quality'.
3. Donno, *Complete Poems*, 229; Bradbrook and Lloyd-Thomas, 29; Schwenger takes the lover to be homosexual and thus frustrated by a 'forbidden' love, 370, and finds that the poem 'fuses both emblematic and armorial elements' (364). Anne E. Berthoff, 'The Voice of Allegory: Marvell's "The Unfortunate Lover"', *MLQ* 27 (1966), 41–50, 42, suggests that 'The poem is a continued metaphor by which is figured the necessary suffering of the time-bound soul, the lover in his world of sacrifice'; she, too, finds it 'emblematic' (42). Røstvig, '"In Ordine"',245, says that the poem is about 'the irresistible power of love.'
4. Hunt, 62–3.
5. Schwenger,368; cf. n.3, *supra*.
6. E.g. Colie, *My Ecchoing Song* (Princeton, NJ, 1970) is the most thoroughgoing in that approach; for her cfs. to Otto Van Veen's, Herman Hugo's and Quarles' Emblems, *see* esp. 110–12. Cf. also Friedman, 41; Donno, *Complete Poems*, 229; Røstvig, '"In Ordine"', compares Marvell's poem with Giordano Bruno's "emblematic" sonnet-sequence, *Heroic Frenzies*, as a lover's "biography".
7. Reported by Bradbrook and Lloyd-Thomas, 29n.; Legouis, 32n., dismisses this interpretation and states that Syfret herself had abandoned it.
8. Annabel Patterson, *Marvell and the Civic Crown*, 20–5.
9. Margoliouth, I. 256, and Donno, *Complete Poems*, 229, concur in dating the poem by means of a reference in line 57 to Lovelace's 'Dialogue—Lucasta, Alexis', which appeared in the volume to which Marvell contributed his commendatory verses.
10. E. E. Duncan-Jones, 'A Reading of Marvell's "The Unfortunate Lover"', *I. A. Richards: Essays in His Honour*, ed. Reuben Brower, Helen Vendler and John Hollander (New York, 1973), 213–26, 225.
11. Reeves and Seymour-Smith, *Selected Poems*, 166, remark that it was 'probably written for an exclusive literary group' because of its enigmatic assurance.
12. Cf Ch.1 above. For Marvell's courtly circle at this time, cf. Burdon, 17–18; Kelliher, 32–4.

13. Cf. n. 9, *supra*.

14. Schwenger, 373, citing and rejecting such derogation, for different reasons.

15. Apart from Marvell's references to masque-techniques in *Appleton House*, which imply some familiarity with masques on his part, Marvell moved in a circle with access to the Inns (cf. n. 12, *supra*), where masques were sometimes performed. In *May*, 37–8, he alludes to an incident which took place at a masque at the Inns of Court (1633/4), when May was assaulted by the Lord Chamberlain. For an account of the incident, *see* Margoliouth, I. 305.

16. Beard, 4, notes that 'they are set aloft as it were upon a stage, to be gazed at of euery commer', Cf. Orgel, *Illusion*, 42–3.

17. Orgel and Strong, 7, 52.

18. Orgel, *Illusion*, 77–9.

19. *Ibid.*, 79.

20. *Ibid.*, 38.

21. *Ibid.*, 40, *et passim*.

22. *Ibid.*, 88; Thomas, 'Two Cultures?', 175, 182.

23. Orgel, *Illusion*, 44–5; cf. Thomas' account of the Prynne controversy, 'Two Cultures?', 177f. More detailed discussion of the complex of Puritan attitudes is given in Sasek, *op. cit.*

24. Thomas, 'Two Cultures?', 175.

25. *Ibid.*, 185.

26. Orgel, *Illusion*, 44.

27. *Ibid.*, 80.

28. *Ibid.*, 40, 43: they were 'ideals made apprehensible'.

29. *Ibid.*, 79–83.

30. It is pertinent to note, there, that Orgel (*ibid.*, 42) observes that the Renaissance's theatrical metaphor for princes included 'the notion of the ruler as an exemplary figure'.

31. Colie, *Ecchoing Song*, 110.

32. Orgel, *Illusion*, 24–5: 'the verbal was inseparable from the visual' in the masques.

33. *Ibid.*, 43.

34. Duncan-Jones, 'A Reading', 224; Hunt, 62, finds it 'grotesque and hilarious'; Legouis, *Andrew Marvell*, 32, says 'Raillery, if it exists, is tinged with sympathy, and we even think that sympathy predominates', despite the 'grotesque verve' of the poem.

35. Orgel, *Illusion*, 72–3.

36. Orgel and Strong, 52.

37. *Ibid.*, 54.

38. *Ibid.*, 54–6.

39. *Love's Triumph Through Callipolis* (1631), Ben Jonson and Inigo Jones, repro. in Orgel and Strong, 405–7; 11. 99–101 (406).

40. *Love's Triumph*, 11. 30–3.

41. *Ibid.*, 11. 34–43.

42. *Ibid.*, 1. 92; editors' comment, 407; and cf. 54.

43. Orgel and Strong, 56.

44. Cf. Orgel and Strong's account of sea-imagery in the masques, 54.
45. By Davenant and Inigo Jones, repro. in Orgel and Strong, 730–4.
46. Cf. the comments of Orgel and Strong, 72.
47. Orgel, *Illusion*, 21.
48. Orgel and Strong, 73.
49. *Salmacida*, 11. 22–68.
50. *Ibid.*, 11. 107–10.
51. *Ibid.*, 11. 1–4.
52. *Ibid.*, 11. 132–41: 'How am I grieved the world should everywhere/Be vexed into a Storm, save only here!/Thou over-lucky, too-much-happy isle,/. . .thy long health can never altered be/But by thy surfeits on felicity./And I to stir the humours that increase/In thy full body, overgrown with peace,/Will call those Furies hither who incense/The guilty and disorder innocence.
53. *Ibid.*, 11. 8, 13–15.
54. *Ibid.*, 11. 18–21.
55. Cf. Orgel and Strong, 72.
56. *Salmacida*, Entry 16, Entry 14 (732).
57. The allusion is explained in *Salmacida*, 71–110.
58. Margoliouth, 1. 256.
59. Patterson, *Marvell and the Civil Crown*, 24–5.
60. *RT*, Grosart, II. 398.
61. Cf. Milton, *PL.* i. 515–16, iii. 562: and the notes thereon in Carey and Fowler.
62. Berthoff, 42–3, noted this; cf. *OED*, 1b.
63. *Salmacida*, 439–48.
64. Orgel, *Illusion*, 49–51, discusses the development of the relationship between masque and antimasque in this period, and its use of pastoral elements. Cf. also Ronald Bayne, 'Masque and Pastoral', *The Cambridge History of English Literature*, ed. A. W. Ward and A. R. Waller (Cambridge, 1950), VI. 328–72.
65. *Ibid.*, 39–40.
66. *Ibid.*, 54–5, 71.
67. *Ibid.*, 71.
68. An example of such poetry is Wyatt's 'The Lover Compareth his State To A Ship in Perilous Storm Tossed on the Sea'; Surrey 'Complaint of the Absence of her Lover, being upon the Sea'. Cf. Shakespeare, Sonnet CXVI, 6.
69. Cf. also Lord Bridgman's speech (as reported in *GP*, 268) on the threat of war as 'clouds' and 'storm'; also cf. Dryden's *Astraea Redux*, in which the political turbulence of the Civil War and rebellion is conveyed in the images of wind, storm, and tempestuous seas, and where again waters symbolize the state. Halifax, 63, uses the imagery of the 'winds' of unrest, harnessed to the Ship of State motif.
70. Beard, 4–5.
71. As Orgel and Strong note, 71, ship-money was one of the topical issues that preoccupy the masques.
72. For example, Berthoff, 'Voice', 47.

73. Margoliouth, I. 255.
74. Schwenger, 368.
75. Cf. Margoliouth, I. 255. *Salmacida* is a fine example of such imagery, in fact.
76. Thus Schwenger states this motif as the complete meaning of the lines, 371.
77. Cf. Marvell's use of the image in *Bermudas*, Ch.6. iii, above. For an account of the sea as a metaphor for Fortune and Providence, *see* Williams, 'Spenser: Some uses', 136–7. Cf. Orgel and Strong, 71.
78. Williams, 'Some Uses', 138.
79. *Ibid.*, 136; Orgel and Strong, 71f.
80. Milton, *De Doctrina*, IV. 449; cf. Luke 21:25–6. Cf. Jeremy Taylor, 279: 'The thunders of the dying and groaning heavens, and the crack of the dissolving world, when the whole fabrick of nature shall shake into dissolution and eternal ashes.'
81. Schwenger, 371.
82. Cf. also Herle, *David's Song*, 3.
83. Cf. also Marvell's 'jarring Elements' of war and desolation in *Blake* (35); discussed in Ch.6. iii, above; Cf. Donne's *First Anniversary*, where 'Both Elements and passions liv'd at peace/In her, who caus'd all Civill war to cease' (321–2].
84. For their identification in this period, see *OED*, 6A.
85. *OED*, 2 (fig.).
86. Adams, *Spiritual Navigator*, 15. Cf. Bernard Gilpin, *Antichrists of the Reformation* (1552), repro. in Chandos, who says that the oppressors of the faithful poor are 'couetous cormorants' (33). And cf. n. 90, below.
87. See *RT*, 187; *Smirke*, 72, 77; *Last Instructions*, 489'-90.
88. *A Medicine for Malignancy* (1644), quoted in Whiting, 235.
89. Compare with the ideas in these stanzas also Nixon, *Christian Navy*, where in the Sea of the World the 'Rock' of *pride* (cf. absolutism) causes 'wrecks', and is especially dangerous to princes (A4v.–B). And on this Rock are (cf. Marvell's Cormorants) 'Most lothsome fowles that haue no other foode,/But feede vpon the fame of euery man' (sig. C2v.): Nixon makes them images of antichristian detractors (sig. C2v.-3). He also allegorizes a 'wofull rocke' of heresy. Cf. also Noodt, *Theatre for Worldlings*, Spenserian verses, *Minor Poems*, I. 503, where he comments upon Revelation 19:17–18: that it is prophesied for the Latter Days that 'birdes from air descending downe on earth/Should warre vpon the kings, and eate their flesh.' All these uses of the motif originate, like Marvell's in Revelation 19:17–18.
90. For the 'consciences' episode, and its bearing on Strafford's fate, *see* Hibbert, *Charles I*, pp. 155–6.
91. For the clash between Williams and Laud, *see*, for example, Claire Cross, *Church and People*, 178. On Fairfax's acrimony, *see* Margoliouth, I. 285.
92. Røstvig, '"In Ordine"', 249.
93. Cf. n. 84, *supra*.
94. See e.g. Whittick, *Symbols*; Ferguson, *Signs and Symbols*.

95. *See* Stocker, 'Poet of the Latter Days', Ch.4.i. For a positive version of the pelican-ministry image, see *Death O.C.*, 80, where Cromwell outdoes 'bleeding Pelicans' by his care of the state.

96. Cf. Sibbes, *Bride*, 64: where 'birds of prey' attack Christ the 'Turtle-Dove', being those antichristian enemies who 'beare a speciall and implacable malice against Gods Church and Children', drawing the 'heart-blood' of Christianity by their usurpation of it. The idea is very similar to Marvell's, especially as Sibbes mentions also the Church 'as a ship in the midst of the waves'.

97. Purchas, 'Virginia's Verger', 236: describing dissensions in the community there.

98. Cf., for example, Samuel Daniel's Sonnet 27, 'Th'Ocean of my teares must drowne me burning'.

99. Margoliouth, I. 48.

100. Røstvig, '"In Ordine"', 250, noticed the pun.

101. Revelation 19:13; cf. Noodt, Spenser, *Minor Poems*, I. 503: 'His precious robe I saw embrued with bloud', a verse paraphrase of this Revelation text.

102. Temple, 4.

103. Crutwell, 188–9.

104. *See* Hunt, 196n.

105. Milton, *Eikonoklastes*, Bohn edn, I. 313.

106. *Ibid.*, I. 312.

107. Orgel and Strong, 75.

108. *See*, for example, Crutwell,188.

109. For example, *Declaration of the Army in Scotland*, Woodhouse, 477.

110. For examples of different interpretations of the last stanza, *see*, for example, N. A. Salerno, 'Marvell's "The Unfortunate Lover"', *Explicator* 18 (1960), Item 42; and J. M. Patrick, 'Marvell's "The Unfortunate Lover"', *Explicator* 20 (1962), Item 65. Røstvig, '"In Ordine"', 249, concludes that 'All we can say is that the heraldic image. . .must be climactic and triumphant'. Colie, *Ecchoing Song*, 113, and Toliver, 166–7, take refuge in impressionism. Berthoff, 'Voice', 45, says that the lover is 'dying into art'; Schwenger, 364, remarks 'the puzzling quality of this crucial summation'.

111. This quotaton was noticed by Duncan-Jones, 'A Reading', 224n., who does not elaborate.

112. Cf. the Geneva Bible (1599) version: 'he. . .fighteth righteously'.

113. Duncan-Jones, 'A Reading', 222, records this occasion in relation to the poem, but comes to a different conclusion.

114. Margoliouth, I. 256.

115. Geneva Bible (1599) gloss on II Kings 23:29. Cf. II Chronicles 35:20–5.

116. II Kings 22:1–2. The Geneva Bible (1599) comments: 'beeing but eight yeare old, he sought the God of his father Dauid'. Thus his youth and his orphaned state are "associated" with his piety.

117. II Chronicles 35:25, and the Geneva bible (1599) gloss on verse 24.

118. Cf. Margoliouth, I. 256.

119. Chapman, *Hero and Leander*, VI. 287–91; where a similar elevation is accorded to these lovers, as 'the first that ever poet sung' (293).
120. This pendant is illustrated in the frontispiece to Christopher Hibbert's *Charles I*. The mixture of ideas and images in this stanza might have been prompted by Bacon's essay 'Of Adversity', in which he notes that 'it is more pleasing to have a *lively work upon a sad and solemn ground*. . .Certainly *virtue is like precious odours*, most fragrant when they are incensed or crushed: for prosperity doth best discover vice; but adversity doth best discover virtue'. He touches there also upon 'Christian resolution, that saileth in the frail bark of the flesh through the waves of the world'. (Francis Bacon, *Essays*, ed. Michael J. Hawkins [1972], 16, 15).

Bibliography

All books are published in London unless otherwise specified.

(1) PRIMARY SOURCES

Abelard, Peter, *The letters of Abelard and Heloise*, transl. Betty Radice (Harmondsworth, 1974)

Adams, Thomas, *The Blacke Devill* . . . *The Wolfe worrying the Lambes and the Spiritual Navigator Bound for the Holy Land* (1615)

——*Heaven-Gate; or, The Passage to Paradise*, repr. in *Works*, Nichol's Series of Standard Divines, Puritan Period (Edinburgh, 1982), III. 74–84

Anon., *A Discovery of the Great Fantasie* . . . *Together with a Discovery of the great Arch-Whore, and her Paramours or Lovers* (1642), *Thomason Tracts*, E.124 (28)

Anon., *An Honest Discourse between Three Neighbours, Touching the Present Government in these Three Nations* (1655)

Aubrey, John, *Brief Lives*, ed. Andrew Clark, 2. vols. (Oxford, 1898)

Augustine, St., *The City of God*, ed. and transl. D. Knowles & H. Bettenson (Harmondsworth, 1972)

——*The Confessions*, transl. E. B. Pusey (1907)

——*Letters*, transl. Sister Wilfrid Parsons, 5 vols., Fathers of the Church (New York, 1951–5)

——*Selected Letters*, Loeb edn. (1953)

Bacon, Francis, *The Advancement of Learning*, ed. G. W. Kitchin (1915)

——*Essays*, ed. M. J. Hawkins (1972)

——*New Atlantis*, in *Works*, ed. James Spedding, R. L. Ellis & D. D. Heath, 14 vols. (1857–74), III.129–66

Beard, Thomas, *The Theatre of God's Judgements*, third, rev. edn. (1631)

Benlowes, Edward, *Theophila: or, Love's Sacrifice* (1652)

Bernard, St., *A Rule of Good Life (1633)*, repr. in facsim. (Menston, 1971)

Bernard, Richard, *A Key of Knowledge . . . of St. John's mysticall Revellation* (1617)

Bettenson, Henry, (ed.), *The Early Christian Fathers* (Oxford 1969)

Bible: *Authorized version (1611)* (Oxford, n.d.)

——*Geneva Bible (1560)*, repr., in facsim. (1969)

——*Geneva Bible* (1599)

——*Vulgate Bible* (Cologne, 1638)

——*Apocrypha* (Cambridge, n.d.)

——*The Apocryphal New Testament*, transl. and ed. M. R. James (1975)

Blackwood, Christopher, *Expositions and Sermons upon . . . Matthew* (1659)

Brightman, Thomas, *A Revelation of the Revelation* (1615)

——*A Commentary on the Canticles* (Amsterdam, 1644)

Brocardo, G., *The Reuelation on S.Iohn Reueled* (1582)

Broughton, Hugh, *A Revelation of the Holy Apocalyps* (1610)

Browne, Thomas, *Selected Writings*, ed. Geoffrey Keyneş (1970)

——*Pseudodoxia Epidemica*, ed. Simon Wilkins, 2 vols. (1894)

——*Certain Miscellany Tracts* (1684)

Bunyan, John, *The Pilgrim's Progress & The Holy War* (n.d.)

Burnet, Thomas, *The Sacred Theory of the Earth*, ed. Basil Willey (1965)

Burroughs, Jeremiah, *Four Books on the Eleventh of Matthew* (1658)

Burton, Henry, *The Seven Vials; Or, a briefe and plaine Exposition . . .* (1628)

Burton, Robert, *The Anatomy of melancholy*, ed. Holbrook Jackson (1972)

Butler, Charles, *The Feminine Monarchie: or, A Treatise Concerning Bees, and the due Ordering of them* (Oxford, 1609)

Chase, Thomas, *Spiritual Whoredom Discovered in a Sermon before the House of Commons* (1647)

Chandos, John (ed.), *In God's Name: Examples of Preaching in England 1534–1662* (1971)

Chapman, George, *Chapman's Homer*, ed. Allardyce Nicholl, 2 vols. (1967)

Chaucer, Geoffrey, *Works*, ed. F. N. Robinson, 2nd edn. (1957)

Cheynell, Francis, *Sion's Memento, and God's Alarum* (1643), repr. in facsim. in *The English Revolution, I: Fast Sermons to Parliament*, ed. R. Jeffs, 34 vols. (1970–71) vol. VI.

Cowley, Abraham, *Essays, Plays & Sundry Verses* ed. A. R. Waller (1906)

————*The Civil War*, ed. Allan Pritchard (Toronto, 1973)

Crashaw, Richard, *The Complete Poetry*, ed. G. W. Williams (New York, 1970)

Daniel, Samuel, *Poems & A Defence of Rhyme*, ed. A. C. Sprague (Chicago, 1962)

Dante, *The Divine Comedy*, transl. & ed. D. L. Sayers, 3 vols. (Harmondsworth, 1949).

Davies, R. T. (ed.), *Medieval English Lyrics* (1963)

Day, William, *An Exposition of the Book of the Prophet Isaiah* (1654)

Daye, John, *The Parliament of Bees . . . Being an allegorical description of the actions of good & bad men in these our daies* (1641)

Donne, John, *Complete Poetry & Selected Prose*, ed. John Hayward (1903)

Elyot, Thomas, *The Book Named the Governor*, ed. S. E. Lehmberg (1962)

Evelyn, John, *The History of Religion, A rational account of the true religion*, 2 vols. (1850)

————*Miscellaneous Writings* (n.d.; probably 18th.C.)

————*Silva* (n.d.)

————*Terra: A Philosophical Discourse of Earth* (York, 1787)

Fairfax, Edward, *Godfrey of Bulloigne: a translation of Tasso's Jerusalem Delivered*, ed. Henry Morley (1890)

Fairfax, Thomas, Poems & Transcriptions, Bodleian MS. *Fairfax* 40

————'The Poems', ed. E. Bliss Reed, *Transactions of the Connecticut Academy of Arts and Sciences*, XIV (July, 1909), 239–89

Forbes, Patrick, *An Exquisite Commentarie vpon the Reuelation of Saint Iohn* (1613)

Golding, Arthur, *Shakespeare's Ovid: Arthur Golding's Translation of the "Metamorphoses" (1567)*, ed. W. H. D. Rouse (1961)

Goodwin, John, *Anti-Cavalierisme; Or, Truth Pleading As well the Necessity, as the Lawfulness of this present War . . .* (1642)

Goodwin, Thomas, *Works*, 12 vols., Nichol's Series of Standard Divines, Puritan Period (Edinburgh, 1861–6)

Greenhill, William, *The Axe at the Root* (1643), repr. in facsim., *Fast Sermons*, vol. VI.

Halifax, Marquess of (George Savile), *Complete Works*, ed. J. P. Kenyon (Harmondsworth, 1969)

Hartlib, Samuel, *A Description of the famous Kingdome of Macaria, shewing its excellent Government* (1641)

————*The Reformed Common-Wealth of Bees* (1655)

——*The Reformed Husband-Man; or a Briefe Treatise of the Errors, Defects, and Inconveniences of our English Husbandry* (1651)

Hawkins, Henry, *Partheneia Sacra (1633)*, repr. in facsim. (Menston, 1971)

Henry, Matthew, *Commentary: Acts of Revelation*, ed. D. Winter (1975)

——*Commentary: The Four Gospels*, ed. D. Winter (1974)

Herbert, George, *The English Poems*, ed. F. E. Hutchinson (2nd edn. Oxford, 1945)

Hesiod, *Hesiod and Theognis*, transl. D. Wender (Harmondsworth, 1976)

Herle, Charles, *David's Song of Three Parts* (1643), repr. in facsim., *Fast Sermons*, vol. VI.

Hobbes, Thomas, *Leviathan*, ed. K. R. Minogue (1973)

Horace, *Odes and Epodes*, Loeb edn. (1914)

Hutchinson, Lucy, *Memoirs of the Life of Colonel Hutchinson* (1908)

Johnson, Robert, *Nova Britannia. Offring Most Excellent fruites by Planting in Virginia* (1609)

Jonson, Ben, *The Fortunate Isles, and their Union: Celebrated in a Masque Design'd for the Court on the Twelfth Night, 1626*, in *Works*, 6 vols. (1716) VI.54–75.

Lactantius, *The Divine Institutes I–VII*, transl. Sister M.F. McDonald, Fathers of the Church (Washington, 1964)

Lucianus, *Verae Historiae*, in *Works*, Loeb edn. (1913), vol. I.

Marshall, Stephen, *Reformation and Desolation: Or, a Sermon tending to the Discovery of the Symptomes of a People to whom God will by no means be reconciled* (1642), repr. in facsim., *Fast Sermons*, vol. II.

——*The Song of Moses . . . and the Song of the Lambe* (1643), repr. in facsim., *Fast Sermons*, vol. VI.

Malynes, Gerald de, *The Commonwealth of Bees* (1655)

Marvell, Andrew, The Poems and Letters, ed. H. M. Margoliouth, Pierre Legouis & E. E. Duncan-Jones, 2 vols. (Oxford, 1971)

——*The Latin Poetry of Andrew Marvell*, ed. William A. McQueen & K. A. Rockwell (Chapel Hill, 1964)

——*Miscellaneous Poems (1681)*, repr. in facism. (Menston, 1973)

——*The Complete Poems*, ed. E. S. Donno (Harmondsworth, 1972)

——*Selected Poetry*, ed. Frank Kermode (1967)

——*Poems*, ed. James Reeves & Martin Seymour-Smith (1969)

——*Selected Poems*, ed. Joseph Summers, The Laurel Poetry Series

(New York, 1961)

Marvell, Andrew, *Mr. Smirke, Defence of Howe, General Councils, The Growth of Popery*, repr. in *Works*, ed. A. B. Grosart, 4 vols. (Fuller Worthies Library, 1868–75), vol. IV.

——*the Rehearsal Transpros'd, and The Rehearsal Tranpros'd The Second Part*, ed. D. I. B. Smith (1971)

Mason, Thomas, *A Reuelation of the Reuelation* (1619)

Mayer, John, *Ecclesiastica Interpretatio* (1627)

Mede, Joseph, *The Key of the Revelation (Clavis Apocalyptica)* (1643)

Milton, John, *Poetical Works*, ed. Douglas Bush (1970)

——*The Poems*, ed. John Carey & Alistair Fowler (1968)

——*The Prose Works*, ed. J. A. St. John *et al.*, Bohn edn., 5 vols. (1848–53)

More, P. E. & Cross, F. L. (eds.), *Anglicanism: The Thought and Practice of the Church of England, illustrated from the religious literature of the Seventeeth Century* (1957)

Napier, John, *Napier's Narration* (1641)

Newcomen, Matthew, *A Sermon tending to set forth the right use of the Disasters that befall our Armies* (1644)

Nixon, Anthony, *The Christian Navy: Wherein is playnely described the perfit course to sayle to the Hauen of eternall happinesse* (1602)

North, Thomas, *Plutarch's Lives . . . translated by Sir Thomas North*, 8 vols (Oxford, 1928)

Ovid, *Metamorphoses*, Loeb edn. (1916, 1921)

Owen, John, *The Advantages of the Kingdom of Christ* (1651)

——*The Shaking and Translating of Heaven and Earth* (1649)

Pinto, V. de Sola & Rodway, A. E. *The Common Muse* (Harmondsworth, n.d.)

Pliny, *Naturalis Historia*, Loeb edn. (1942–9)

Plutarch, *Lives*, Loeb edn. (1919)

Purchas, Samuel (The Elder), *Hakluytus Posthumous: Or, Purchas His Pilgrimes*, 20 vols. (Glasgow, 1905–7)

Purchas, Samuel (The Younger), *A Theatre of Politicall Flying-Insects* (1657)

Quarles, Francis, *Emblemes* (1696)

——*Hieroglyphics of the Life of Man (1638)*, repr. in facsim., ed. John Horden (1975)

——*Hosanna (1647) & Threnodes (1641)*, repr. in facsim., ed. John Horden (Liverpool, 1960)

——*Schola Cordis & Hieroglyphics . . .* (1845)

Sallust, *Bellum Catilinae*, Loeb edn. (1931)

Sedgwick, Obadiah, *Haman's Vanity* (1643), repr. in facsim., *Fast Sermons* vol. VI.

Shakespeare, William, *The Tempest*, ed. Frank Kermode, The Arden Shakespeare (1964)

Sibbes, Richard, *Light from Heaven . . . in Four Treatises* (1638)

——*The Brides Longing for her Bride-groomes second Comming . . .* (1638)

Sidney, Philip, *A Defence of Poetry*, ed. Jan van Dorsten (Oxford, 1966)

Smith, John, *The True Travels, Adventures, & Observations of Captain John Smith*, repr. in *Works*, ed. Edward Aber, 2 vols. (1895).

Southerne, Edmund, *A Treatise Concerning the Right Use and Ordering of Bees* (1593)

Spenser, Edmund, *Poetical Works*, ed. E. de Selincourt, 3 vols. (Oxford, 1910)

——*The Works: A Variorum Edition*, ed. E. Greenlaw, C. G. Osgood, F. M. Padelford, R. Heffner, 9 vols. (Baltimore, 1932–57)

Sterry, Peter, *The Clouds in which Christ Comes* (1647)

Suetonius, *Works*, Loeb edn. (1913)

Symonds, William, *Virginia* (1609)

Taylor, Jeremy, *The Golden Grove: Selected Passages from the Sermons and Writings*, ed. L. Pearsall Smith (Oxford, 1930)

Temple, Thomas, *Christ's Government in and over his People* (1642), repr. in facsim., *Fast Sermons*, vol. IV.

Varro, *De Lingua Latina*, Loeb edn. (1938)

Vaughan, Henry, *The Complete Poems*, ed. Alan Rudrum (Harmondsworth, 1976)

Virgil, *Opera* (Oxford, 1969)

Waller, Edmund, *The Poems*, ed. G. Thorn Drury (New York, 1968)

Whitaker, Alexander, *Good Newes From Virginia* (1613)

Wilkins, John, *A Discourse Concerning the Beauty of Providence in all the rugged passages of it* (1649)

Wilson, Thomas, *Jerichoes Down-Fall* (1643)

Winstanley, Gerrard, *The Law of Freedom & Other Writings*, ed. Christopher Hill (Harmondsworth, 1973)

——Selections from the Works, ed. L. D. Hamilton (1944)

(2) SECONDARY MATERIAL

(i) *History and Religion*

Ashley, Maurice, *Oliver Cromwell and His World* (1972)

——*The Greatness of Oliver Cromwell* (1958)

Aylmer, G. E. (ed.), *The Interregnum: The Quest for Settlement 1646–1660* (1974)

Ball, Bryan W., *A Great Expectation: Eschatological Thought in English Protestantism to 1660* (Leiden, 1975)

Broase T. R., *Death in the Middle Ages* (1972)

Breslow, M. A., *A Mirror of England: English Puritan Views of Foreign Nations, 1618–1640* (Camb., Mass., 1970)

Capp, B. S., *The Fifth Monarchy Men* (1972)

Clark, George, *The Later Stuarts, 1660–1714* (Oxford, 1956)

Cohn, Norman, *The Pursuit of the Millennium* (1957)

Cross, Claire, *Church and People 1450–1660* (Glasgow, 1976)

——'Parochial Structure and the Dissemination of Protestantism in Sixteenth-century England', *Studies in Church History* 16 (1978), 269–78.

Davies, Godfrey, *The Early Stuarts, 1603–1660* (Oxford, 1959)

Eurich, Nell P. *Science in Utopia: A Mighty Design* (Camb., Mass., 1967)

Frye, R. M., 'The Teachings of Classical Puritanism on Conjugal Love', *Studies in the Renaissance* 2 (1955), 148–59

Gardiner, S. R. (ed.), *The Constitutional Documents of the Puritan Revolution 1625–1660* (3rd edn., Oxford, 1906)

Gardner, Jane F., *Leadership and the Cult of the Personality* (1974)

George, C. H. & K., *The Protestant Mind of the English Reformation 1570–1640* (Princeton, 1961)

Haley, K. H. D., *William of Orange and the English Opposition, 1672–4* (Oxford, 1953)

Haller, W. & M., 'The Puritan Art of Love', *HLQ* IV (1941–2), 235–72.

Hibbert, Christopher, *Charles I* (1968)

Hill, Christopher, *Antichrist in Seventeenth-Century England* (1971)

——'The Diary of John Evelyn', *History* 42 (1957), 12–18.

——*God's Englishman: Oliver Cromwell and the English Revolution* (Harmondsworth, 1972)

——*Puritanism and Revolution* (1969)

——*Milton and the English Revolution* (1979)

——*The World Turned Upside Down* (Harmondsworth, 1975)

Jones, J. R. (ed.), *The Restored Monarchy, 1660–1688* (1979)

Kenyon, J. P., *The Stuart Constitution* (Cambridge, 1966)

——*The Stuarts: A Study in Kingship* (1958)

Lamont, William M., *Godly Rule: Politics and Religion 1603–1660* (1969)

Lamont, William M. and Oldfield, Sybil, *Politics, Religion, and Literature in the Seventeenth Century* (1975)

Manning, Brian (ed.), *Politics, Religion and the English Civil War* (London, 1973)

Mascall, E. L. & Box, H. S., *The Blessed Virgin Mary* (1963)

Masson, Georgina, *Queen Christina* (1974)

Miller, Edward, *Portrait of a College: A History of the College of Saint John the Evangelist, Cambridge* (Cambridge, 1961)

Miller, Perry, *Errand into the Wilderness* (Camb., Mass., 1956)

Morton, A. L., *The English Utopia* (1978)

Murray, Iain H., *The Puritan Hope* (1971)

Reeves, Marjorie, *The Influence of Prophecy in the Later Middle Ages* (Oxford, 1969)

Russell, Conrad (ed.), *Origins of the English Civil War* (1973)

Shaw, Howard, *The Levellers* (1968)

Simon, Edith, *The Saints*, (Harmondsworth, 1972)

Simpson, Alan, *Puritanism in Old and New England* (Chicago, 1961)

Tawney, R. H., *Religion and the Rise of Capitalism* (Harmondsworth, 1973)

Thomas, Keith, *Religion and the Decline of Magic* (Harmondsworth, 1973)

Tonkin, Humphrey, 'Utopias: Notes on a Pattern of Thought', *The Centennial Review* 14 (1970), 385–95

Toon, Peter (ed.), *Puritans, the Millennium, and the Future of Israel: Puritan Eschatology 1600–1660* (Cambridge, 1970)

Trevor-Roper, H. R., 'The Fast Sermons of the Long Parliament', *Essays in British History*, ed. H. R. Trevor-Roper (1965), 85–138

——'Witches and Witchcraft', *Encounter* (May, 1967)

——*The European Witch-Craze of the Sixteenth and Seventeenth Centuries* (Harmondsworth, 1969)

Trollope, Anthony, *The West Indies and the Spanish Main* (1968)

Tuveson, E. L., *Millennium and Utopia: A Study in the Background of the Idea of Progress* (New York & London, 1964)

Walzer, Michael, *The Revolution of the Saints: A Study in the Origins of Radical Politics* (1966)

Watkins, Owen C., *The Puritan Experience* (1972)

Webster, Charles, *The Great Instauration: Science, Medicine and Reform, 1626–1660*, (1975)

Wedgwood, C. V., *The Trial of Charles I* (1967)

Werkmeister, William H. (ed.), *Facets of the Renaissance* (New York, Evanston & London, 1963)

Wilson, John F., *Pulpit in Parliament: Puritanism during the English Civil War 1640–48* (Princeton, NJ, 1969)

Wind, Edgar, *Pagan Mysteries in the Renaissance* (1968)

Woodhouse, A. S. P. (ed.), *Puritanism and Liberty: Being the Army Debates (1647–9) from the Clarke Manuscripts with supplementary documents* (1938)

Wright, Louis B., *Religion and Empire: The Alliance between Piety and Commerce in English Expansion 1558–1625* (Chapel Hill, 1943)

Zagorin, Perez, *The Court and the Country: the beginning of the English Revolution* (1969)

(ii) *Art*

Gibson, Walter S., *Hieronymus Bosch* (1973)

James, M. R., *The Apocalypse in Art* (1931)

Kauffmann, C. M., *An Altar-piece of the Apocalypse* (1968)

D'Ancona, Mirelli Levi, *The Garden of the Renaissance: Botanical Symbolism in Italian Painting* (Florence, 1977)

Panofsky, Erwin, *Meaning in the Visual Arts* (Harmondsworth, 1970)

——*Studies in Iconology: Humanistic Themes in the Art of the Renaissance* (New York & London, 1972)

Pope-Hennessy, John, *A Sienese Codex of the Divine Comedy* (Oxford, 1947)

Ripa, Cesare, *Iconologia, repr. as Baroque & Rococo Pictoral Imagery*, ed. E. A. Maser (New York, 1971)

Seznec, Jean, *The Survival of the Pagan Gods: The Mythological Tradition and its Place in Renaissance Humanism and Art* (New York, 1961)

Whittick, Arnold, *Symbols: Signs and their Meaning and Uses in Design* (1971)

Wölfflin, Heinrich, *The Art of Albrecht Dürer*, transl. A. & H. Grieve (1971)

(iii) *Literary Criticism*

Allen, Don Cameron, *Image and Meaning: Metaphoric Traditions in Renaissance Poetry* (Baltimore, 1960)

——'Symbolic Color in the Literature of the English Renaissance', *PQ* 15 (1936), 81–92

——'Love in a Grave', *MLN* 74 (1959), 485–6

Allentuck, M. E., Marvell's "Pool of Air" ', *MLN* 74 (1959), 587–9

Anselment, Raymond A., ' "Betwixt Jest and Earnest": Ironic reversal in Andrew Marvell's "The Rehearsal Transpos'd" ', *MLN* 66 (1971), 282–93

——'Satiric Strategy in Marvell's "The Rehearsal Transpros'd" ', *MP* 68 (1970–71), 137–50

Bagguley, W. H. (ed.), *Andrew Marvell, 1621–78: Tercentenary Tributes* (1922)

Bain, Carl E., 'The Latin Poetry of Andrew Marvell', *PQ* 38 (1959), 436–49

Bayne, Ronald, 'Masque and Pastoral', *The Cambridge History of English Literature*, ed. A. W. Ward and A. R. Waller (Cambridge, 1950), VI 328–72

Benjamin, Edwin B., 'Marvell's "Bermudas" ', *CEA Critic* 29 (1967), 10, 12; reply to Parish, 30 (1967), 10

Berthoff, Anne E., *The Resolved Soul: A Study of Marvell's Major Poems* (Princeton, NJ, 1970)

——'The Voice of Allegory: Marvell's "The Unfortunate Lover" ', *MLQ* 27 (1966), 41–50

Blanch, R. J., 'Precious Metal and Gem Symbolism in "Pearl" ', *Lock Haven Review* 7 (1965), 1–12

Bradbrook, F. W., 'The Poetry of Marvell,' *The Pelican Guide to English Literature*, ed. Boris Ford, vol. 3 (Harmsworth, 1956)

Bradbrook, M. C., 'Marvell and the Poetry of Rural Solitude,' *RES* XVII, 65 (1941) 37–46

Bradbrook, M. C. & Lloyd-Thomas, M. G., *Andrew Marvell* (Cambridge, 1961)

Braden, Gordon, ' "Vivamus, mae Lesbia" in the English Renaissance,' *ELR* IX. 2 (1979), 199–224.

Brett, R. L., (ed.), *Andrew Marvell; Essays on the Tercentenary of his Death* (Oxford, 1979)

Browne, J. N., 'A Note on Symbolic Numbers in Spenser's "Aprill" ', *N&Q* CCXXV (1980), 301–4

Buhler, C. F., 'A Letter by Marvell,' *N&Q* (11 Oct. 1952), 451

Burdon, P. H., 'Andrew Marvell and Richard Flecknoe in Rome,' *N&Q* 19 (Jan. 1972), 16–18

Bush, Douglas, *English Literature in the Earlier Seventeenth Century, 1600–1660* (Oxford, 1945)

Carens, James F., 'Andrew Marvell's Cromwell Poems', *BuR* 7 (1957), 41–70

Carey, John, (ed.), *Andrew Marvell: A Critical Anthology* (Harmondsworth, 1969

Carpenter, Margaret, 'From Herbert to Marvell: Poetics in "A Wreath" and "The Coronet" ', *JEGP* 69 (1970), 50–62

Carroll, J. J., 'The Sun and the Lovers in "To His Coy Mistress" ', *MLN* 74 (1959), 4–7

Chambers, A. B., ' "I was but an Inverted Tree": Notes toward the

History of an Idea', *Studies in the Renaissance*, 8 (1961) 291–9

Chernaik, Warren, *The Poet's Time: Politics and Religion in the work of Andrew Marvell* (Cambridge, 1983)

Cinquemani, A. M., 'Marvell's "The Mower Against Gardens" ', *Explicator* 20 (1961), Item 77

Colie, Rosalie L., *"My Ecchoing Song"*: *Marvell's Poetry of Criticism* (Princeton, NJ, 1970)

——'Marvell's "Bermudas" and the Puritan Paradise', *Renaissance News* 10 (1957), 75–9

Collinge, N. E., *The Structure of Horace's Odes*, (1961)

Comparetti, Domenico, *Virgil in the Middle Ages*, transl. E. F. M. Benecke (1966)

Coolidge, J. S., 'Marvell and Horace', *MP* 63 (1965), III–120

Corder, J. M., 'Marvell and Nature', *N&Q* n.s. 6 (1959), 58–61

Cruttwell, Patrick, *The Shakespearean Moment and its place in the poetry of the Seventeenth Century* (New York, 1960)

Cullen, Patrick, 'Imitation and Metamorphosis: The Golden-Age Eclogue in Spenser, Milton, and Marvell', *PMLA* LXXXIV (1969), 1559–70

Cummings, R. M., 'The Difficulty of Marvell's "Bermudas" ', *MP* 67 (1970), 331–40

Cunningham, J. V., 'Logic and Lyric', *MP* 51 (1953), 33–41

Daniel, Robert, 'Marvell's "To His Coy Mistress" ', *Explicator* I. 5 (1943), Item 37

(Datta), Kitty Scoular, *Natural Magic: Studies in the Presentation of Nature in English Poetry from Spenser to Marvell* (Oxford, 1965)

——'Marvell's Prose and Poetry: More Notes', *MP* 63 (1965–6), 319–21

——'Marvell and Wotton: A Reconsideration', *RES* n.s. 19 (1968), 403–5

Davies, L. A., 'An Unpublished Poem about Andrew Marvell', *YES* I (1971), 100–101

Davison, Dennis, *The Poetry of Andrew Marvell* (1964)

——'Marvell and Politics', *N&Q* n.s. III. 5 (1955), 201–2

——'Notes on Marvell's "To His Coy Mistress" ', *N&Q* (December, 1958), 521

Day, R. A., 'Marvell's "Glew" ', *PQ* 32 (1953), 344–6

Dobbins, Arthur C., *Milton and the Book of Revelation* (Alabama, 1975)

Donno E. S., (ed.), *Andrew Marvell: The Critical Heritage* (1978)

Duncan-Jones, E. E., 'The erect sword in Marvell's "Horatian Ode" ', *EA* 15 (1962) 172–4

——'The date of Marvell's "To His Coy Mistress" ', *TLS* (5 Dec. 1958), 705

——'Benlowes, Marvell, and the Divine Casimire: A Note', *HLQ* 20 (1957), 183–4

——'Marvell His own Critic', *N&Q* (Sept. 1956), 383–4

——'Marvell: A Great Master of Words', *Proceedings of the British Academy* LXI (1975), 267–90

——'A Reading of Marvell's "The Unfortunate Lover" ', *I.A. Richards: Essays in His Honour*, ed. Reuben Brower, Helen Vendler & John Hollander (New York, 1973), 213–26

Eliot, T. S., *Selected Essays* (1951)

Emperor, John Bernard, *The Catullan Influence in English Lyric Poetry, Circa 1600–1650* (New York, 1973)

Empson, William, *Some Versions of Pastoral* (Harmondsworth, 1966)

Everett, Barbara, 'Marvell's "The Mower's Song" ', *CQ* IV (1962), 219–24

Evett, David, ' "Paradice's Oly Map": The *Topos* of the *Locus Amoenus* and the Structure of Marvell's "Upon Appleton House" ', *PMLA* LXXXV (1970), 504–13

Farnham, Anthony E., 'Saint Teresa and the Coy Mistress', *BUSE* 2 (1956), 226–39

Fizdale, Tay, 'Irony in Marvell's "Bermudas" ', *ELH* 42 (1975), 203–213

Fixler, Michael, *Milton and the Kingdoms of God* (1964)

French, J. Milton, 'Notes on two Puritan Poets, Marvell and Wither', *N&Q* (16 April, 1938), 273–4

Friedenreich, Kenneth, (ed.), *Tercentenary Essays in Honor of Andrew Marvell* (Hamden, Conn., 1977)

Friedman, Donald M., *Marvell's Pastoral Art* (1970)

Frye, R. M., *Milton's Imagery and the Visual Arts: Iconographic Tradition in the Epic Poems* (Princeton, NJ, 1978)

Galdon, Joseph A., *Typology and Seventeenth Century Literature* (The Hague, 1975)

Gilbert, Allan H., *The Symbolic Persons in the Masques of Ben Jonson* (New York, 1969)

Godshalk, W. L., 'Marvell's "The Mower to the Glow-worms" ', *Explicator* (October, 1966), Item 12

Gwynn, Frederick L., 'Marvell's "To His Coy Mistress", 33–46', *Explicator* (May, 1953) Item 49

Hankins, John E., 'Spenser and the Revelation of St. John', *PMLA* LX (1945), 364–81

Harding, Davis P., *The Club of Hercules: Studies in the Classical*

Background of "Paradise Lost" (Urbana, 1962)

——*Milton and the Renaissance Ovid* (Urbana, 1946)

Hibbard, G. R., 'The County-House Poem of the Seventeenth Century', *JWCI* XIX (1956), 159–74

Hodge, R. I. V., Foreshortened Time: Andrew Marvell and *Seventeeth-Century Revolutions* (Cambridge, 1978)

Höltgen, K. J., 'Floral Horologues prior to Marvell's Garden', *N&Q* n.s. 16.10 (1969), 381–2

Howarth, R. G., 'Marvell: An Emendation', *N&Q* (Aug. 1953), 330

Hunt, John Dixon, *Andrew Marvell: His Life and Writings* (1978)

Hyman, L. W., *Andrew Marvell* (New York, 1964)

——'Marvell's "Coy Mistress" and Desperate Lover', *MLN* 75 (1960), 8–10

——'Politics and Poetry in Andrew Marvell', *PMLA* LXXIII (1958), 475–9

Kawasaki, Toshihiko, 'Marvell's "Bermudas"—A Little World, or a New World?', *ELH* 43 (1976), 38–52

Keast, William R., *Seventeenth-century English Poetry: Modern Essays in Criticism* (1971)

Keister, Don A., 'Marvell's "The Garden" ', *Explicator* 10.4 (1952), Item 24

Kelliher, W. Hilton, 'Marvell's "A Letter to Dr. Ingelo" ', *RES* n.s. 20 (1969), 50–57

——'A New Text of Marvell's "To His Coy Mistress" ', *N&Q* 17 (1970), 254–6

——*Andrew Marvell: Poet and Politician, 1621–78* (British Library, 1978)

Kermode, Frank, *Renaissance Essays* (1973)

——'A Note on Marvell', *N&Q* (May 1962), 218

——'Two Notes on Marvell', *N&Q* (March 1952), 136–8

——*The Sense of an Ending: Studies in the Theory of Fiction* (1967)

King, A. H., 'Some Notes on Andrew Marvell's "Garden" ', *ES* 20 (1938), 118–21

King, Bruce, *Marvell's Allegorical Poetry* (New York & Cambridge, 1977)

——'In Search of Andrew Marvell', *REL* 8 (1967), 31–41

——' "The Mower Against Gardens" and the Levellers', *HLQ* 33 (1970), 237–42

Knights, L. C., *Public Voices: Literature and Politics, with special reference to the Seventeenth Century* (London, 1971)

Knott, John R. Jr, *Milton's Pastoral Vision: An Approach to "Paridise Lost"* (Chicago, 1971)

Kolve, V. A., *The Play Called Corpus Christi* (1966)

Kropf, C. R., 'Libel and Satire in the Eighteenth Century', *Eighteenth-Century Studies*, VIII. 2 (1974–5), 153–68

Leavis, F. R., *Revaluation* (1936)

Legouis, Pierre, *Andrew Marvell: Poet, Puritan, Patriot* (Oxford, 1968)

——'Marvell's "Little T. C. in a Prospect of Flowers", an "Eclogue of the Golden Age"?', *PMLA* LXXXVI (1971), 275–7

——'Marvell's Grasshoppers', *N&Q* n.s. 5.3 (1958), 108–9

——'Marvell and "the two learned brothers of St. Marthe" ' *PQ* 38 (1959), 450–58

——'Marvell and the New Critics', *RES* n.s. 8.32 (1957), 382–9

——'Marvell's Maniban', *RES* 2.7 (1926), 328–35

Leishman, J. B., *The Art of Marvell's Poetry* (1966)

Lippincott, Henry F. Jr, 'Marvell's "On Paradise Lost" ', *ELN* (June 1972), 265–72

Lord, George de F., (ed.), *Andrew Marvell: A Collection of Critical Essays* (Englewood Cliffs, NJ, 1968)

MacCaffrey, Isabel G., 'Some Notes on Marvell's Poetry, Suggested by a Reading of his Prose', *MP* 61 (1964), 261–9

Malekin, Peter, *Liberty and Love: English Literature and Society, 1640–88* (1981)

Margoliouth, H. M., 'Notes on Marvell', *N&Q* (May 1953), 220

Marinelli, Peter V., *Pastoral* (1971)

Martz, Louis, *The Poetry of Meditation* (New Haven, 1962)

Maxwell, J. C., 'Marvell and Logic', *N&Q* (July, 1970) 256

Mazzeo, J. A., 'Cromwell as Machiavellian Prince in Marvell's "An Horatian Ode" ', *JHI* 20.1 (1960), 1–17

——'Cromwell as Davidic King', *Reason and Imaginaiton*, ed. J. A. Mazzeo (1962) 29–55

McChesney, John, 'Marvell's "The Garden" ', *Explicator* 10.1 (1951), Item 4

Meagher, John C., *Method and Meaning in Jonson's Masques* (1966)

Miller, Bruce E., 'Logic in Marvell's "To His Coy Mistress" ', *NDQ* 30 (1962), 48–9

Miner, Earl, (ed.), *Illustrious Evidence: Approaches to English Literature of the Early Seventeenth Century* (1975)

——(ed.), *Literary Uses of Typology: from the Late Middle Ages to the Present* (Guildford, 1977)

——'The "Poetic Picture, Painted Poetry" of "The Last Instructions to a Painter" ', *MP* 63 (1965–6), 288–94

Mitchell, C., 'Marvell's "The Mower to the Glow-worms" ',

Explicator (May 1960), Item 50

Moldenhauer, Joseph J., 'The Voices of Seduction in "To His Coy Mistress": A Rhetorical Analysis', *Texas Studies in Literature and Language* 10 (1968), 189–206

Molesworth, Charles, 'Property and Virtue: The Genre of the Country-House Poem in the Seventeenth Century', *Genre* I (1968), 141–57

——'Marvell's "Upon Appleton House": The Persona as Historian, Philosopher, and Priest', *SEL* 13 (1973), 149–62

Muir, Kenneth, 'A Virgilian Echo in Marvell', *N&Q* 196 (1951), 115

Nisbet, R. G. M. & Hubbard, Margaret, *A Commentary on Horace: Odes Book I* (Oxford, 1970)

Nixon, Paul Morris, 'Studies in Chaucer's Colour Vocabulary', M.Phil. thesis, York 1977

Orgel, Stephen, *The Illusion of Power: Political Theater in the English Renaissance* (Berkeley, 1975)

Orgel, Stephen and Strong, Roy, (eds.), *Inigo Jones: The Theatre of the Stuart Court*, 2 vols. (Berkeley, 1973)

Orwen, W. R., 'Marvell's Bergamot', *N&Q* (Aug. 1955), 340–41

——'Marvell's "The Garden" ', *N&Q* (Dec. 1946), 247–9

——'Marvell's "Narrow Case" ', *N&Q* n.s. 2 (1955), 201

Palomo, Dolores, 'The Halcyon Moment of Stillness in Royalist Poetry', *HLQ* 44 (1981), 205–21

Parish, John E., 'Back to the "Bermudas" ', *CEA Critic* 30 (1967), 10

Patrick, J. M., 'Marvell's "The Unfortunate Lover" ', *Explicator* 20 (April 1962), Item 65

Patrides, C. A., (ed.), *Approaches to Marvell: The York Tercentenary Lectures* (1978)

——*The Grand Design of God: The Literary Form of the Christian View of History* (1972)

——(ed.), *Aspects of Time* (Manchester, 1976)

Patterson, Annabel, *Marvell and the Civic Crown* (Princeton, NJ, 1978)

——' "Bermudas" and "The Coronet": Marvell's Protestant Poetics', *ELH* 44 (1977), 478–99

Pitman, M. R., 'Andrew Marvell and Sir Henry Wotton', *RES* n.s. XIII (1962), 157–8

Proudfoot, L., 'Marvell: Sallust and the Horatian Ode', *N&Q* 196 (29 Sept. 1951), 434

Putnam, Michael C. J., *Virgil's Pastoral Art: Studies in the Eclogues* (Princeton, NJ, 1970)

Rainbow, M. F. E., 'Marvell and Nature', *DUJ* 37 (1945), 22–7

Rand, E. K., 'Milton in Rustication', *SP* 19 (1922), 109–35

Rees, Christine, 'The Metamorphosis of Daphne in Sixteenth- and Seventeenth-century English Poetry', *MLR* 66 (1971), 251–63

Richardson, J. M., 'More Symbolic Numbers in Spenser's "Aprill" ', *N&Q* (Oct. 1982) 411–12

Robbins, Caroline, 'A Note on a Hitherto Unprinted Speech by Andrew Marvell', *MLR* 31 (1936), 549–50

Rollinson, Philip, 'The Traditional Contexts of Milton's "Two-Handed Engine" ', *ELN* 9 (1971–2)), 28–35

Rosenberg, John D., 'Marvell and the Christian Idiom', *Boston University Studies in English*, 4 (1960), 152–61

Røstvig, Maren-Sophie, *The Happy Man: Studies in the Metamorphosis of a Classical Ideal, 1600–1700*, 2 vols. (Oslo, 1962)

——'Benlowes, Marvell, and the Divine Casimire', *HLQ* 18 (1954), 13–35

——' "Upon Appleton House" and the Universal History of Man', *ES* 42 (1961), 337–51

Roth, Frederick H., Jr, 'Marvell's "Upon Appleton House": A Study in Perspective', *Texas Studies in Literature and Language* XIV.2 (1972), 269–81

Salerno, N. A., 'Marvell's "The Unfortunate Lover", VIII', *Explicator* 18 (1960), Item 42

——'Andrew Marvell and the Grafter's Art', *EA* 21 (1968), 125–32

Sasek, Lawrence A., *The Literary Temper of the English Puritans* (New York, 1961)

——'Marvell's "To His Coy Mistress" ', *Explicator* 14 (April 1956), Item 47

Schmitter, Dean Morgan, 'The Occasion for Marvell's "Growth of Popery" ', *JHI* XXI (1960), 568–70

Schulz, Howard, 'Christ and Antichrist in "Paradise Regained" ', *PMLA* LXVII, 790–808

Schwenger, Peter T., 'Marvell's "Unfortunate Lover" as Device', *MLQ* 35 (1974), 364–75

Sedelow, W. A., Jr, 'Marvell's "To His Coy Mistress" ', *MLN* 71 (1956), 6–8

Sharrock, Roger, 'The date of Marvell's "To His Coy Mistress" ', *TLS* (31 Oct. 1958), 625; *TLS* (16 Jan. 1959), 33

Simeone, William, 'A Probable Antecedent of Marvell's "Horatian Ode" ', *N&Q* 197 (1952), 316–18

Simmons, J. L., 'Marvell's "The Picture of Little T. C. in a Prospect of Flowers" ', *Explicator* 22 (1964), Item 62

Smith, Donal, 'The Political Beliefs of Andrew Marvell', *UTQ* 36

(1966–7), 55–67

——'Marvell', *English Poetry: Select Bibliographical Gides*, ed. A. E. Dyson (1971), 96–110

Smith, Barbara Herrnstein, *Poetic Closure: A Study of How Poems End* (Chicago & London, 1968)

Solomon, J., 'A Reading of Marvell's "Garden" ', *English Studies in Africa*, II. 2 (1968), 151–60

Spitzer, Leo, 'Marvell's "Nymph Complaining for the Death of her Faun": Sources versus Meaning', *MLQ* 19 (1958), 231–43

Starnes, DeWitt T. & Talbert, E. W., *Classical Myth and Legend in Renaissance Dictionaries* (Chapel Hill, 1955)

Stewart, Stanley, *The Enclosed Garden: The Tradition and the Image in Seventeenth-Century Poetry* (Milwaukee and London, 1966)

——'Marvell and the *Ars Moriendi*', *Seventeenth-Century Imagery*, ed., Earl Miner (Berkeley, 1971), 133–50

Summers, Claude J., 'The Frightened Architects of Marvell's Horatian Ode', *Seventeenth-Century News* 28 (1970), 4

Summers, Joseph, *The Heirs of Donne and Jonson* (1970)

Tillyard, E. M. W., *The Metaphysicals and Milton* (1956)

Toliver, Harold E., *Marvell's Ironic Vision* (New Haven & London, 1965)

Tuve, Rosemond, *Images and Themes in Five Poems by Milton* (Camb., Mass., 1957)

——'Spenser and Some Pictorial Conventions', *SP* 37 (1940), 149–76

Wain, John, (ed.), *Interpretations* (1955)

Walker, Robert G., 'Rochester and the Issue of Deathbed Repentance in the Restoration', *South Atlantic Review* 47.1 (1982), 21–37

Wall, L. N., 'A Note on Marvell's Letters', *N&Q* n.s. 5.3 (1958), III

——'Thomas Randolph and Marvell's "Coy Mistress" ', *N&Q* n.s. 15 (1968), 103

Wallace, John M., *Destiny His Choice: The Loyalism of Andrew Marvell* (Cambridge, 1968)

——'Marvell's "lusty Mate" and the Ship of the Commonwealth', *MLN* 76 (1961), 106–110

Wallerstein, Ruth, *Studies in Seventeenth-Century Poetic* (Madison, Wis., 1950)

Walton, Geoffrey, 'The Poetry of Andrew Marvell: A Summing Up', *Politics and Letters*, 4 (1948), 22–35

Warnke, Frank J., 'Play and Metamorphosis in Marvell's Poetry',

SEL 5 (1965), 23–30

Waters-Bennett, Josephine, 'Britain among the Fortunate Isles', *SP* 53 (1956), 114–40

——*The Evolution of the "Faerie Queene"* (New York, 1960)

Werblowsky, R. J. Zwi, *Lucifer and Prometheus: A Study of Milton's Satan* (1973)

West, Michael, 'The Internal Dialogue of Shakespeare's Sonnet 146', *SQ* 25 (1974), 109–23

Wheatcroft, John, 'Andrew Marvell and the Winged Chariot', *BuR* 6 (1956), 22–53

Whiting, G. W., *Milton's Literary Milieu* (New York, 1964)

Wilding, Michael, (ed.), *Marvell: Modern Judgements* (1969)

——Review of George de F. Lord (ed.), *Andrew Marvell: Complete Poetry* (New York, 1968), *MLR* 66 (1971), 664–5

Willey, Basil, *The Seventeenth-Century Background* (Harmondsworth, 1962)

Williams, Kathleen, 'Spenser: Some Uses of the Sea and the Storm-tossed Ship', *Research Opportunities in Renaissance Drama*, XIII–IV (1970–71), 135–42

Wilson, A. J. N., 'Andrew Marvell: "An Horatian Ode . . . "': The Thread of the Poem and Its Use of Classical Allusion', *CQ* II (1969), 325–41

Wilson, R., 'Marvell's Denton', *TLS* (26 Nov. 1971), 1481; replies by John Newman (28 Jan. 1972), 99; A. A. Tait (11 Feb. 1972), 157; James Turner (31 Mar. 1972), 367

Winterton, J. B., 'Some Notes on Marvell's "Bermudas" ', *N&Q* n.s. 15 (1968), 102

Wittreich, Joseph A., Jr, *Visionary Poetics: Milton's Tradition and His Legacy* (San Marino, Calif., 1979)

Yates, Frances A., *Astraea: The Imperial Theme in the Sixteenth Century* (Harmondsworth, 1977)

Index

absolutism, and popery, 5, 25; and
civil war, 9, 259-303 *passim*
activism, as zeal, 9, 15, 93; and
quietism, 12, 125-37, 149-61,
240-55 *passim;* problems of,
11-12, 21-3, 108-10, 21, 52, 201,
203-5, 221-31 *passim*
Adams, Thomas, 174, 192, 193
Allen, D.C., 65
Americas, 176-7
Antichrist, and aesthetics, 162-3;
bondage by, 5; desolation of,
114; devouring, 20; illusion, 50;
imposture, 87; and Islam, 23-4;
persecution by, 23, 114, 191; as
reversion, 16; and sectarians,
23-4; temporal and spiritual, 32,
116-21, 125-6; *see also* Empire
Arminianism, 2, 51, 154, 199, 287-8
Astraea, 122-4, 137-60, 172
Aubrey, John, 34, 36, 250
Augustan Pax, 73, 122
Augustine, St, on history, 43, 105,
113; on providence, 43, 67-8; on
time, 107-8, 110-11; 122, 248
Augustus (Octavius Caesar), 83-5,
86, 95, 96-7, 103, 122
Ayloffe, John, 29

Bacon, Francis, 44, 104, 109, 113,
175, 195
Beard, Thomas, 55
Blood, Thomas, 29
Browne, Thomas, 38, 41, 231, 241

Caesar, Julius, 84, 93, 276
Calvinism, 45
Cambridge, University, 3-4

carpe diem genre, 202-3, 204, 205,
222-3, 230-1
Catullus, 202, 203, 208, 215, 230-1
Charles I, 28; as martyr, 265-6,
293-6, 303; M. on, 8-9, 71-103
passim; 257-305; in masques,
258-305; piety, 9; as prince, 173;
in propaganda, 114, 294-7;
regicide, 7-8, 20, 26, 89-92, 258,
298, 301; respect for his office, 7;
trial, 103; as tyrant 40
Charles II, 9, 29, 34, 98, 168, 171-3
Christina, Queen of Sweden, 10,
124, 137
Church Militant, 59, 151, 174
Civil War, the English, and Ireland,
92-3; as Latter Day war, 1-2,
46-7, 53, 101-2, 115, 222, 225,
234, 244, 258-301; loyalties in,
7-8, 25-6; and national sin, 2-3,
46, 64, 85, 128, 130, 131, 150,
290-2; and poetry, 37-8, 155;
psychological effects of, 8, 37-8,
41, 47-8, 56-7, 151-3, 155; as vial,
87
civil war, the Roman, 68, 72, 122,
123, 150-1, 276
conversion, spiritual, 116-21, 128,
203-31 *passim*, 239, 242, 250
Country House poems, 66, 161
Country party, 27
Cowley, Abraham, 37
Cromwell, Oliver, 115, 187, 221,
222, 228, 225; contemporary
attitudes to, 8, 27, 68, 78-9, 80,
82, 102, 103-4; foreign policy,
10, 176, 178, 186; and M. 7, 25-7,
180, 186, *see also* M., *Blake,*

377